ELFQUEST:
THE GRAND
QUEST
VOLUME TWELVE

ELFQUEST CREATED BY
**WENDY &
RICHARD PINI**

ELFQUEST:
**THE GRAND
QUEST**
VOLUME **TWELVE**

WRITTEN BY
WENDY & RICHARD PINI and DON STRAIT

ART BY
WENDY PINI & DON STRAIT

LETTERING BY
RICHARD PINI

ELFQUEST: THE GRAND QUEST VOLUME TWELVE
Published by DC Comics. Cover, timeline, character
bios, and compilation copyright © 2005 Warp
Graphics, Inc. All Rights Reserved.

Originally published in single magazine form in
ELFQUEST: KINGS OF THE BROKEN WHEEL 8-9.
Copyright © 1991 Warp Graphics, Inc. All Rights
Reserved. All characters, their distinctive
likenesses and related elements featured in this
publication are trademarks of Warp Graphics, Inc.
The stories, characters and incidents featured in
this publication are entirely fictional. DC Comics
does not read or accept unsolicited submissions
of ideas, stories or artwork.

DC Comics, 1700 Broadway, New York, NY 10019
A Warner Bros. Entertainment Company
Printed in Canada. First Printing.
ISBN: 1-4012-0508-9

Cover illustration by Wendy Pini

The ElfQuest Saga is an ever-unfolding story spanning countless millennia that follows the adventures of humans, trolls and various elfin tribes. Some of the events that occur prior to the time of this volume are outlined below using the very first published ElfQuest story as a benchmark.

OUR STORY BEGINS HERE...
7 YEARS LATER

Recognition gives Cutter and Leetah twin children, *Ember* and *Suntop*. The Wolfriders set out to find and unite other elfin tribes. They discover fabled Blue Mountain where they meet bizarre, winged *Tyldak* and the beautiful, enigmatic Winnowill, who jealously protects her control over the mountain's secrets.

On the way to the frozen northlands, brutal mountain trolls attack and the Wolfriders are barely saved by the *Go-Back* elves. Their leader, *Kahvi*, allies the Go-Backs with the Wolfriders and forest trolls to win the Palace.

The Wolfriders' lives are peaceful again – until Glider *Aroree* kidnaps *Windkin* to give to Winnowill. The betrayal propels Cutter and his tribe into another conflict. Meanwhile, Rayek seeks out Winnowill, whom he naively regards as an equal. The Black Snake seduces him into serving her cause – to turn Blue Mountain into a spaceship to return all pure-blooded elves to their starhome.

In the final battle between Cutter and Winnowill, Blue Mountain itself is destroyed along with most of the Glider elves, and Winnowill is banished forever to a deserted island in the middle of the ocean. The elves are left to pick up the tattered threads of their lives.

Rayek returns to the Palace, where the spirits of the dead Gliders restore it to its original glory. At the same time, Suntop receives a psychic cry of distress from unknown elves. Rayek convinces Cutter and the Wolfriders to let him fly the Palace to the source of the mysterious cry, using Suntop as his compass. Realizing he can solve two of his problems with one stroke, Rayek transports the Crystal Palace – along with Leetah and the two cubs – 10,000 years into the future, where the mortal Cutter can't survive to stop him.

3,000 – 2,000 YEARS BEFORE

Goodtree, eighth chief of the Wolfriders, founds a new Holt deep in the woods and creates the Father Tree where the Wolfriders can all live. Her son, *Mantricker,* reopens the struggle with nomadic humans. Mantricker's son, *Bearclaw,* discovers Greymung's trolls living in the tunnels beneath the Holt. Bearclaw becomes the Wolfriders' tenth chief.

In the distant Forbidden Grove near Blue Mountain, *Petalwing* and the preservers tirelessly protect their mysterious wrapstuff bundles.

9,000 YEARS BEFORE

Wolfrider chief Timmorn feels the conflict between his elf and wolf sides, and leaves the tribe to find his own destiny. *Rahnee the She-Wolf* takes over as leader, followed by her son *Prey-Pacer*.

10,000 YEARS BEFORE

Over time, the High Ones become too many for their faraway planet to support. *Timmain's* group discovers the World of Two Moons, but as their crystalline ship approaches, the High Ones crash-land far in the new world's past. Primitive humans greet them with brutality. The elfin High Ones and their troll attendants scatter into the surrounding forest. To survive, Timmain magically takes on a wolf's form and hunts for the other elves. *Timmorn*, first chief of the Wolfriders, is born.

0
1,000
2,000
3,000
4,000
5,000
6,000
7,000
8,000
9,000
10,000

FIRE & FLIGHT

| 0 |

The peace is an illusion, and humans burn the Wolfriders from their forest home. Cutter and his band are driven into a vast desert where they discover new elves, the Sun Folk. Cutter Recognizes the Sun Folk's healer Leetah, and the two groups unite.

475

600

1,000

6 YEARS BEFORE

The feud between elves and humans ends — seemingly — with the death of Bearclaw. Cutter assumes leadership of the tribe.

2,000

25 YEARS BEFORE

Joyleaf gives birth to a son, *Cutter*, who forms a fast friendship with *Skywise*. The two become brothers "in all but blood."

3,000

475 YEARS BEFORE

Bearclaw begins a long feud with a tribe of humans who live near the Holt. Although both sides suffer over the years, neither gives in.

4,000

600 YEARS BEFORE

In the oasis Sun Village deep in the desert to the south of the Holt, *Rayek* is born. *Leetah* is born twelve years later.

5,000

4,000 YEARS BEFORE

Freefoot leads the Wolfriders during a prosperous, quiet time. Freefoot's son, Oakroot, subsequently becomes chief and later takes the name *Tanner*.

7,000 YEARS BEFORE

Swift-Spear, fourth chief, goes to war for the first time against humans of a nearby village. The humans leave, and he takes the name *Two-Spear*. When his sister *Huntress Skyfire* challenges his chieftainship, the tribe splits. Two-Spear leaves, and Skyfire becomes chief.

6,000

7,000

8,000

10,000 – 8,000 YEARS BEFORE

Descendants of the High Ones wander the world. *Savah* and her family settle the Sun Village in the desert. *Lord Voll* and the Gliders move into Blue Mountain and shut themselves away from the world.

Guttlekraw becomes king of the trolls. Over time, the trolls tunnel under the future Holt of the Wolfriders.

9,000

Greymung rebels against Guttlekraw, who flees north. *Winnowill* gives birth to Two-Edge.

10,000

The ElfQuest saga spans thousands of years and to date has introduced readers to hundreds of characters. At the time of the stories in this volume, these are the major characters you will meet and get to know.

THE WOLFRIDERS

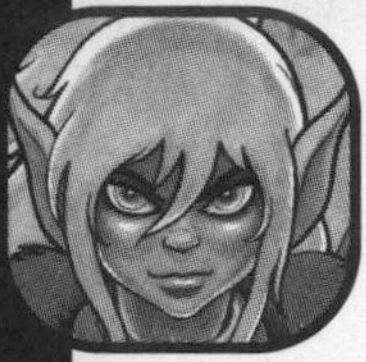

CUTTER

While his name denotes his skill with a sword, Cutter is not a cold and merciless death-dealer. Strong in his beliefs, he will nevertheless bend even the most fundamental of them if the well-being of his tribe is at stake. Skywise believes that what sets Cutter apart from all past Wolfrider chieftains is his imagination and ability to not only accept change, but take advantage of it.

LEETAH

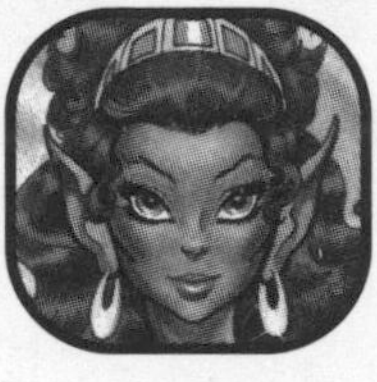

Her name means "healing light" and – as the Sun Folk's healer – she is the village's most precious resource. For over 600 years she has lived a sheltered life, surrounded by love and admiration, knowing little of the world beyond her desert oasis. Though delicate-seeming, beneath her beauty lies a wellspring of strength that has yet to be tested. She dislikes the death she has caused but understands it is The Way.

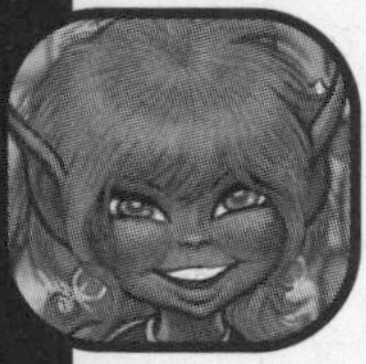

EMBER

Named for her fire-red hair, Ember is destined to be the next chief of the Wolfriders. As such, she constantly watches and learns from her father's actions; she also learns gentler skills from Leetah. As Cutter was a unique blend of his own parents' qualities, so too is Ember. She has recently begun experiencing what it will mean to lead.

SUNTOP

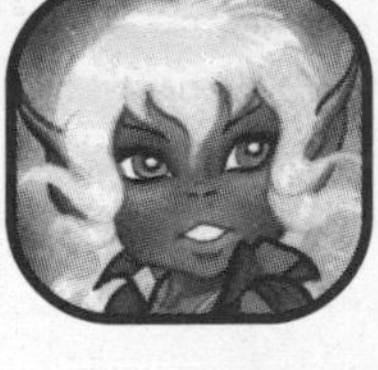

Suntop is the gentle, enigmatic son of Cutter and Leetah. Although a true Wolfrider, Suntop was born in the Sun Village and considers it home. Content that Ember will become chief of the Wolfriders, he says of himself, "I'll be what I'll be." Suntop has powerful mental abilities; his "magic feeling," as he calls it, alerts him when magic is being used by other elves.

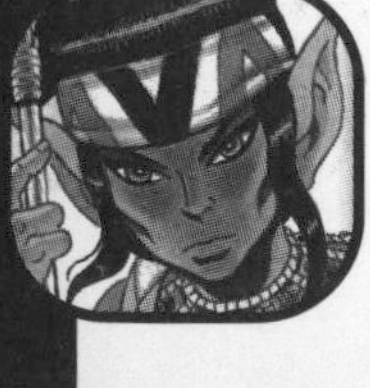

RAYEK

Vain and prideful, Rayek was chief hunter for the Sun Village. The same age as Leetah, he has spent nearly all those years as the healer's friend – always hoping that she will see him as more than simply that. He is a superb athlete, and skilled in both magic and weaponry. He sired a daughter, Venka, with the Go-Backs' chief Kahvi, but believes her to be dead. Ever boastful, he now resides within the Palace, seeking power and enlightenment.

SKYWISE

Orphaned at birth, Skywise is the resident stargazer of the Wolfriders, and only his interest in elf maidens rivals his passion for understanding the mysteries of the universe. Skywise is Cutter's counselor, confidant, and closest friend. While he is capable of deep seriousness, nothing can diminish Skywise's jovial and rakish manner.

STRONGBOW

Strongbow is the reserved, silent master archer of the Wolfriders. Ever the devil's advocate, he is often proved right but finds no value in saying "I told you so." Strongbow is extremely serious, rarely smiles, and prefers sending to audible speech. He is completely devoted to his lifemate, Moonshade, and intensely proud of their son Dart. Having taken an elf's life in the battle of Blue Mountain, however, his soul is now shaken.

SCOUTER

Scouter has the sharpest eyes of all the Wolfriders. He is steadfast, loyal, and often overprotective. He is also extremely intolerant of anyone, tribemates included, whom he perceives as putting his loved ones in jeopardy. Dewshine and Scouter have been lovemates for most of their lives, yet are not Recognized.

DEWSHINE

Swift and graceful as a deer, Dewshine is the most agile and free-spirited of the Wolfriders — and that takes some doing! She has a beautiful voice, full of melody and laughter. Song and dance are passions with her, and she has a talent for mimicking birdsong. Dewshine came to Recognition early and unexpectedly, with the shapechanged Glider Tyldak. That union produced a son, Windkin.

CLEARBROOK

Calm, dignified and thoughtful, choosing her words carefully, Clearbrook is the eldest female Wolfrider. Her quiet advice is always welcomed. When she lost her lifemate, One-Eye, in the quest for the Palace, Clearbrook turned into a fierce and vengeful angel of death. Both mother figure and warrior, Clearbrook is now an advocate of forgiveness and letting go of the past — but her path to that understanding has been harrowing.

EKUAR

Ekuar is one of the most ancient elves on the World of Two Moons. He is a rock-shaper, who long ago was abducted by trolls who forced him to use his powers to search for precious metals and gems. To keep him in line, the trolls tortured and maimed the gentle elf, but rather than becoming bitter, Ekuar has turned his misfortune into an outlook that is amazingly life-affirming!

AROREE

Aroree was one of the Gliders' Chosen Eight. When she met Skywise, he opened her eyes to a wider world. Aroree saw in Skywise a spark, one that was missing from her own life. She desperately wanted to flee Blue Mountain and lead a life far from its shadow, but her abduction of Windkin in Winnowill's service has brought her great shame.

FRIENDS

PETALWING

Petalwing is a Preserver — a carefree, fairylike creature that arrived on the World of Two Moons with the original High Ones. Petalwing lives under the grand illusion that "highthings" (elves) cannot live without it, and must be watched over and protected. Petalwing is the closest thing that the Preservers have to a leader. Cutter considers Petalwing to be a major annoyance; the sprite is unperturbed by this.

THE TROLLS

PICKNOSE

His name was inspired by his most prominent facial feature, which resembles the curved business end of a pick. The success of Picknose's interactions with the Wolfriders has been mixed at best, for while he does possess a sort of honor, he is also an opportunist of the first water. Currently King of the mountain trolls, Picknose is ever seeking opportunity.

OLD MAGGOTY

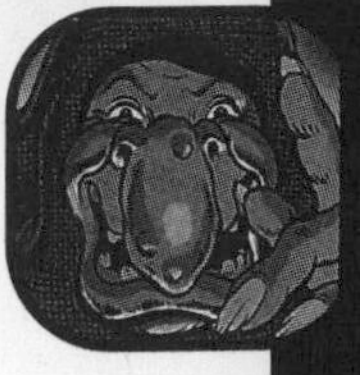

Old Maggoty was caught by Bearclaw one night stealing dreamberries near the Wolfriders' Holt. The two then became liaisons for their respective peoples in matters of trade. Old Maggoty is a master of herb lore and is renowned for brewing dreamberry wine, a potent lavender distillation that can set even the strongest-stomached elf on his pointed ear.

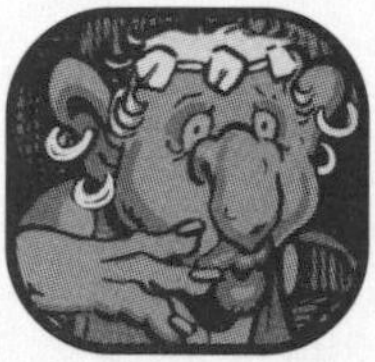

ODDBIT

Oddbit embodies all the troll maidenly virtues: she's greedy, deceptive, manipulative, coy, vain and fickle. She is the ultimate material girl, adorning the footstools of both King Guttlekraw and, later, King Greymung. After Picknose rescued her, Oddbit kept the lovesick troll dangling for years.

TRINKET

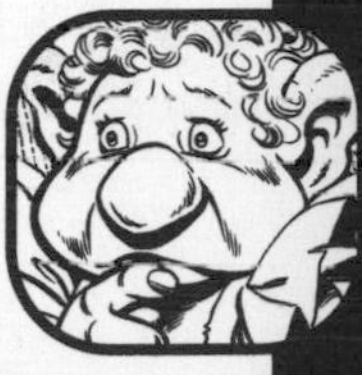

Trinket is the dreamberry of her father Picknose's eye and she knows it. She had been extremely spoiled from birth by her parents and knows that if all else fails, her copious tears and hysterical screams can cause the sternest adult to quail. She considers Ember a great playmate, and the two are often seen trading insults and ugly faces. Trinket is a typical child, always getting into trouble.

IN THE PREVIOUS VOLUME

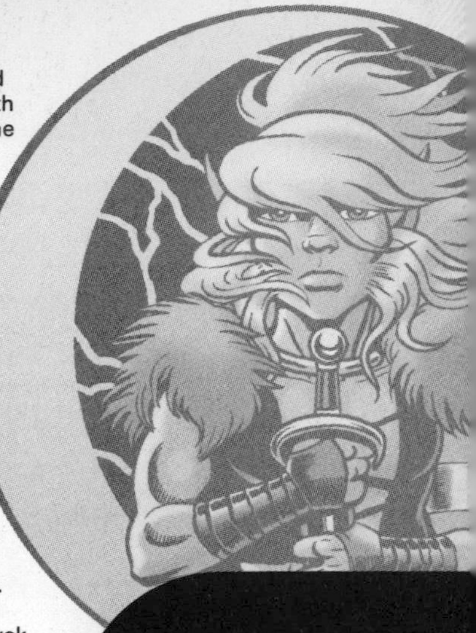

Rayek levitates the Crystal Palace, using Suntop's telepathic connection to the painful Cry From Beyond as a compass. They touch down in a foreign land with a thick, bountiful forest, but they still cannot locate the source of the cry.

Timmain sends to Skywise to look for one voice among the many, which gives Rayek a clue. Finally, he realizes that the cry is the collective voice of the High Ones, reaching through time. He realizes that time is a circle and that the cry comes from the future – at the moment when the High Ones first intended to land on the World of Two Moons. He reasons that if he goes forward in time, to that moment, he can prevent the accident that sent the High Ones far into the past and began the cycle that forced elves and trolls into their harsh ways of life.

Cutter disagrees with Rayek's plan, especially as – if completed – it will negate the existence of various elf tribes that don't measure up to Rayek's standards.

Regardless, when the opportunity presents itself, Rayek uses his great power to send the Palace – with Leetah, Ember, Suntop and Skywise – into the future, to the moment the cry originates. Cutter and the other Wolfriders are left behind, unable to follow through time itself.

As the moons pass, Cutter's despair over losing his family and friends is so great that the arrival of Nightfall and Redlance's daughter, Tyleet, is no cause for joy.

Time passes far too slowly for the wolf chief. His adventures do nothing to dull the ache in his heart. The entire tribe is affected by his gray mood. All hope seems lost as he realizes he will not survive until the Palace reappears.

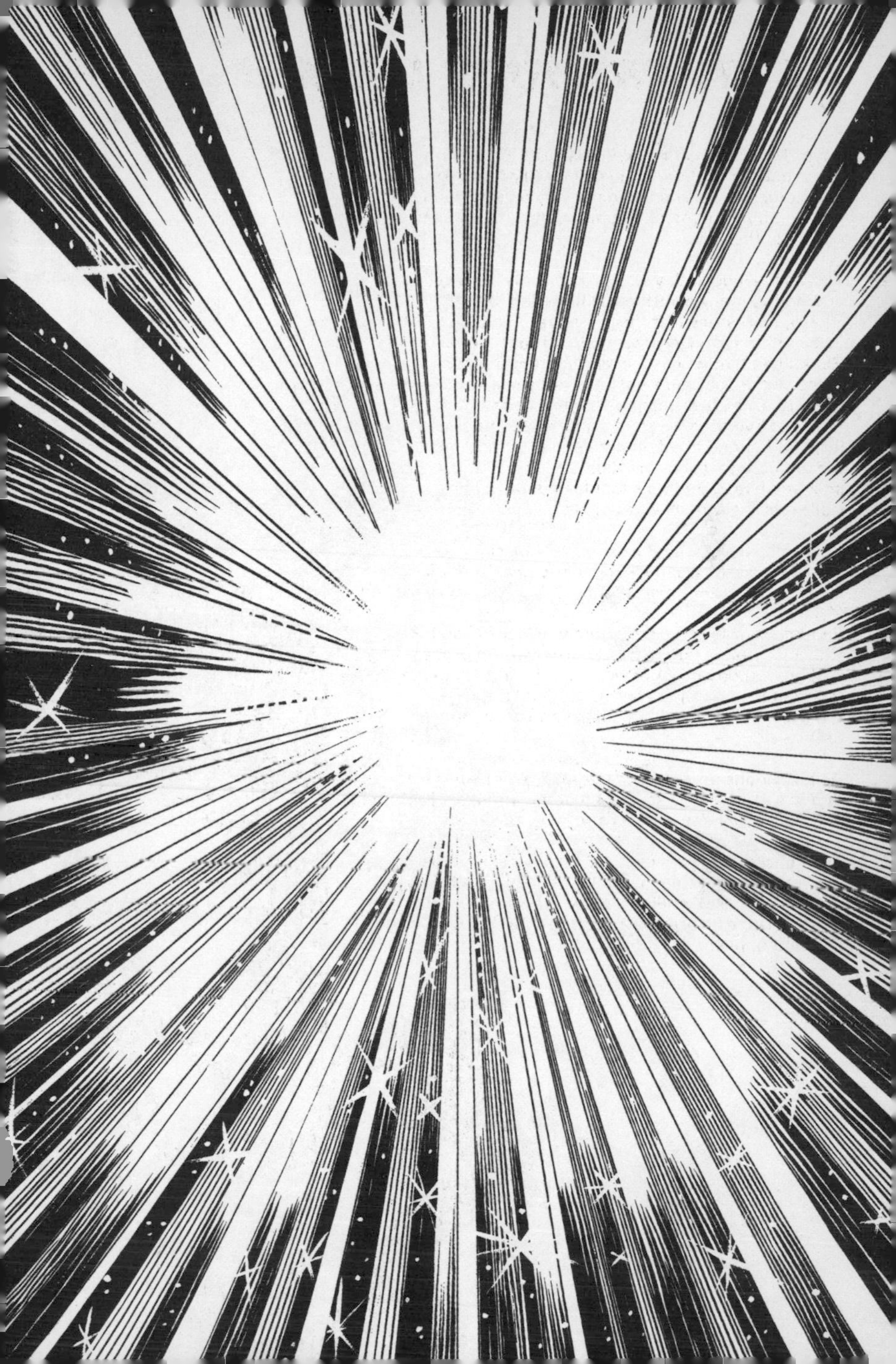

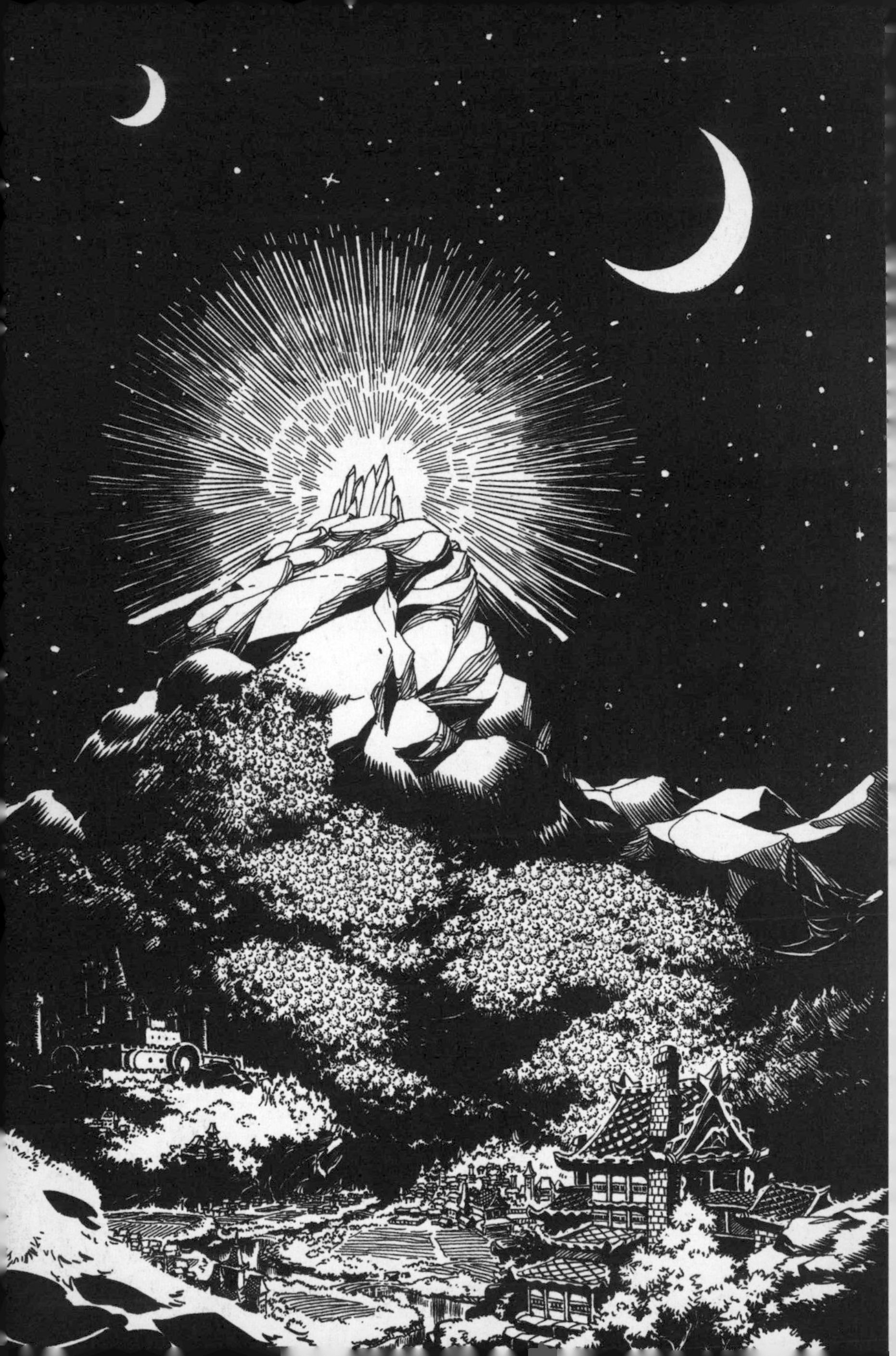

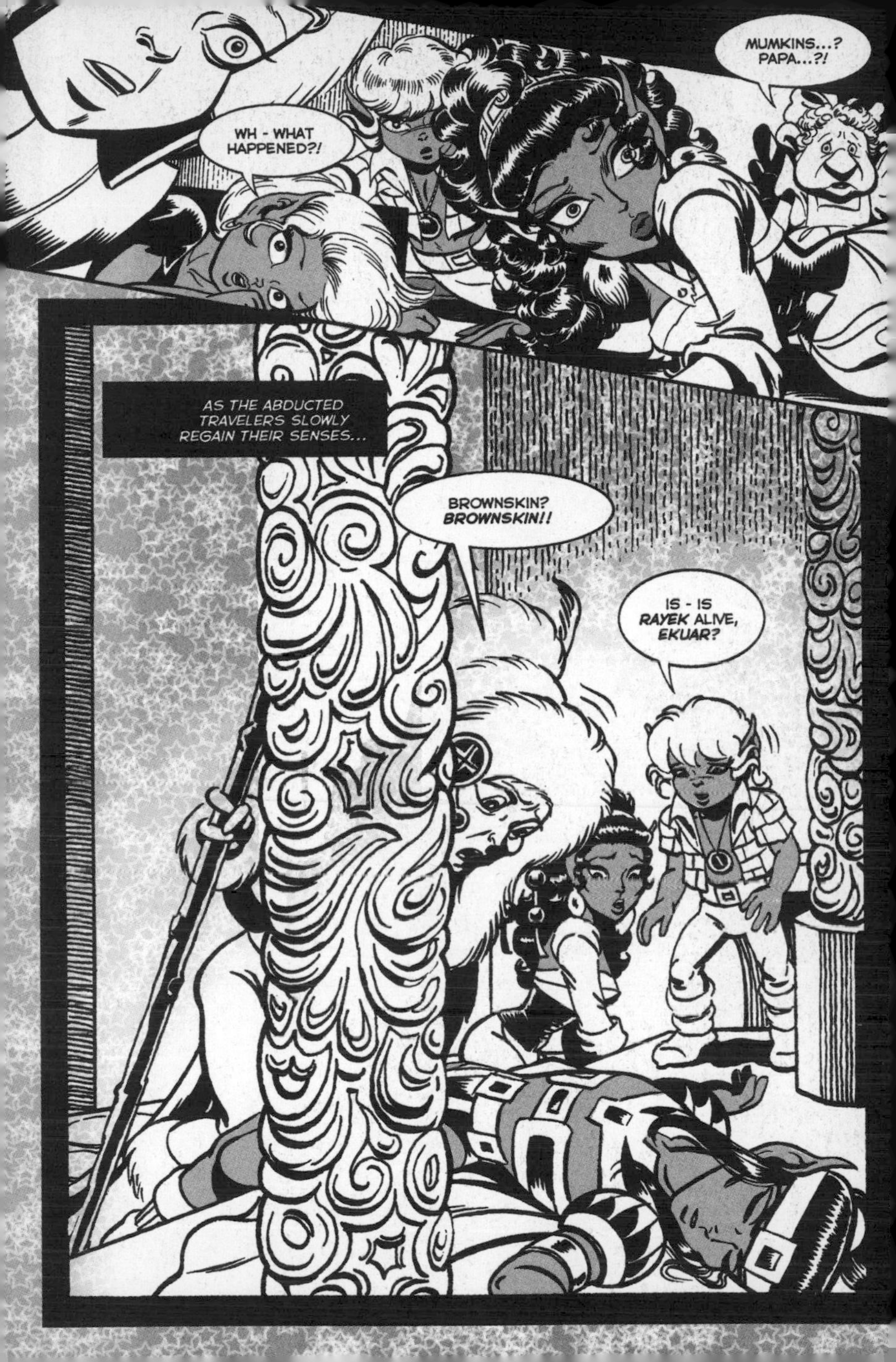
MUMKINS...? PAPA...?!
WH - WHAT HAPPENED?!
AS THE ABDUCTED TRAVELERS SLOWLY REGAIN THEIR SENSES...
BROWNSKIN? BROWNSKIN!!
IS - IS RAYEK ALIVE, EKUAR?

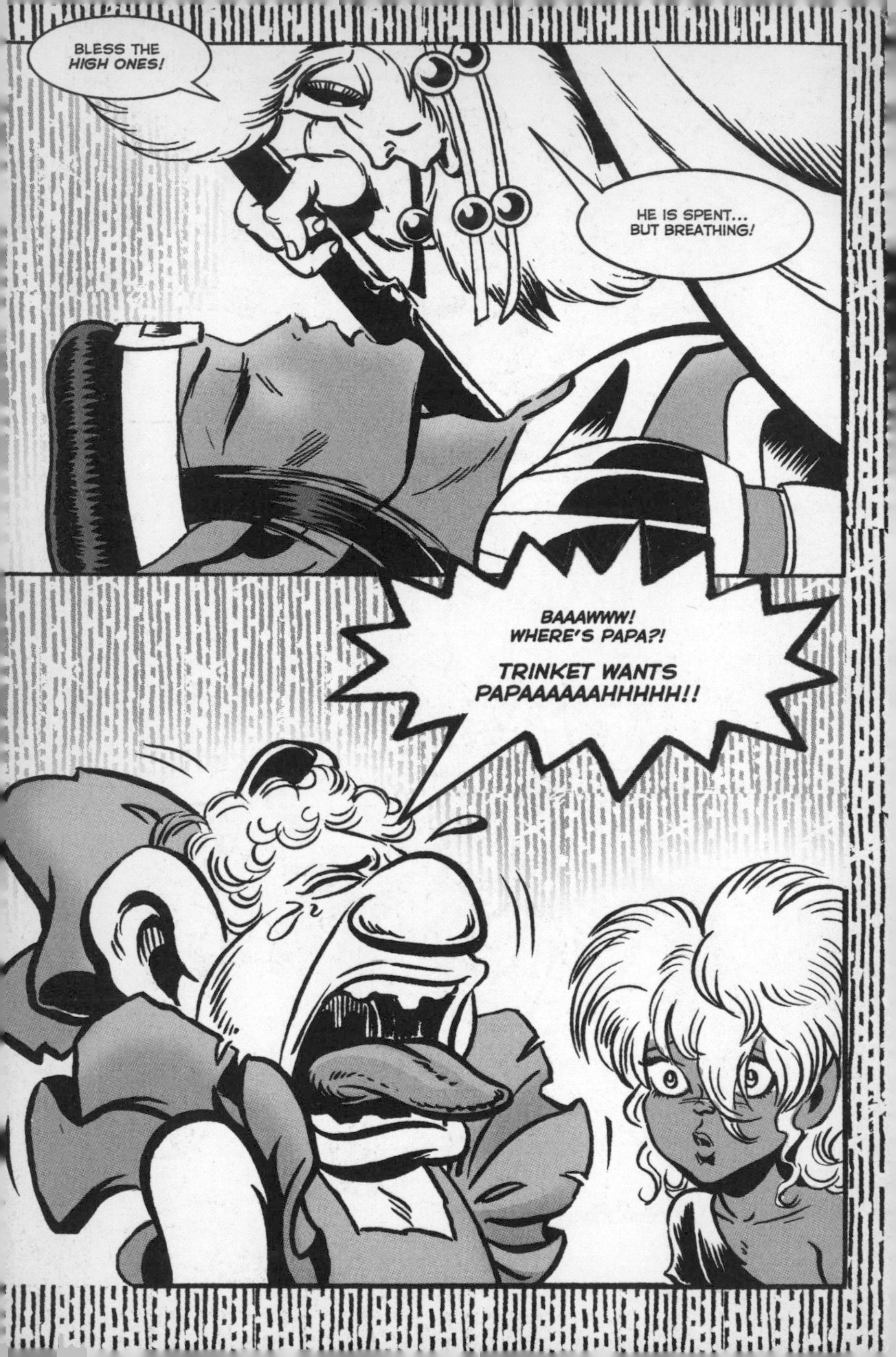
BLESS THE *HIGH ONES!*
HE IS SPENT... BUT BREATHING!
BAAAWWW! WHERE'S PAPA?!
TRINKET WANTS PAPAAAAAAHHHHH!!

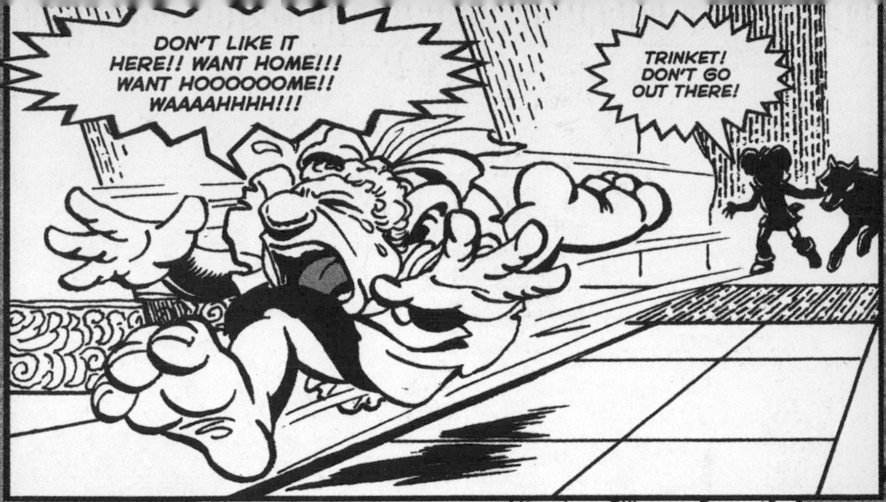
DON'T LIKE IT HERE!! WANT HOME!!! WANT HOOOOOOME!! WAAAAHHHH!!!
TRINKET! DON'T GO OUT THERE!

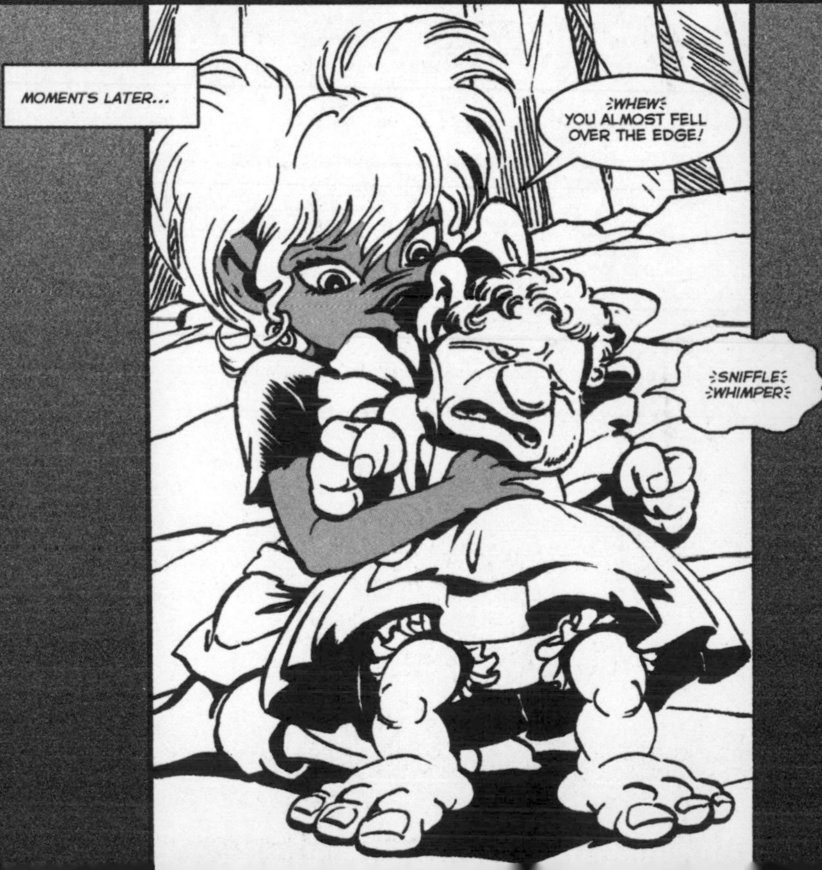
MOMENTS LATER...
WHEW YOU ALMOST FELL OVER THE EDGE!
SNIFFLE WHIMPER

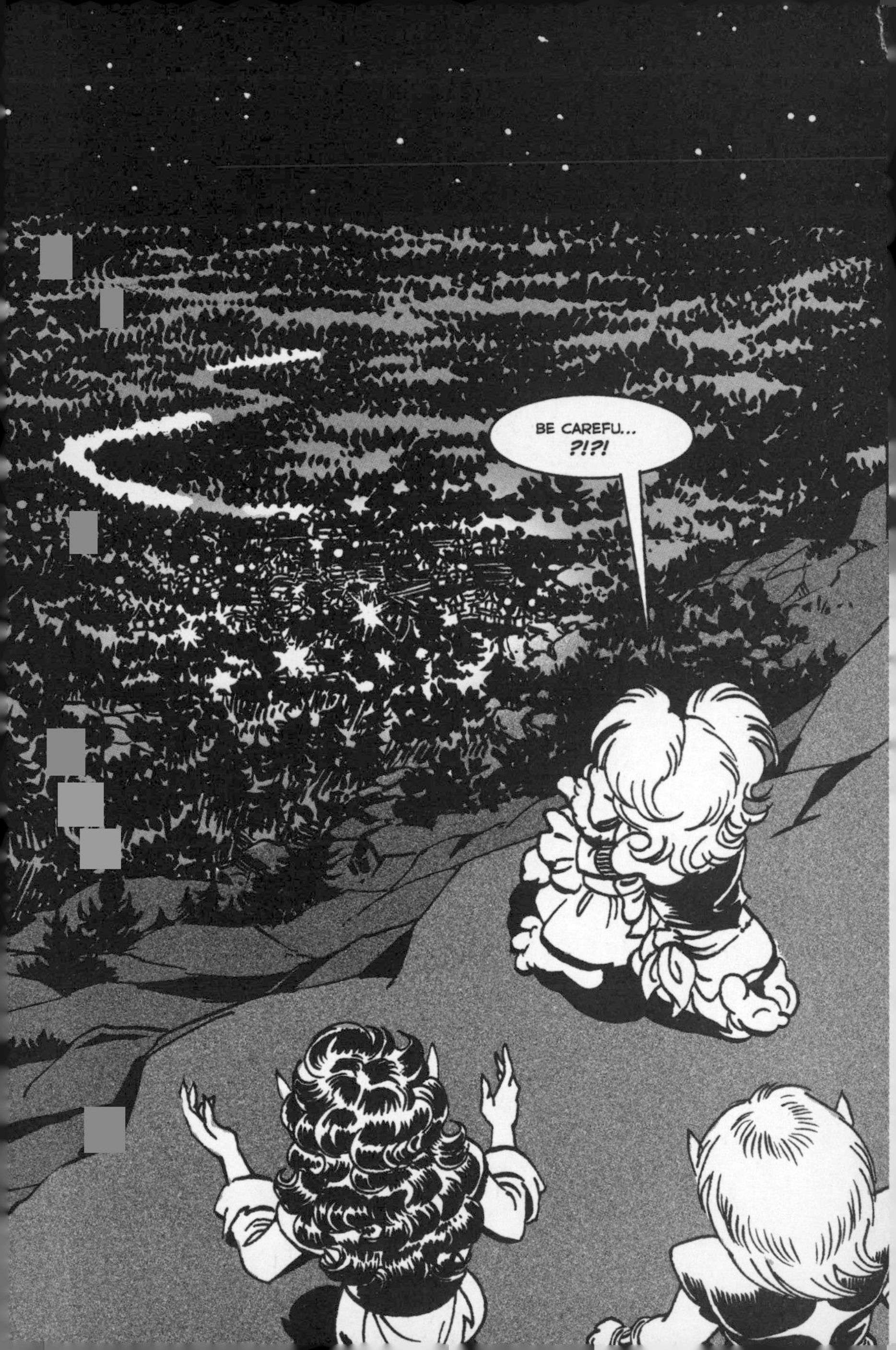
BE CAREFU... ?!?!

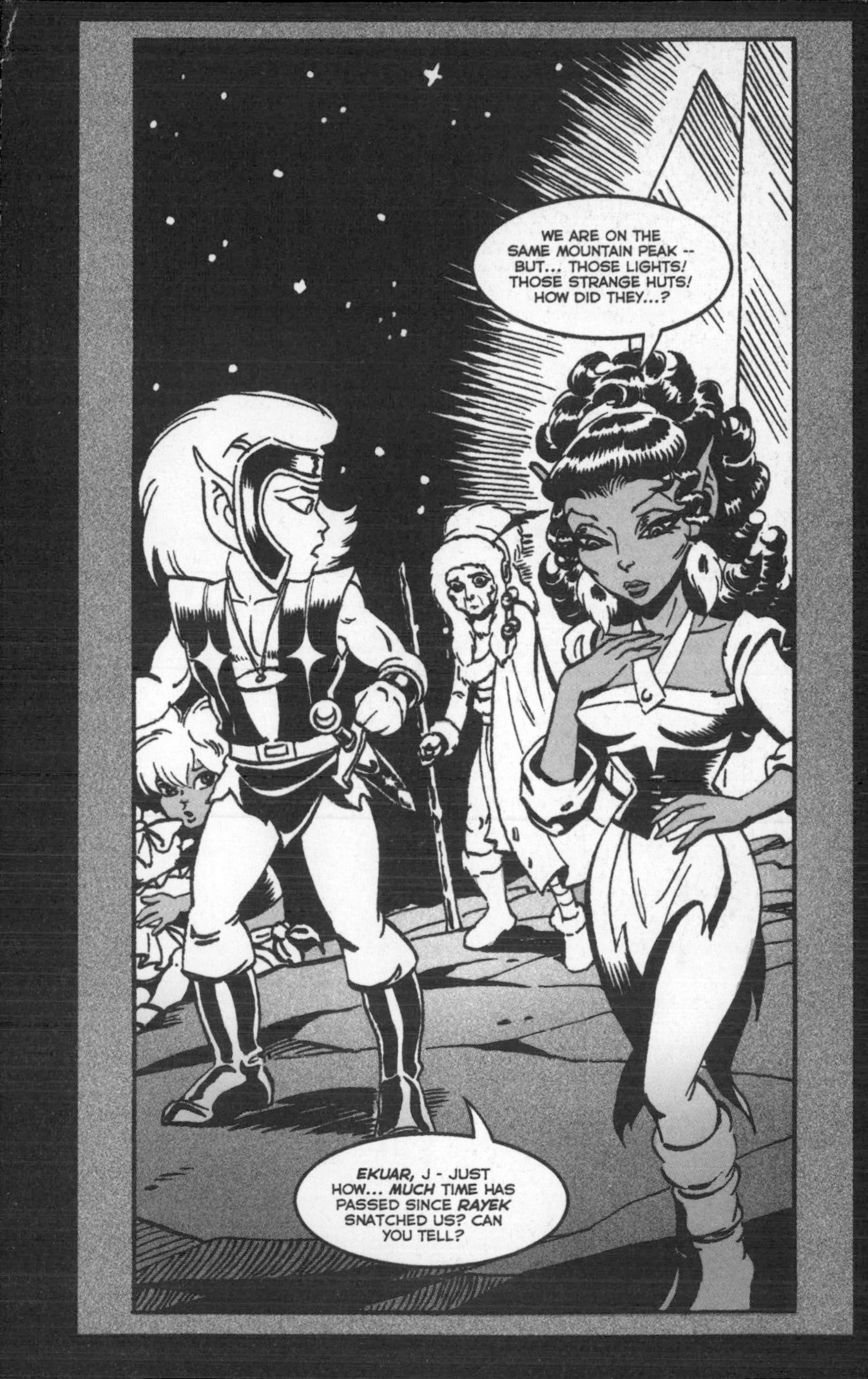
WE ARE ON THE SAME MOUNTAIN PEAK -- BUT... THOSE LIGHTS! THOSE STRANGE HUTS! HOW DID THEY...?
EKUAR, J - JUST HOW... MUCH TIME HAS PASSED SINCE RAYEK SNATCHED US? CAN YOU TELL?

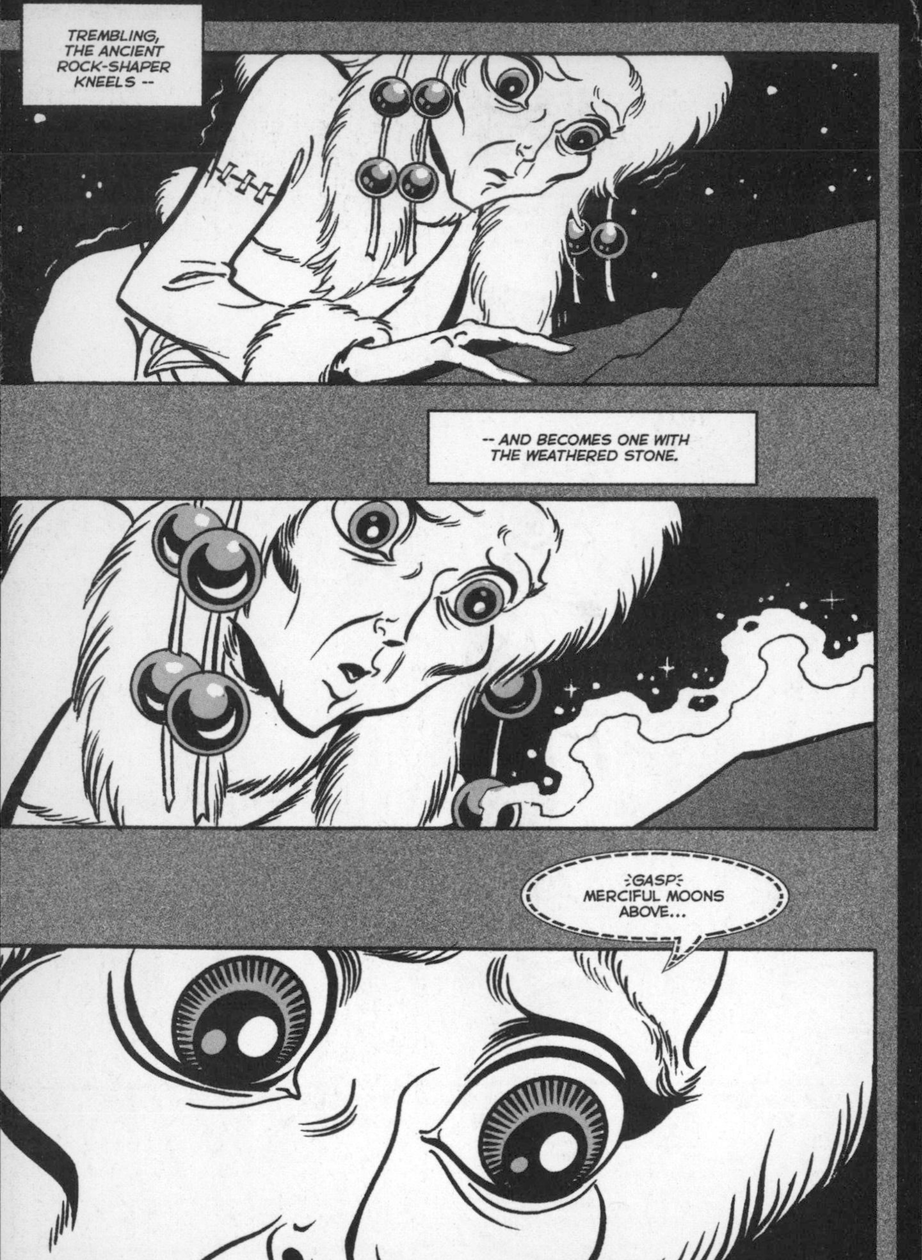
TREMBLING, THE ANCIENT ROCK-SHAPER KNEELS --
-- AND BECOMES ONE WITH THE WEATHERED STONE.
GASP
MERCIFUL MOONS ABOVE...

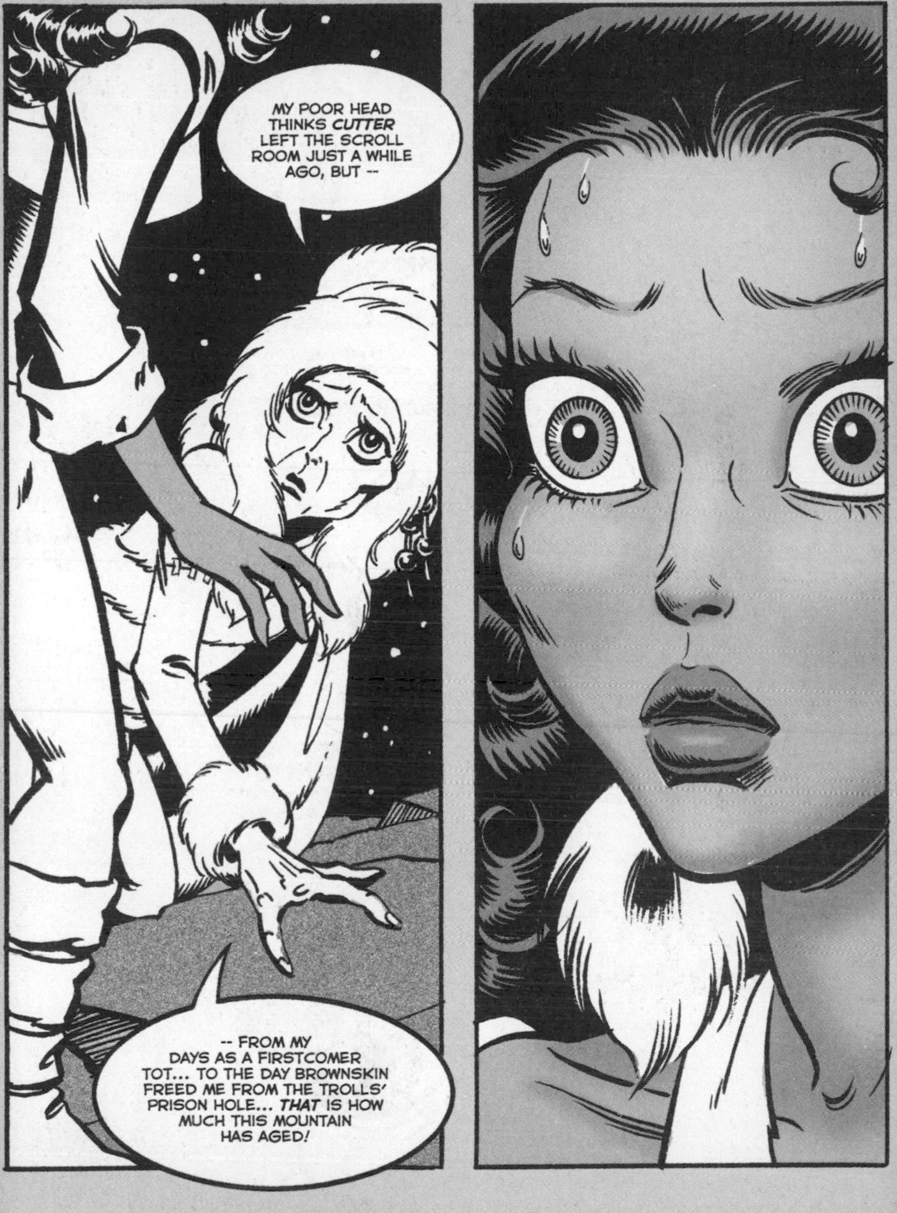
MY POOR HEAD THINKS *CUTTER* LEFT THE SCROLL ROOM JUST A WHILE AGO, BUT --
-- FROM MY DAYS AS A FIRSTCOMER TOT... TO THE DAY BROWNSKIN FREED ME FROM THE TROLLS' PRISON HOLE... *THAT* IS HOW MUCH THIS MOUNTAIN HAS AGED!

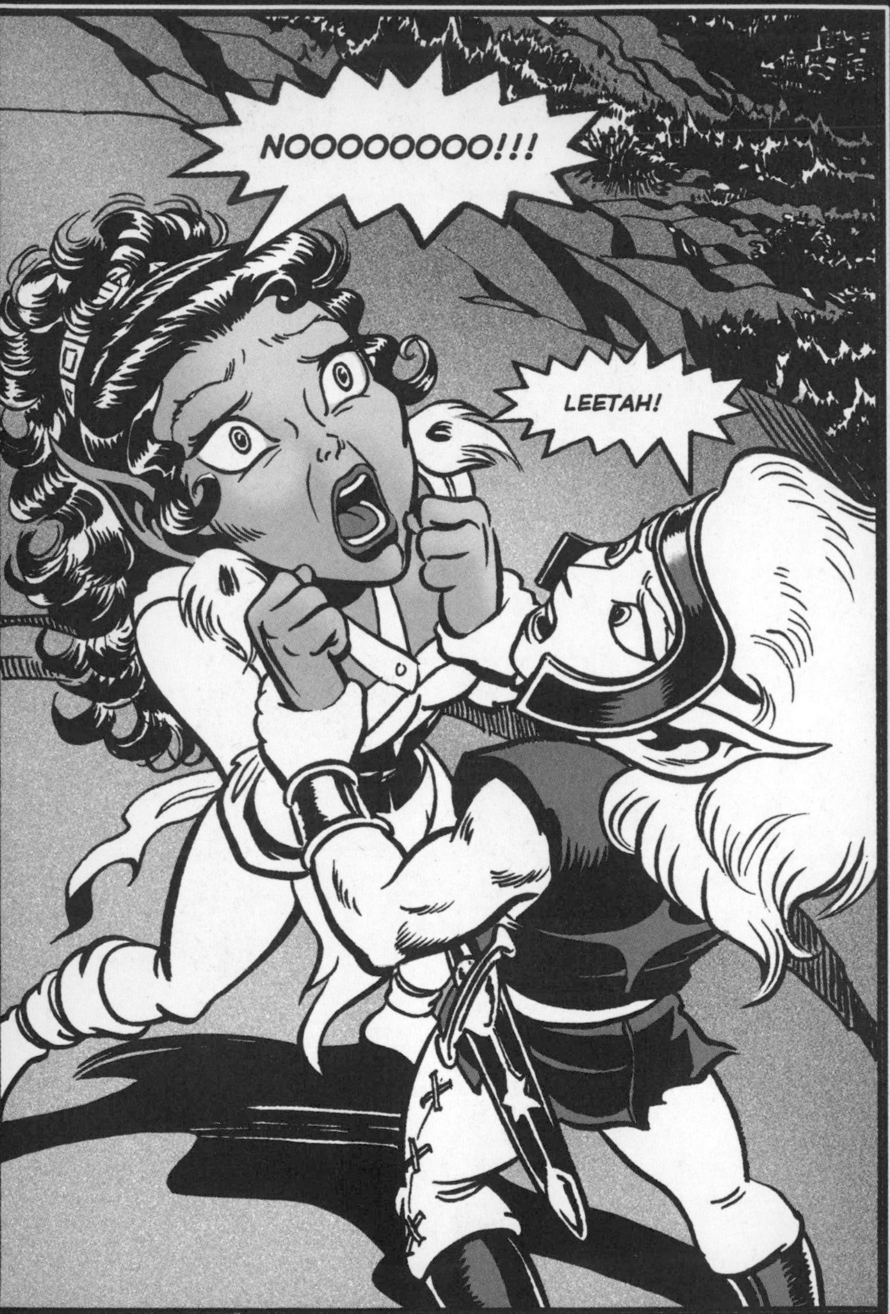
NOOOOOOOO!!!
LEETAH!

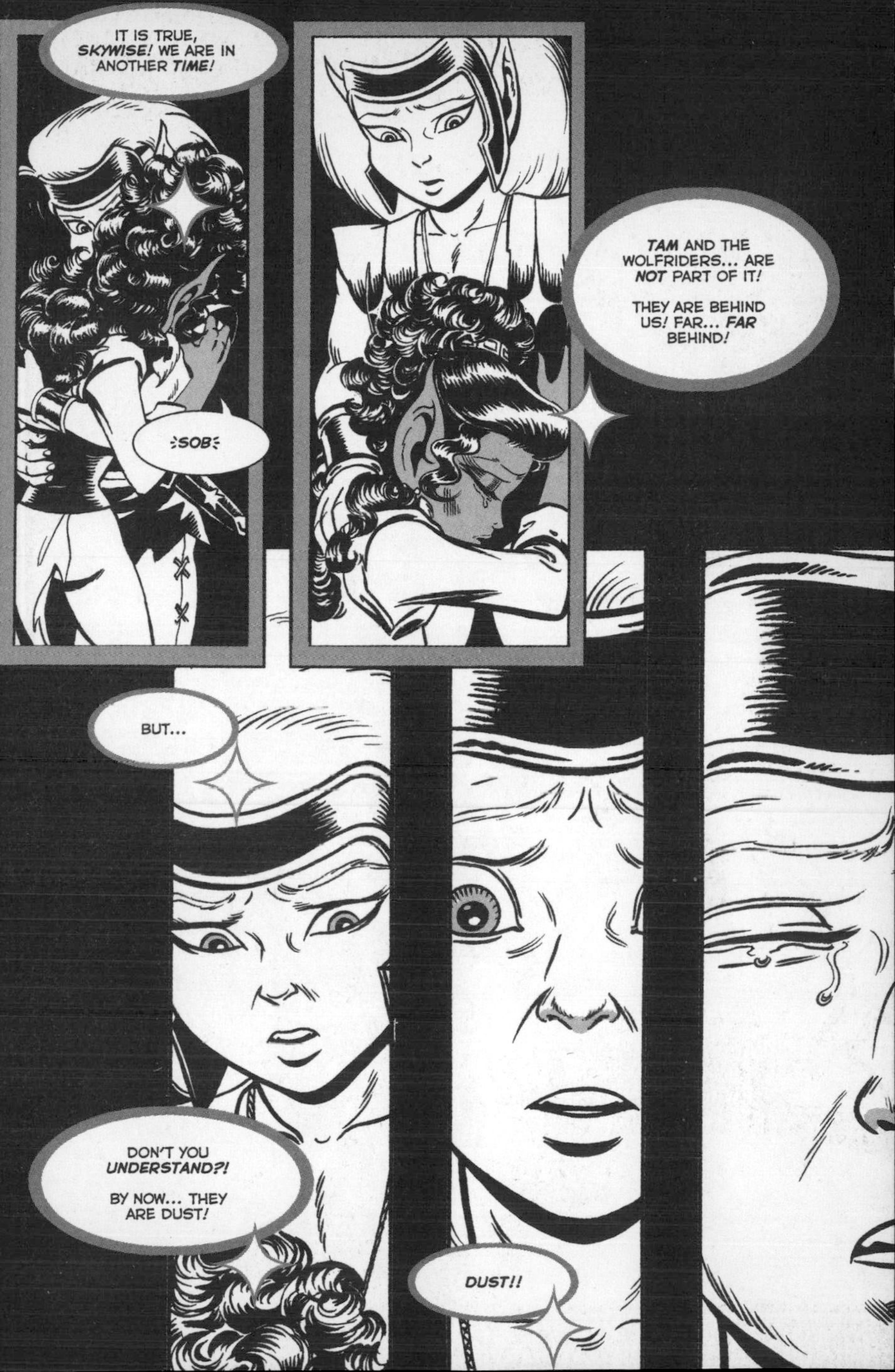

IT IS TRUE, *SKYWISE!* WE ARE IN ANOTHER *TIME!*
SOB
TAM AND THE WOLFRIDERS... ARE *NOT* PART OF IT!
THEY ARE BEHIND US! FAR... *FAR* BEHIND!
BUT...
DON'T YOU *UNDERSTAND?!*
BY NOW... THEY ARE DUST!
DUST!!

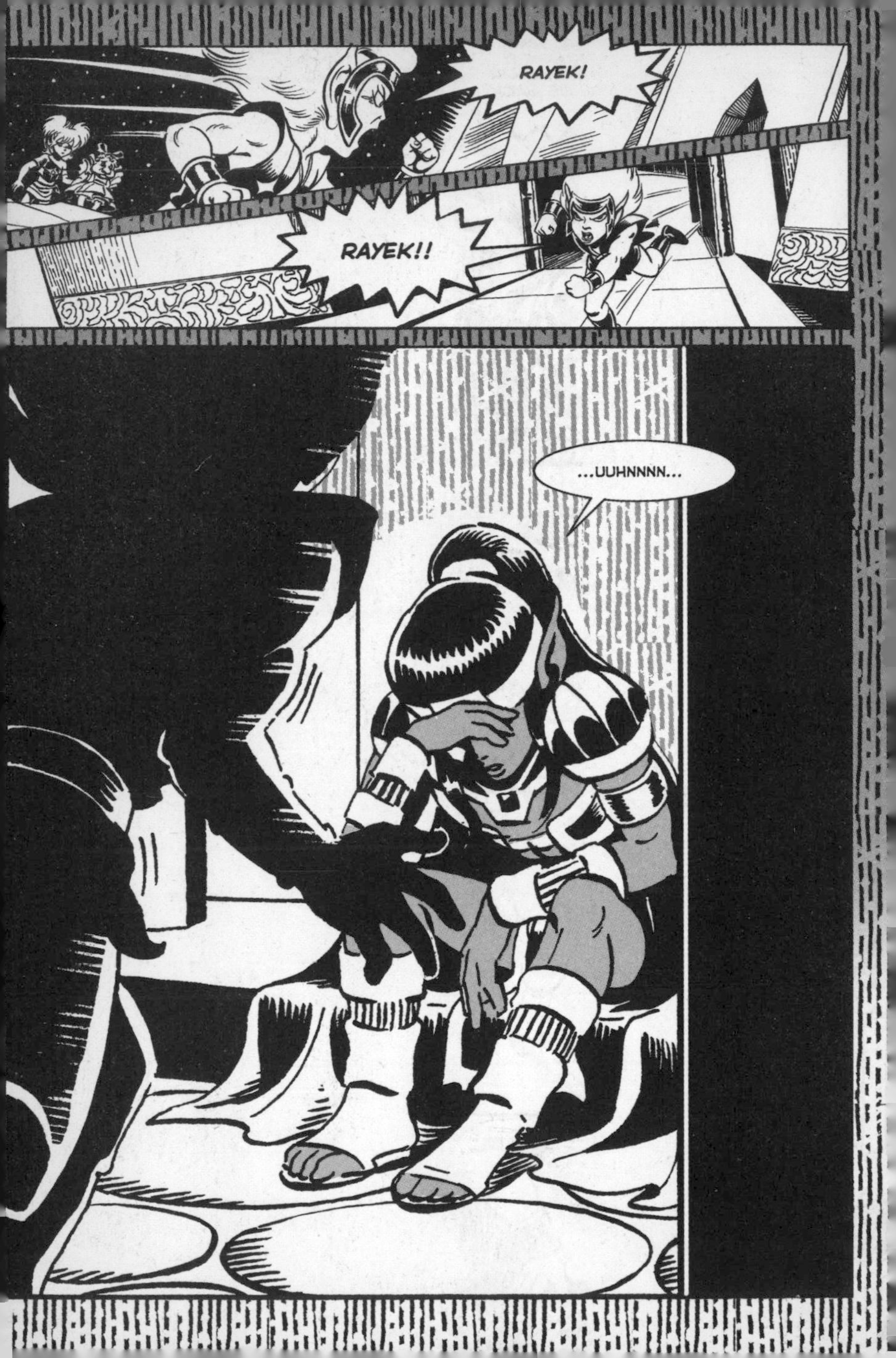
RAYEK!
RAYEK!!
...UUHNNNN...

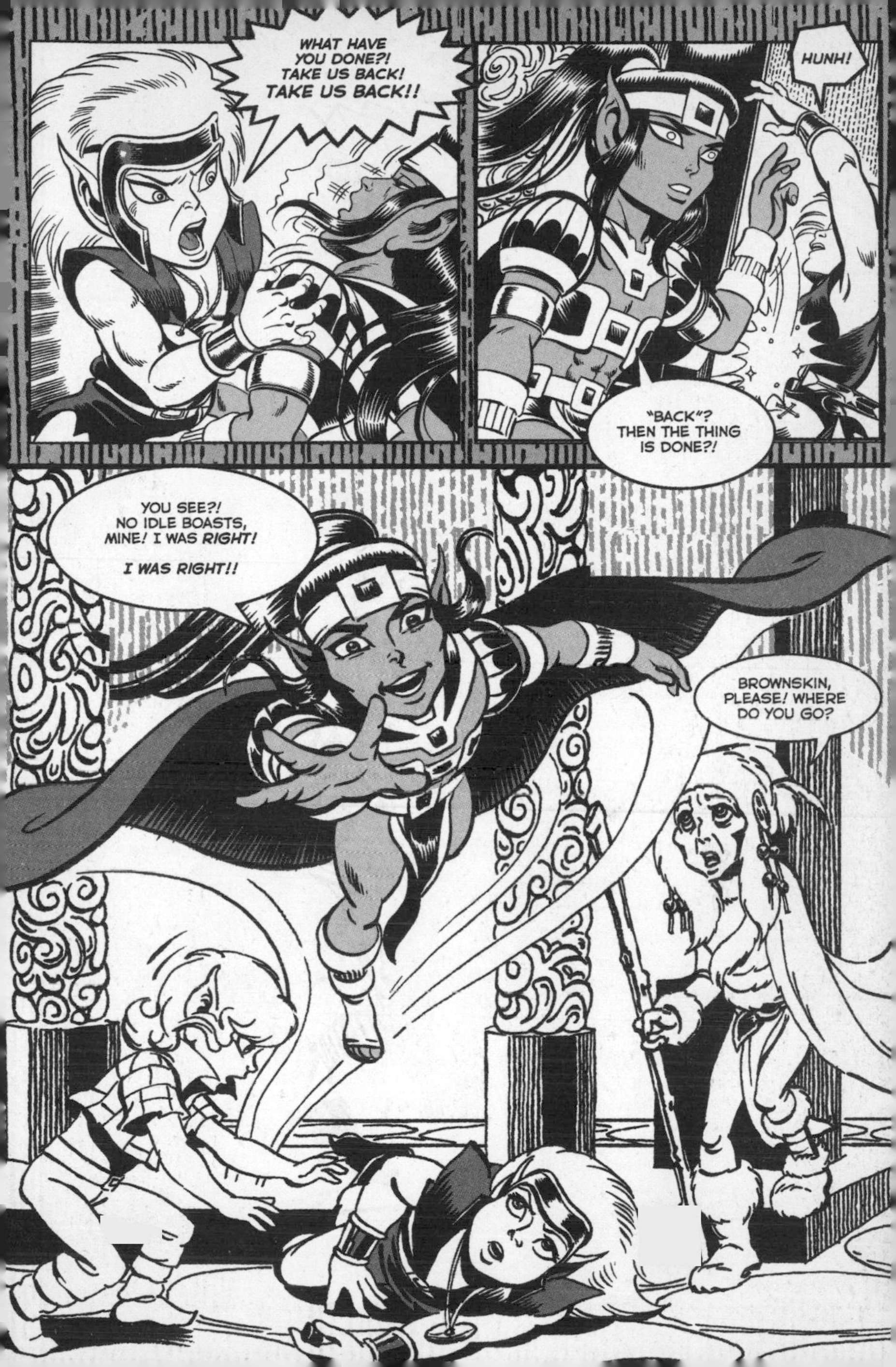
WHAT HAVE YOU DONE?! TAKE US BACK! TAKE US BACK!!
HUNH!
"BACK"? THEN THE THING IS DONE?!
YOU SEE?! NO IDLE BOASTS, MINE! I WAS RIGHT!
I WAS RIGHT!!
BROWNSKIN, PLEASE! WHERE DO YOU GO?

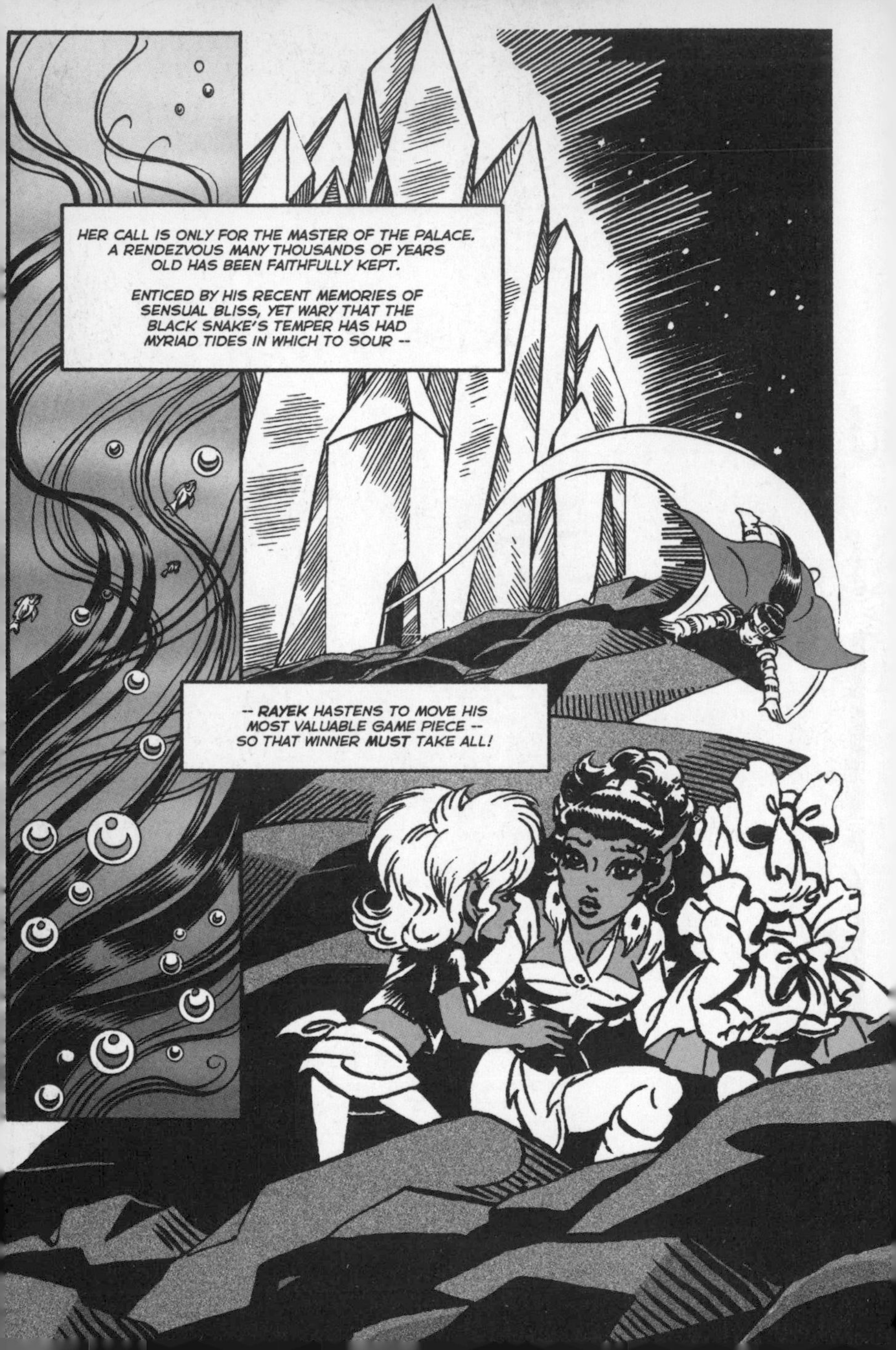
HER CALL IS ONLY FOR THE MASTER OF THE PALACE. A RENDEZVOUS MANY THOUSANDS OF YEARS OLD HAS BEEN FAITHFULLY KEPT.
ENTICED BY HIS RECENT MEMORIES OF SENSUAL BLISS, YET WARY THAT THE BLACK SNAKE'S TEMPER HAS HAD MYRIAD TIDES IN WHICH TO SOUR --
-- RAYEK HASTENS TO MOVE HIS MOST VALUABLE GAME PIECE -- SO THAT WINNER MUST TAKE ALL!

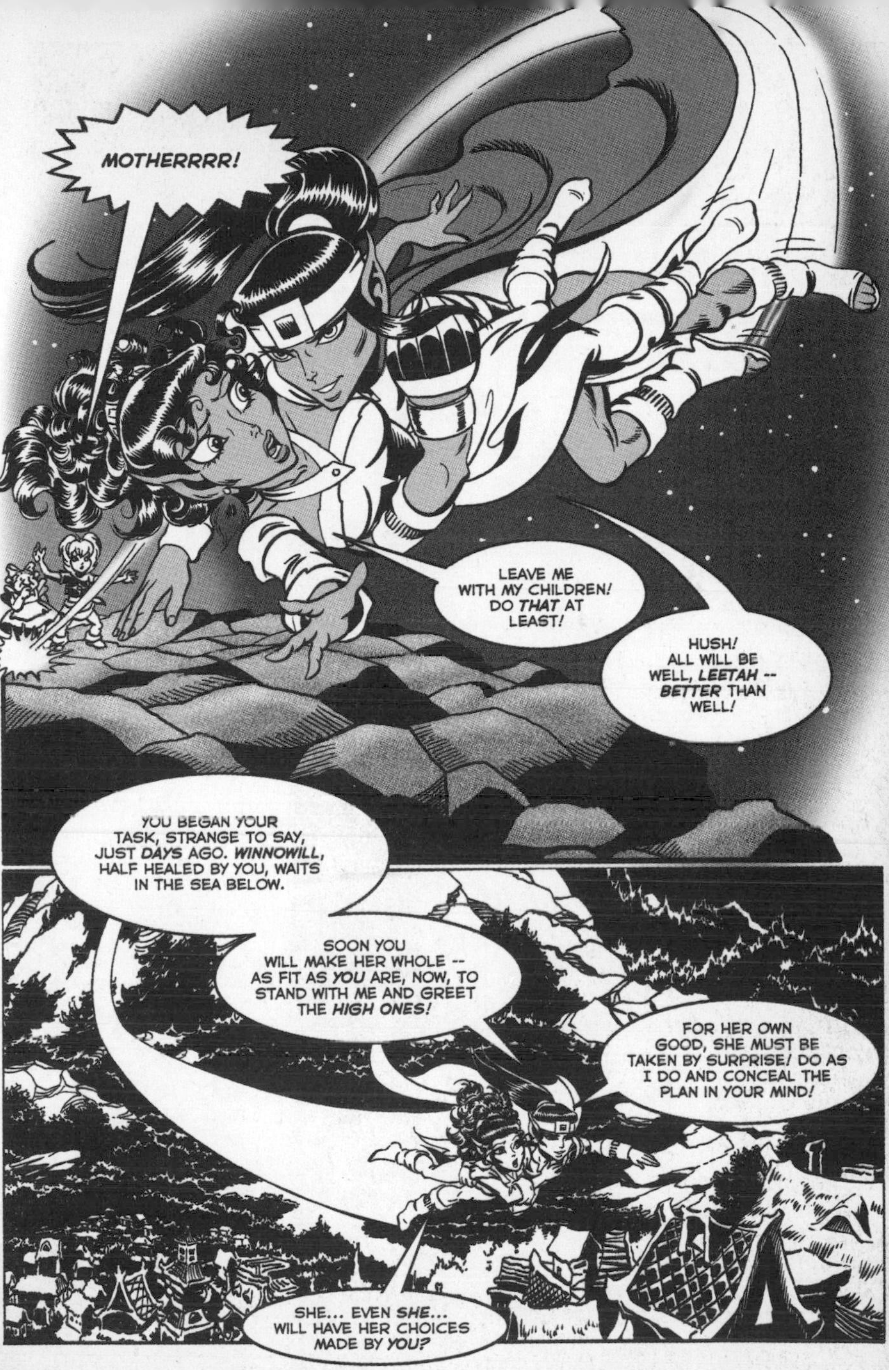
MOTHERRRR!
LEAVE ME WITH MY CHILDREN! DO THAT AT LEAST!
HUSH! ALL WILL BE WELL, LEETAH -- BETTER THAN WELL!
YOU BEGAN YOUR TASK, STRANGE TO SAY, JUST DAYS AGO. WINNOWILL, HALF HEALED BY YOU, WAITS IN THE SEA BELOW.
SOON YOU WILL MAKE HER WHOLE -- AS FIT AS YOU ARE, NOW, TO STAND WITH ME AND GREET THE HIGH ONES!
FOR HER OWN GOOD, SHE MUST BE TAKEN BY SURPRISE! DO AS I DO AND CONCEAL THE PLAN IN YOUR MIND!
SHE... EVEN SHE... WILL HAVE HER CHOICES MADE BY YOU?

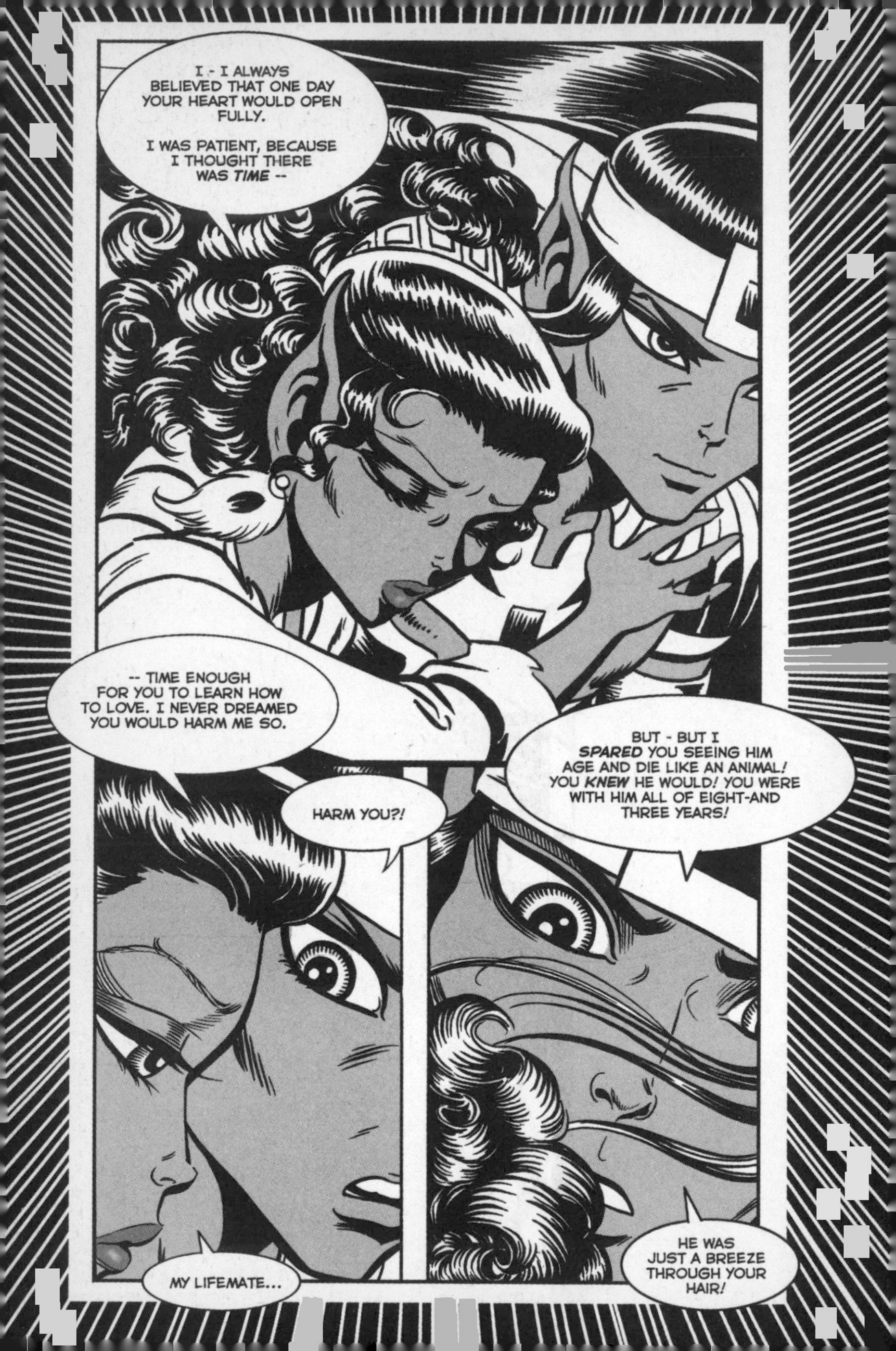
I - I ALWAYS BELIEVED THAT ONE DAY YOUR HEART WOULD OPEN FULLY.
I WAS PATIENT, BECAUSE I THOUGHT THERE WAS *TIME* --
-- TIME ENOUGH FOR YOU TO LEARN HOW TO LOVE. I NEVER DREAMED YOU WOULD HARM ME SO.
HARM YOU?!
BUT - BUT I ***SPARED*** YOU SEEING HIM AGE AND DIE LIKE AN ANIMAL! YOU ***KNEW*** HE WOULD! YOU WERE WITH HIM ALL OF EIGHT-AND THREE YEARS!
MY LIFEMATE...
HE WAS JUST A BREEZE THROUGH YOUR HAIR!

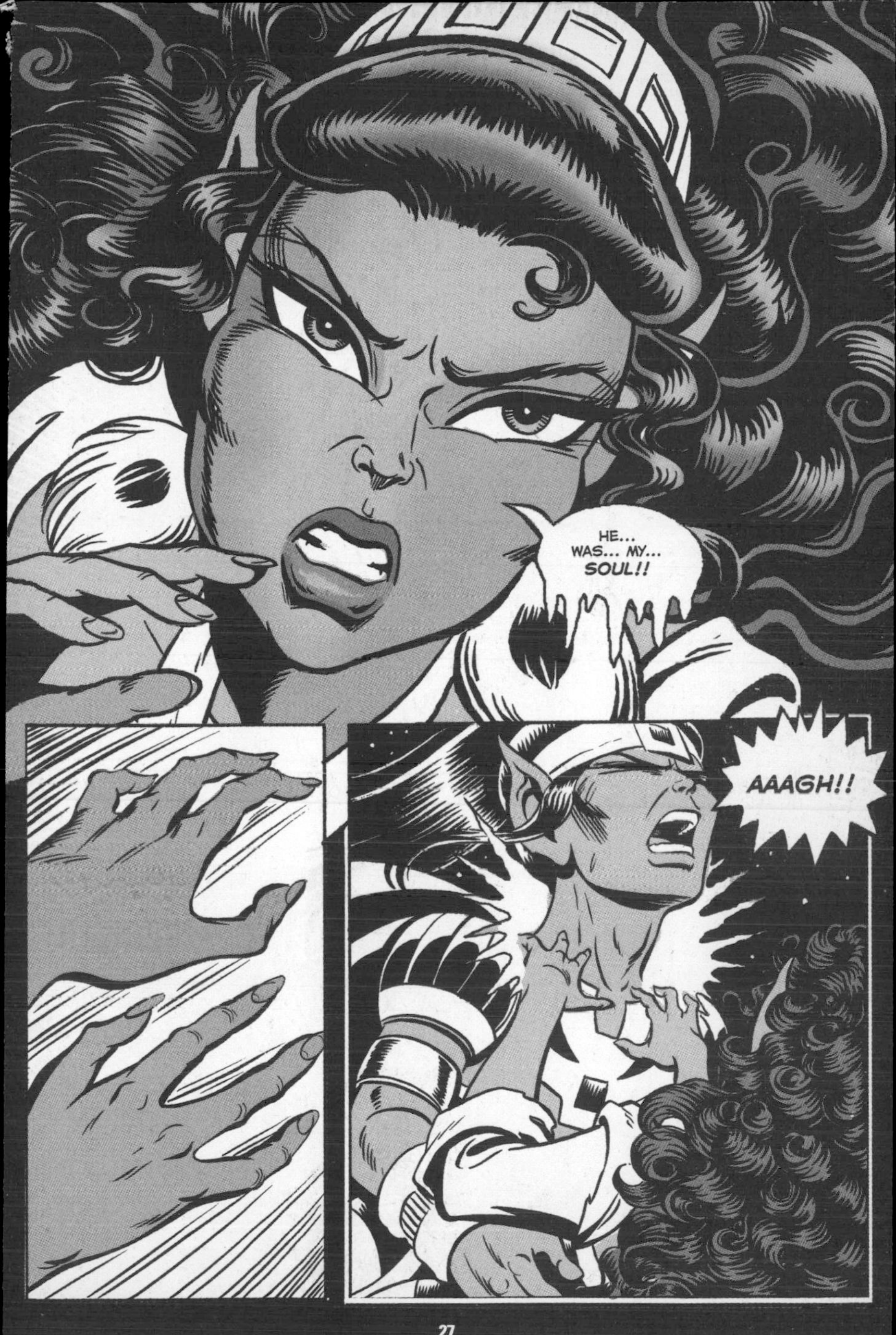
HE... WAS... MY... SOUL!!
AAAGH!!

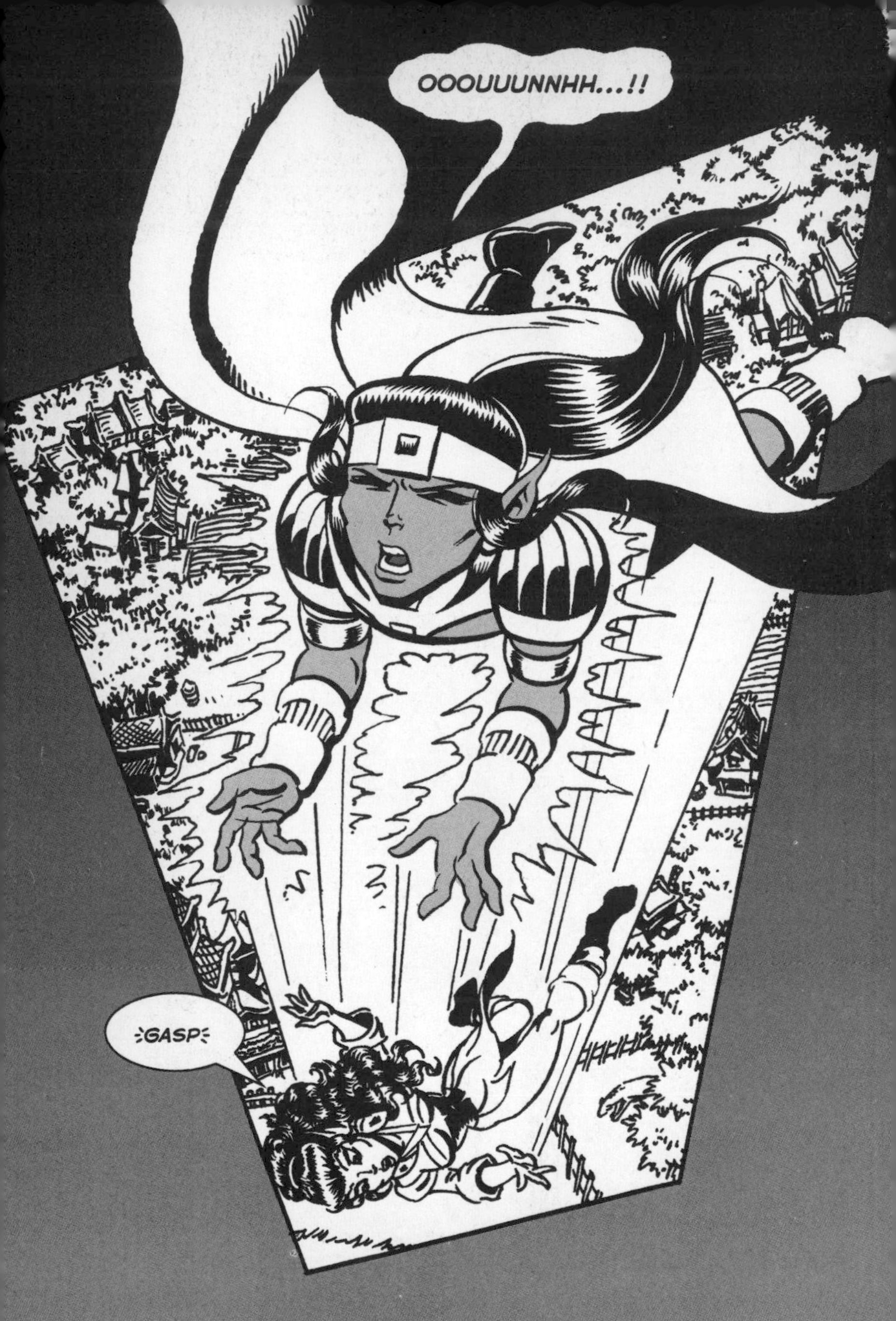
OOOUUUNNHH...!!
GASP

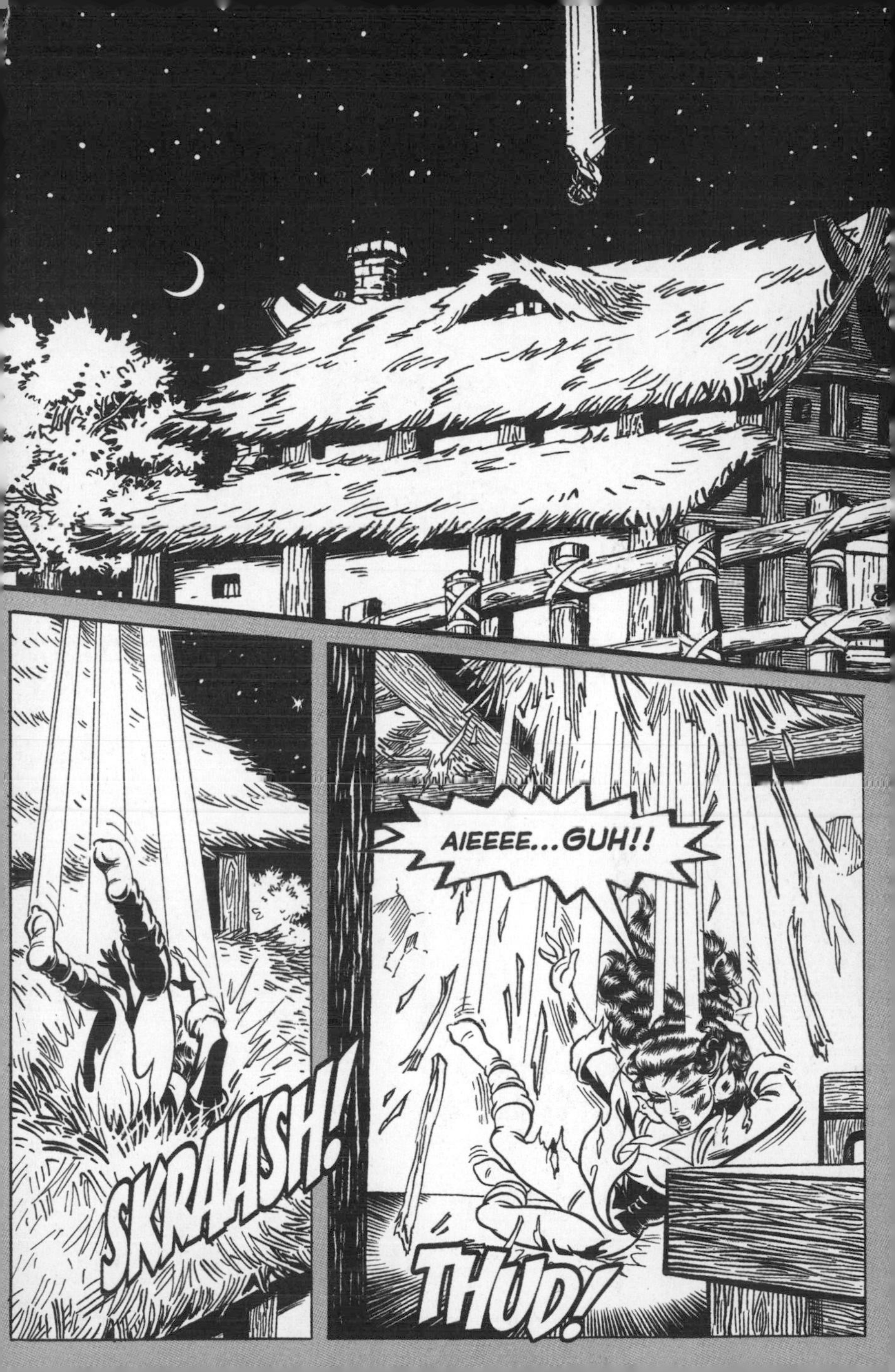
SKRAASH!
AIEEEE...GUH!!
THUD!

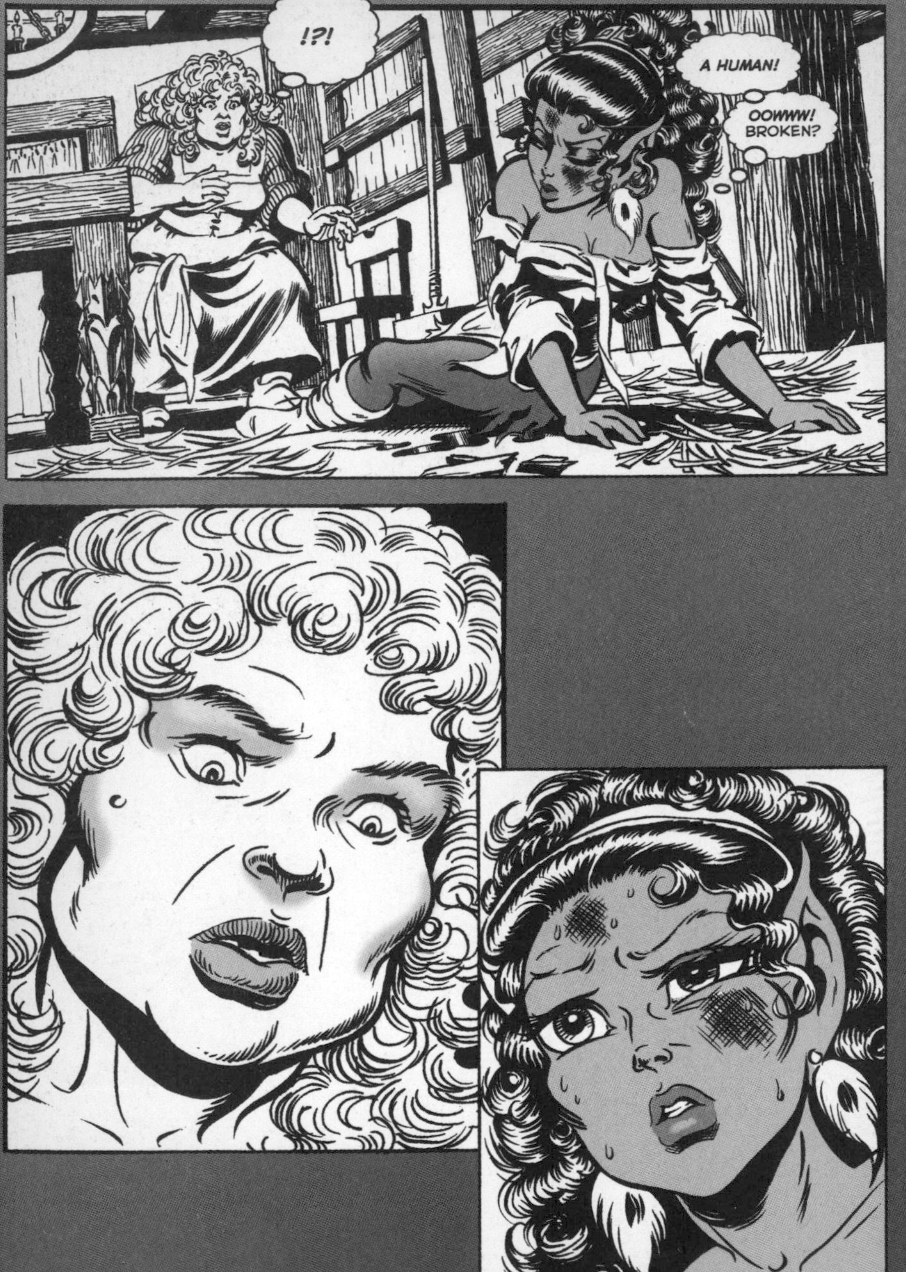
!?!
A HUMAN!
OOWWW! BROKEN?

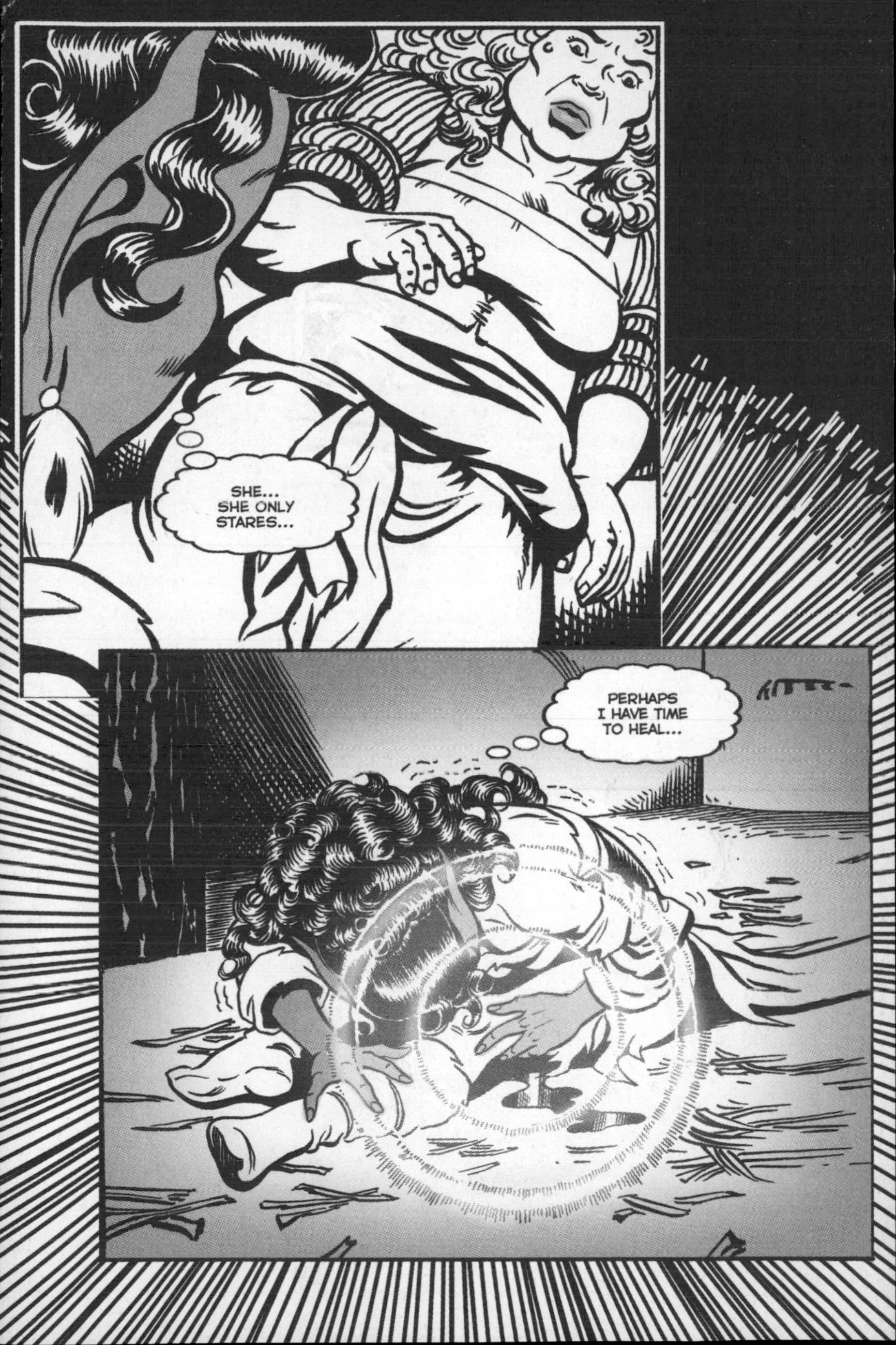
SHE... SHE ONLY STARES...
PERHAPS I HAVE TIME TO HEAL...

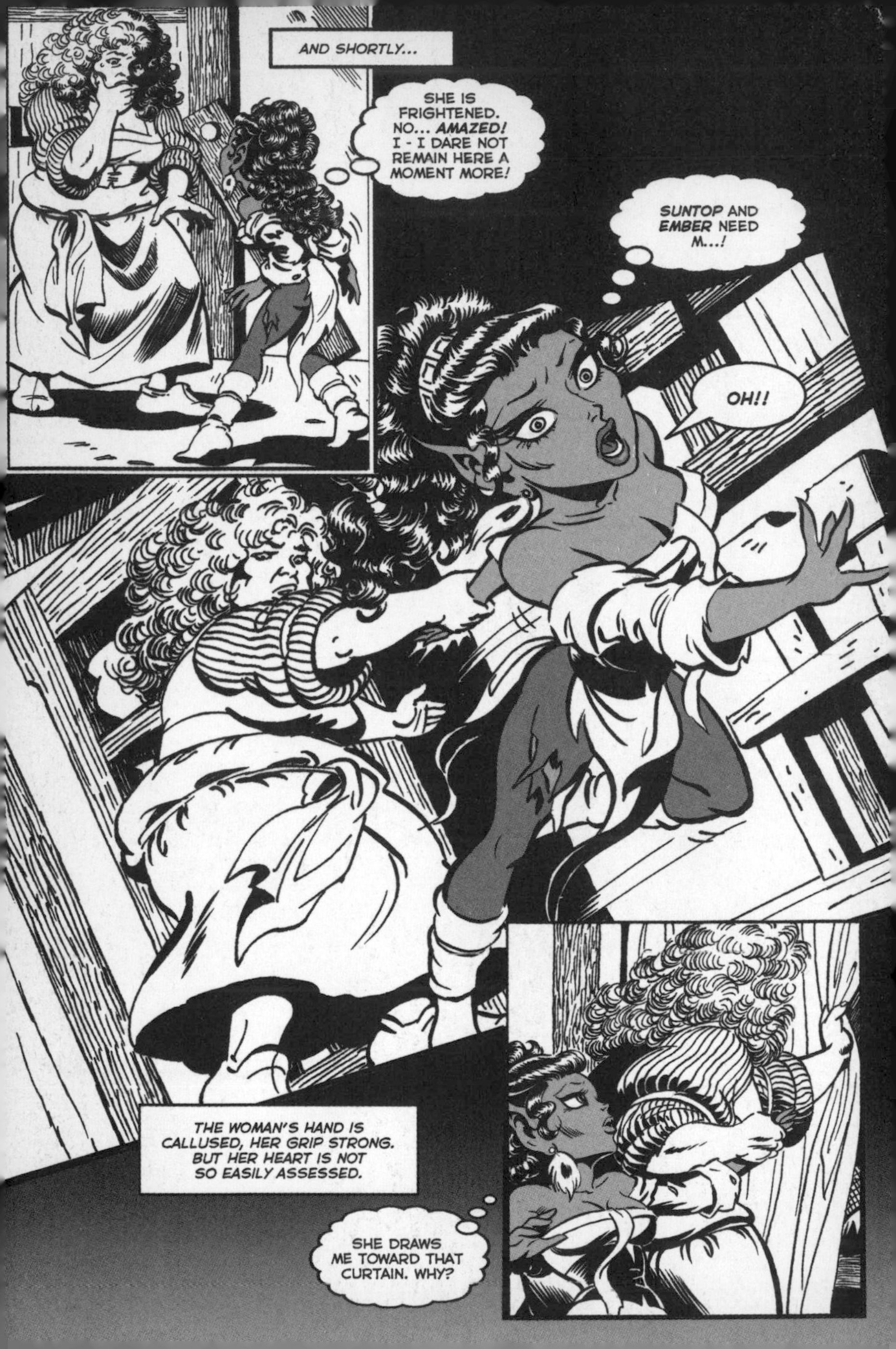
AND SHORTLY...
SHE IS FRIGHTENED. NO... AMAZED! I - I DARE NOT REMAIN HERE A MOMENT MORE!
SUNTOP AND EMBER NEED M...!
OH!!
THE WOMAN'S HAND IS CALLUSED, HER GRIP STRONG. BUT HER HEART IS NOT SO EASILY ASSESSED.
SHE DRAWS ME TOWARD THAT CURTAIN. WHY?

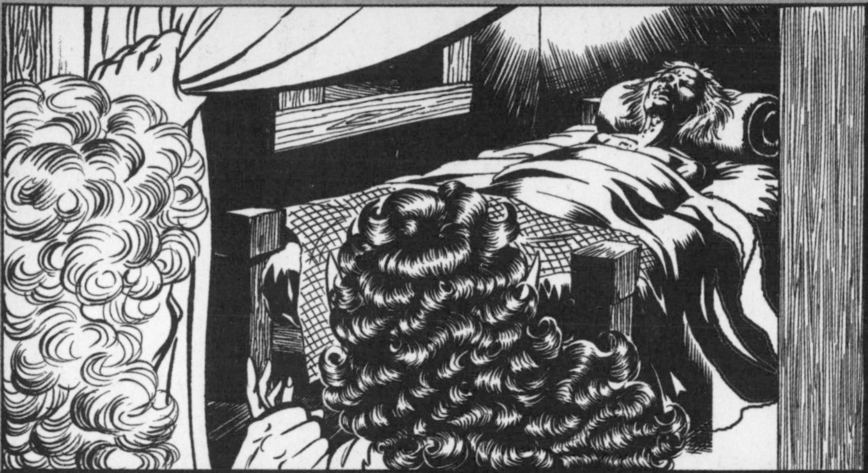

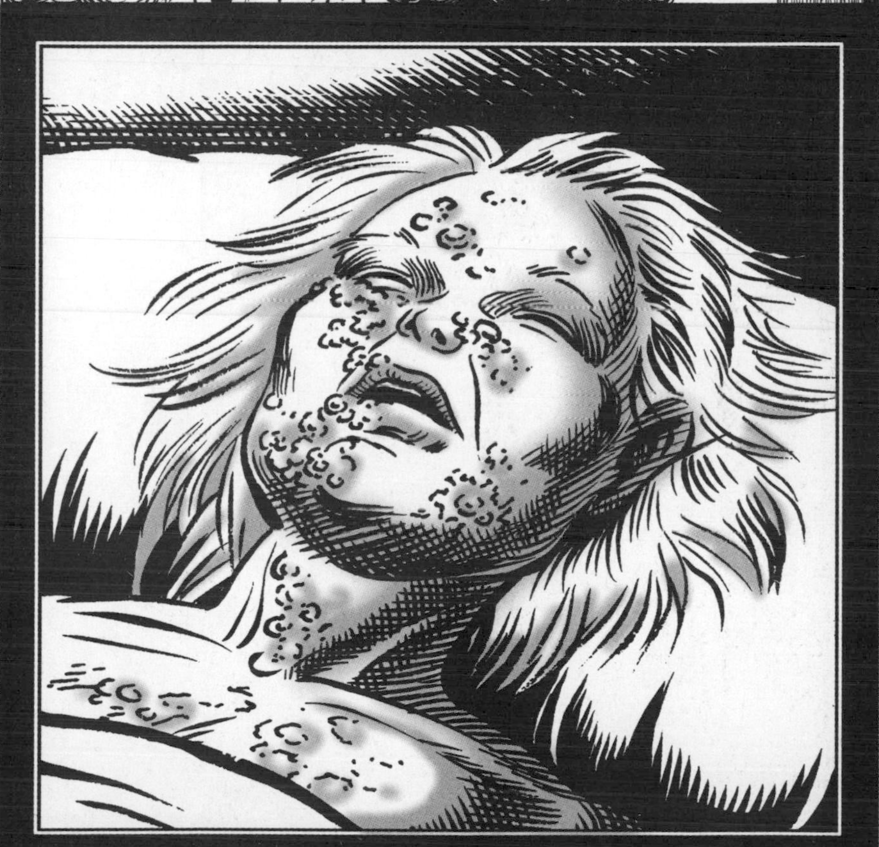

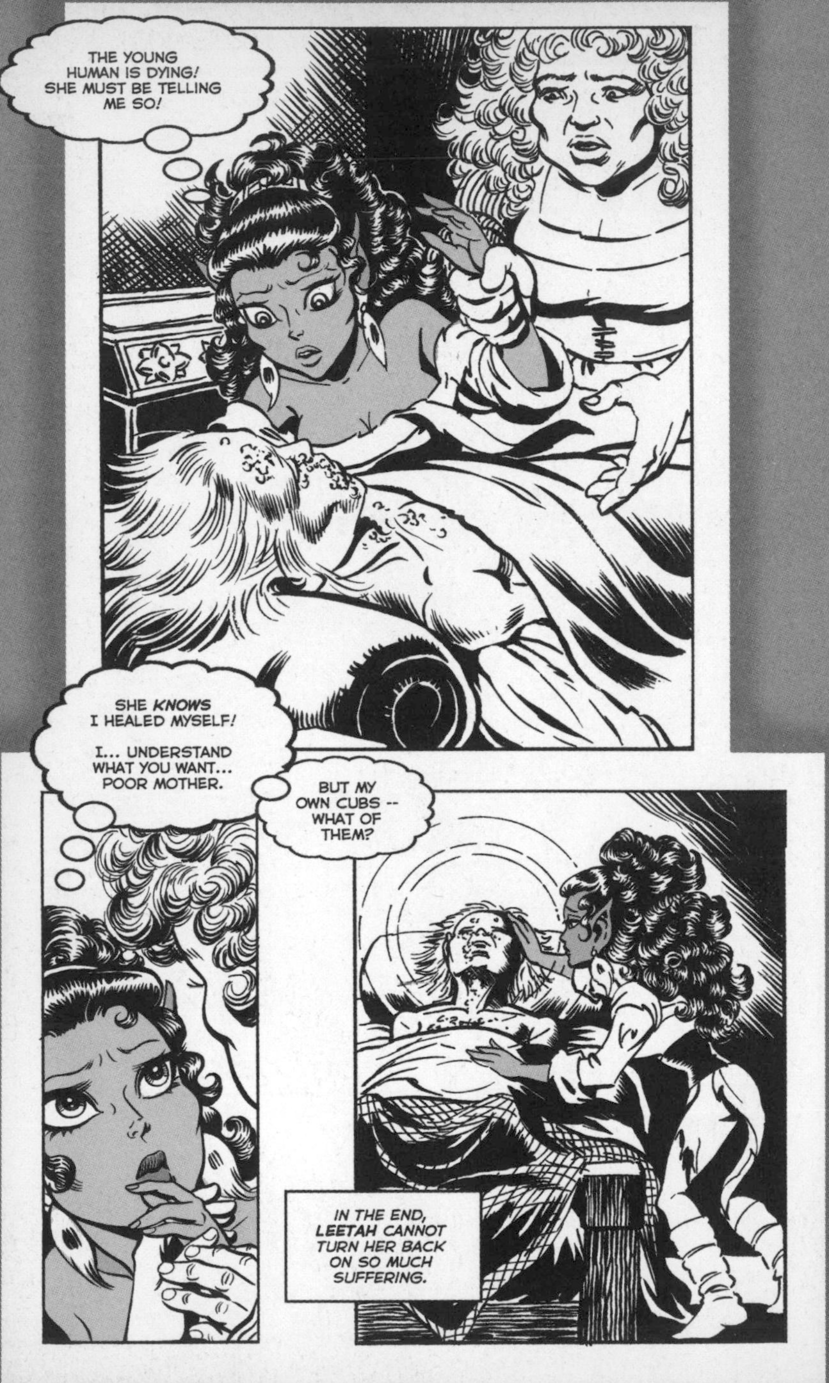
THE YOUNG HUMAN IS DYING! SHE MUST BE TELLING ME SO!
SHE *KNOWS* I HEALED MYSELF!
I... UNDERSTAND WHAT YOU WANT... POOR MOTHER.
BUT MY OWN CUBS -- WHAT OF THEM?
IN THE END, LEETAH CANNOT TURN HER BACK ON SO MUCH SUFFERING.

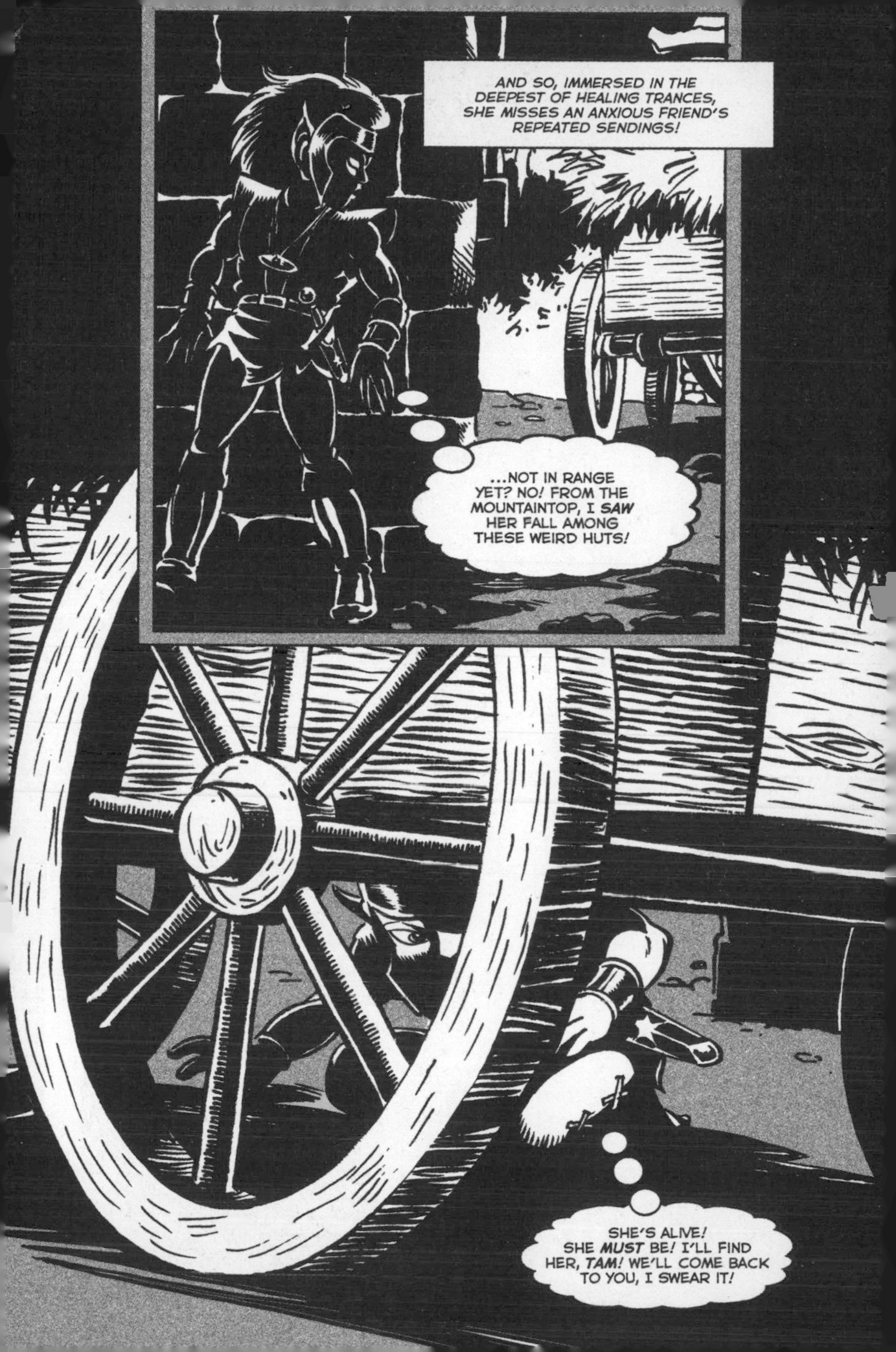
AND SO, IMMERSED IN THE DEEPEST OF HEALING TRANCES, SHE MISSES AN ANXIOUS FRIEND'S REPEATED SENDINGS!
...NOT IN RANGE YET? NO! FROM THE MOUNTAINTOP, I *SAW* HER FALL AMONG THESE WEIRD HUTS!
SHE'S ALIVE! SHE *MUST* BE! I'LL FIND HER, *TAM!* WE'LL COME BACK TO YOU, I SWEAR IT!

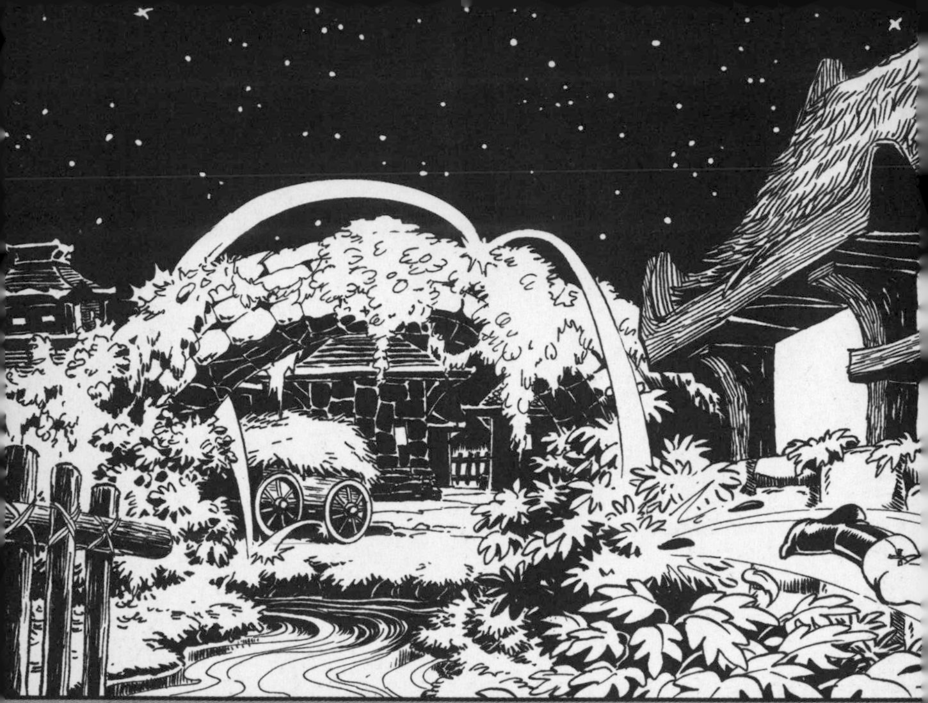

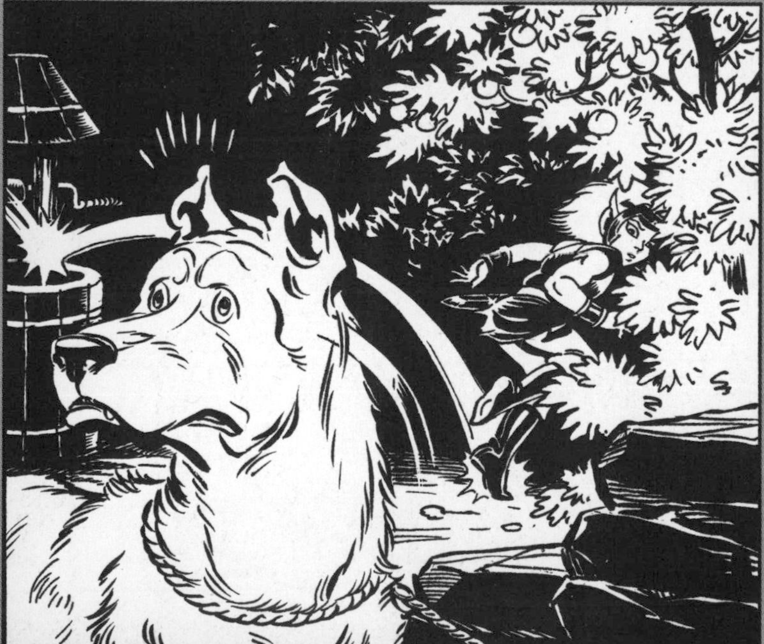

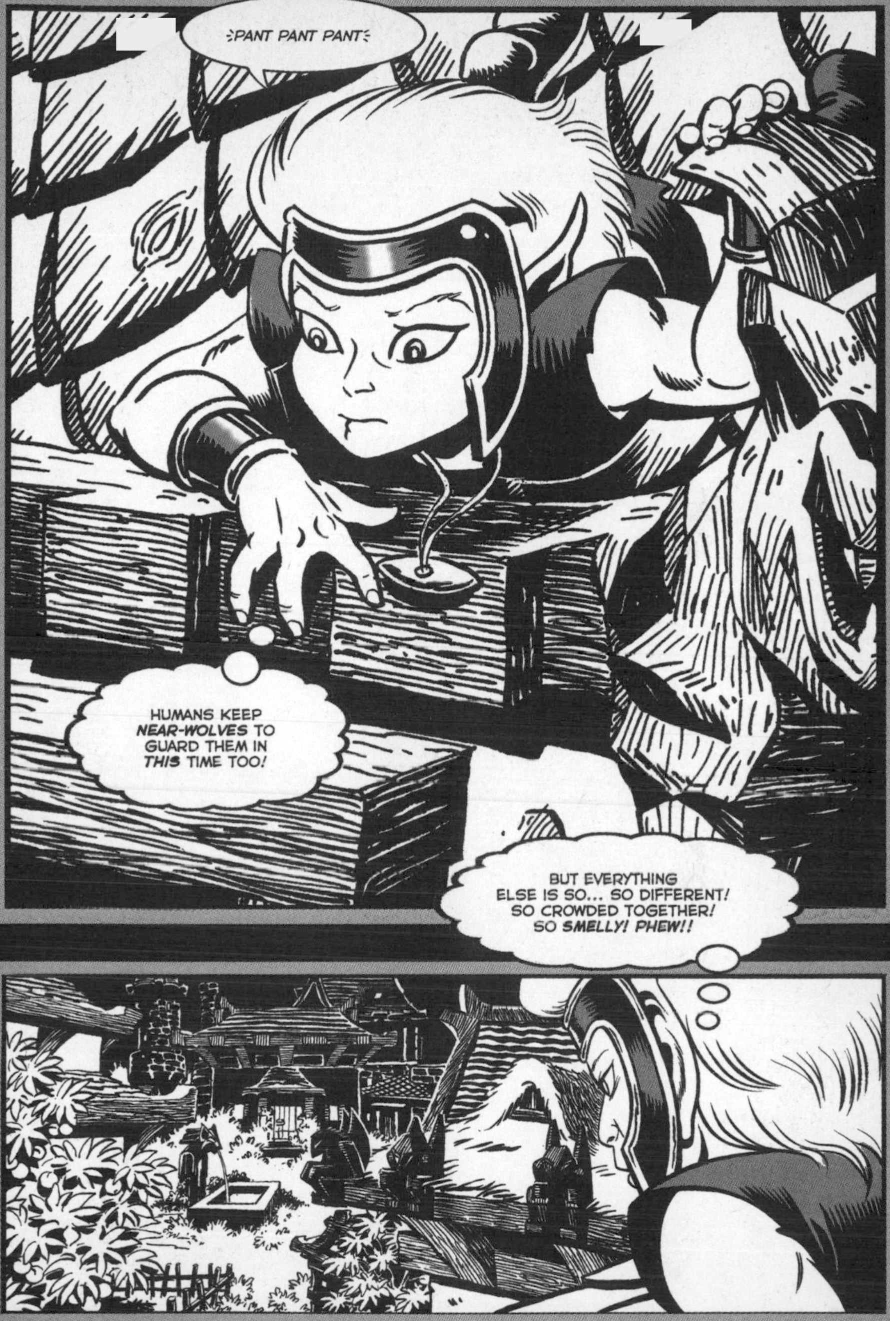
PANT PANT PANT
HUMANS KEEP NEAR-WOLVES TO GUARD THEM IN THIS TIME TOO!
BUT EVERYTHING ELSE IS SO... SO DIFFERENT! SO CROWDED TOGETHER! SO SMELLY! PHEW!!

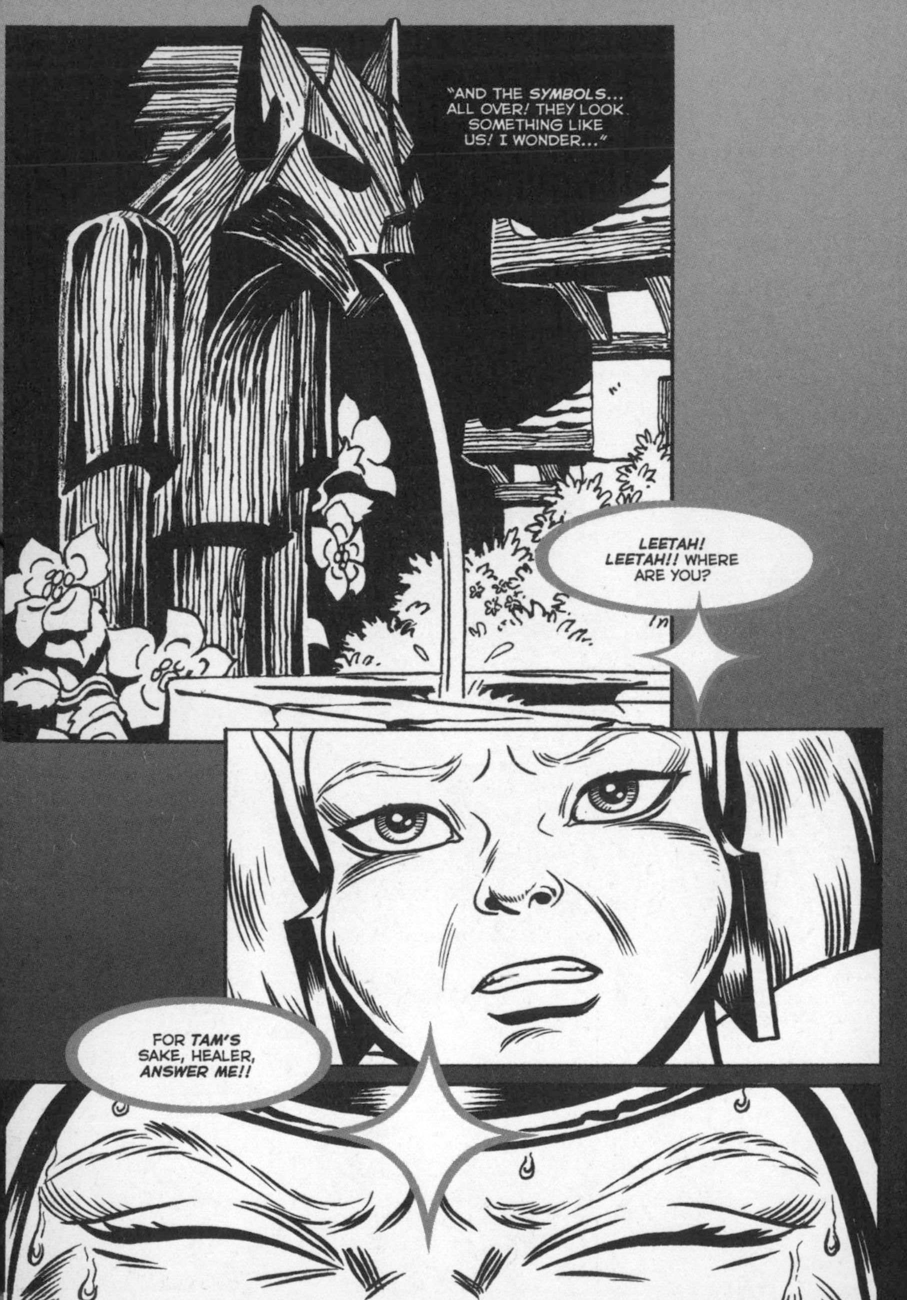

"AND THE SYMBOLS... ALL OVER! THEY LOOK SOMETHING LIKE US! I WONDER..."
LEETAH! LEETAH!! WHERE ARE YOU?
FOR TAM'S SAKE, HEALER, ANSWER ME!!

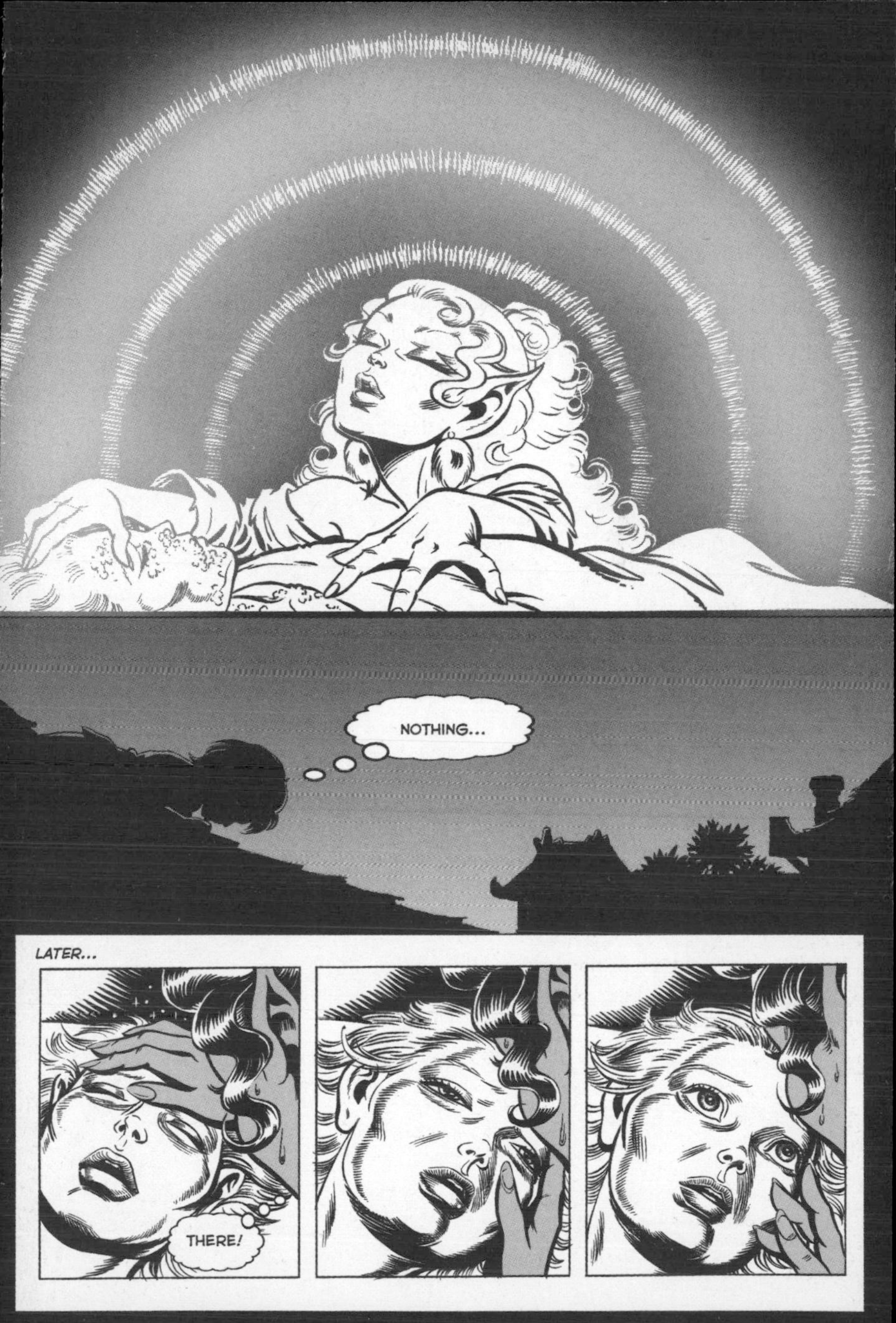
NOTHING...
LATER...
THERE!

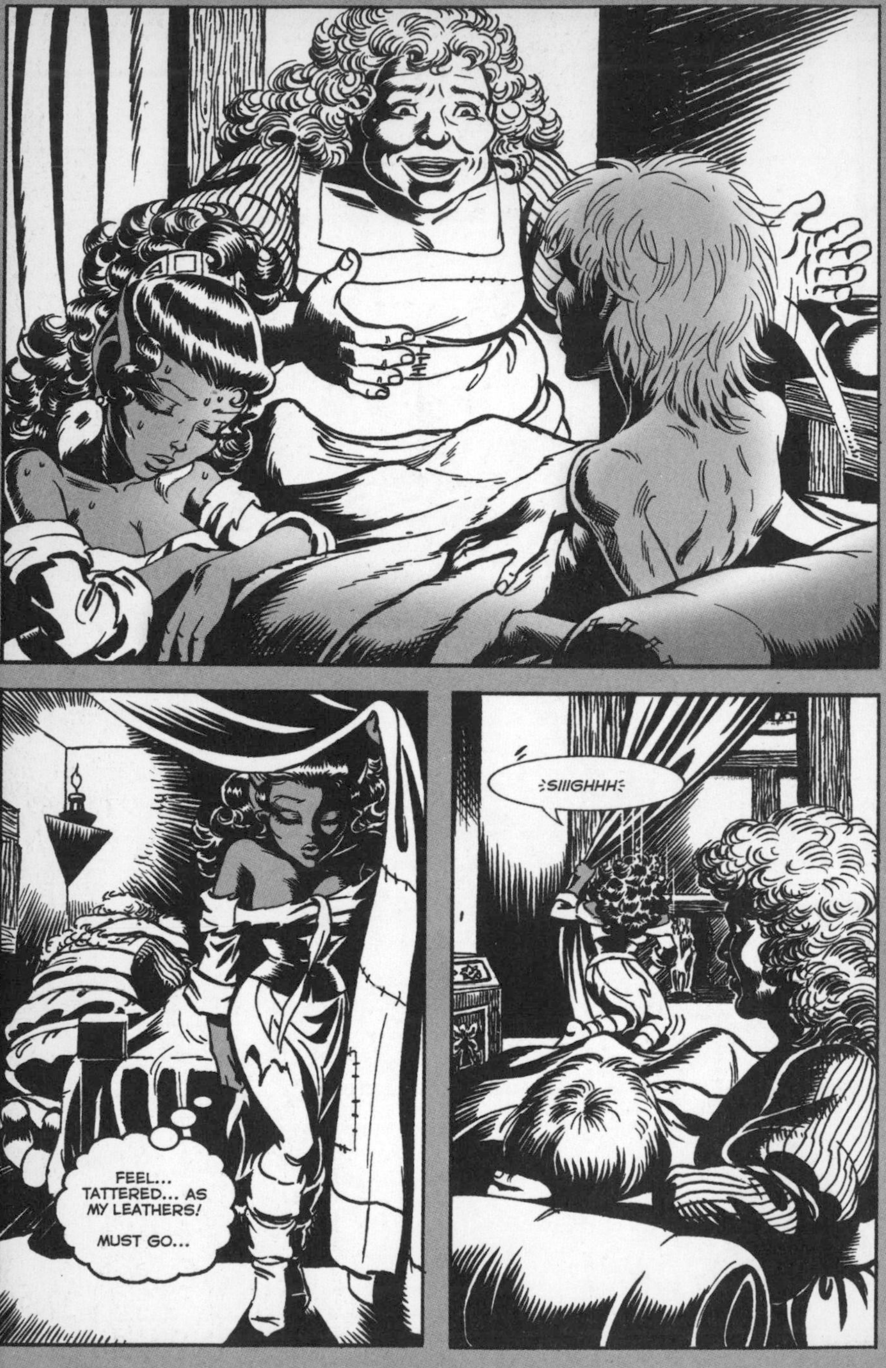
FEEL... TATTERED... AS MY LEATHERS!
MUST GO...
SIIIGHHH

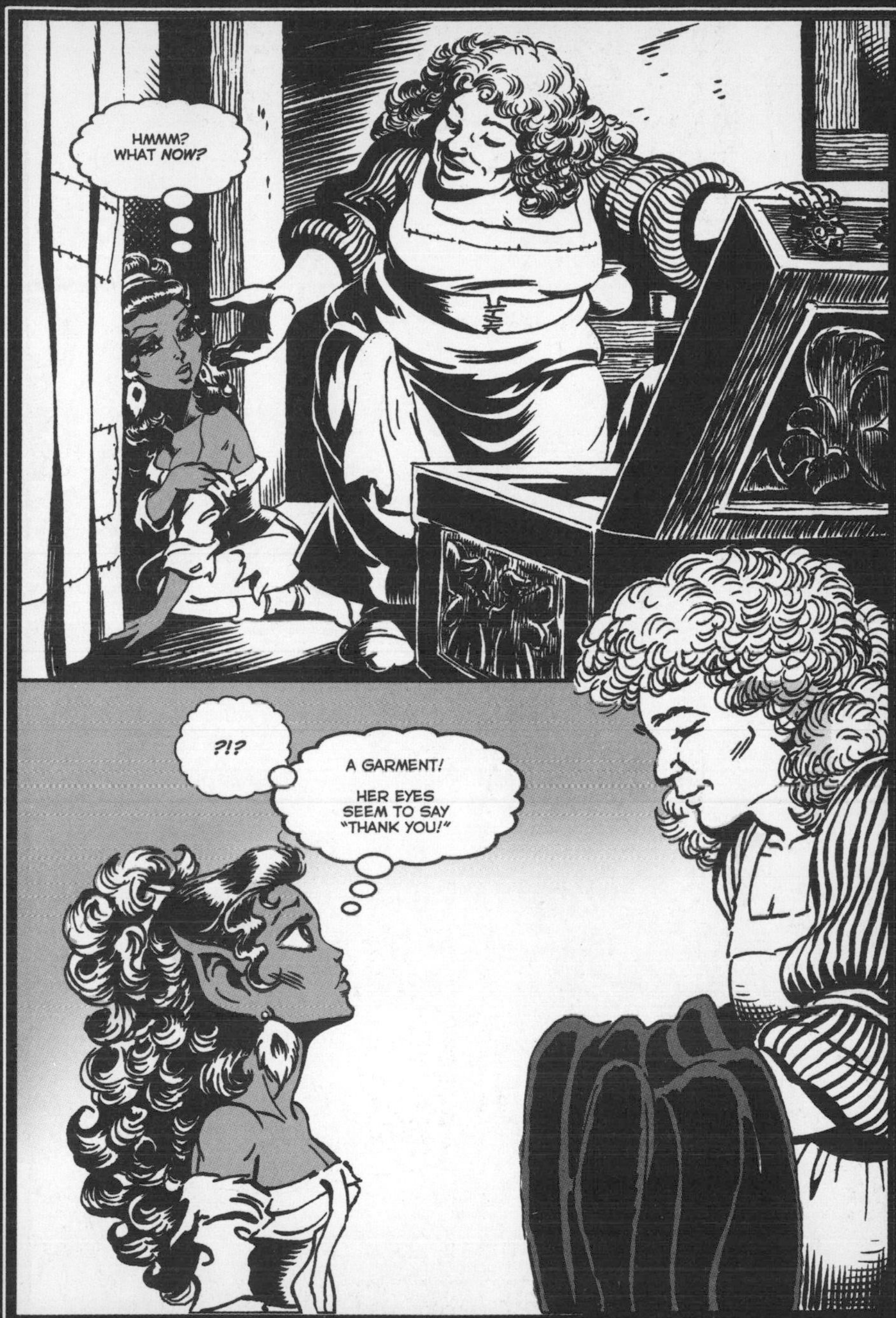
HMMM?
WHAT NOW?
?!?
A GARMENT!
HER EYES SEEM TO SAY "THANK YOU!"

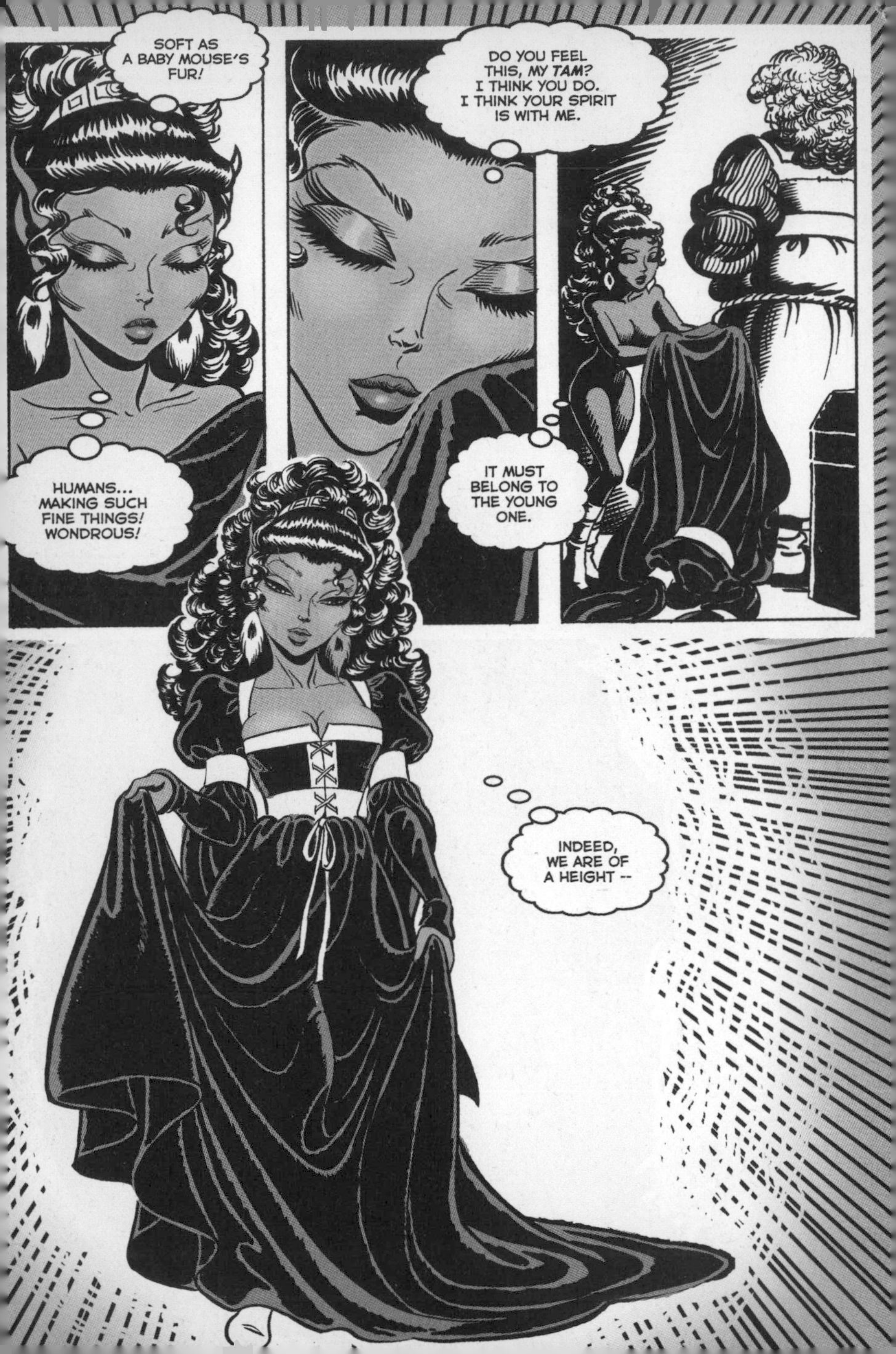
SOFT AS A BABY MOUSE'S FUR!
HUMANS... MAKING SUCH FINE THINGS! WONDROUS!
DO YOU FEEL THIS, MY TAM? I THINK YOU DO. I THINK YOUR SPIRIT IS WITH ME.
IT MUST BELONG TO THE YOUNG ONE.
INDEED, WE ARE OF A HEIGHT --

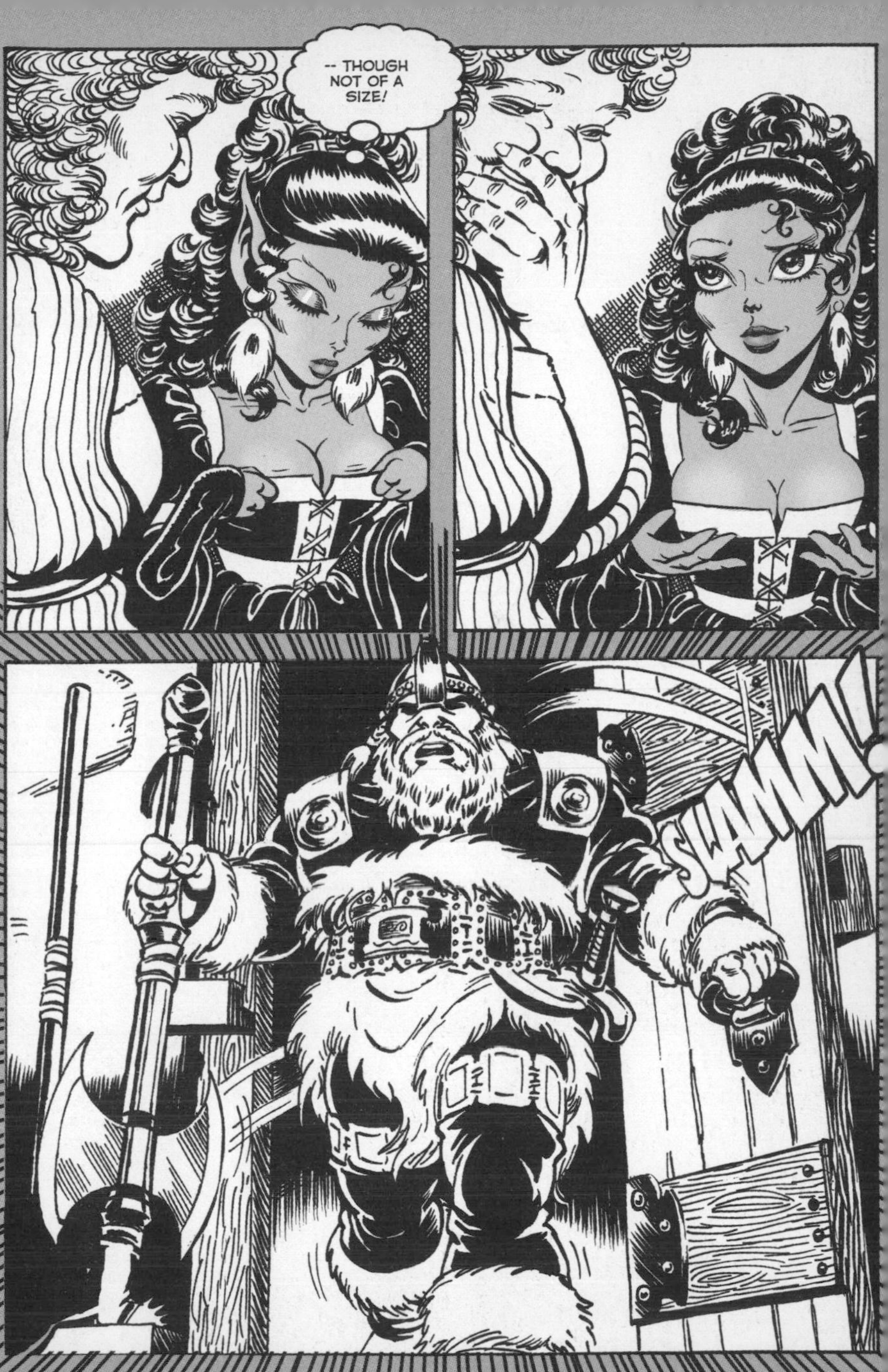
-- THOUGH NOT OF A SIZE!
SLAMM!

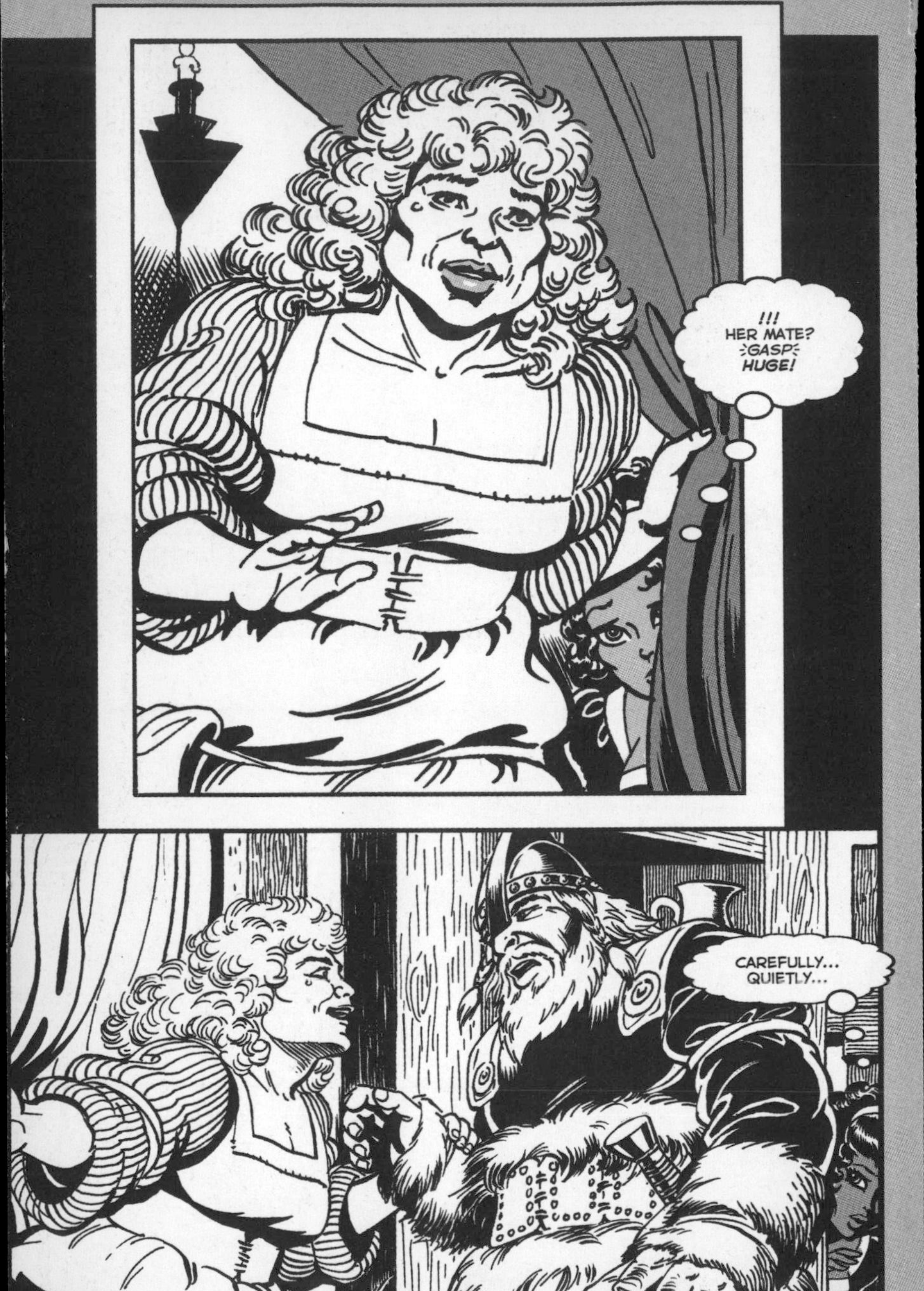
!!!
HER MATE?
GASP
HUGE!
CAREFULLY...
QUIETLY...

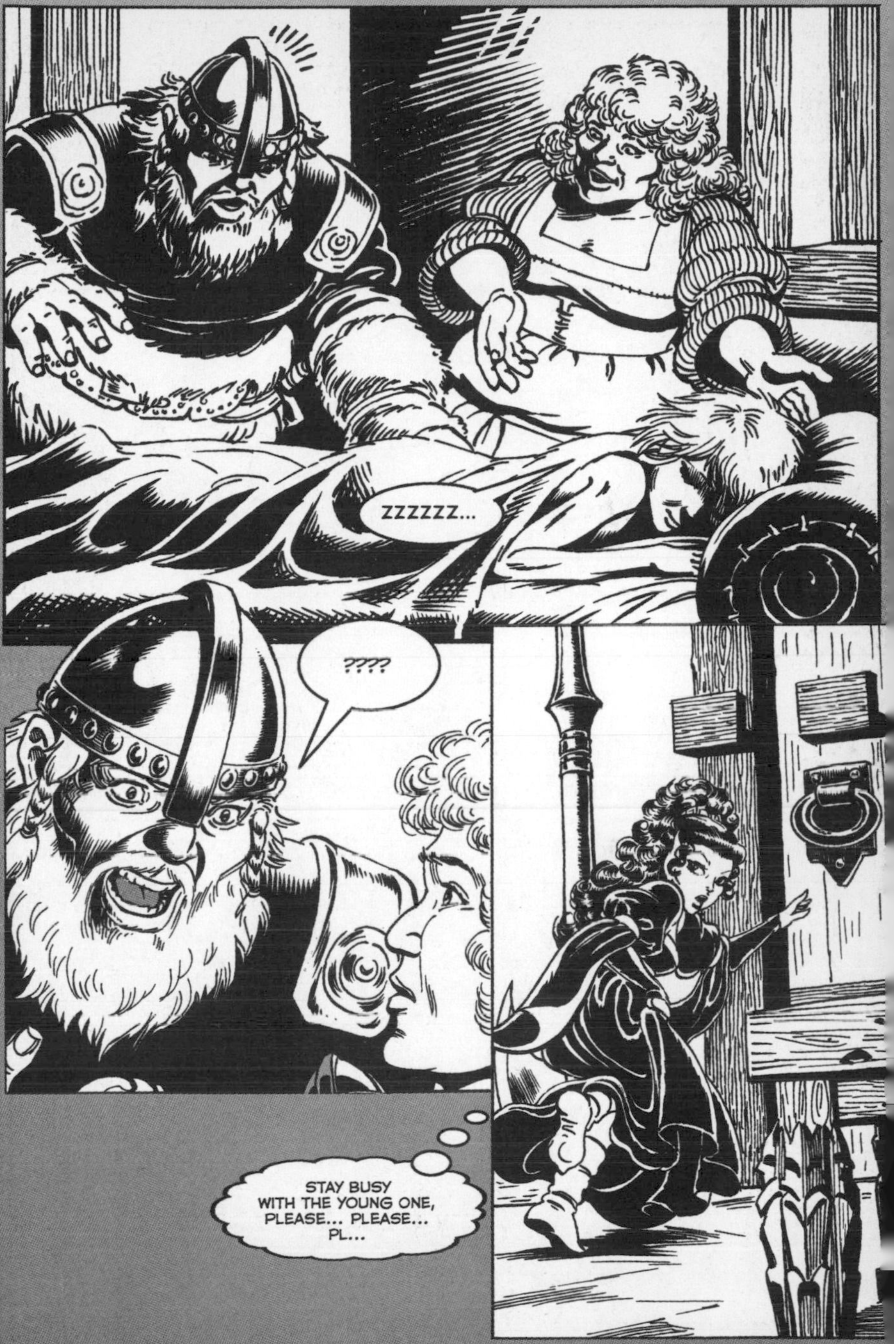
ZZZZZZ...
????
STAY BUSY
WITH THE YOUNG ONE,
PLEASE... PLEASE...
PL...

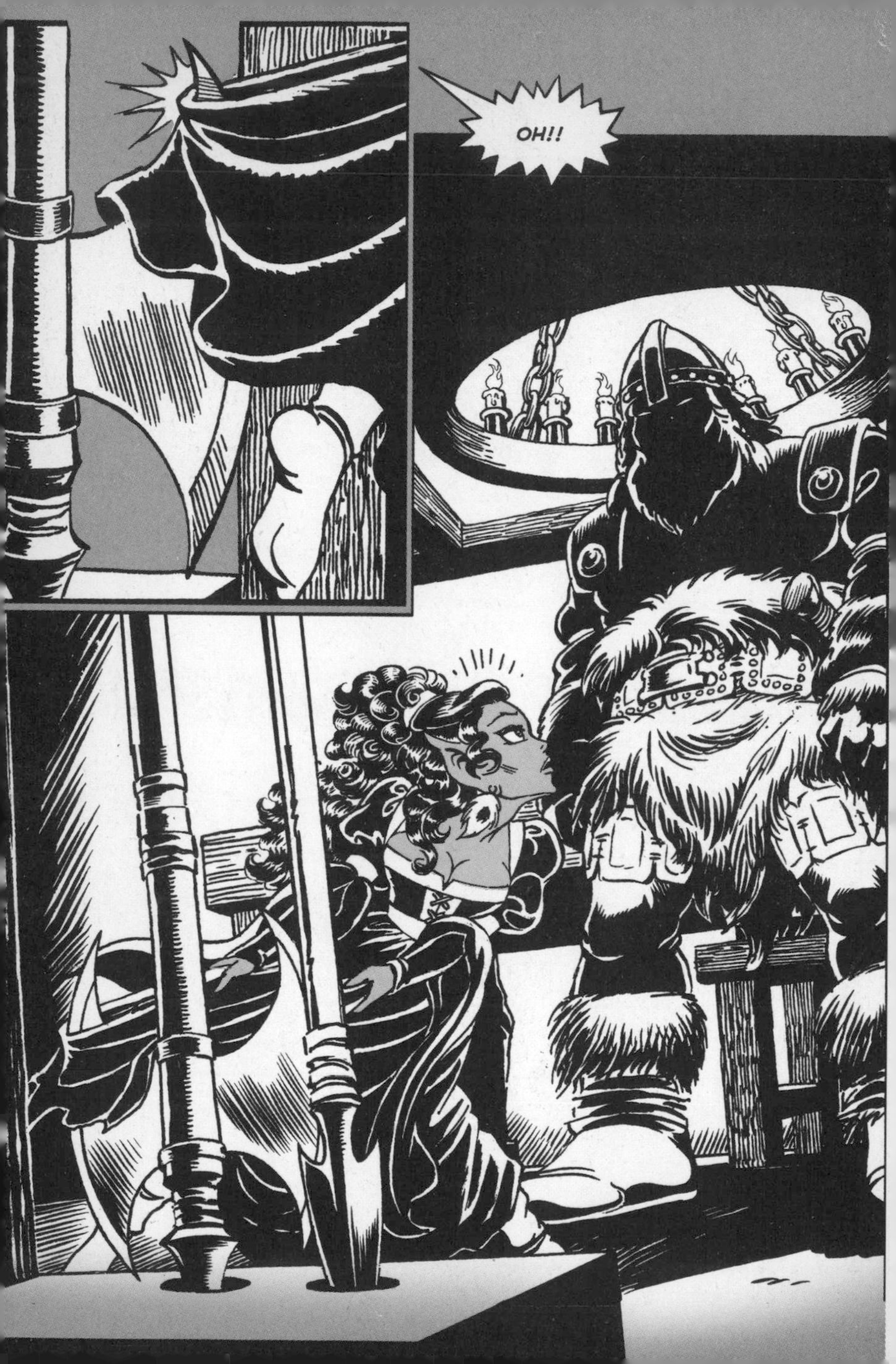
OH!!

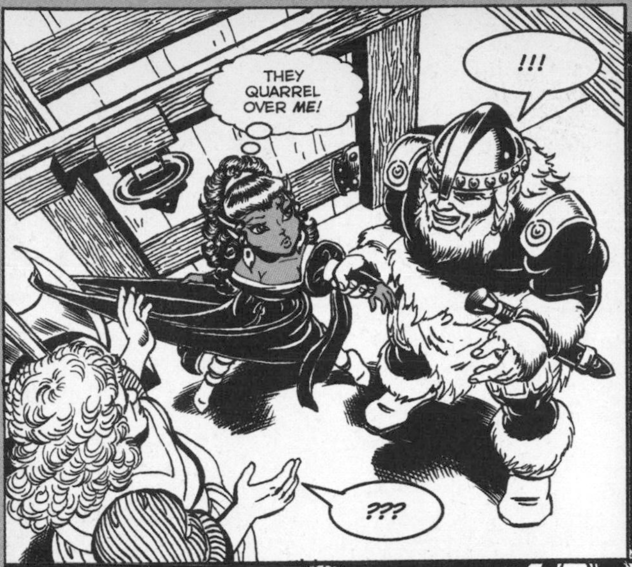
THEY QUARREL OVER ME!
!!!
???

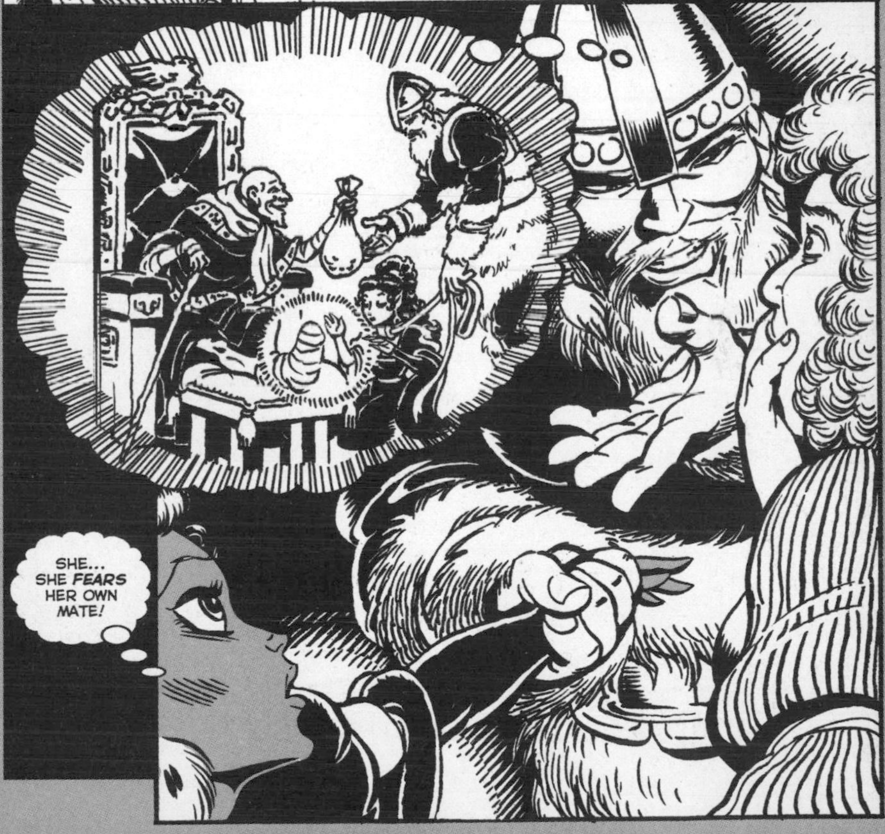
SHE... SHE FEARS HER OWN MATE!

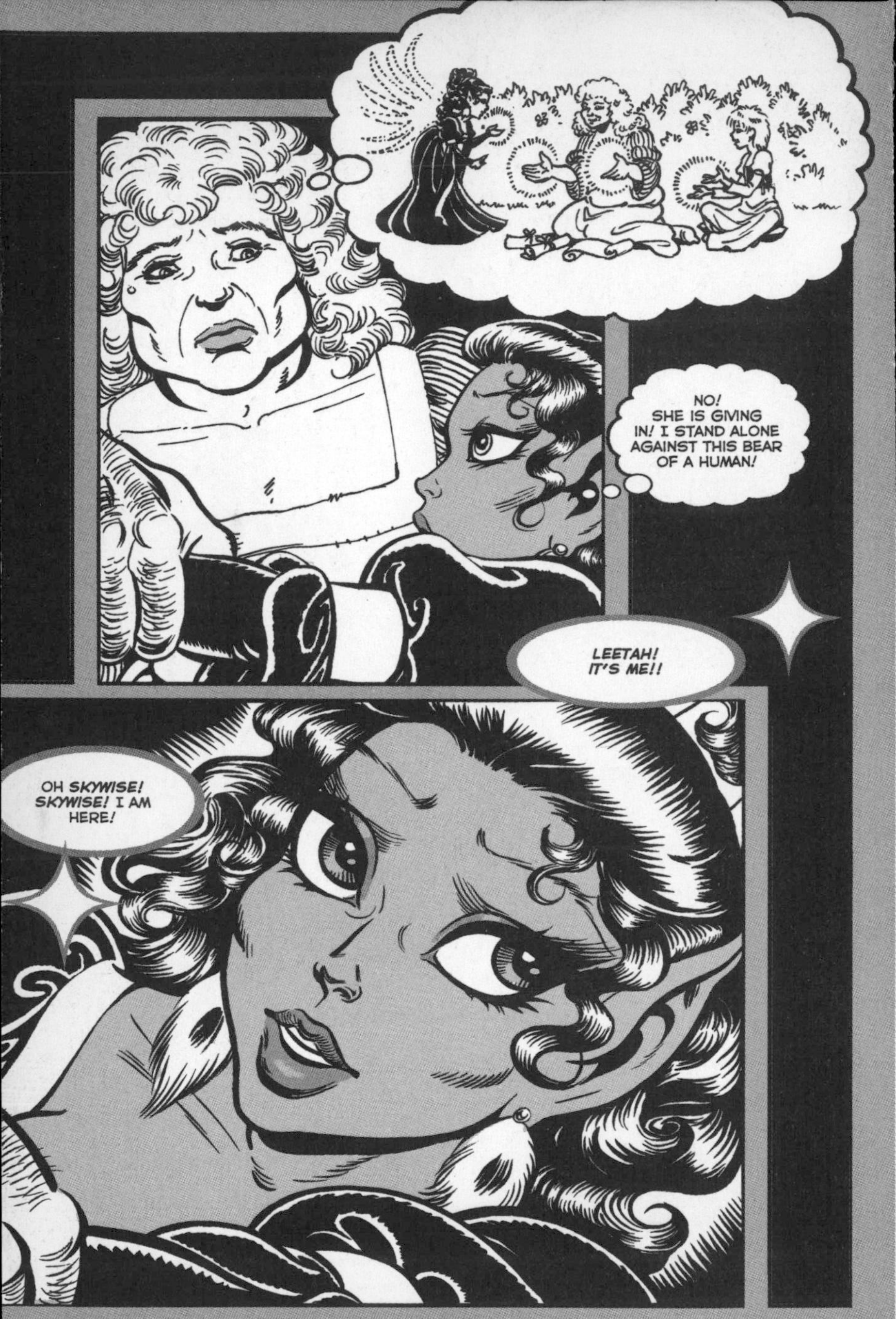
NO! SHE IS GIVING IN! I STAND ALONE AGAINST THIS BEAR OF A HUMAN!
LEETAH! IT'S ME!!
OH SKYWISE! SKYWISE! I AM HERE!

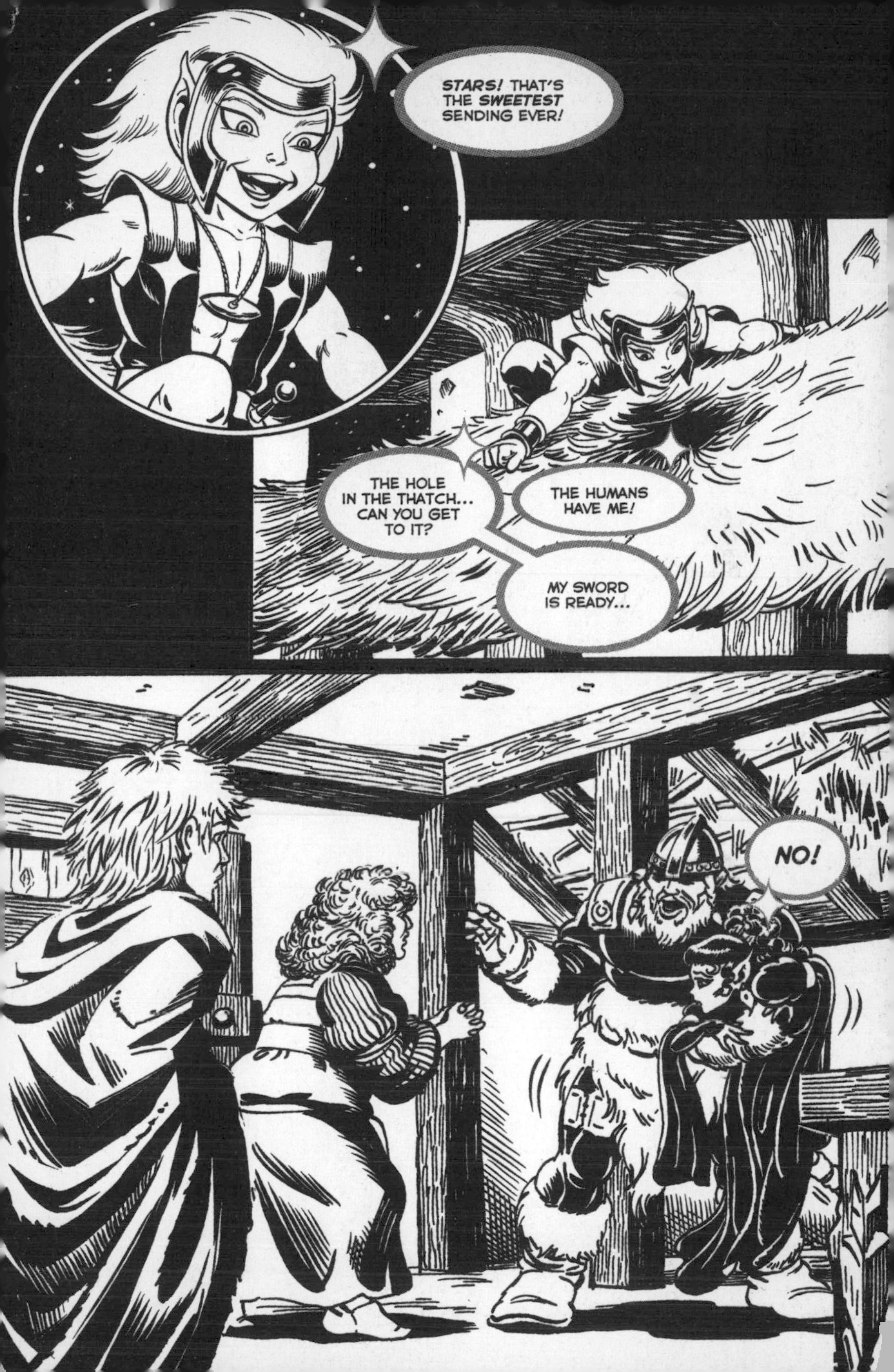
STARS! THAT'S THE SWEETEST SENDING EVER!
THE HOLE IN THE THATCH... CAN YOU GET TO IT?
THE HUMANS HAVE ME!
MY SWORD IS READY...
NO!

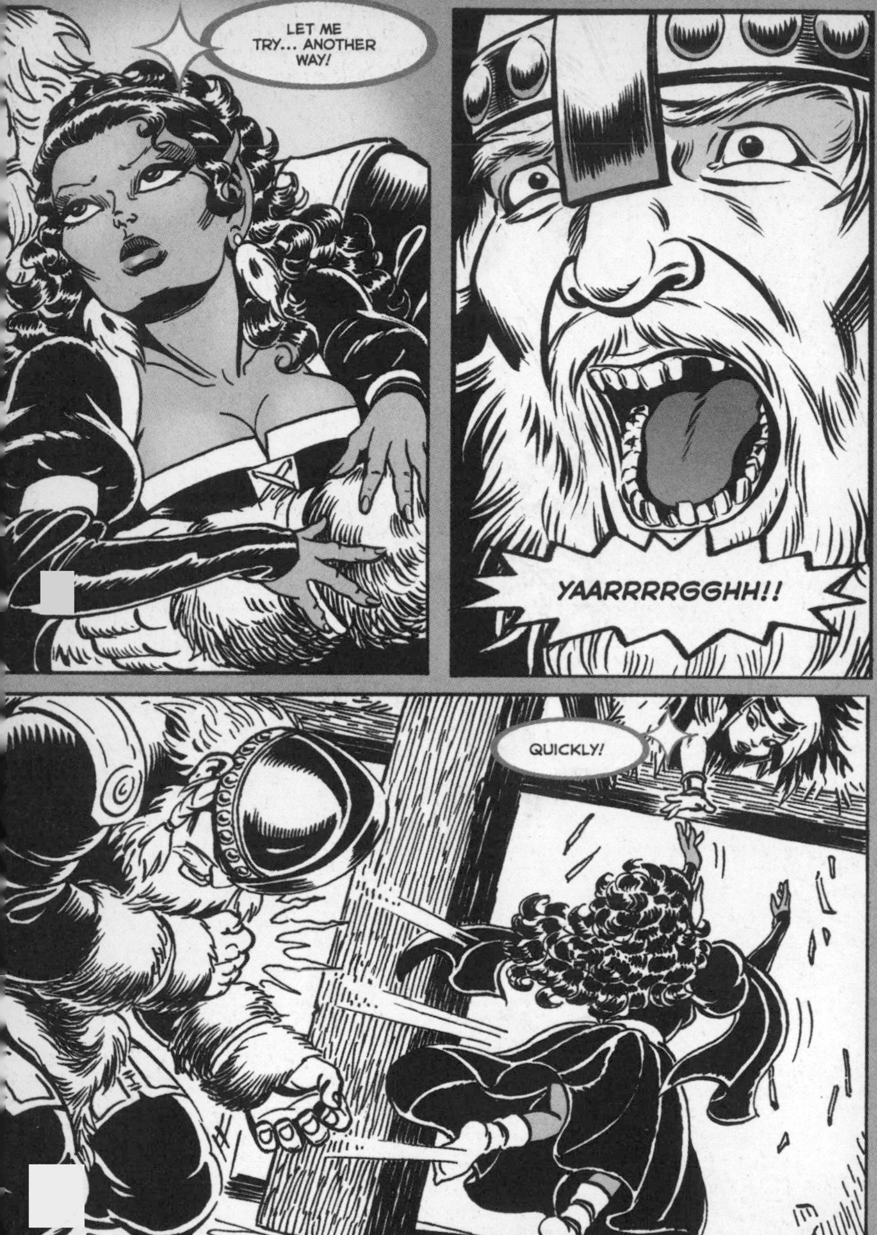
LET ME TRY... ANOTHER WAY!
YAARRRRGGHH!!
QUICKLY!

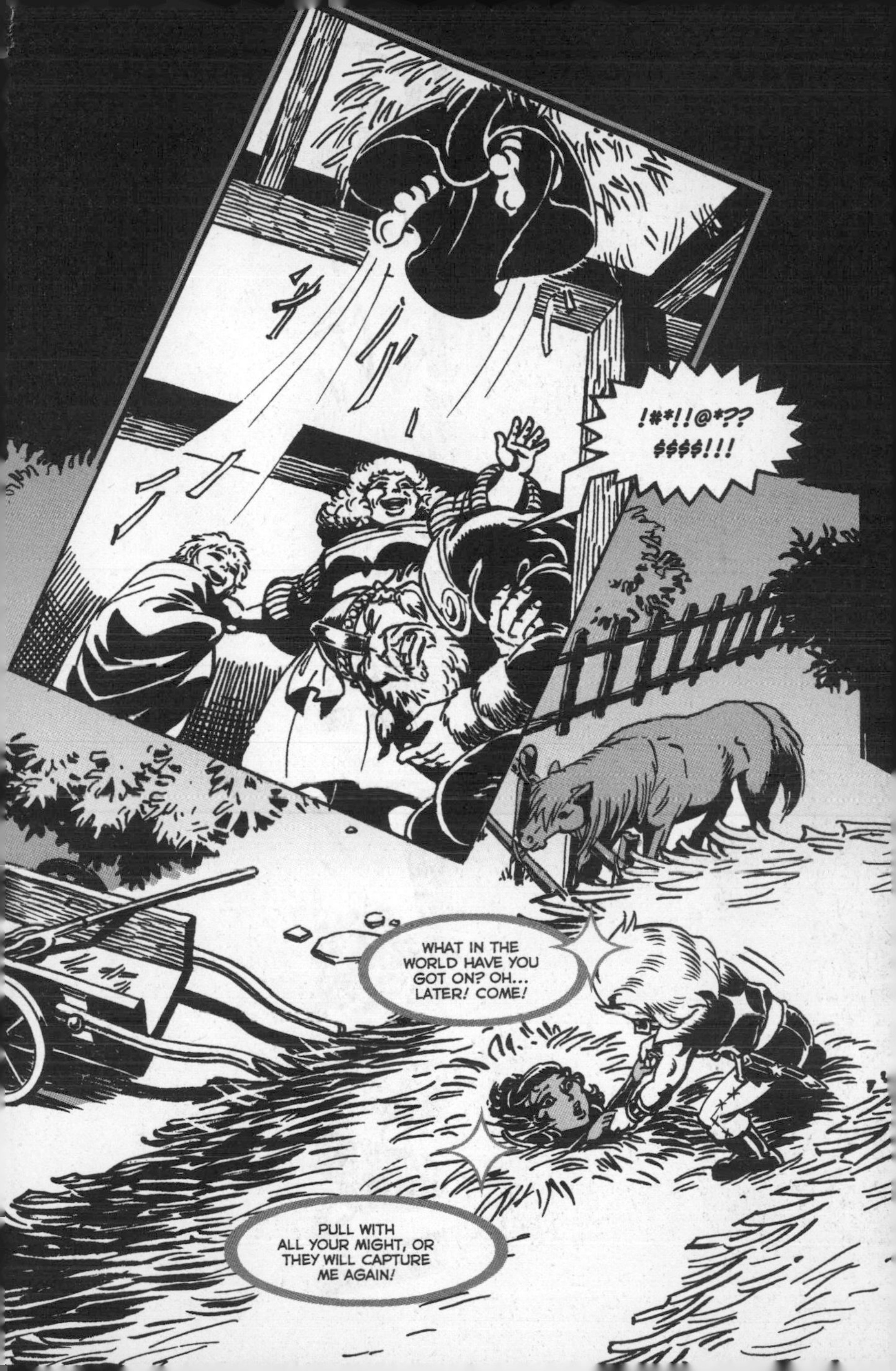
!#*!!@*??
$$$$!!!
WHAT IN THE WORLD HAVE YOU GOT ON? OH... LATER! COME!
PULL WITH ALL YOUR MIGHT, OR THEY WILL CAPTURE ME AGAIN!

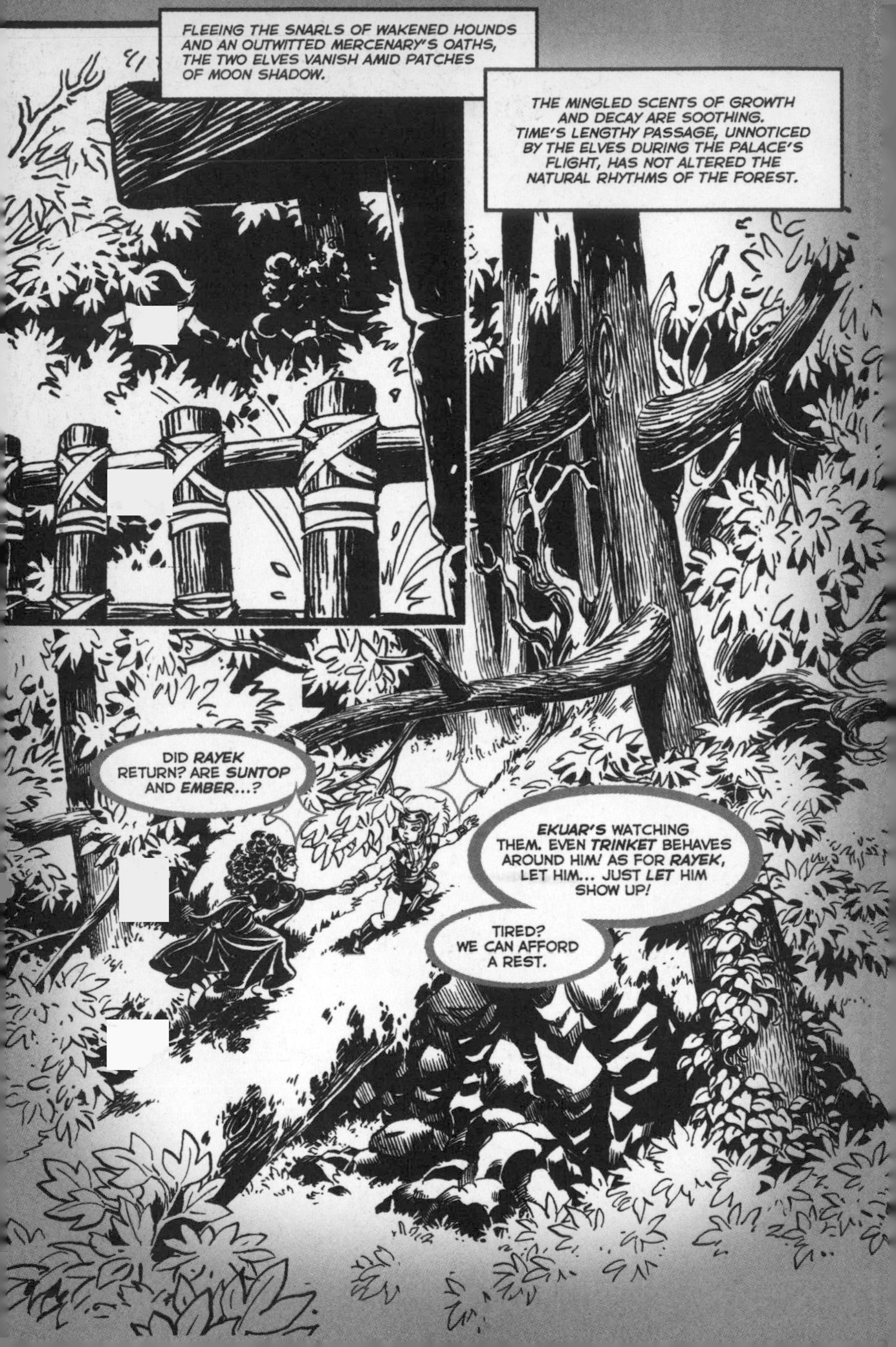
FLEEING THE SNARLS OF WAKENED HOUNDS AND AN OUTWITTED MERCENARY'S OATHS, THE TWO ELVES VANISH AMID PATCHES OF MOON SHADOW.
THE MINGLED SCENTS OF GROWTH AND DECAY ARE SOOTHING. TIME'S LENGTHY PASSAGE, UNNOTICED BY THE ELVES DURING THE PALACE'S FLIGHT, HAS NOT ALTERED THE NATURAL RHYTHMS OF THE FOREST.
DID RAYEK RETURN? ARE SUNTOP AND EMBER...?
EKUAR'S WATCHING THEM. EVEN TRINKET BEHAVES AROUND HIM! AS FOR RAYEK, LET HIM... JUST LET HIM SHOW UP!
TIRED? WE CAN AFFORD A REST.

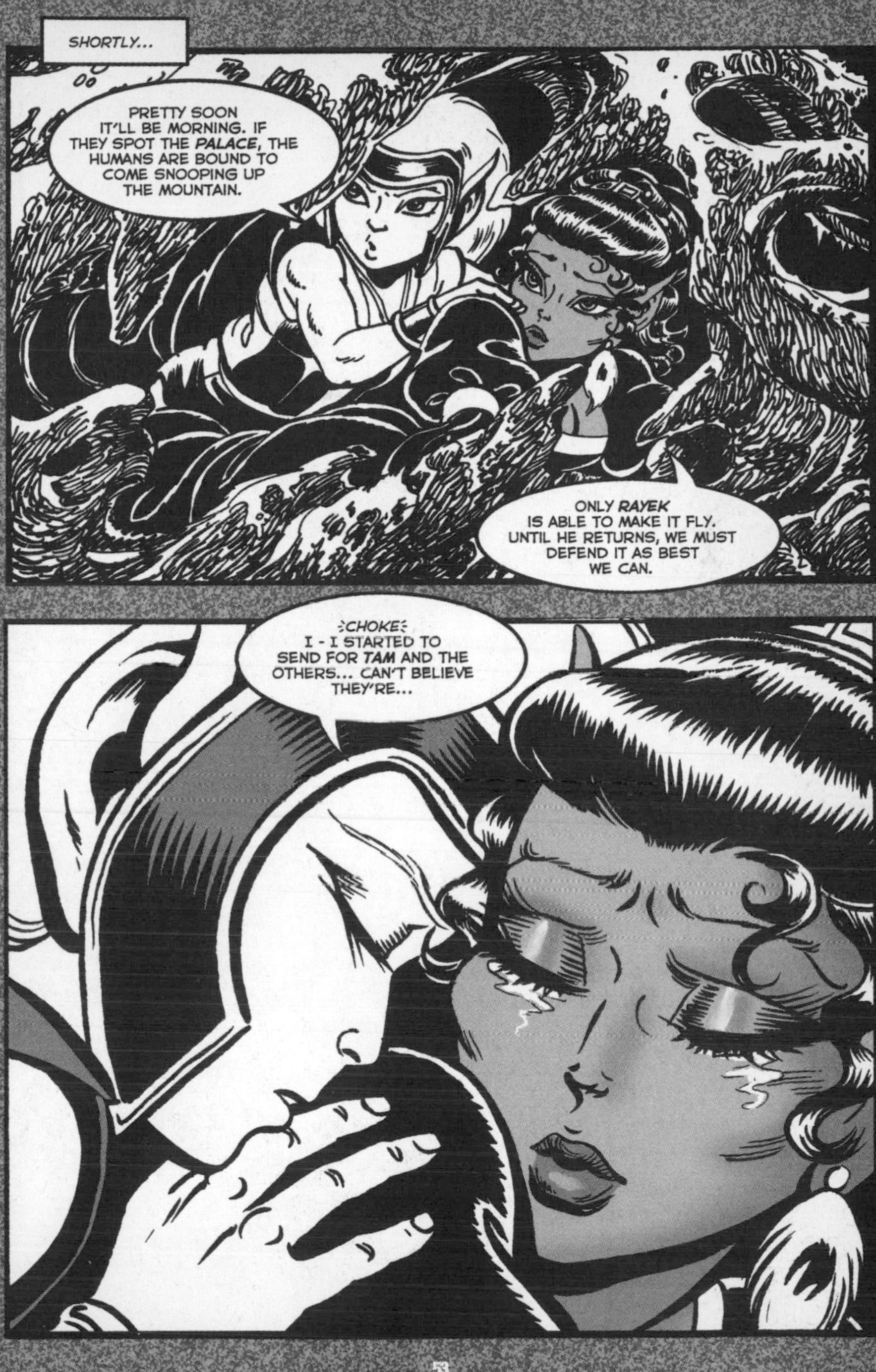
SHORTLY...
PRETTY SOON IT'LL BE MORNING. IF THEY SPOT THE *PALACE*, THE HUMANS ARE BOUND TO COME SNOOPING UP THE MOUNTAIN.
ONLY *RAYEK* IS ABLE TO MAKE IT FLY. UNTIL HE RETURNS, WE MUST DEFEND IT AS BEST WE CAN.
CHOKE
I - I STARTED TO SEND FOR *TAM* AND THE OTHERS... CAN'T BELIEVE THEY'RE...

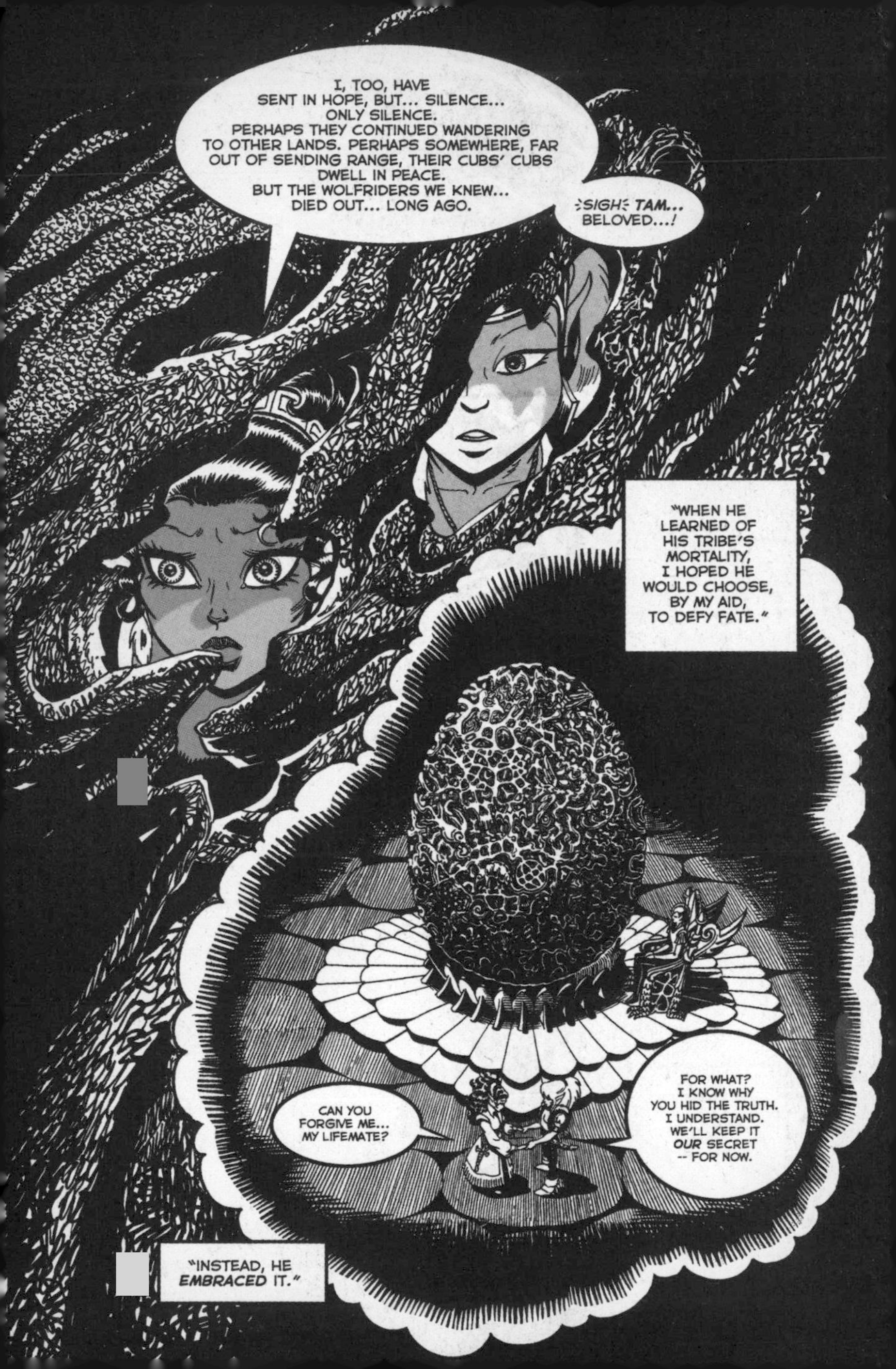
I, TOO, HAVE SENT IN HOPE, BUT... SILENCE... ONLY SILENCE. PERHAPS THEY CONTINUED WANDERING TO OTHER LANDS. PERHAPS SOMEWHERE, FAR OUT OF SENDING RANGE, THEIR CUBS' CUBS DWELL IN PEACE. BUT THE WOLFRIDERS WE KNEW... DIED OUT... LONG AGO.
:SIGH: TAM... BELOVED...!
"WHEN HE LEARNED OF HIS TRIBE'S MORTALITY, I HOPED HE WOULD CHOOSE, BY MY AID, TO DEFY FATE."
CAN YOU FORGIVE ME... MY LIFEMATE?
FOR WHAT? I KNOW WHY YOU HID THE TRUTH. I UNDERSTAND. WE'LL KEEP IT OUR SECRET -- FOR NOW.
"INSTEAD, HE EMBRACED IT."

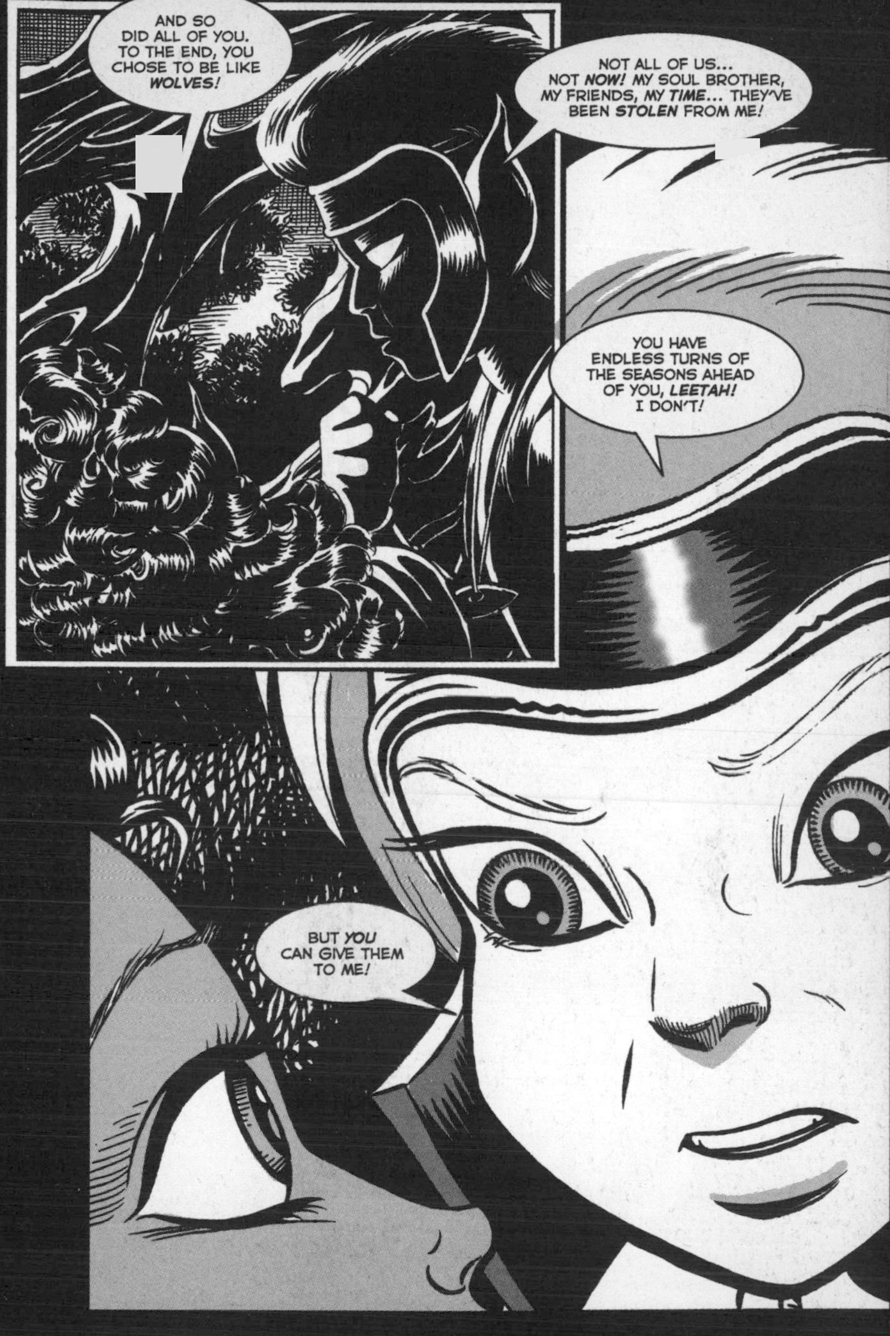
AND SO DID ALL OF YOU. TO THE END, YOU CHOSE TO BE LIKE *WOLVES!*
NOT ALL OF US... NOT *NOW!* MY SOUL BROTHER, MY FRIENDS, MY *TIME*... THEY'VE BEEN *STOLEN* FROM ME!
YOU HAVE ENDLESS TURNS OF THE SEASONS AHEAD OF YOU, *LEETAH!* I DON'T!
BUT *YOU* CAN GIVE THEM TO ME!

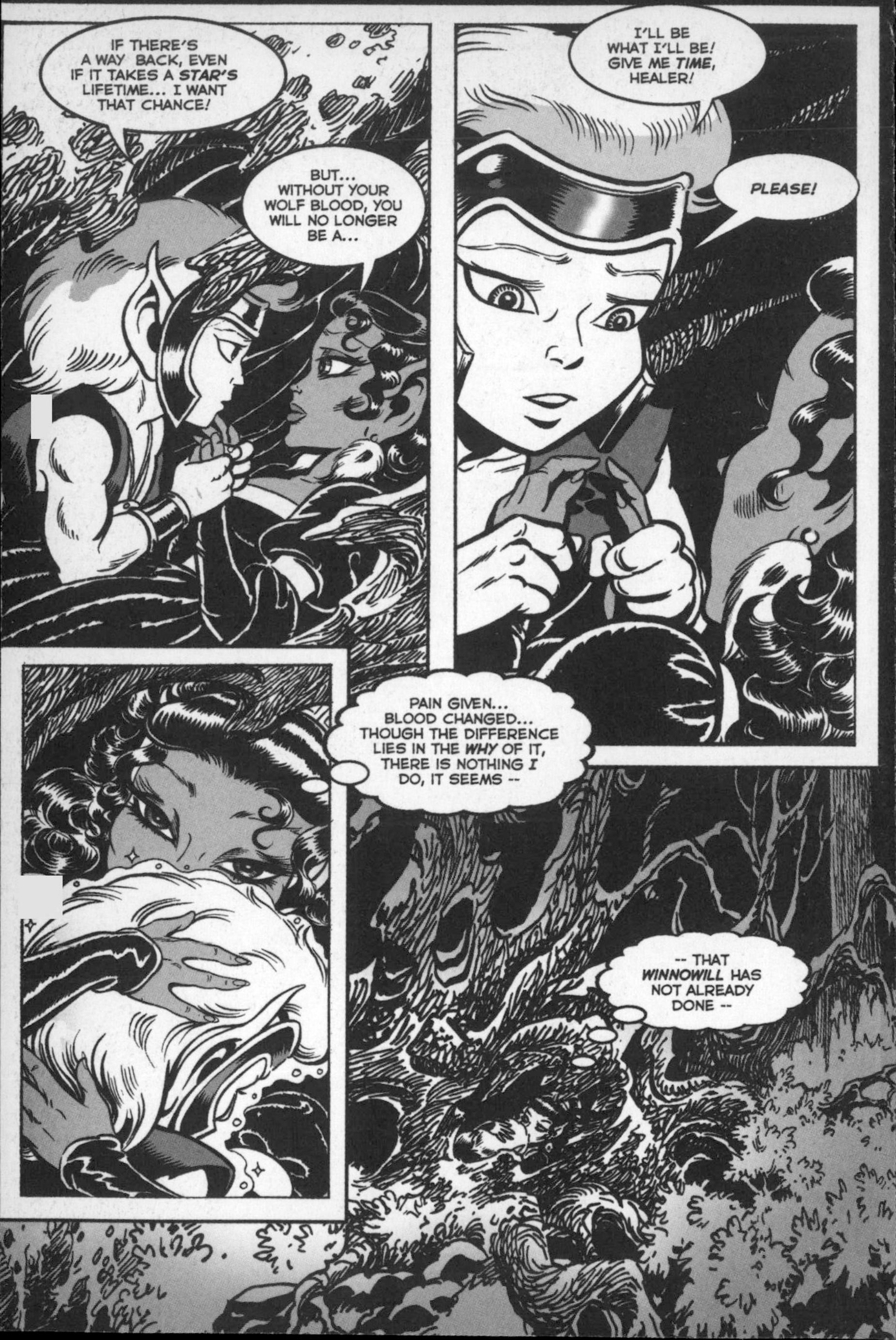
IF THERE'S A WAY BACK, EVEN IF IT TAKES A STAR'S LIFETIME... I WANT THAT CHANCE!
BUT... WITHOUT YOUR WOLF BLOOD, YOU WILL NO LONGER BE A...
I'LL BE WHAT I'LL BE! GIVE ME TIME, HEALER!
PLEASE!
PAIN GIVEN... BLOOD CHANGED... THOUGH THE DIFFERENCE LIES IN THE WHY OF IT, THERE IS NOTHING I DO, IT SEEMS --
-- THAT WINNOWILL HAS NOT ALREADY DONE --

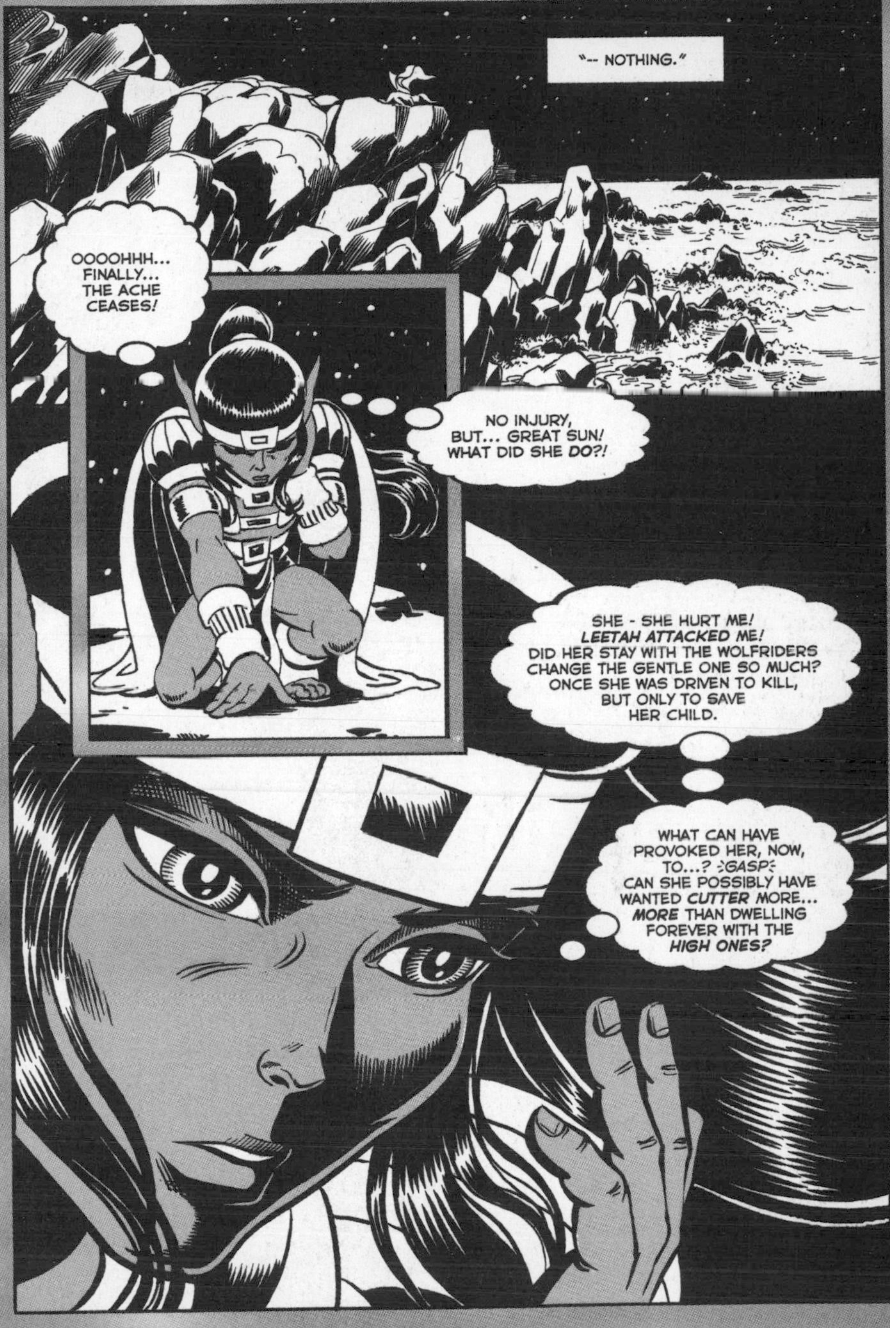
"-- NOTHING."
OOOOHHH... FINALLY... THE ACHE CEASES!
NO INJURY, BUT... GREAT SUN! WHAT DID SHE DO?!
SHE - SHE HURT ME! LEETAH ATTACKED ME! DID HER STAY WITH THE WOLFRIDERS CHANGE THE GENTLE ONE SO MUCH? ONCE SHE WAS DRIVEN TO KILL, BUT ONLY TO SAVE HER CHILD.
WHAT CAN HAVE PROVOKED HER, NOW, TO...? GASP CAN SHE POSSIBLY HAVE WANTED CUTTER MORE... MORE THAN DWELLING FOREVER WITH THE HIGH ONES?

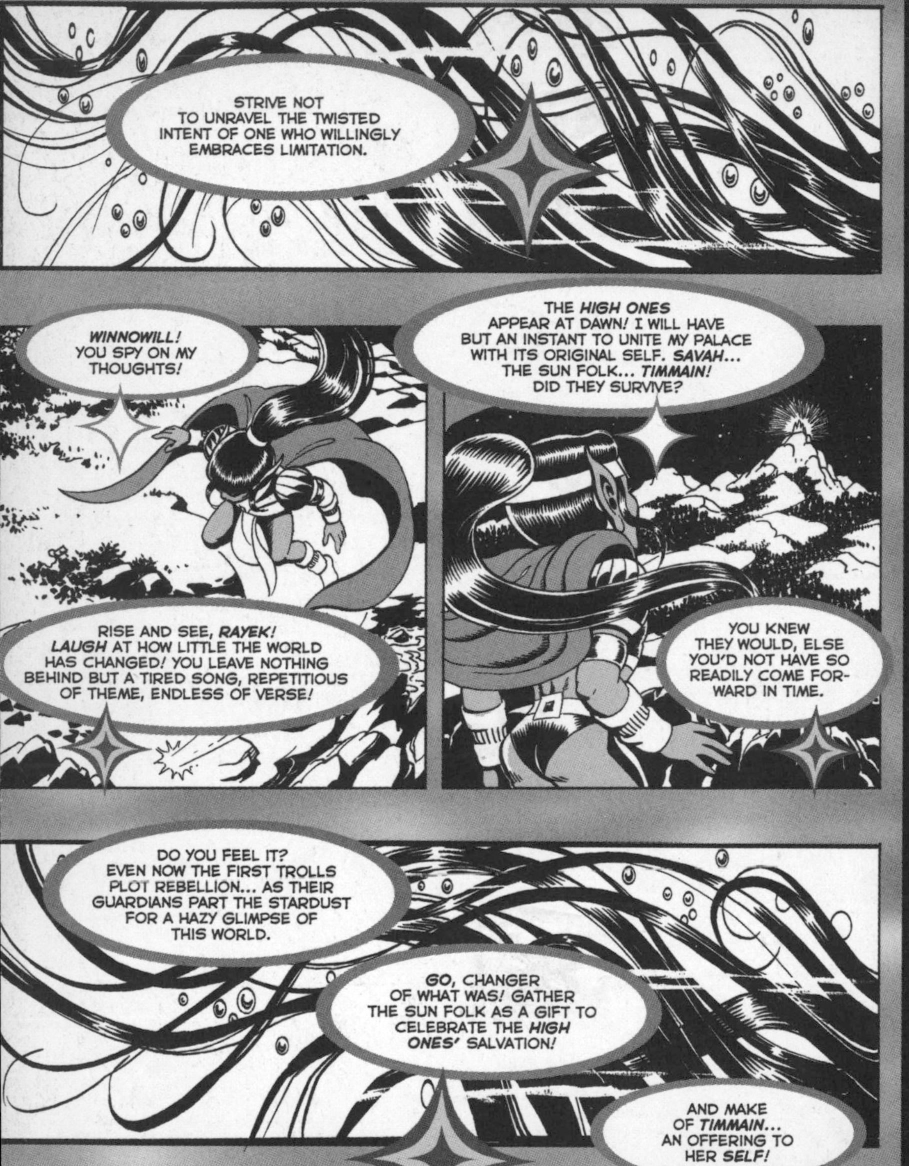
STRIVE NOT TO UNRAVEL THE TWISTED INTENT OF ONE WHO WILLINGLY EMBRACES LIMITATION.
WINNOWILL! YOU SPY ON MY THOUGHTS!
THE HIGH ONES APPEAR AT DAWN! I WILL HAVE BUT AN INSTANT TO UNITE MY PALACE WITH ITS ORIGINAL SELF. SAVAH... THE SUN FOLK... TIMMAIN! DID THEY SURVIVE?
RISE AND SEE, RAYEK! LAUGH AT HOW LITTLE THE WORLD HAS CHANGED! YOU LEAVE NOTHING BEHIND BUT A TIRED SONG, REPETITIOUS OF THEME, ENDLESS OF VERSE!
YOU KNEW THEY WOULD, ELSE YOU'D NOT HAVE SO READILY COME FOR-WARD IN TIME.
DO YOU FEEL IT? EVEN NOW THE FIRST TROLLS PLOT REBELLION... AS THEIR GUARDIANS PART THE STARDUST FOR A HAZY GLIMPSE OF THIS WORLD.
GO, CHANGER OF WHAT WAS! GATHER THE SUN FOLK AS A GIFT TO CELEBRATE THE HIGH ONES' SALVATION!
AND MAKE OF TIMMAIN... AN OFFERING TO HER SELF!

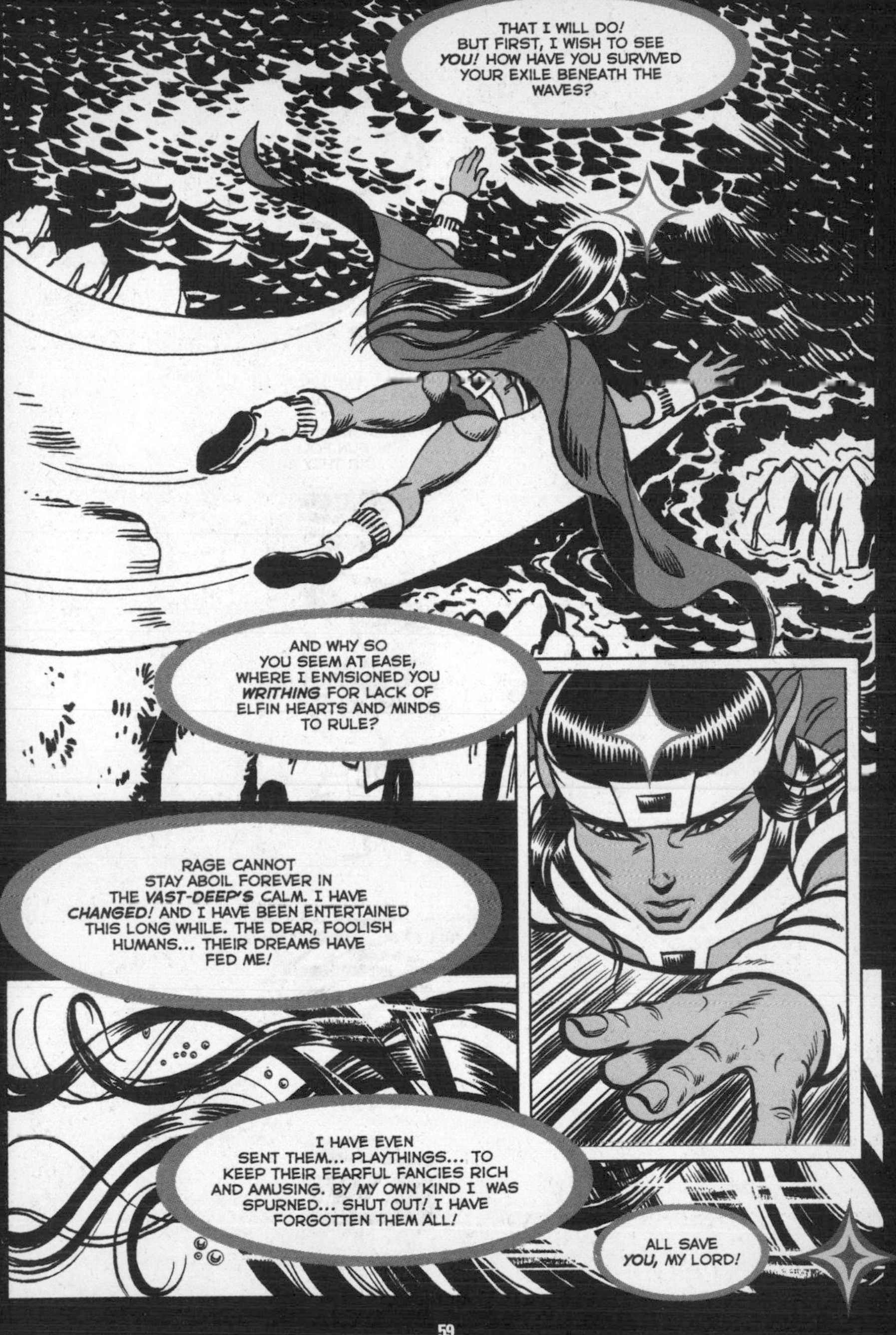
THAT I WILL DO! BUT FIRST, I WISH TO SEE YOU! HOW HAVE YOU SURVIVED YOUR EXILE BENEATH THE WAVES?
AND WHY SO YOU SEEM AT EASE, WHERE I ENVISIONED YOU WRITHING FOR LACK OF ELFIN HEARTS AND MINDS TO RULE?
RAGE CANNOT STAY ABOIL FOREVER IN THE VAST-DEEP'S CALM. I HAVE CHANGED! AND I HAVE BEEN ENTERTAINED THIS LONG WHILE. THE DEAR, FOOLISH HUMANS... THEIR DREAMS HAVE FED ME!
I HAVE EVEN SENT THEM... PLAYTHINGS... TO KEEP THEIR FEARFUL FANCIES RICH AND AMUSING. BY MY OWN KIND I WAS SPURNED... SHUT OUT! I HAVE FORGOTTEN THEM ALL!
ALL SAVE YOU, MY LORD!

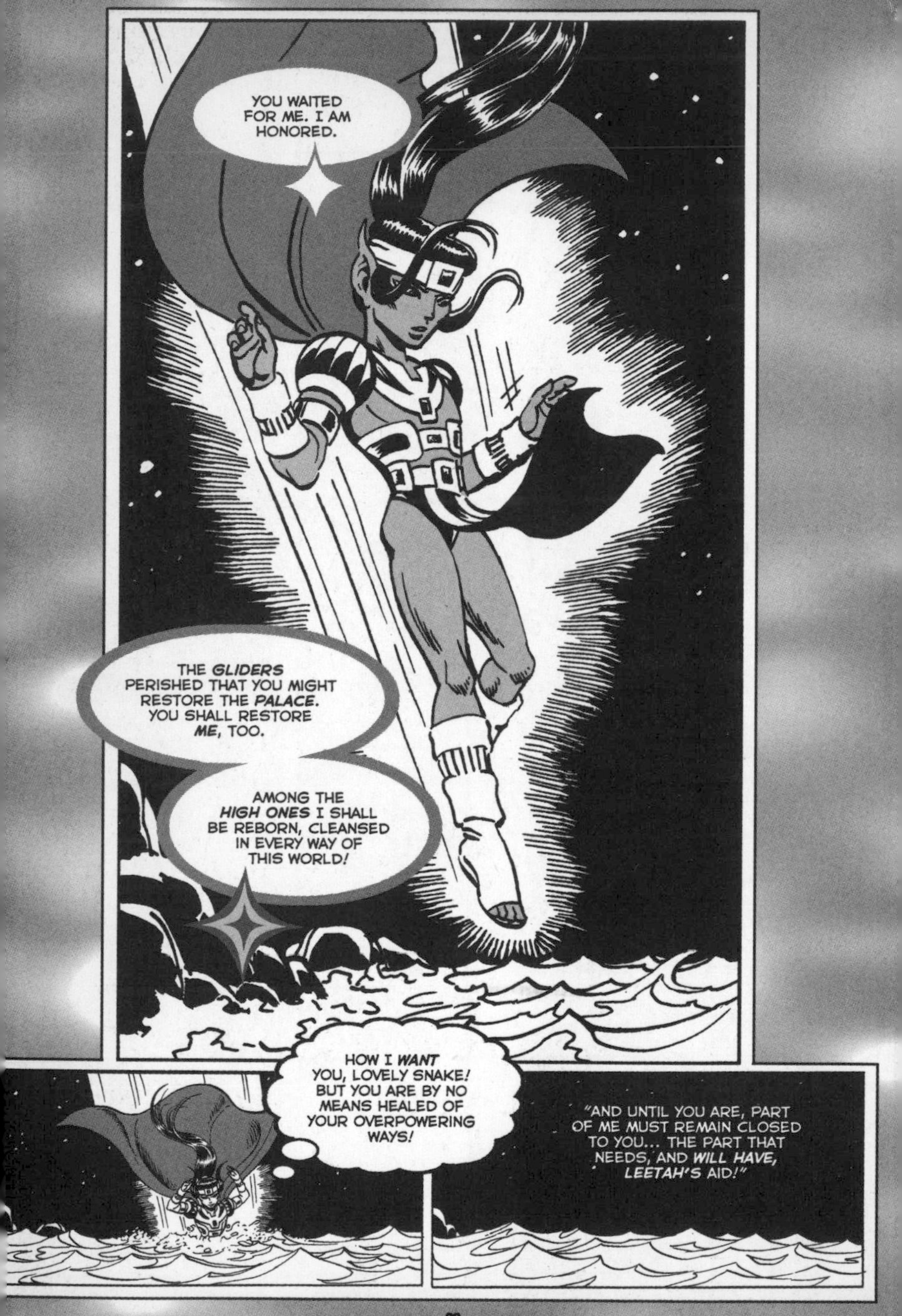
YOU WAITED FOR ME. I AM HONORED.
THE GLIDERS PERISHED THAT YOU MIGHT RESTORE THE PALACE. YOU SHALL RESTORE ME, TOO.
AMONG THE HIGH ONES I SHALL BE REBORN, CLEANSED IN EVERY WAY OF THIS WORLD!
HOW I WANT YOU, LOVELY SNAKE! BUT YOU ARE BY NO MEANS HEALED OF YOUR OVERPOWERING WAYS!
"AND UNTIL YOU ARE, PART OF ME MUST REMAIN CLOSED TO YOU... THE PART THAT NEEDS, AND WILL HAVE, LEETAH'S AID!"

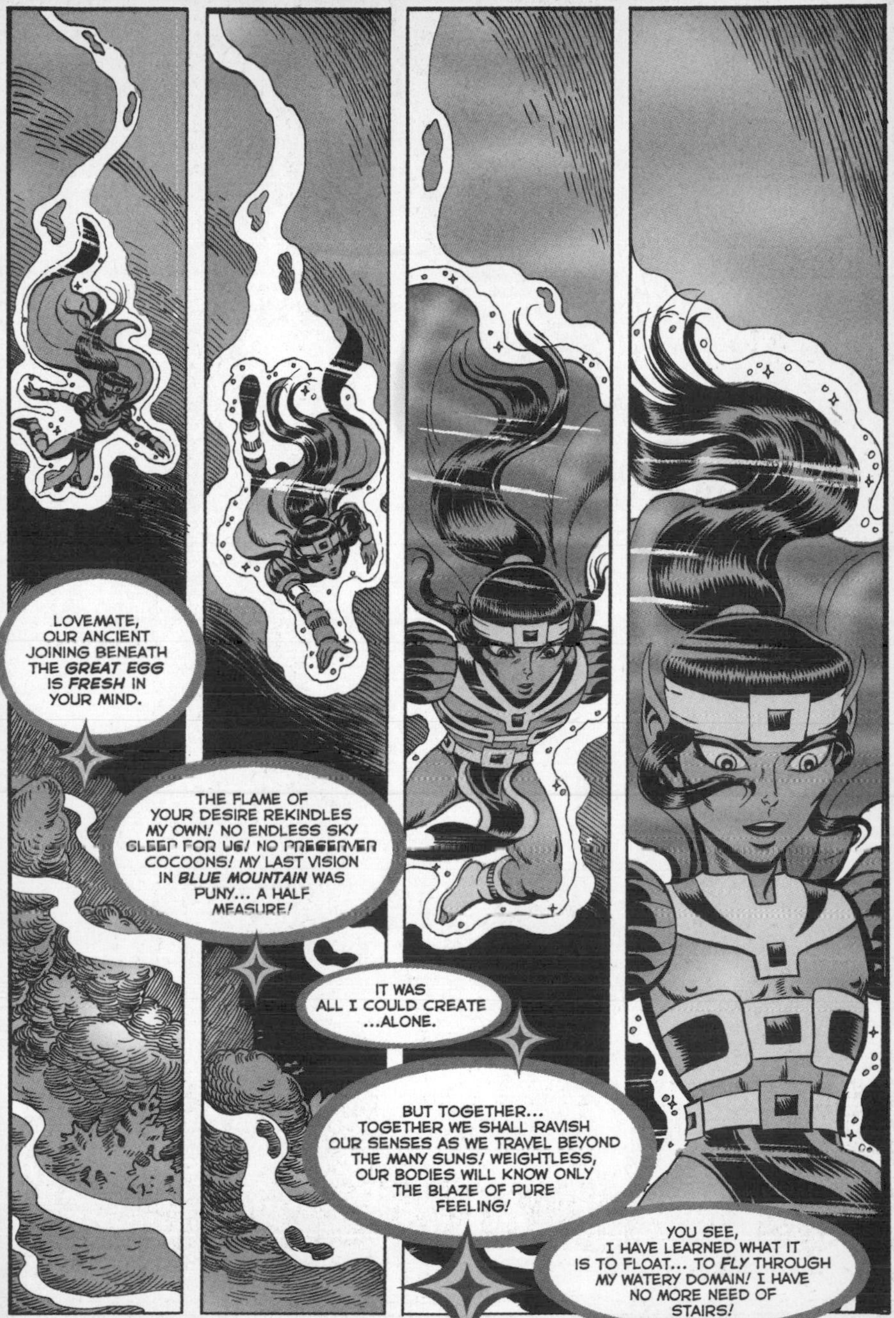
LOVEMATE, OUR ANCIENT JOINING BENEATH THE GREAT EGG IS FRESH IN YOUR MIND.
THE FLAME OF YOUR DESIRE REKINDLES MY OWN! NO ENDLESS SKY SLEEP FOR US! NO PRESERVER COCOONS! MY LAST VISION IN BLUE MOUNTAIN WAS PUNY... A HALF MEASURE!
IT WAS ALL I COULD CREATE ...ALONE.
BUT TOGETHER... TOGETHER WE SHALL RAVISH OUR SENSES AS WE TRAVEL BEYOND THE MANY SUNS! WEIGHTLESS, OUR BODIES WILL KNOW ONLY THE BLAZE OF PURE FEELING!
YOU SEE, I HAVE LEARNED WHAT IT IS TO FLOAT... TO FLY THROUGH MY WATERY DOMAIN! I HAVE NO MORE NEED OF STAIRS!

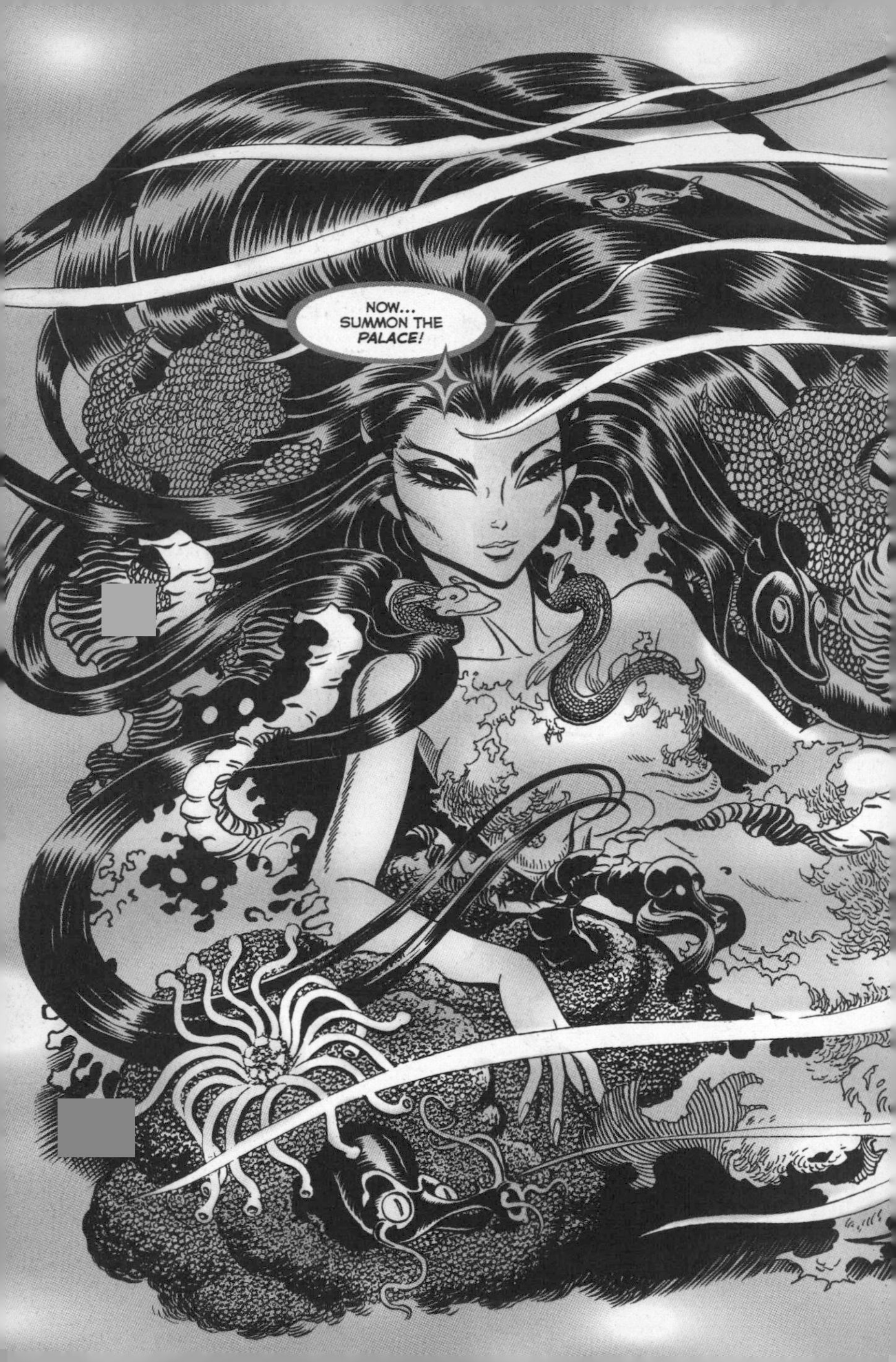
NOW... SUMMON THE PALACE!

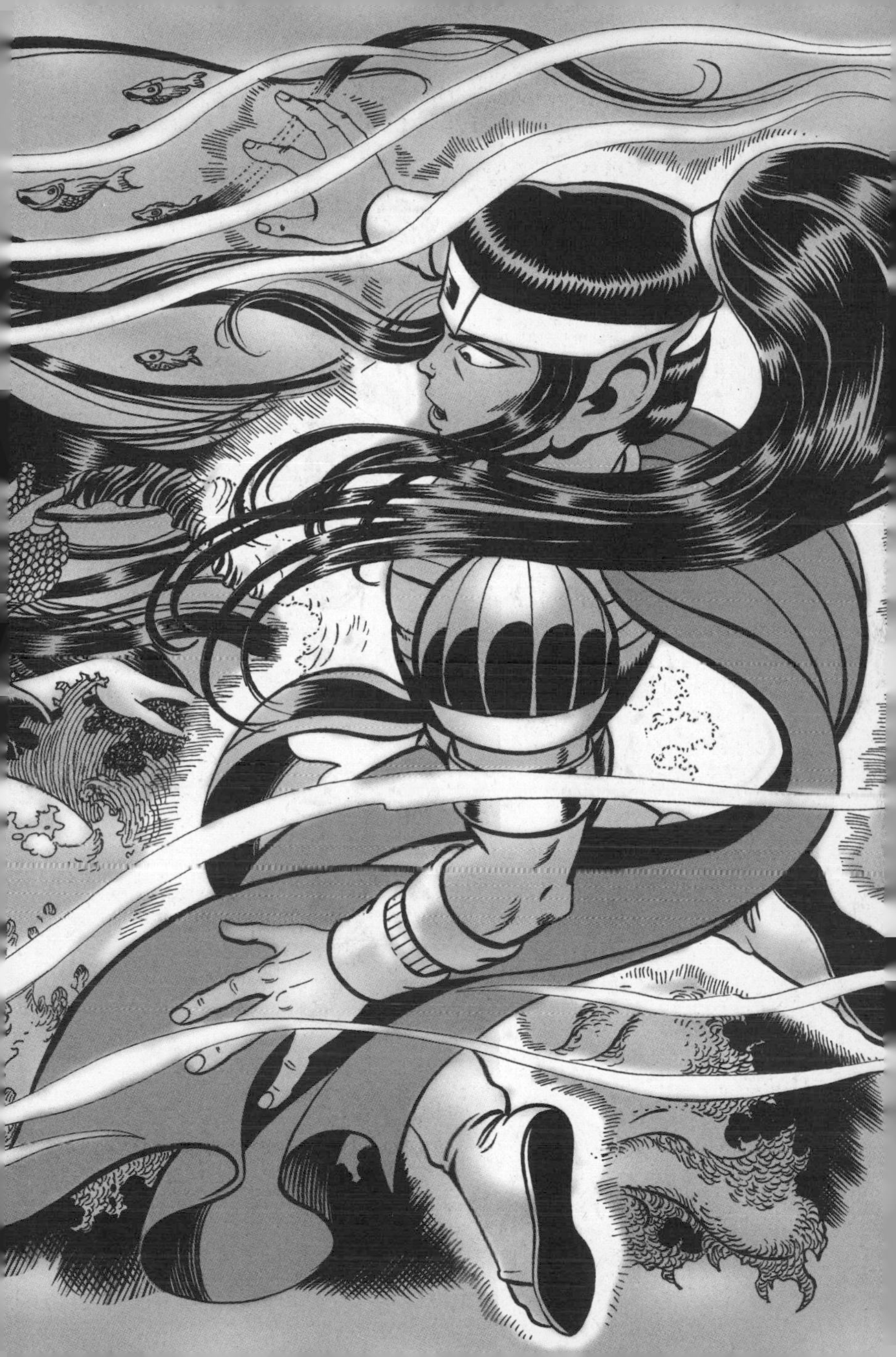

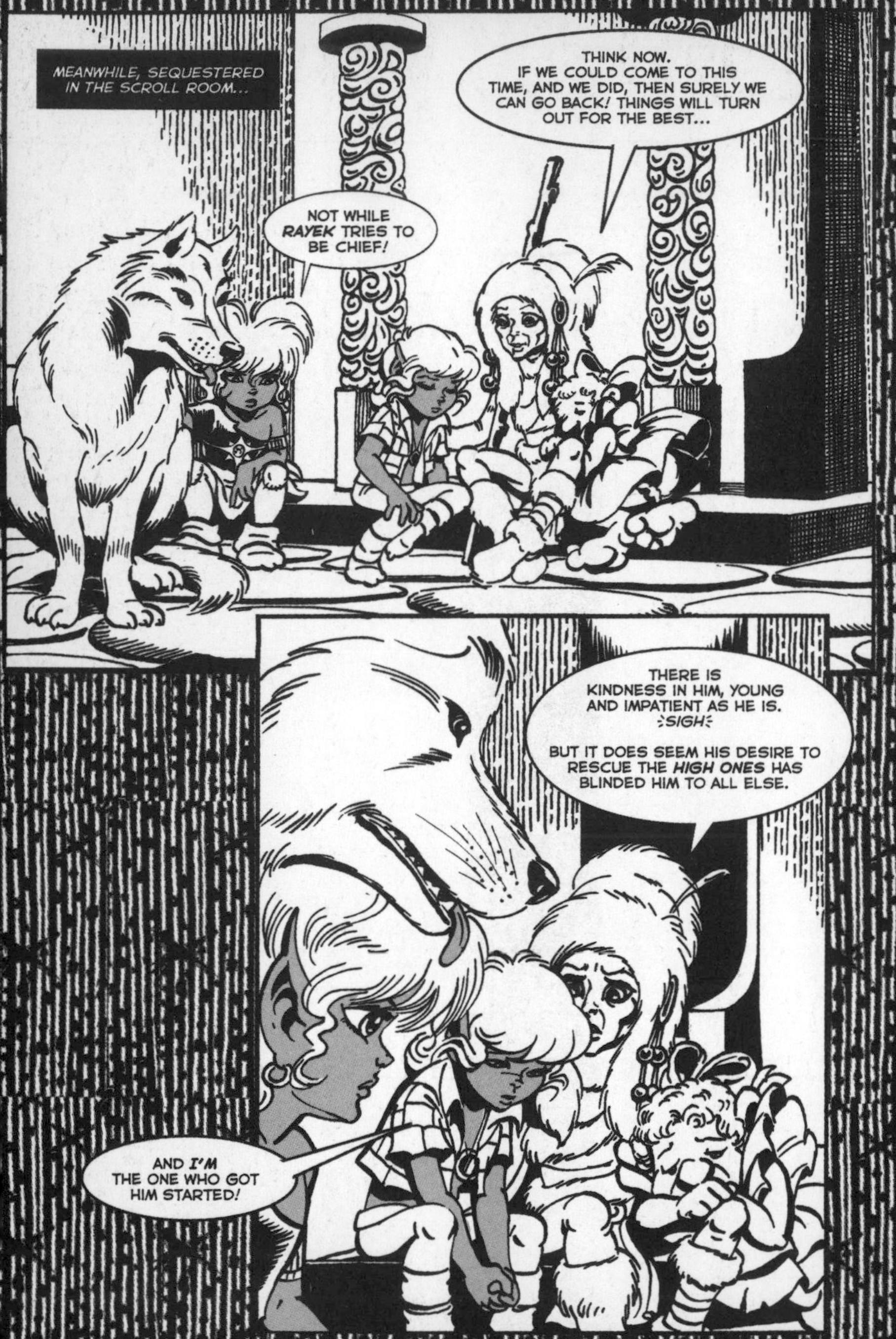
MEANWHILE, SEQUESTERED IN THE SCROLL ROOM...
THINK NOW. IF WE COULD COME TO THIS TIME, AND WE DID, THEN SURELY WE CAN GO BACK! THINGS WILL TURN OUT FOR THE BEST...
NOT WHILE *RAYEK* TRIES TO BE CHIEF!
THERE IS KINDNESS IN HIM, YOUNG AND IMPATIENT AS HE IS. *SIGH*
BUT IT DOES SEEM HIS DESIRE TO RESCUE THE *HIGH ONES* HAS BLINDED HIM TO ALL ELSE.
AND *I'M* THE ONE WHO GOT HIM STARTED!

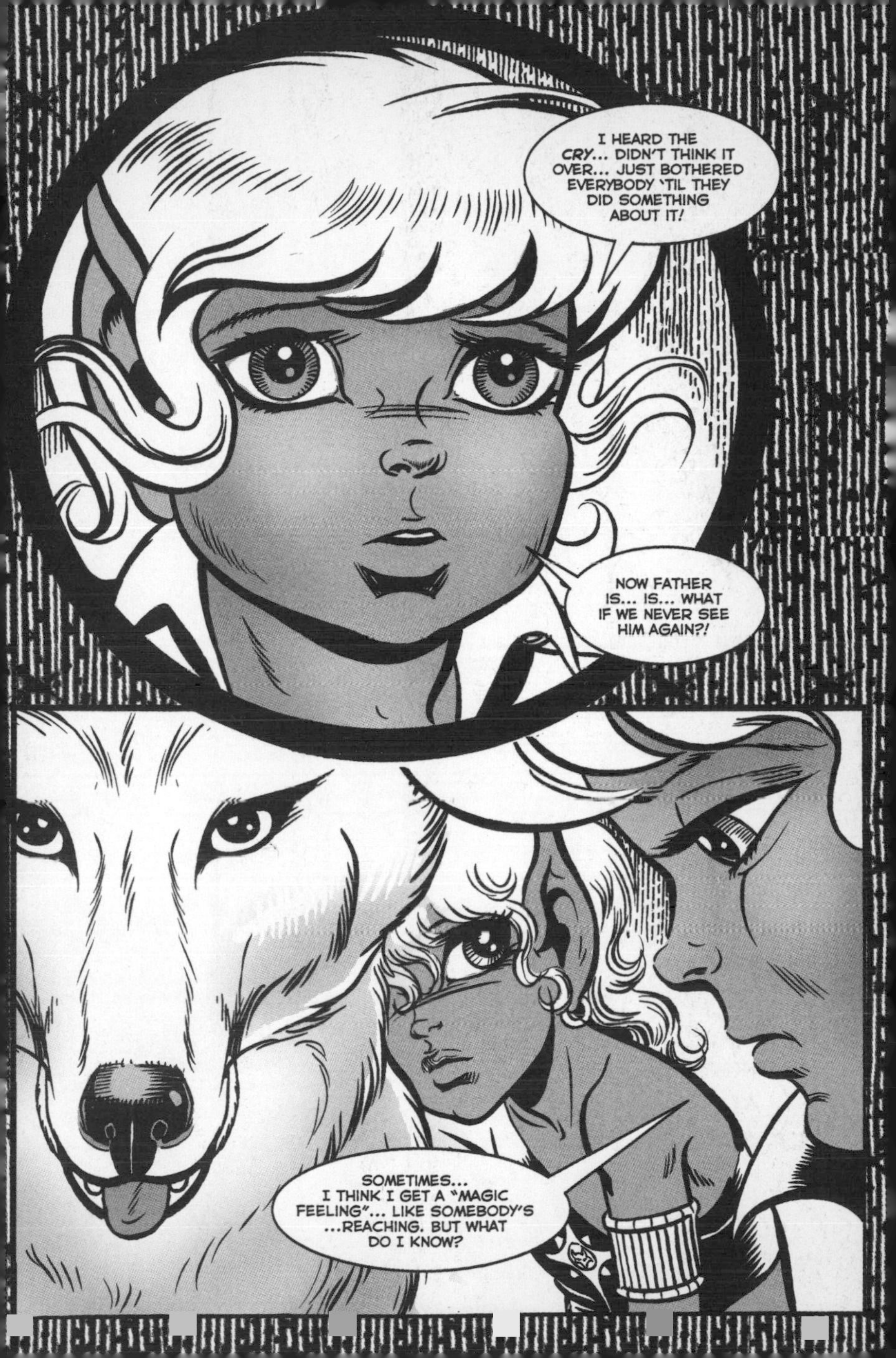
I HEARD THE CRY... DIDN'T THINK IT OVER... JUST BOTHERED EVERYBODY 'TIL THEY DID SOMETHING ABOUT IT!
NOW FATHER IS... IS... WHAT IF WE NEVER SEE HIM AGAIN?!
SOMETIMES... I THINK I GET A "MAGIC FEELING"... LIKE SOMEBODY'S ...REACHING. BUT WHAT DO I KNOW?

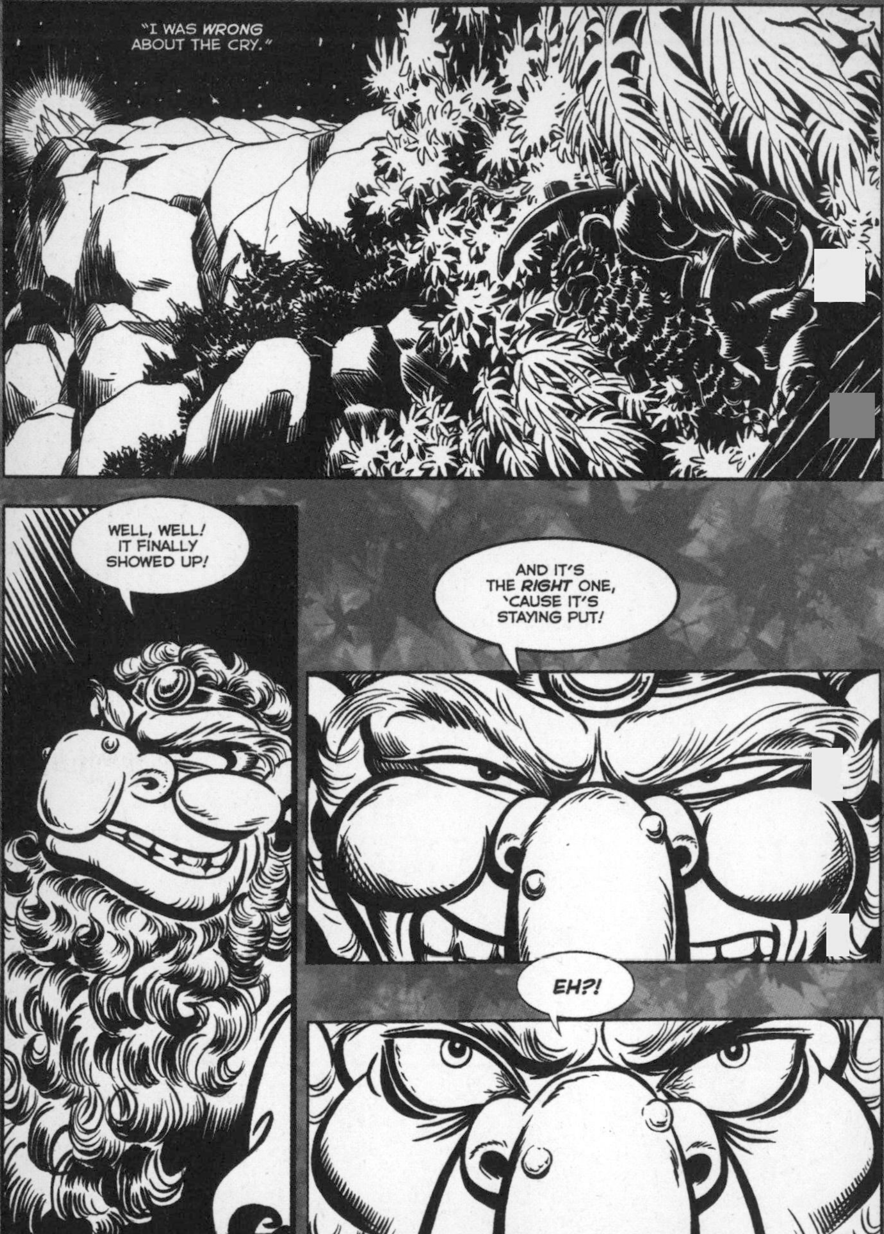
"I WAS WRONG ABOUT THE CRY."
WELL, WELL! IT FINALLY SHOWED UP!
AND IT'S THE RIGHT ONE, 'CAUSE IT'S STAYING PUT!
EH?!

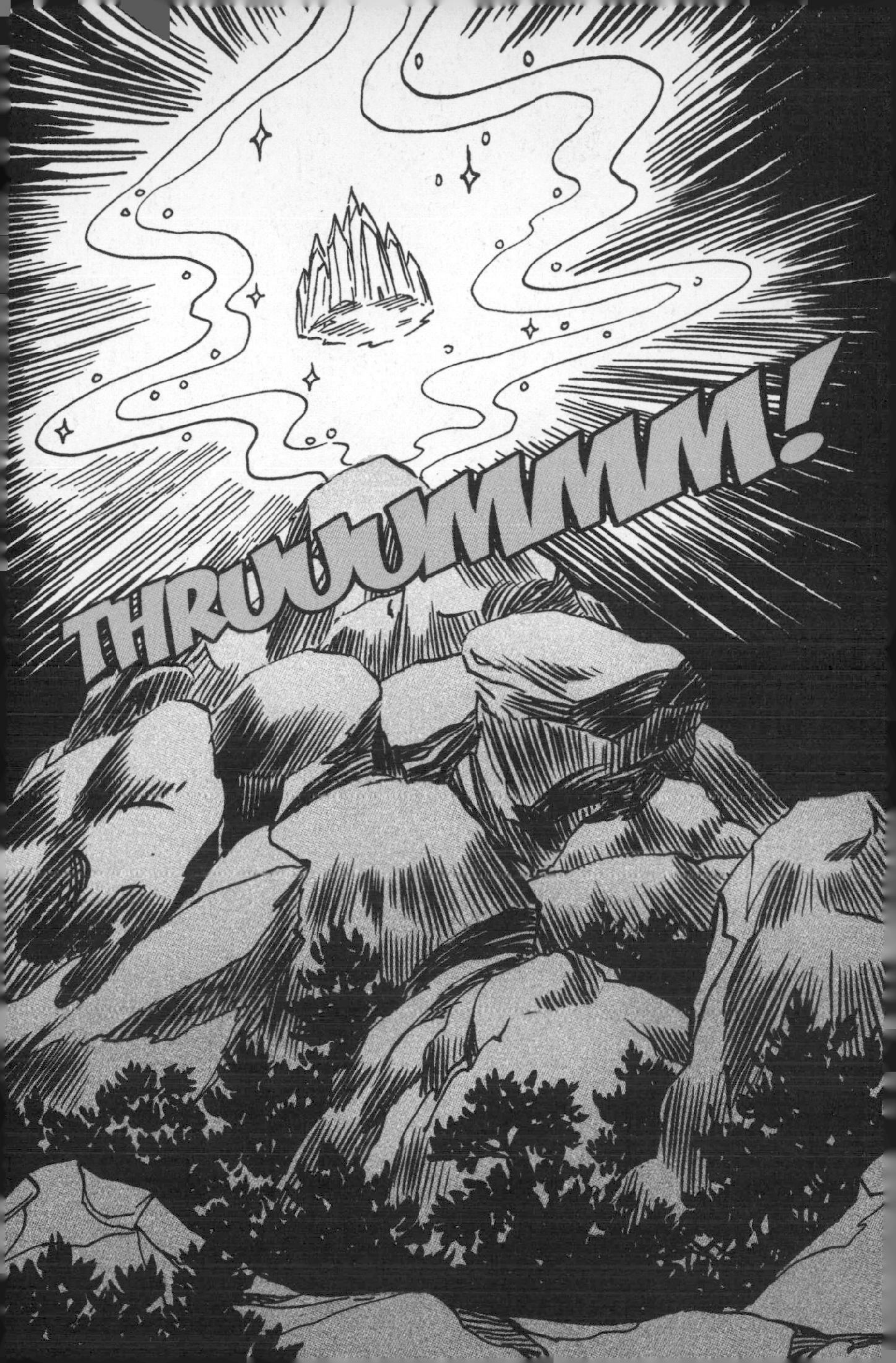
THRUUUMMMMM!

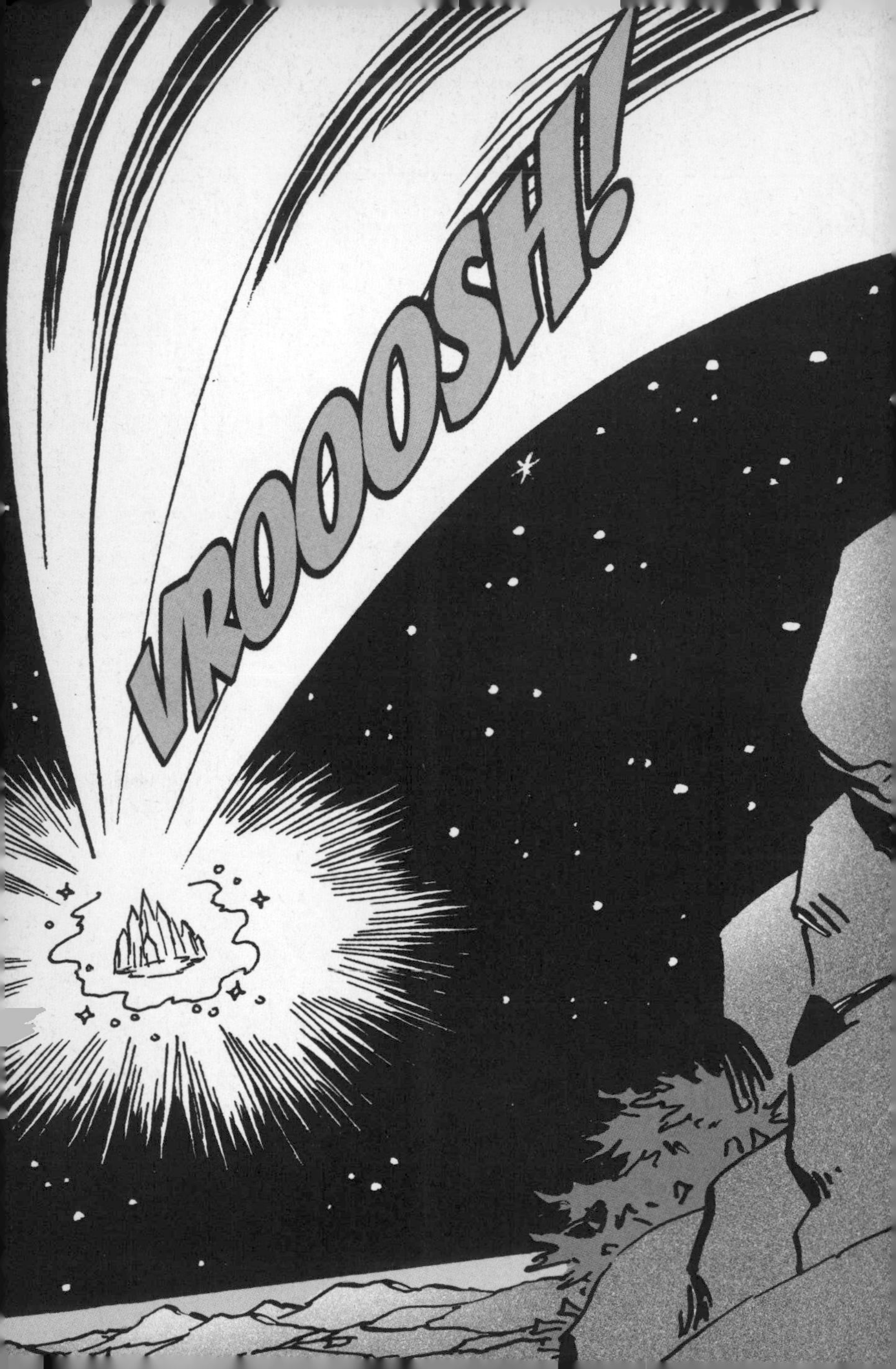
VROOOSH!

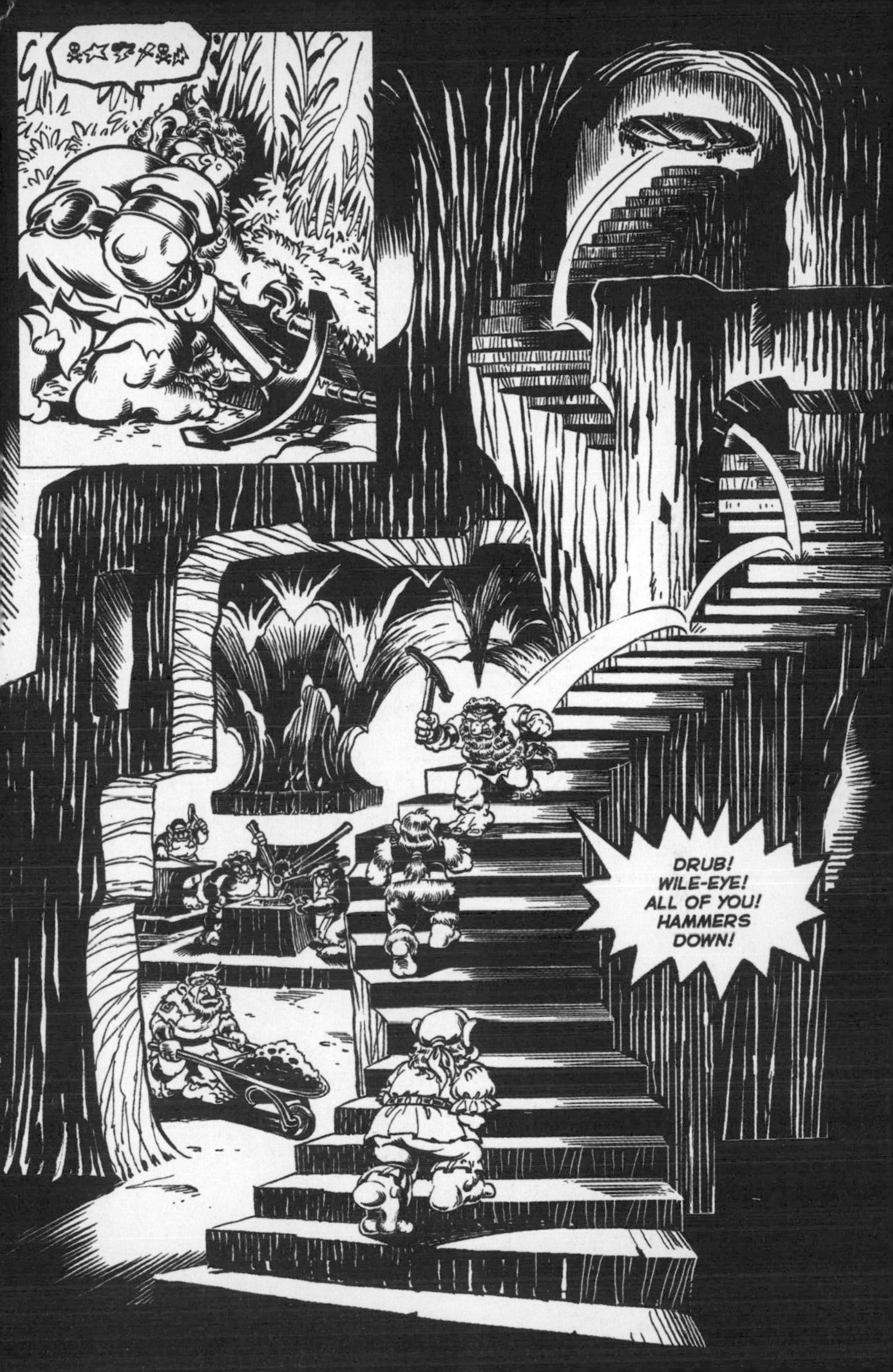
DRUB! WILE-EYE! ALL OF YOU! HAMMERS DOWN!

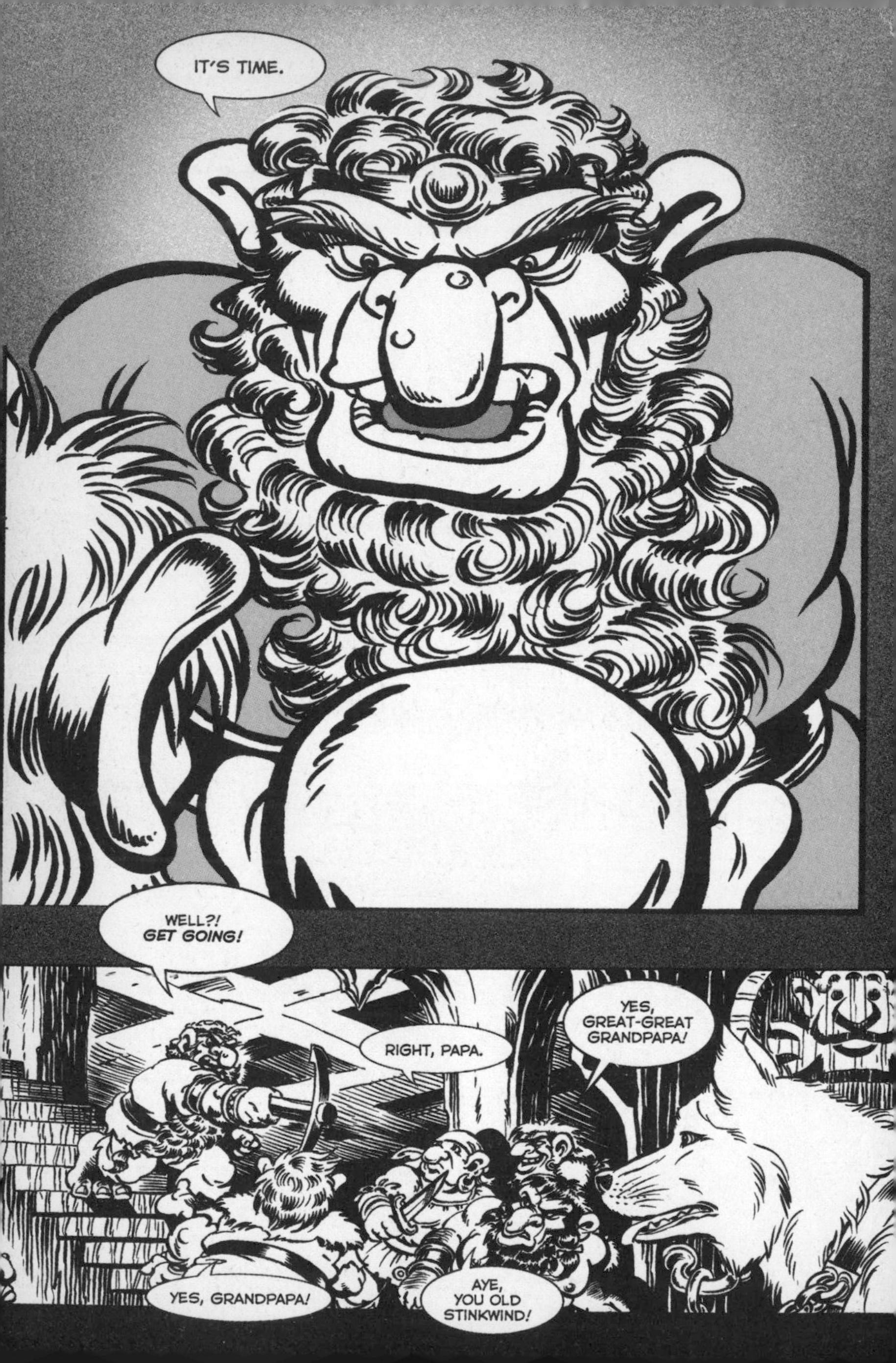
IT'S TIME.
WELL?! GET GOING!
RIGHT, PAPA.
YES, GREAT-GREAT GRANDPAPA!
YES, GRANDPAPA!
AYE, YOU OLD STINKWIND!

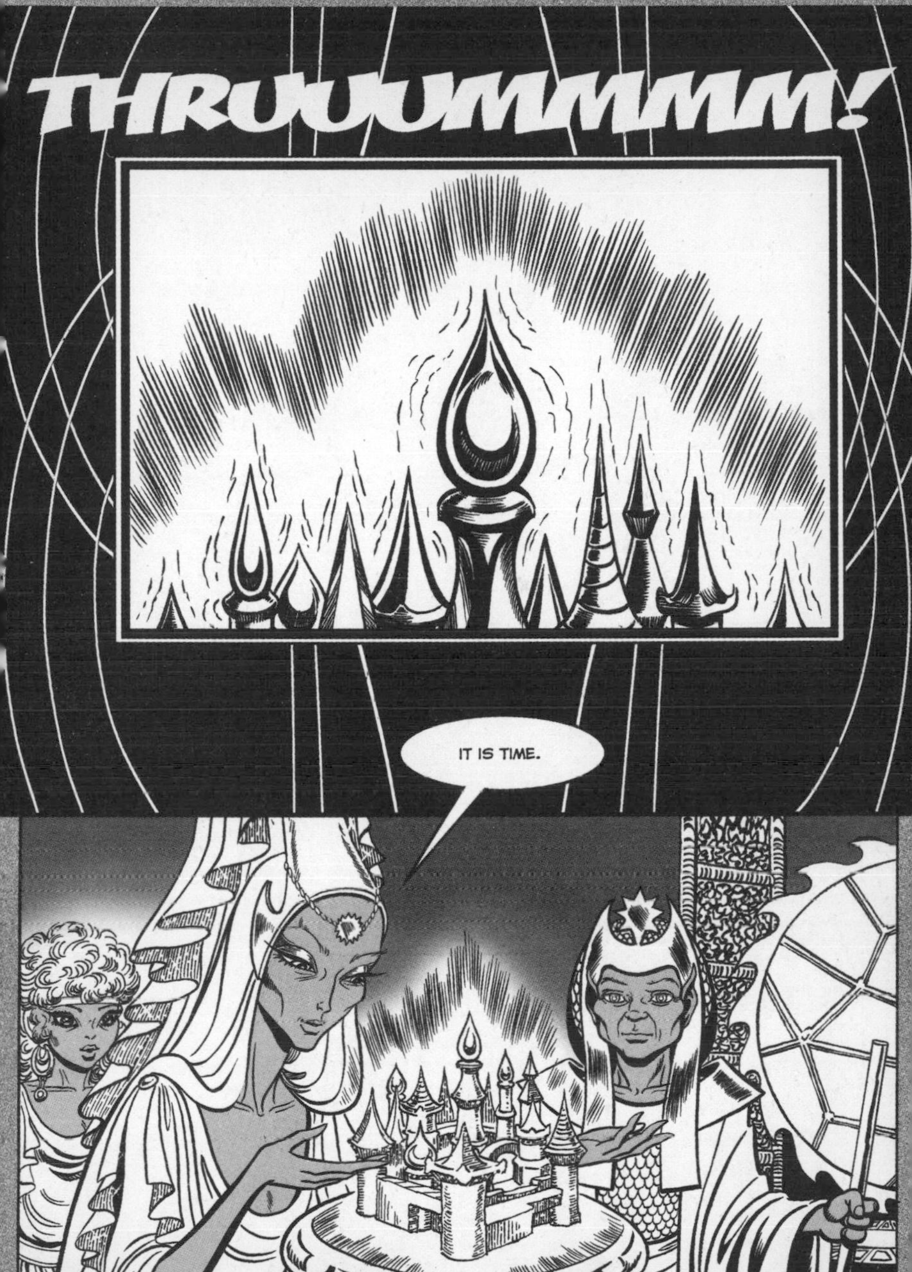
THRUUUMMMMM!
IT IS TIME.

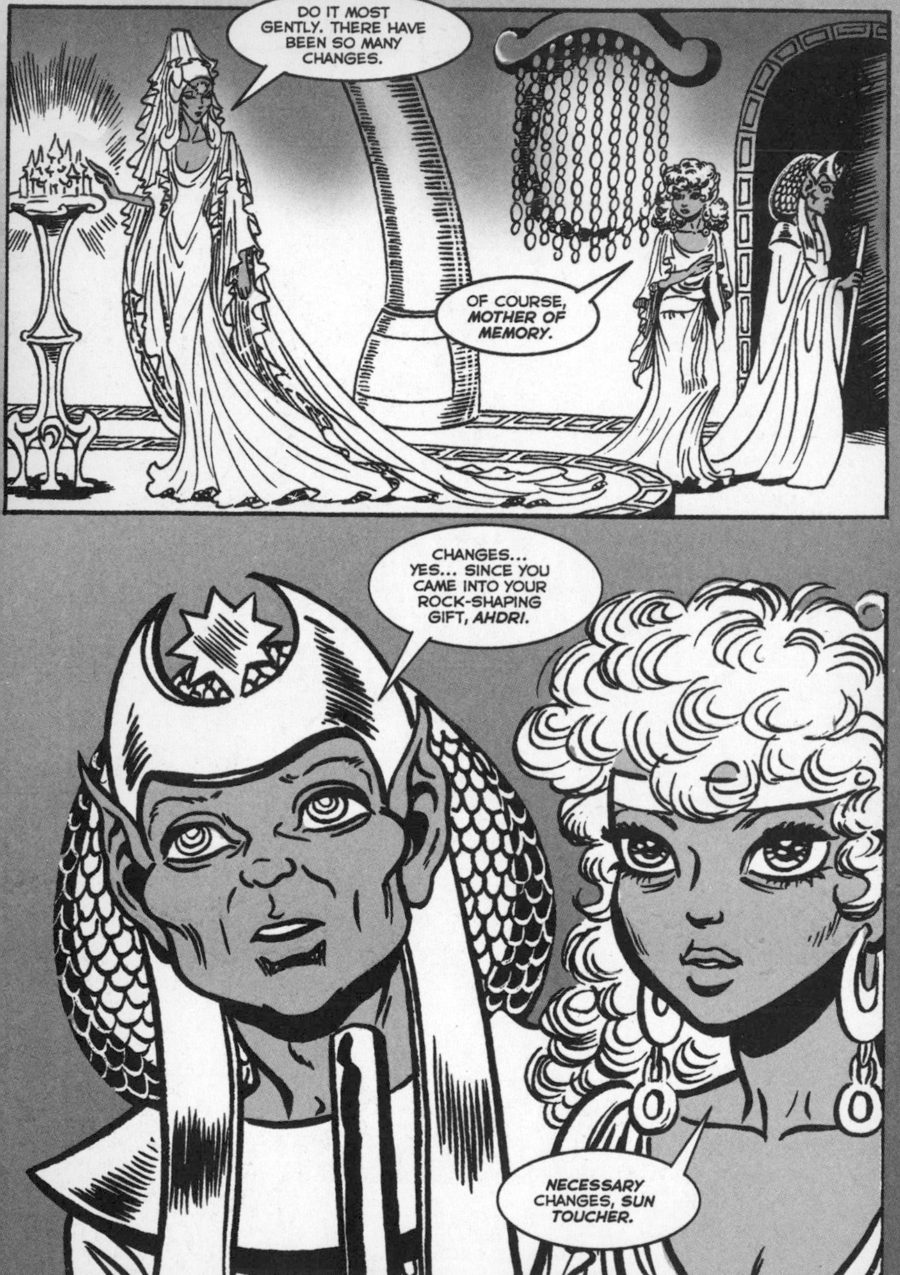
DO IT MOST GENTLY. THERE HAVE BEEN SO MANY CHANGES.
OF COURSE, *MOTHER OF MEMORY.*
CHANGES... YES... SINCE YOU CAME INTO YOUR ROCK-SHAPING GIFT, *AHDRI.*
NECESSARY CHANGES, SUN TOUCHER.

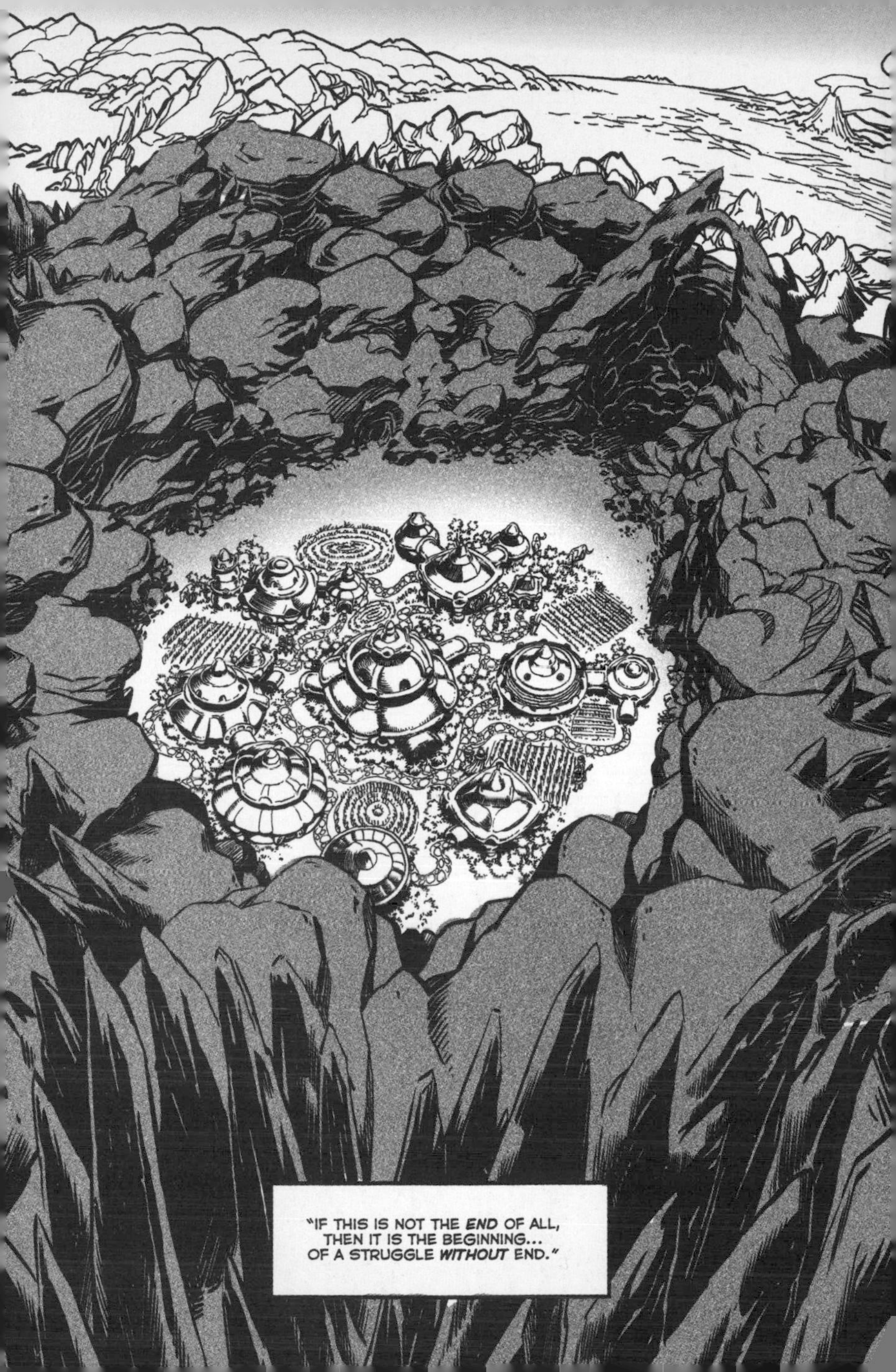
"IF THIS IS NOT THE *END* OF ALL, THEN IT IS THE BEGINNING... OF A STRUGGLE *WITHOUT* END."

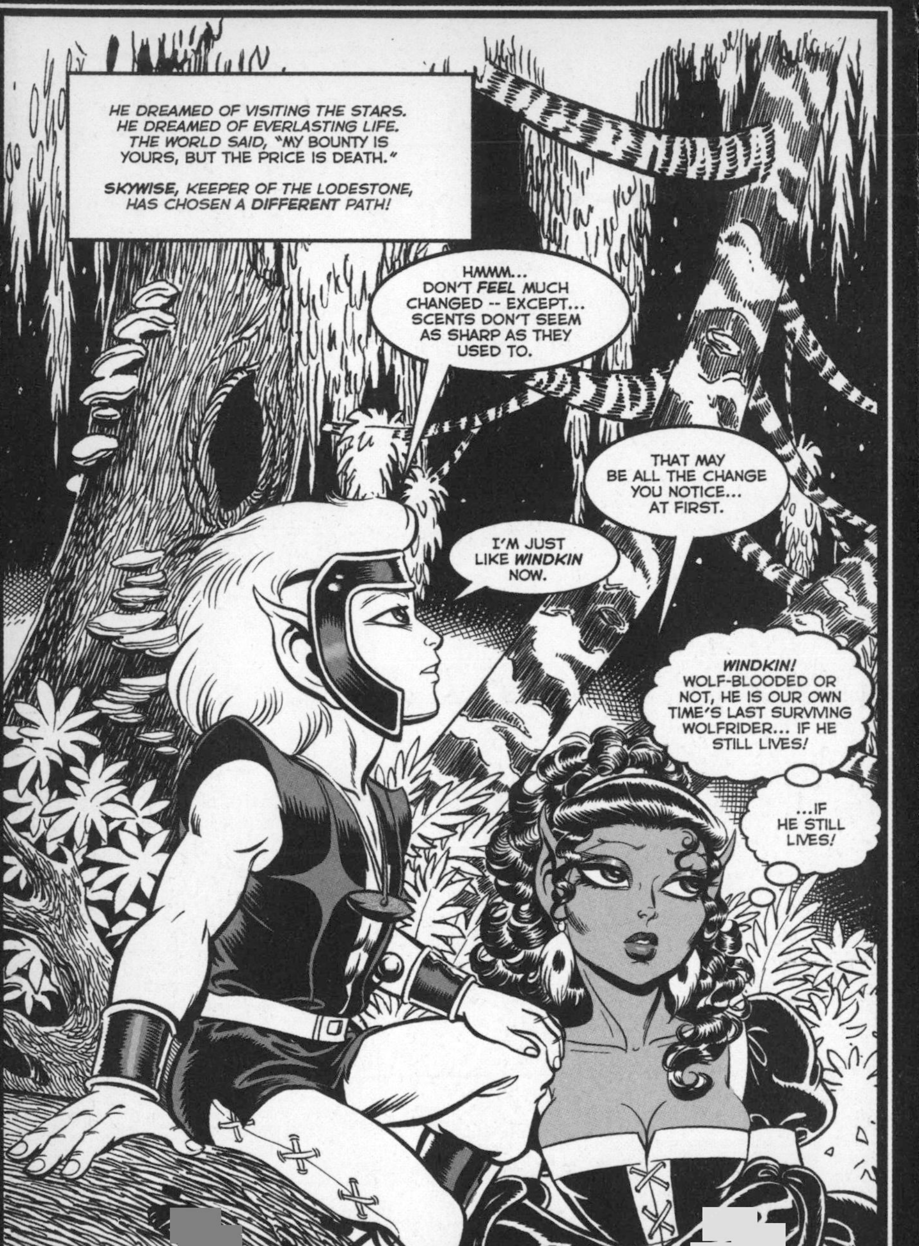
HE DREAMED OF VISITING THE STARS. HE DREAMED OF EVERLASTING LIFE. THE WORLD SAID, "MY BOUNTY IS YOURS, BUT THE PRICE IS DEATH."
SKYWISE, KEEPER OF THE LODESTONE, HAS CHOSEN A DIFFERENT PATH!
HMMM... DON'T FEEL MUCH CHANGED -- EXCEPT... SCENTS DON'T SEEM AS SHARP AS THEY USED TO.
THAT MAY BE ALL THE CHANGE YOU NOTICE... AT FIRST.
I'M JUST LIKE WINDKIN NOW.
WINDKIN! WOLF-BLOODED OR NOT, HE IS OUR OWN TIME'S LAST SURVIVING WOLFRIDER... IF HE STILL LIVES!
...IF HE STILL LIVES!

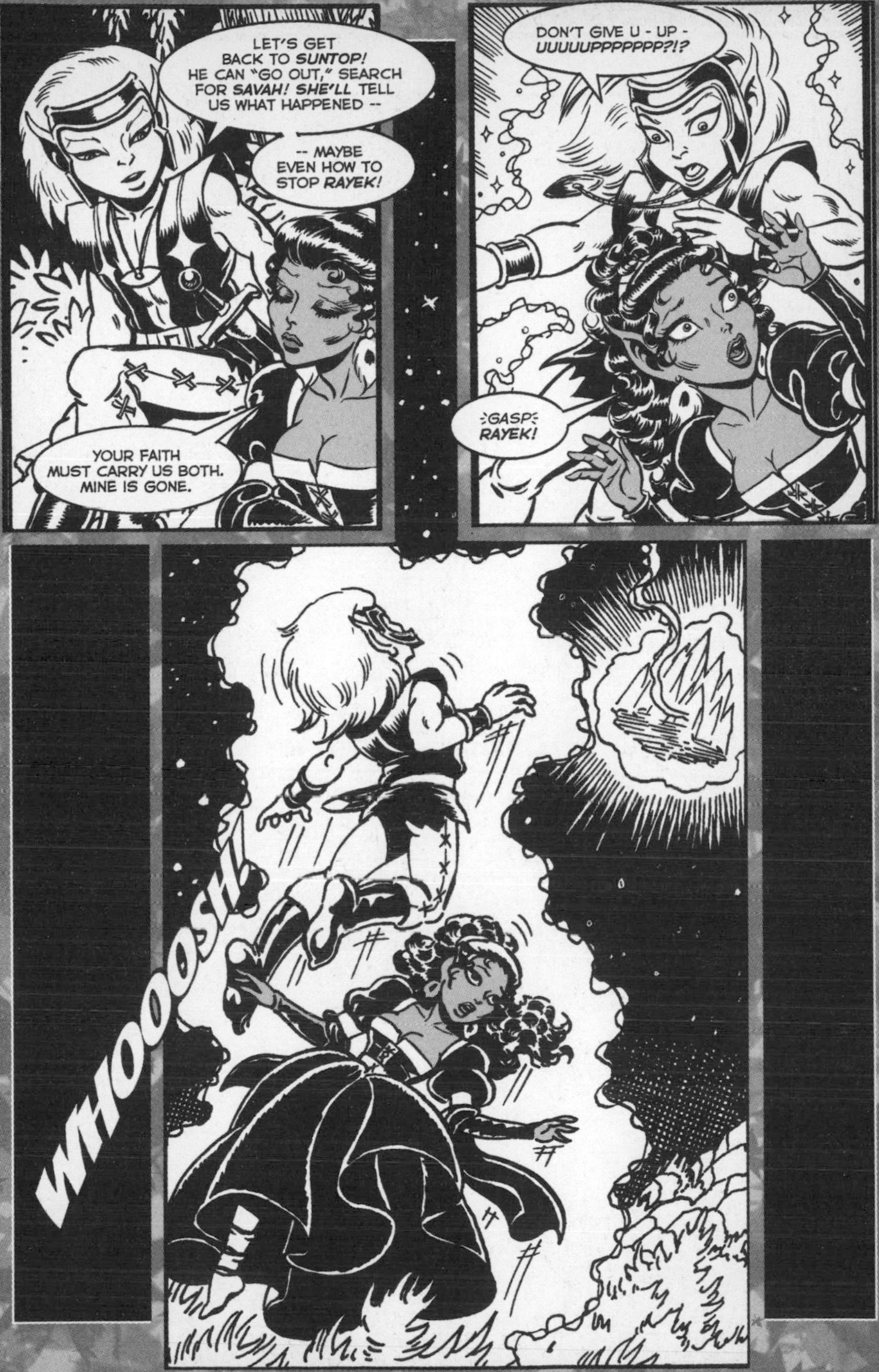
LET'S GET BACK TO SUNTOP! HE CAN "GO OUT," SEARCH FOR SAVAH! SHE'LL TELL US WHAT HAPPENED --
-- MAYBE EVEN HOW TO STOP RAYEK!
YOUR FAITH MUST CARRY US BOTH. MINE IS GONE.
DON'T GIVE U - UP - UUUUUPPPPPPP?!?
GASP RAYEK!
WHOOOSH!

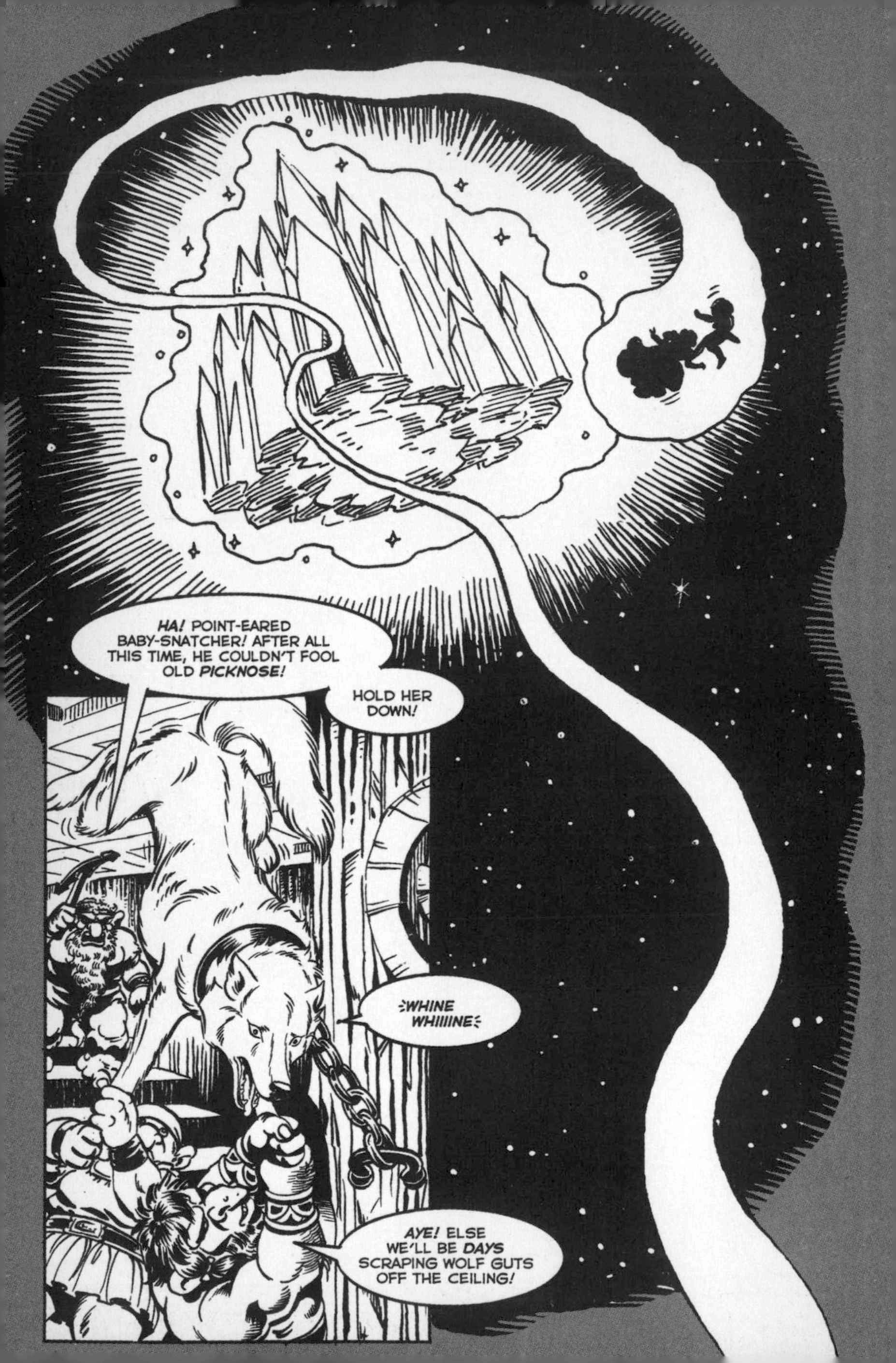
HA! POINT-EARED BABY-SNATCHER! AFTER ALL THIS TIME, HE COULDN'T FOOL OLD PICKNOSE!
HOLD HER DOWN!
WHINE WHIIIINE
AYE! ELSE WE'LL BE DAYS SCRAPING WOLF GUTS OFF THE CEILING!

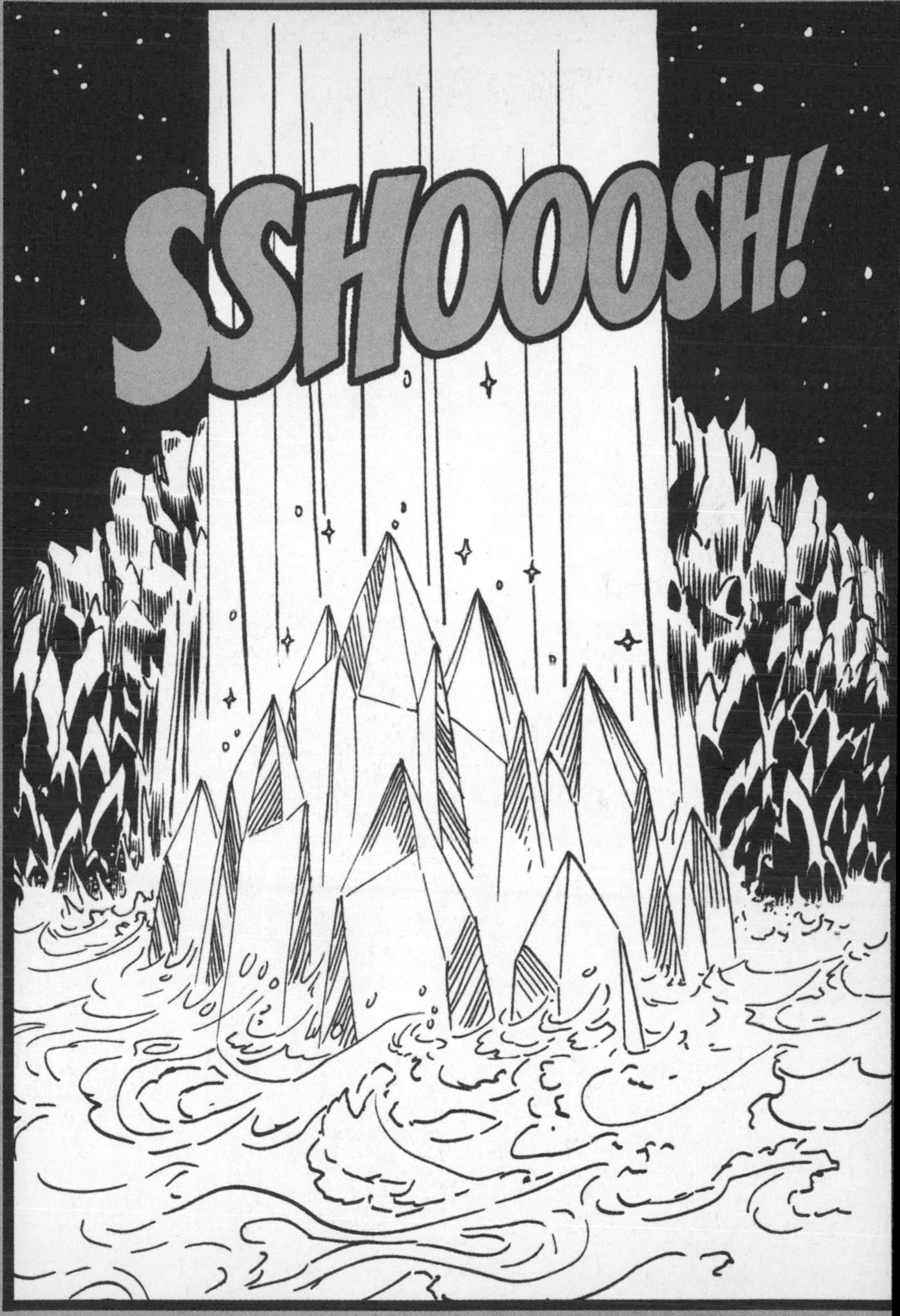
SSHOOOSH!

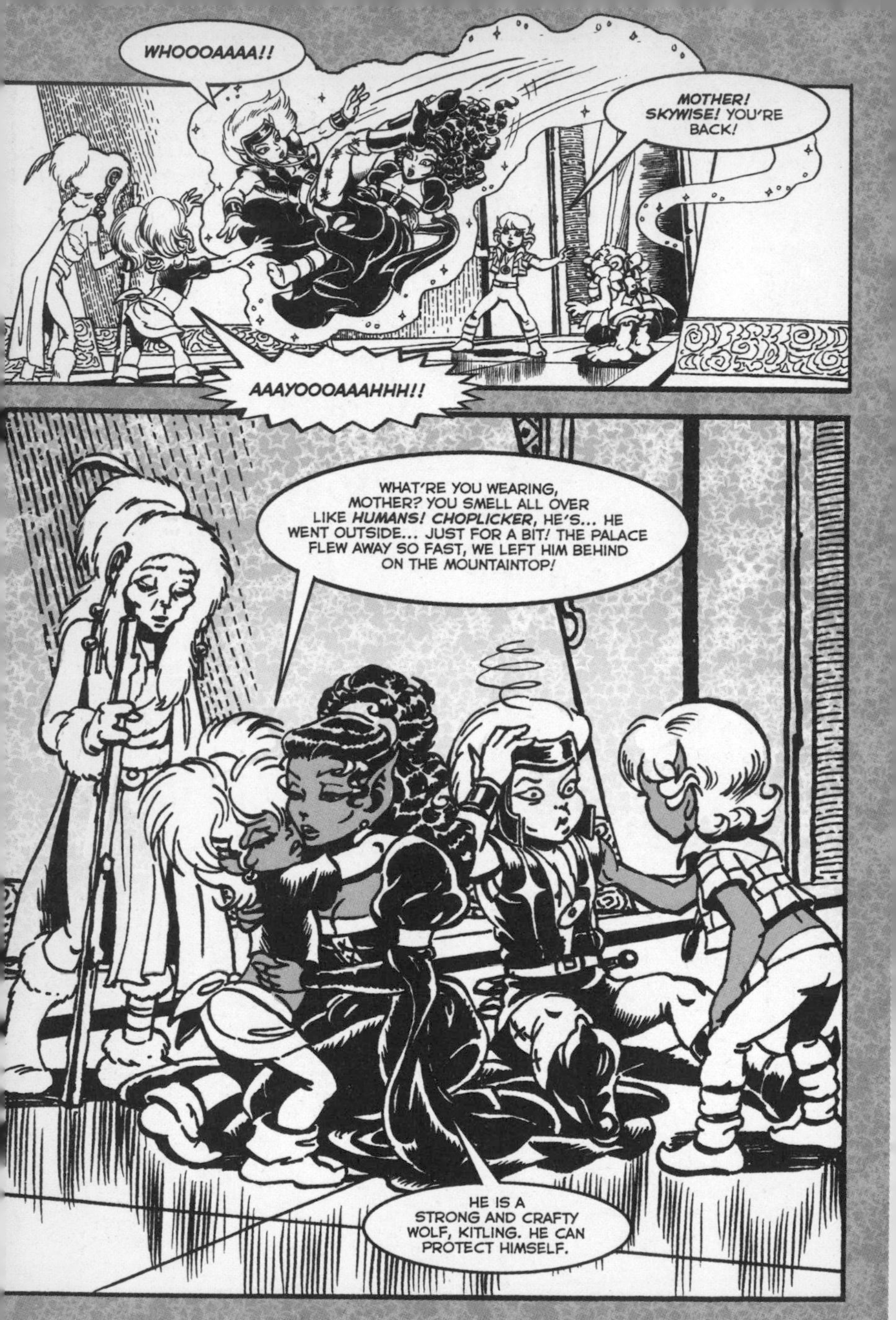
WHOOOAAAA!!
MOTHER! SKYWISE! YOU'RE BACK!
AAAYOOOAAAHHH!!
WHAT'RE YOU WEARING, MOTHER? YOU SMELL ALL OVER LIKE HUMANS! CHOPLICKER, HE'S... HE WENT OUTSIDE... JUST FOR A BIT! THE PALACE FLEW AWAY SO FAST, WE LEFT HIM BEHIND ON THE MOUNTAINTOP!
HE IS A STRONG AND CRAFTY WOLF, KITLING. HE CAN PROTECT HIMSELF.

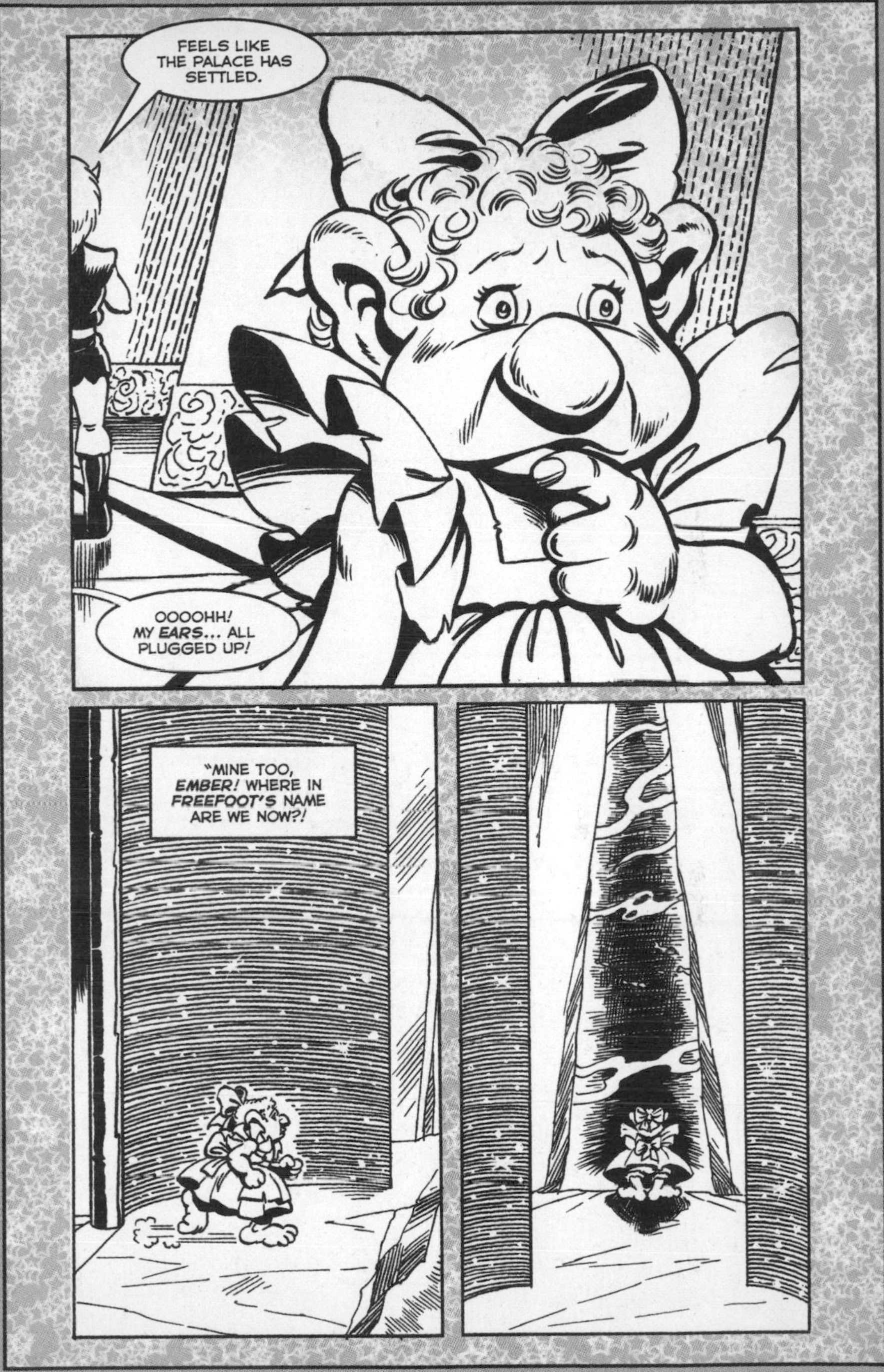
FEELS LIKE THE PALACE HAS SETTLED.
OOOOHH! MY EARS... ALL PLUGGED UP!
"MINE TOO, EMBER! WHERE IN FREEFOOT'S NAME ARE WE NOW?!

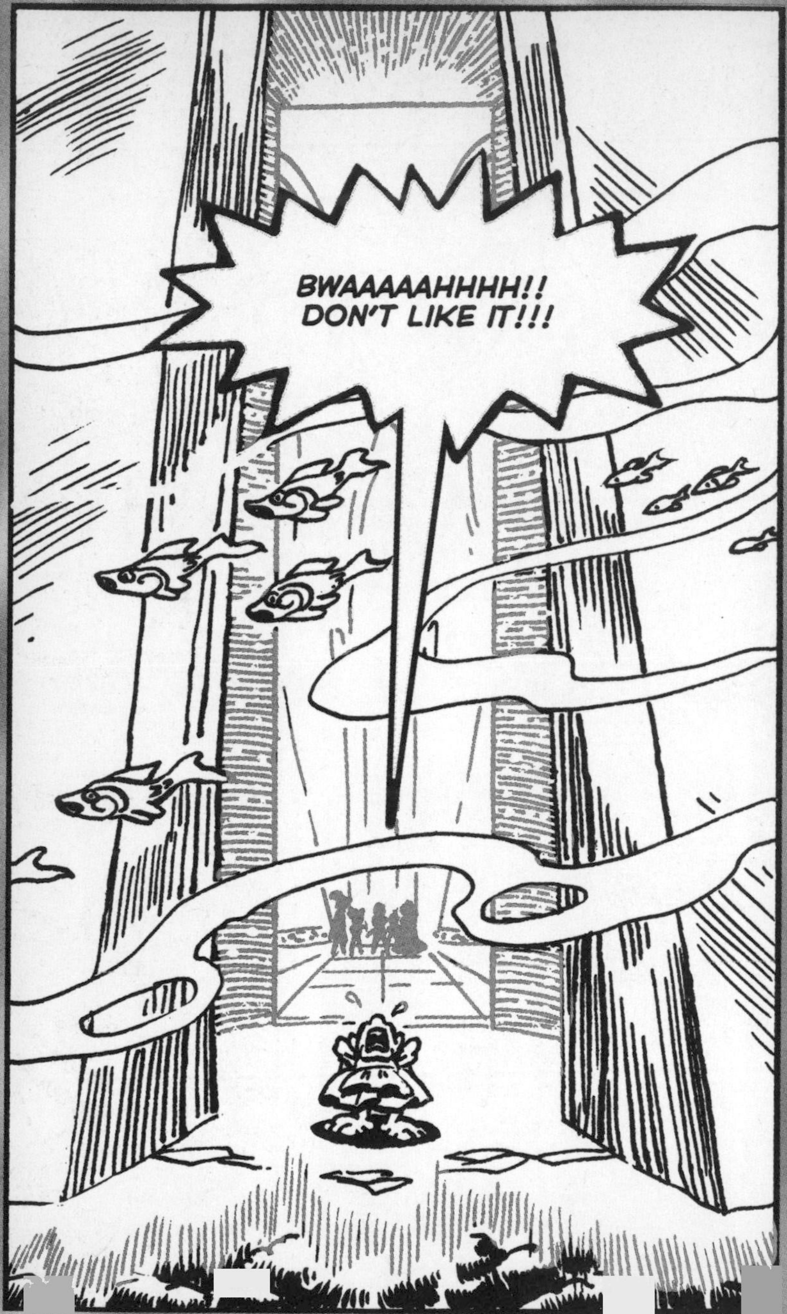
BWAAAAAHHHH!!
DON'T LIKE IT!!!

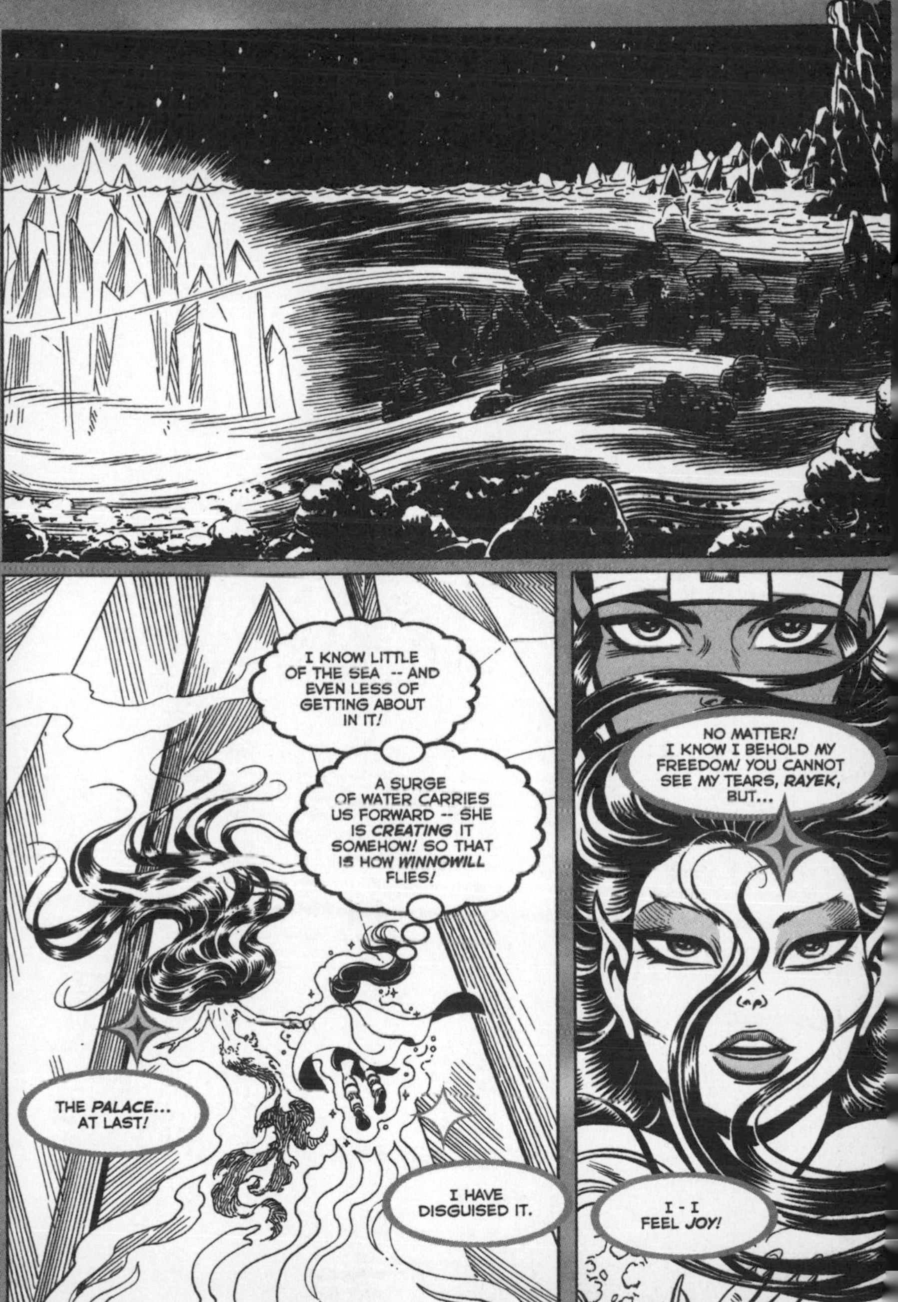

I KNOW LITTLE OF THE SEA -- AND EVEN LESS OF GETTING ABOUT IN IT!
A SURGE OF WATER CARRIES US FORWARD -- SHE IS *CREATING* IT SOMEHOW! SO THAT IS HOW *WINNOWILL* FLIES!
THE *PALACE*... AT LAST!
I HAVE DISGUISED IT.
NO MATTER! I KNOW I BEHOLD MY FREEDOM! YOU CANNOT SEE MY TEARS, *RAYEK*, BUT...
I - I FEEL *JOY!*

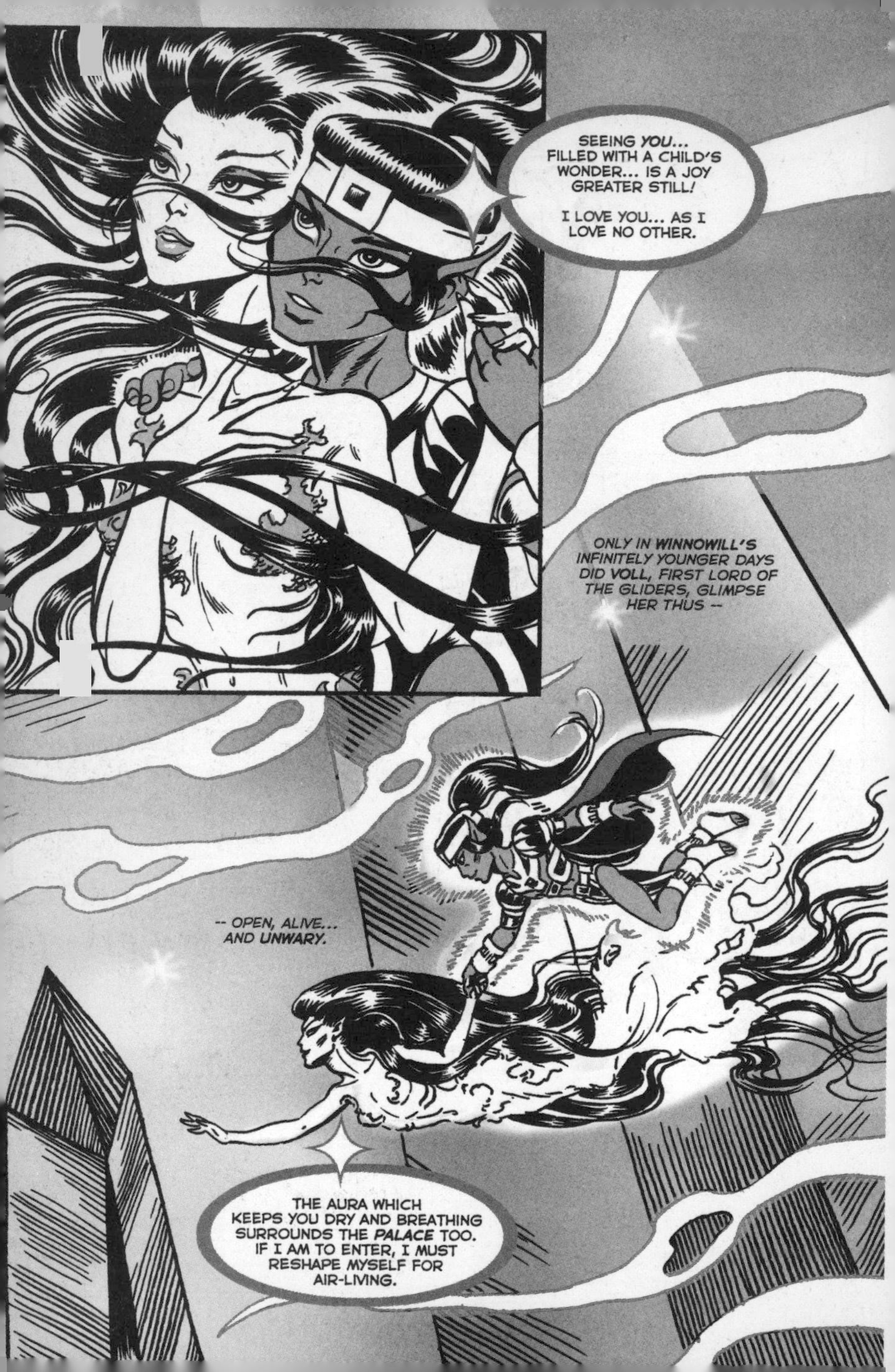
SEEING YOU... FILLED WITH A CHILD'S WONDER... IS A JOY GREATER STILL!
I LOVE YOU... AS I LOVE NO OTHER.
ONLY IN WINNOWILL'S INFINITELY YOUNGER DAYS DID VOLL, FIRST LORD OF THE GLIDERS, GLIMPSE HER THUS --
-- OPEN, ALIVE... AND UNWARY.
THE AURA WHICH KEEPS YOU DRY AND BREATHING SURROUNDS THE PALACE TOO. IF I AM TO ENTER, I MUST RESHAPE MYSELF FOR AIR-LIVING.

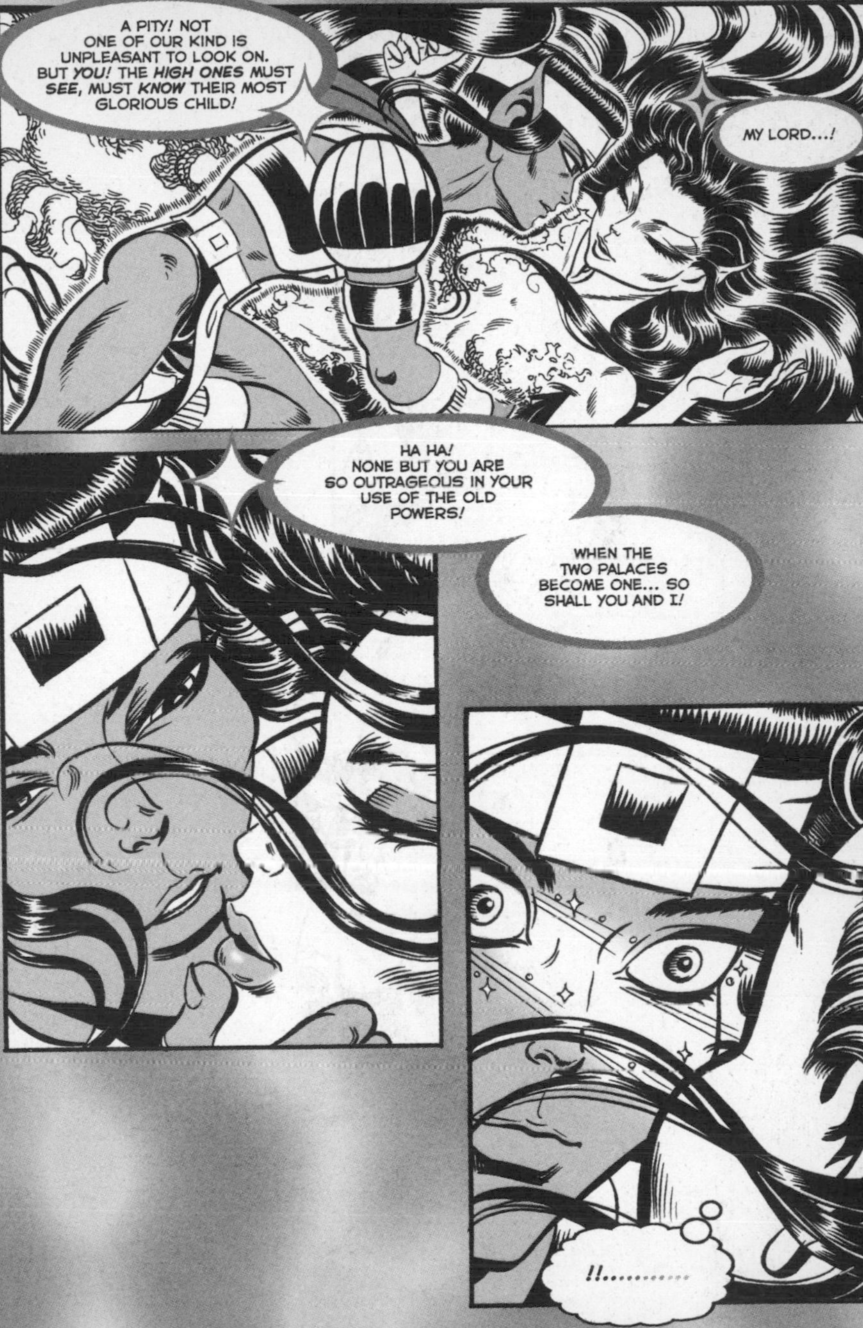
A PITY! NOT ONE OF OUR KIND IS UNPLEASANT TO LOOK ON. BUT YOU! THE HIGH ONES MUST SEE, MUST KNOW THEIR MOST GLORIOUS CHILD!
MY LORD...!
HA HA! NONE BUT YOU ARE SO OUTRAGEOUS IN YOUR USE OF THE OLD POWERS!
WHEN THE TWO PALACES BECOME ONE... SO SHALL YOU AND I!
!!..........

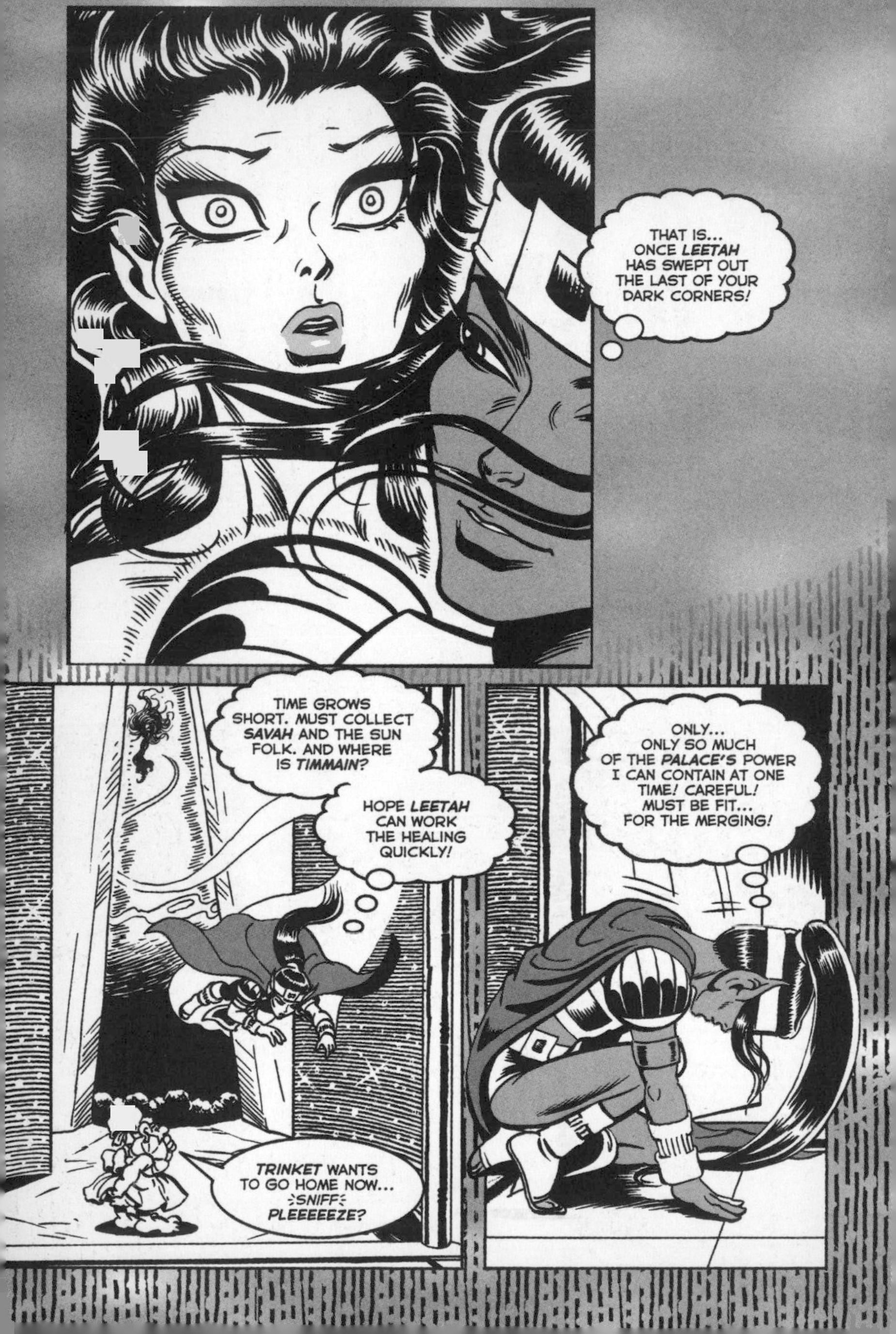
THAT IS... ONCE LEETAH HAS SWEPT OUT THE LAST OF YOUR DARK CORNERS!
TIME GROWS SHORT. MUST COLLECT SAVAH AND THE SUN FOLK. AND WHERE IS TIMMAIN?
HOPE LEETAH CAN WORK THE HEALING QUICKLY!
TRINKET WANTS TO GO HOME NOW... SNIFF PLEEEEEZE?
ONLY... ONLY SO MUCH OF THE PALACE'S POWER I CAN CONTAIN AT ONE TIME! CAREFUL! MUST BE FIT... FOR THE MERGING!

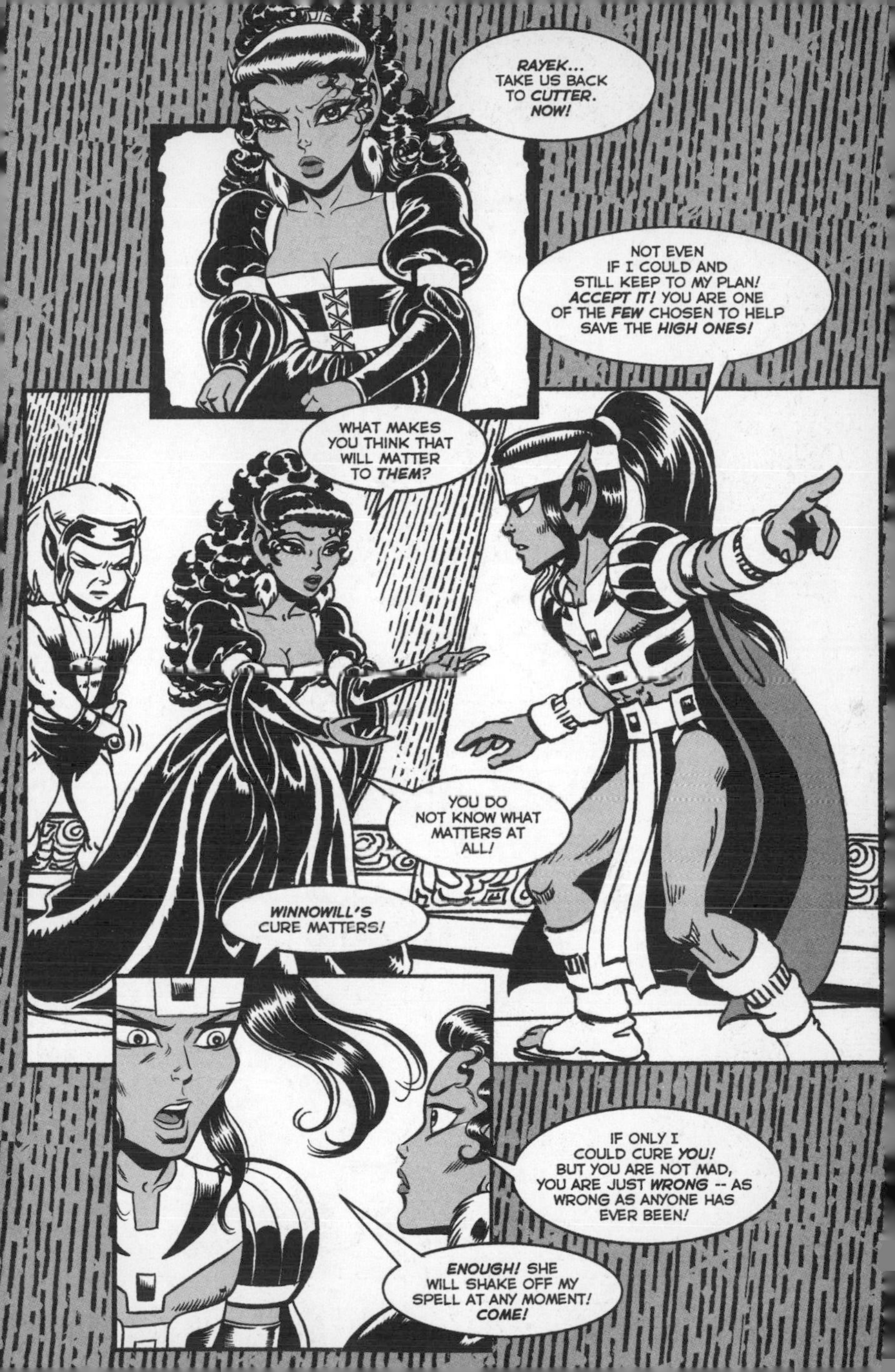

RAYEK... TAKE US BACK TO CUTTER. NOW!
NOT EVEN IF I COULD AND STILL KEEP TO MY PLAN! ACCEPT IT! YOU ARE ONE OF THE FEW CHOSEN TO HELP SAVE THE HIGH ONES!
WHAT MAKES YOU THINK THAT WILL MATTER TO THEM?
YOU DO NOT KNOW WHAT MATTERS AT ALL!
WINNOWILL'S CURE MATTERS!
IF ONLY I COULD CURE YOU! BUT YOU ARE NOT MAD, YOU ARE JUST WRONG -- AS WRONG AS ANYONE HAS EVER BEEN!
ENOUGH! SHE WILL SHAKE OFF MY SPELL AT ANY MOMENT! COME!

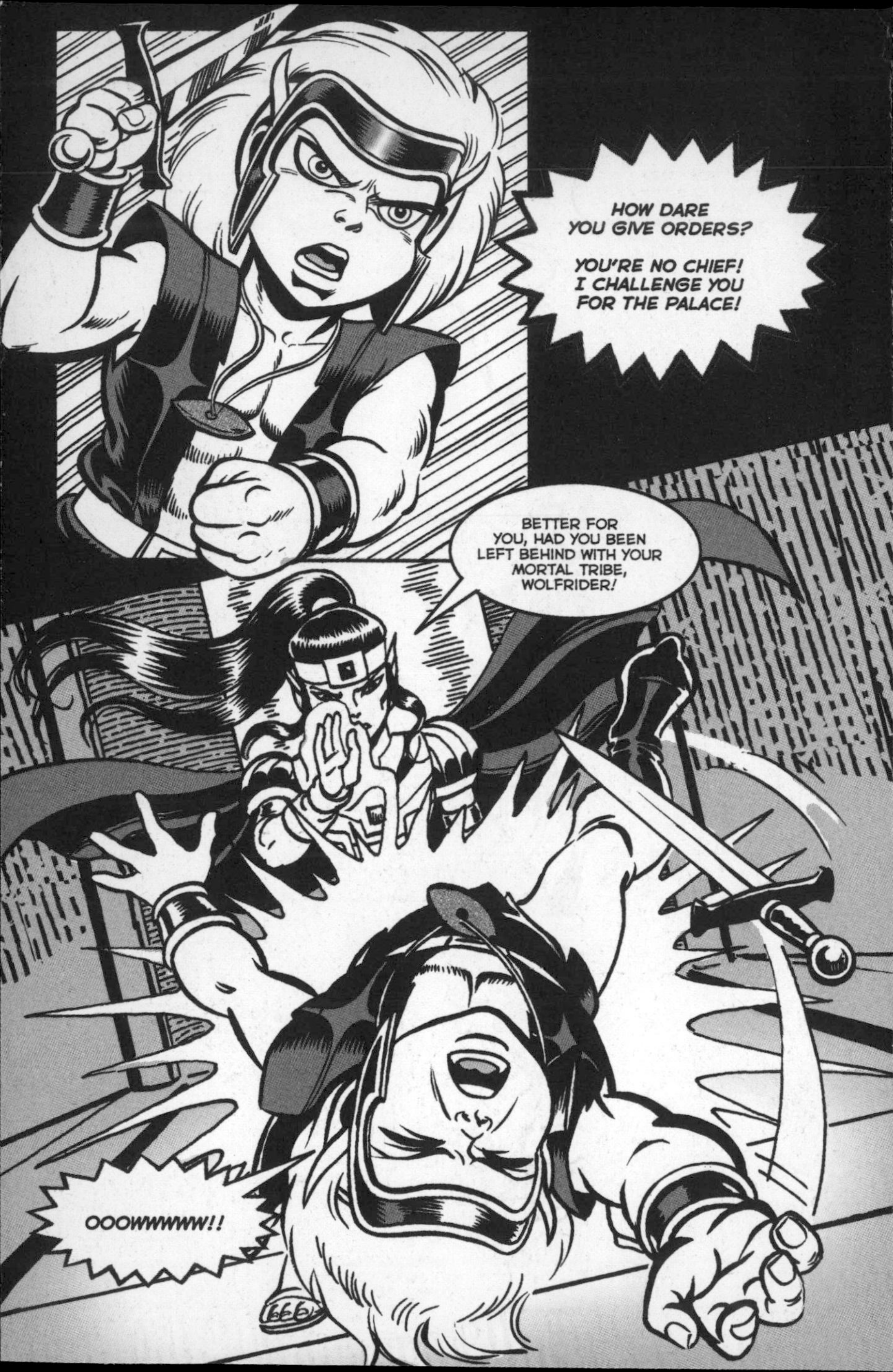
HOW DARE YOU GIVE ORDERS?
YOU'RE NO CHIEF! I CHALLENGE YOU FOR THE PALACE!
BETTER FOR YOU, HAD YOU BEEN LEFT BEHIND WITH YOUR MORTAL TRIBE, WOLFRIDER!
OOOWWWWW!!

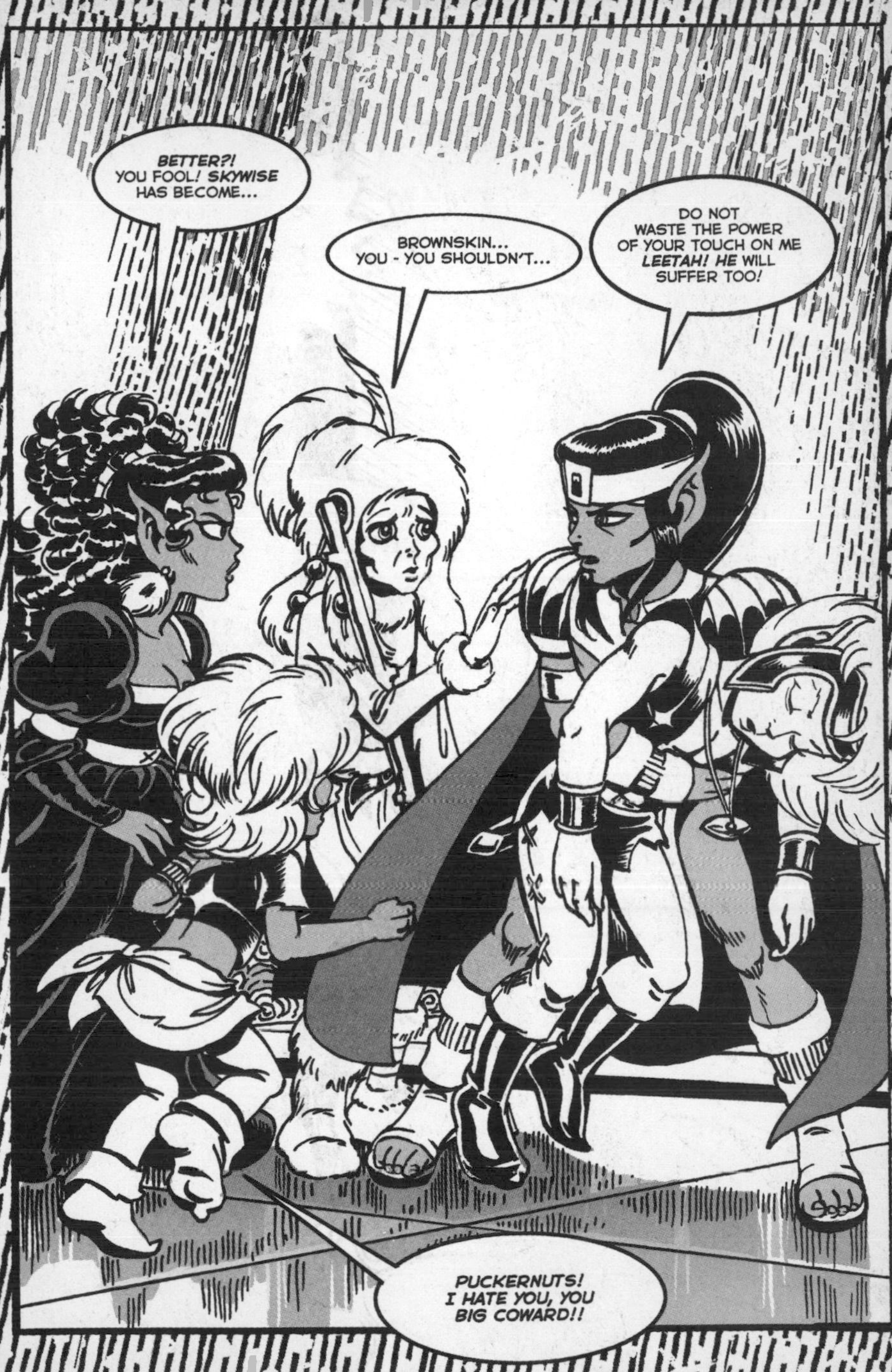
BETTER?! YOU FOOL! SKYWISE HAS BECOME...
BROWNSKIN... YOU - YOU SHOULDN'T...
DO NOT WASTE THE POWER OF YOUR TOUCH ON ME LEETAH! HE WILL SUFFER TOO!
PUCKERNUTS! I HATE YOU, YOU BIG COWARD!!

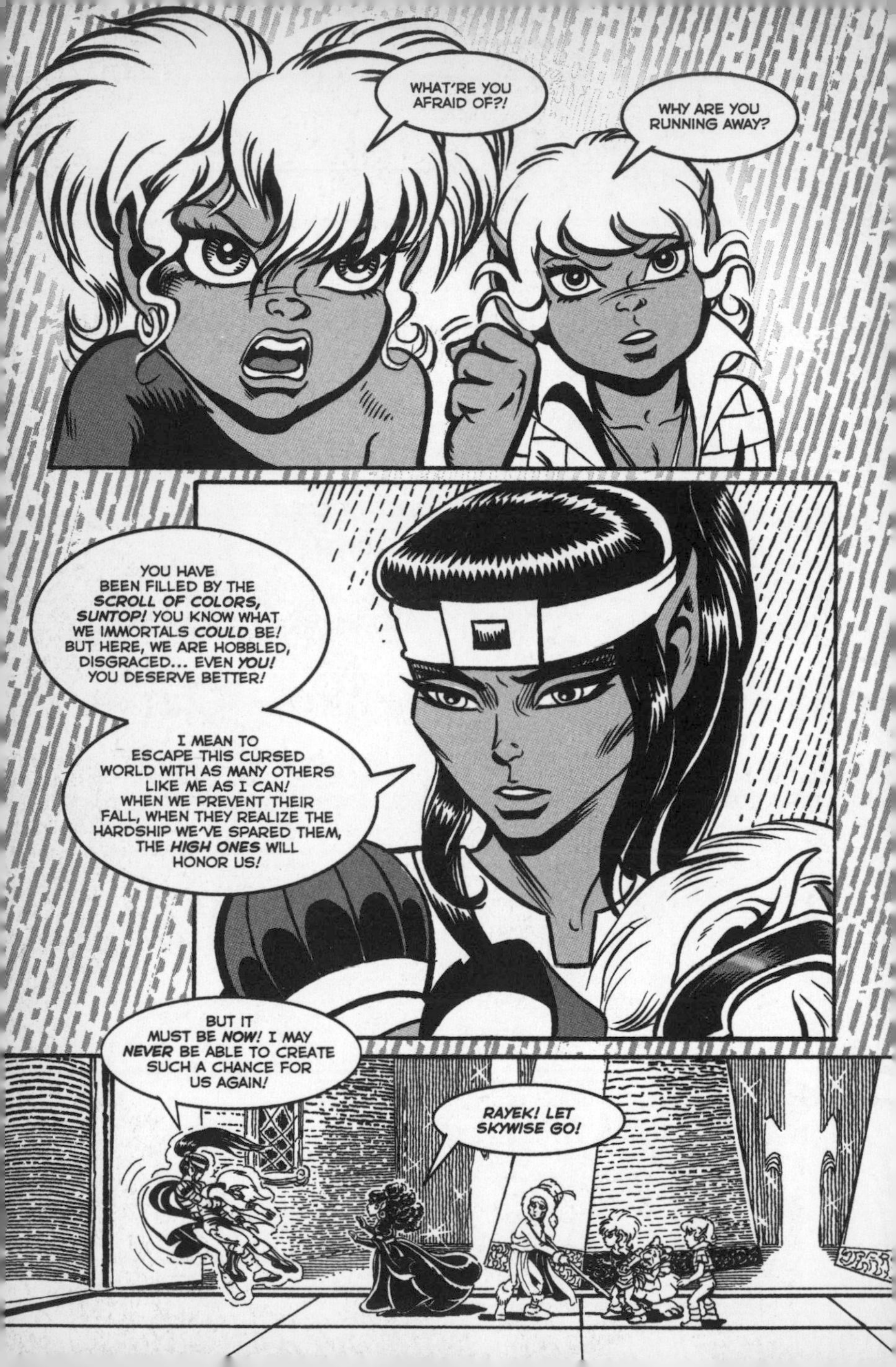
WHAT'RE YOU AFRAID OF?!
WHY ARE YOU RUNNING AWAY?
YOU HAVE BEEN FILLED BY THE SCROLL OF COLORS, SUNTOP! YOU KNOW WHAT WE IMMORTALS COULD BE! BUT HERE, WE ARE HOBBLED, DISGRACED... EVEN YOU! YOU DESERVE BETTER!
I MEAN TO ESCAPE THIS CURSED WORLD WITH AS MANY OTHERS LIKE ME AS I CAN! WHEN WE PREVENT THEIR FALL, WHEN THEY REALIZE THE HARDSHIP WE'VE SPARED THEM, THE HIGH ONES WILL HONOR US!
BUT IT MUST BE NOW! I MAY NEVER BE ABLE TO CREATE SUCH A CHANCE FOR US AGAIN!
RAYEK! LET SKYWISE GO!

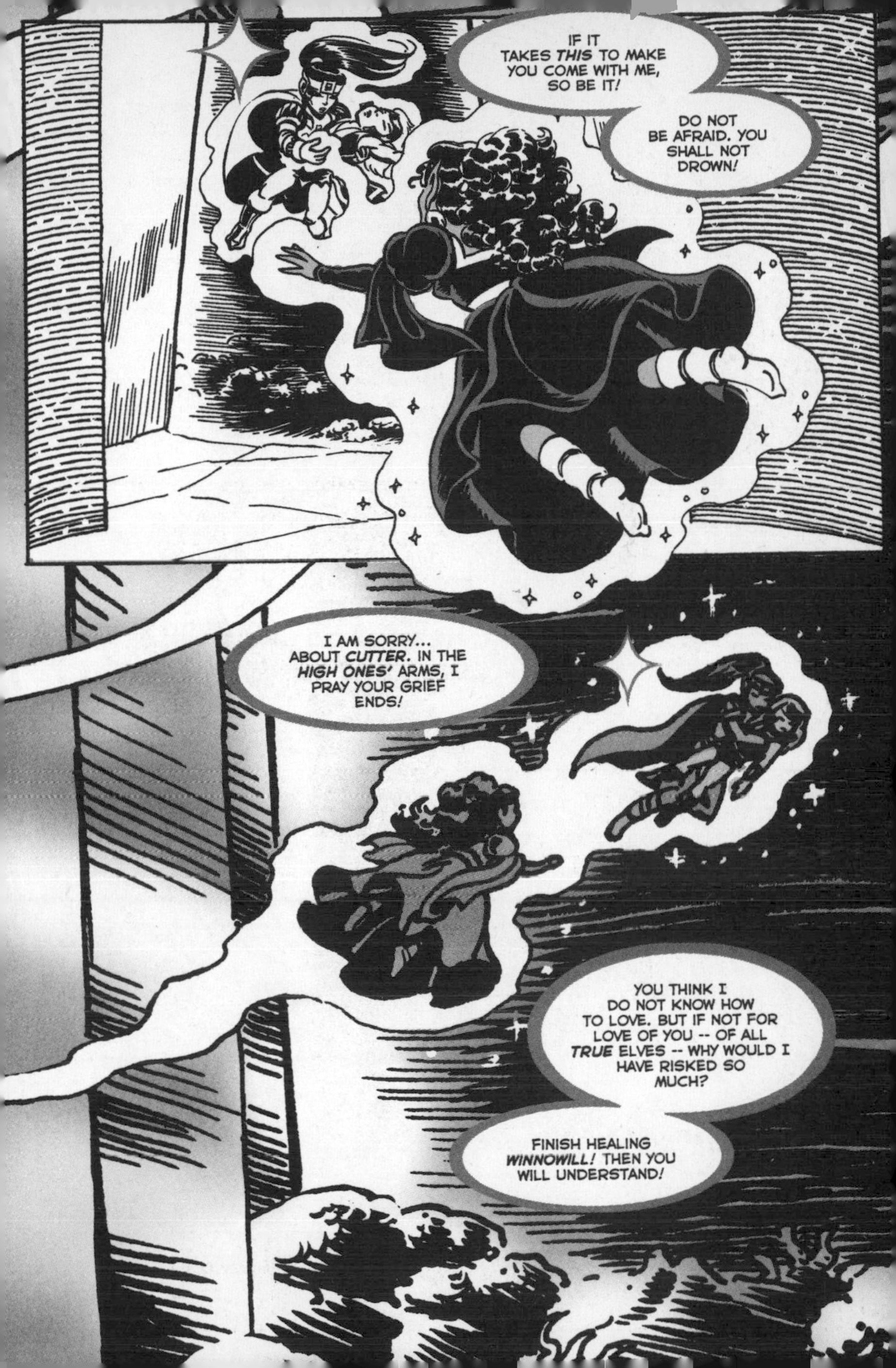
IF IT TAKES THIS TO MAKE YOU COME WITH ME, SO BE IT!
DO NOT BE AFRAID. YOU SHALL NOT DROWN!
I AM SORRY... ABOUT CUTTER. IN THE HIGH ONES' ARMS, I PRAY YOUR GRIEF ENDS!
YOU THINK I DO NOT KNOW HOW TO LOVE. BUT IF NOT FOR LOVE OF YOU -- OF ALL TRUE ELVES -- WHY WOULD I HAVE RISKED SO MUCH?
FINISH HEALING WINNOWILL! THEN YOU WILL UNDERSTAND!

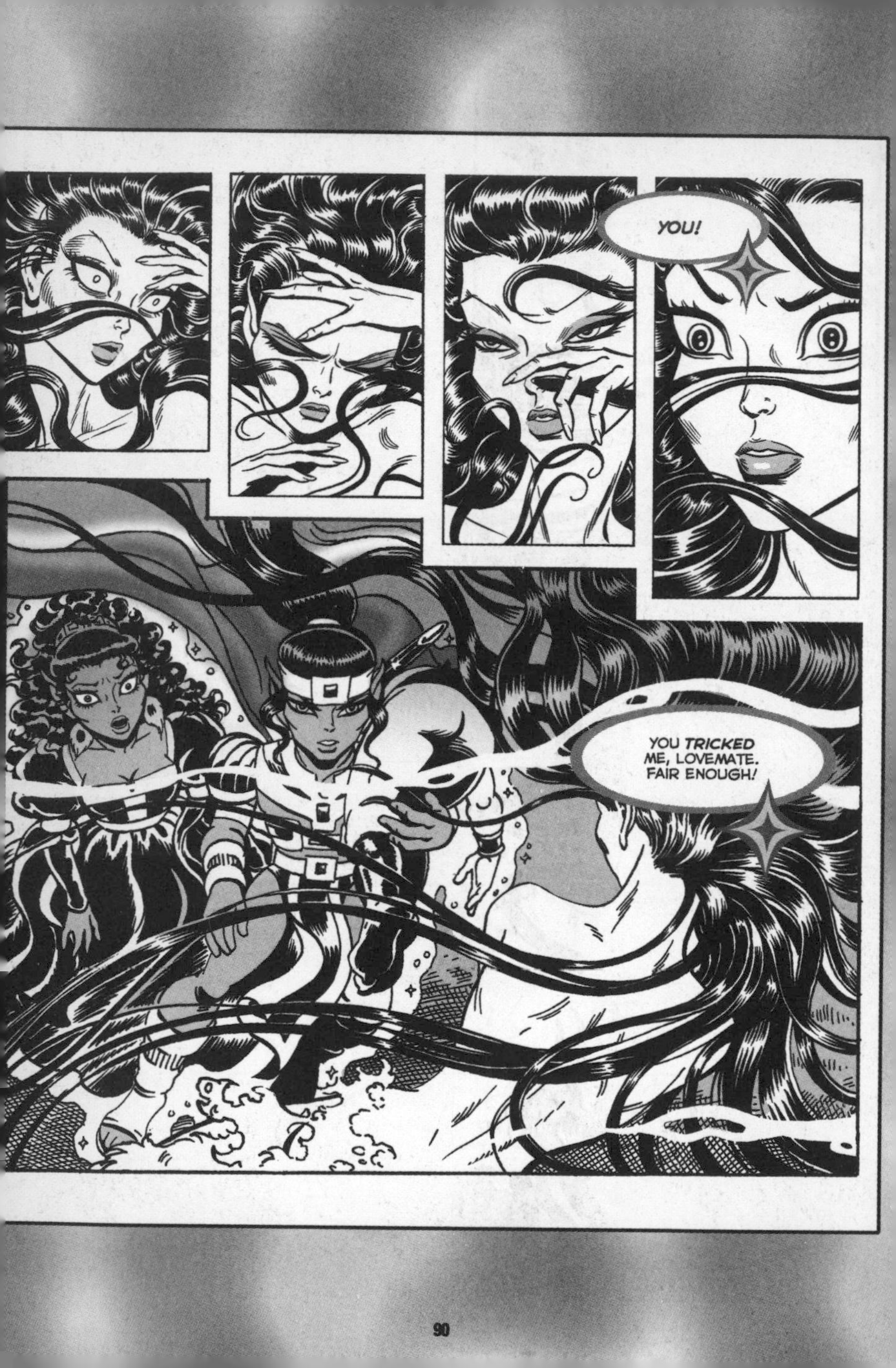
YOU!
YOU TRICKED ME, LOVEMATE. FAIR ENOUGH!

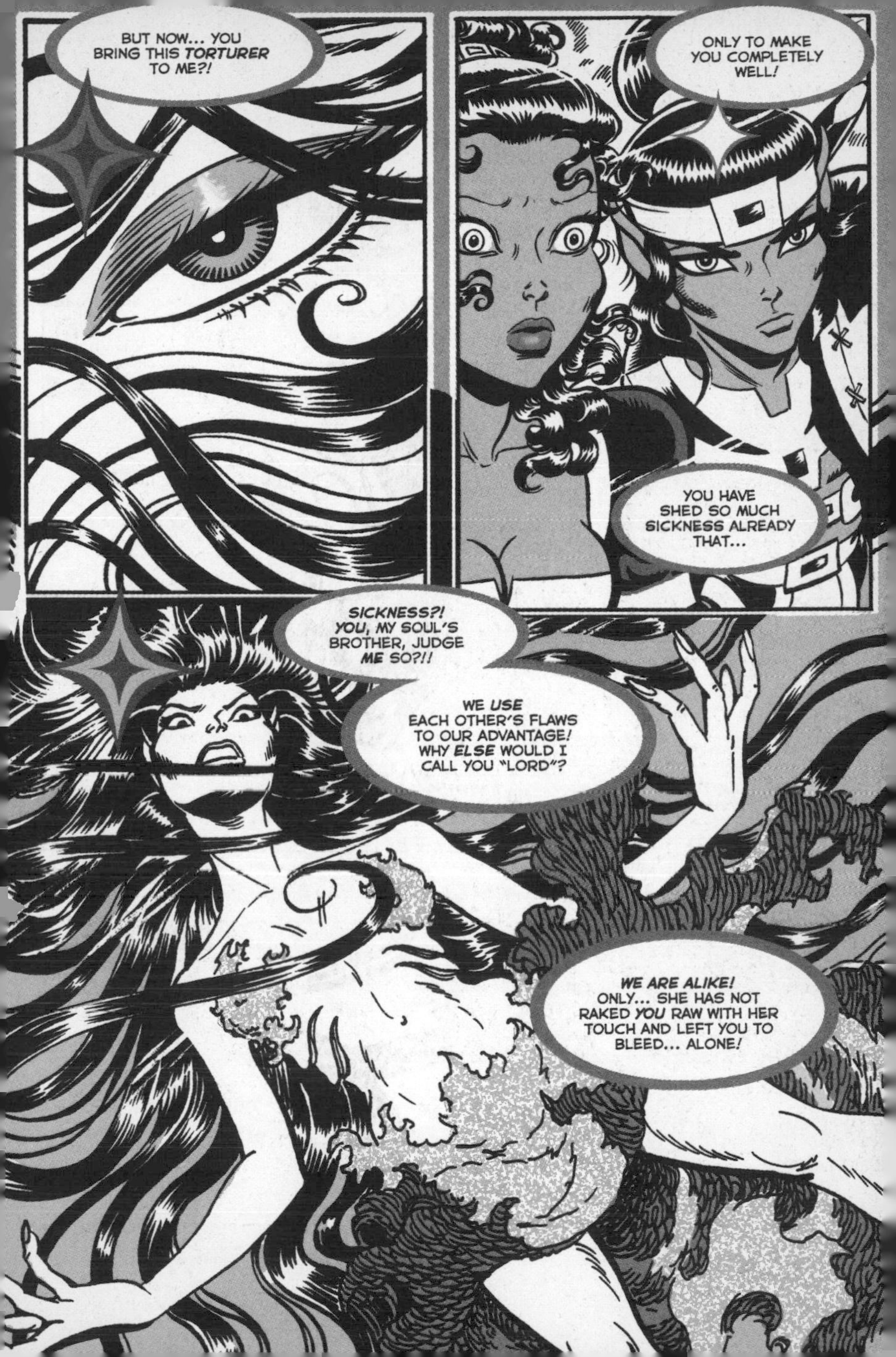
BUT NOW... YOU BRING THIS TORTURER TO ME?!
ONLY TO MAKE YOU COMPLETELY WELL!
YOU HAVE SHED SO MUCH SICKNESS ALREADY THAT...
SICKNESS?! YOU, MY SOUL'S BROTHER, JUDGE ME SO?!!
WE USE EACH OTHER'S FLAWS TO OUR ADVANTAGE! WHY ELSE WOULD I CALL YOU "LORD"?
WE ARE ALIKE! ONLY... SHE HAS NOT RAKED YOU RAW WITH HER TOUCH AND LEFT YOU TO BLEED... ALONE!

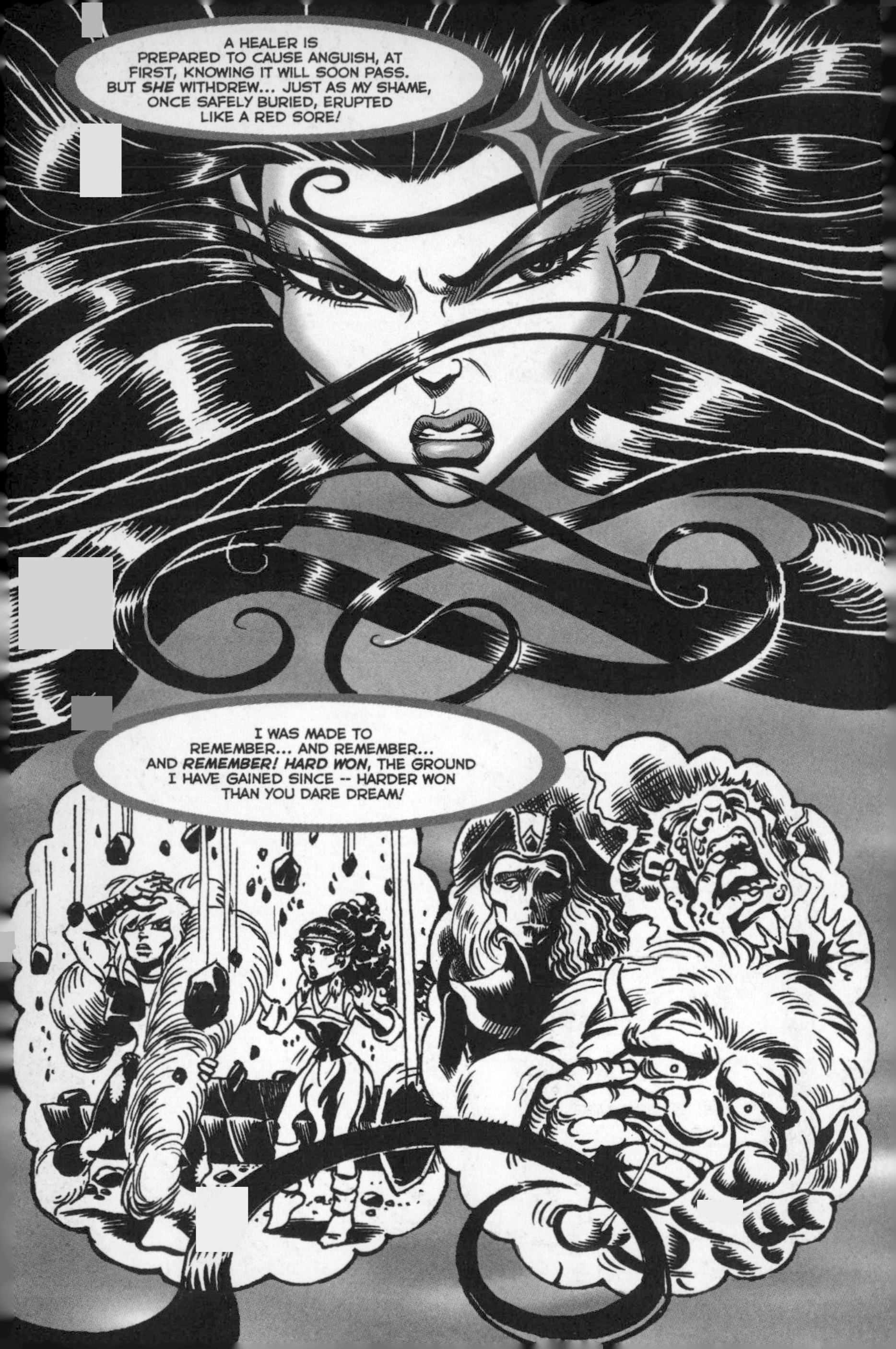
A HEALER IS PREPARED TO CAUSE ANGUISH, AT FIRST, KNOWING IT WILL SOON PASS. BUT *SHE* WITHDREW... JUST AS MY SHAME, ONCE SAFELY BURIED, ERUPTED LIKE A RED SORE!
I WAS MADE TO REMEMBER... AND REMEMBER... AND *REMEMBER! HARD WON*, THE GROUND I HAVE GAINED SINCE -- HARDER WON THAN YOU DARE DREAM!

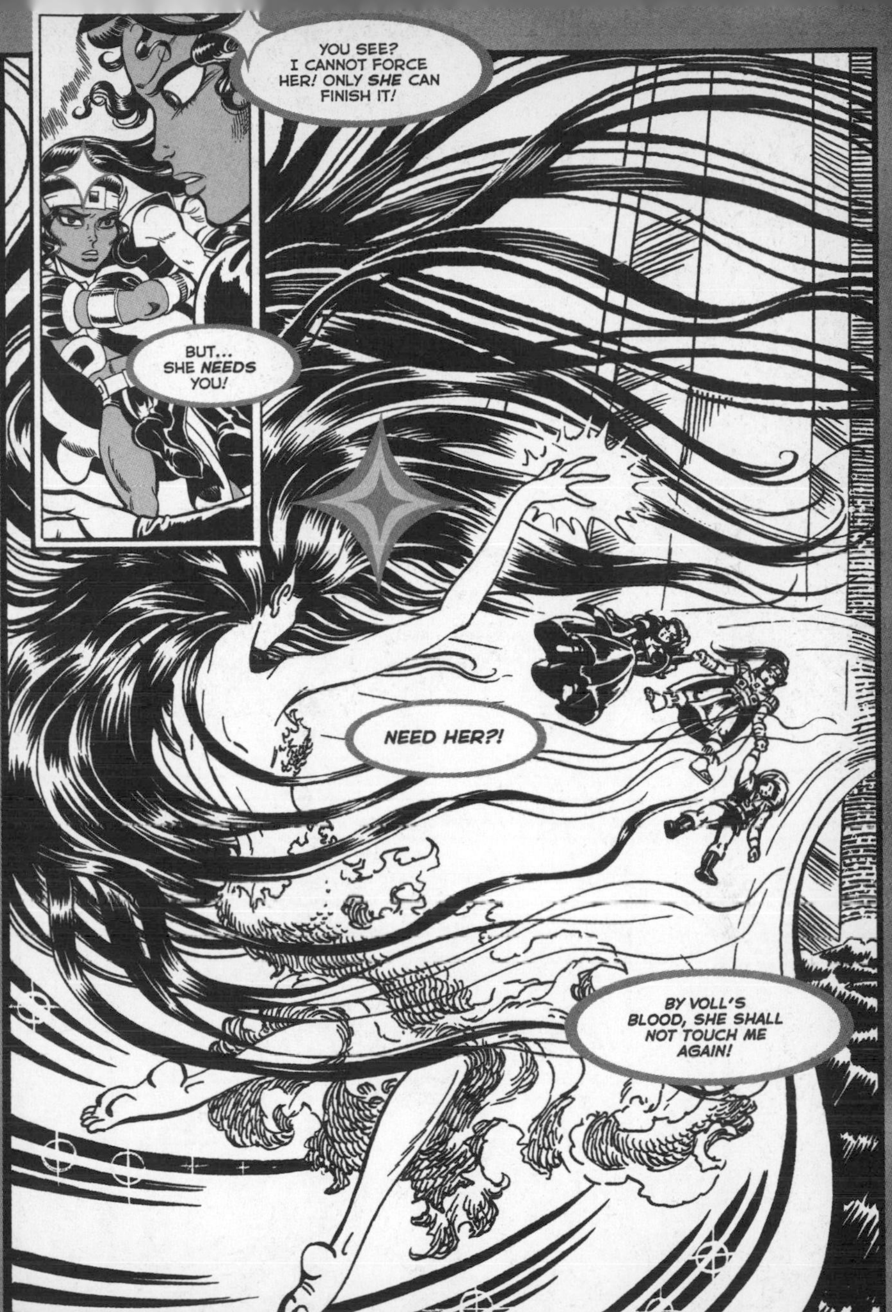

YOU SEE? I CANNOT FORCE HER! ONLY SHE CAN FINISH IT!
BUT... SHE NEEDS YOU!
NEED HER?!
BY VOLL'S BLOOD, SHE SHALL NOT TOUCH ME AGAIN!

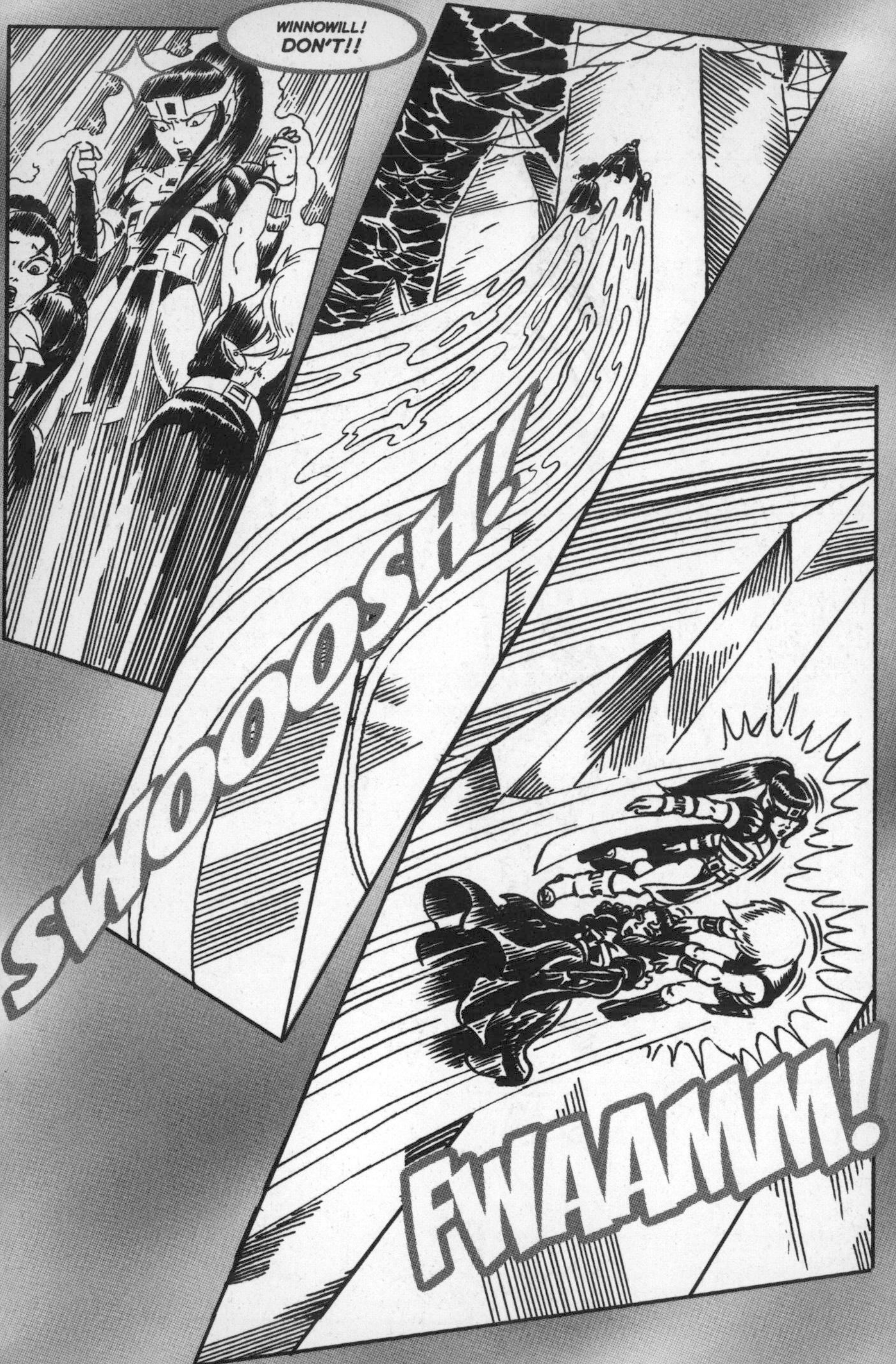

WINNOWILL! DON'T!!
SWOOOOSH!!
FWAAMM!

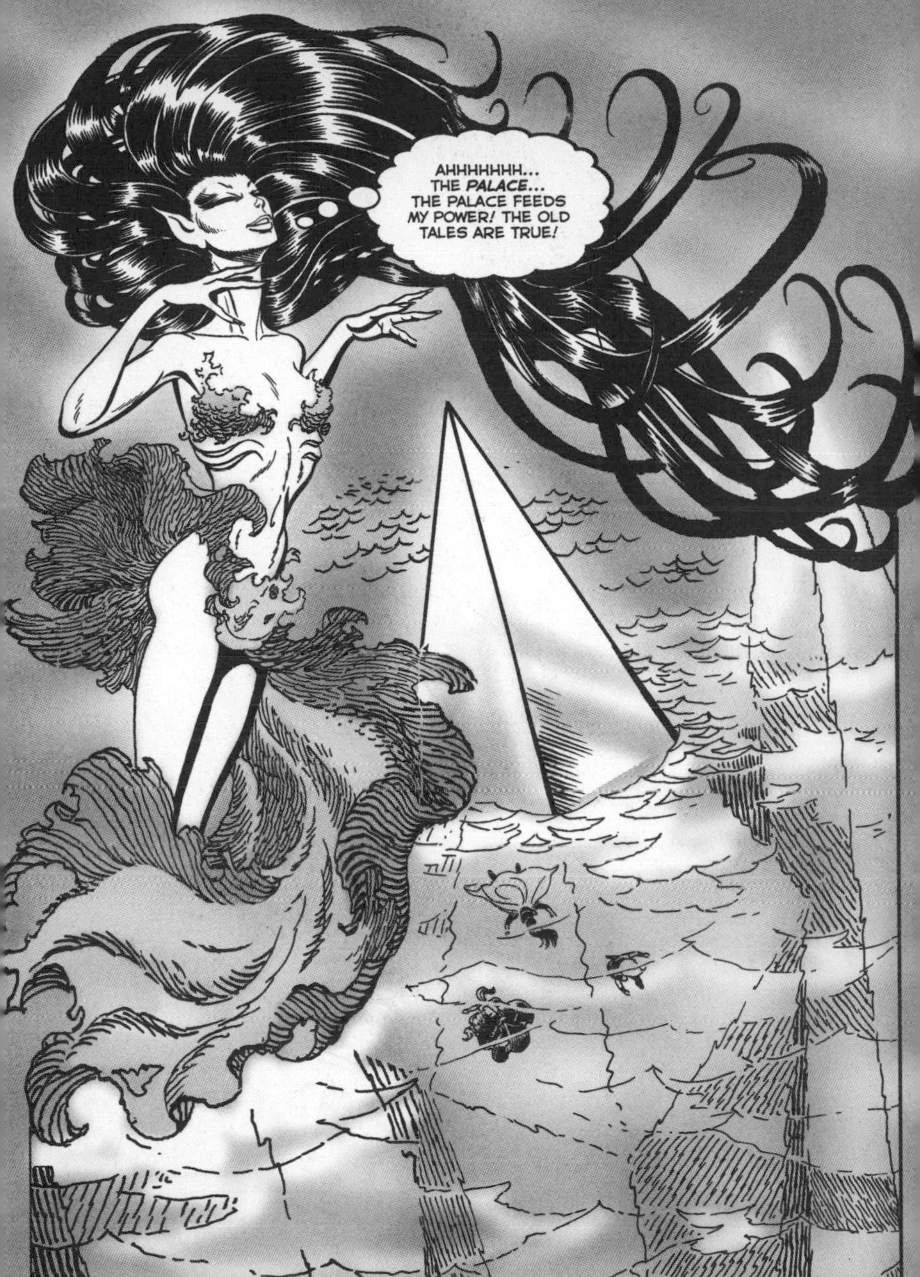
AHHHHHHHH... THE *PALACE*... THE PALACE FEEDS MY POWER! THE OLD TALES ARE TRUE!

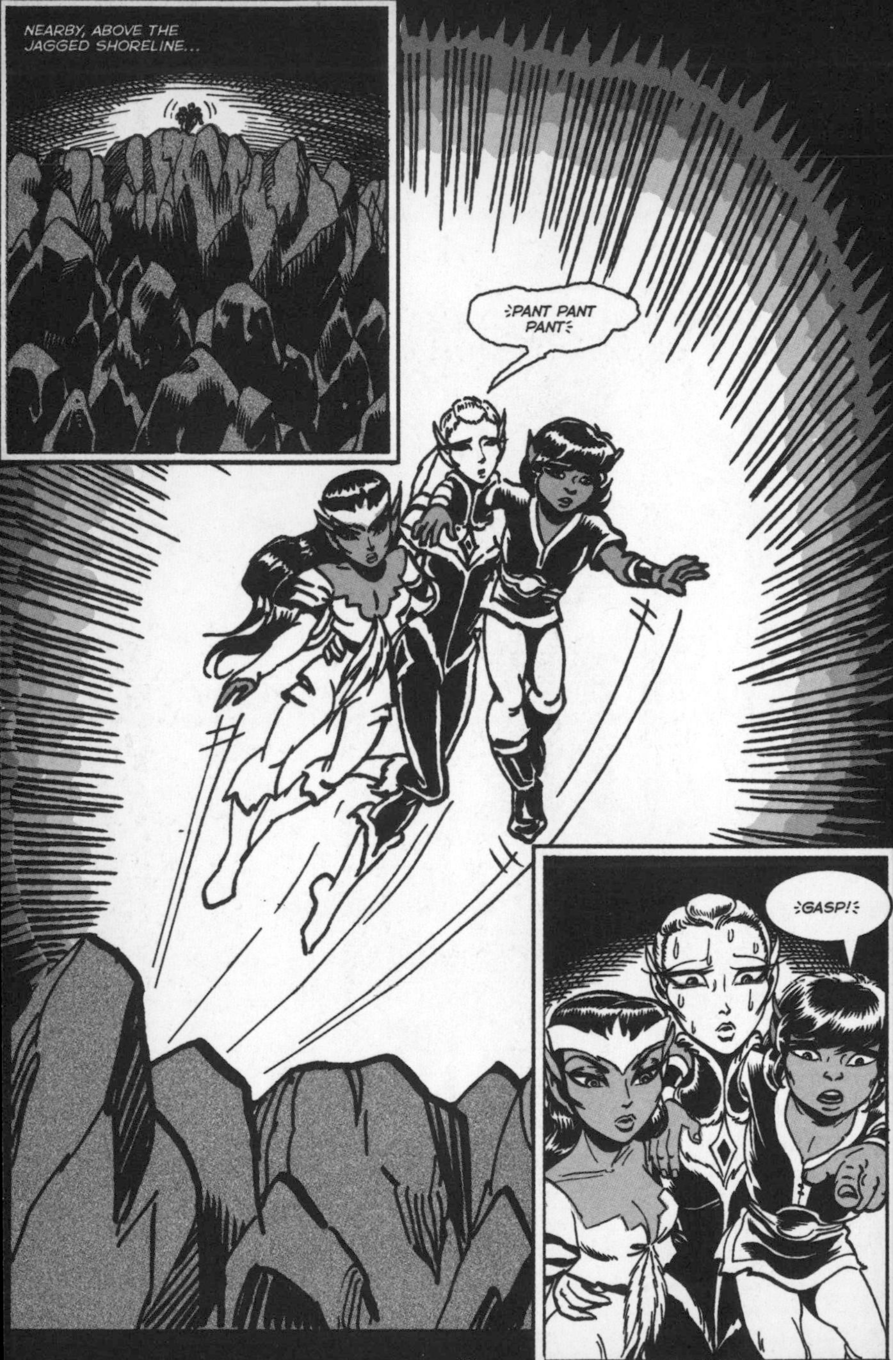
NEARBY, ABOVE THE JAGGED SHORELINE...
PANT PANT PANT
GASP!

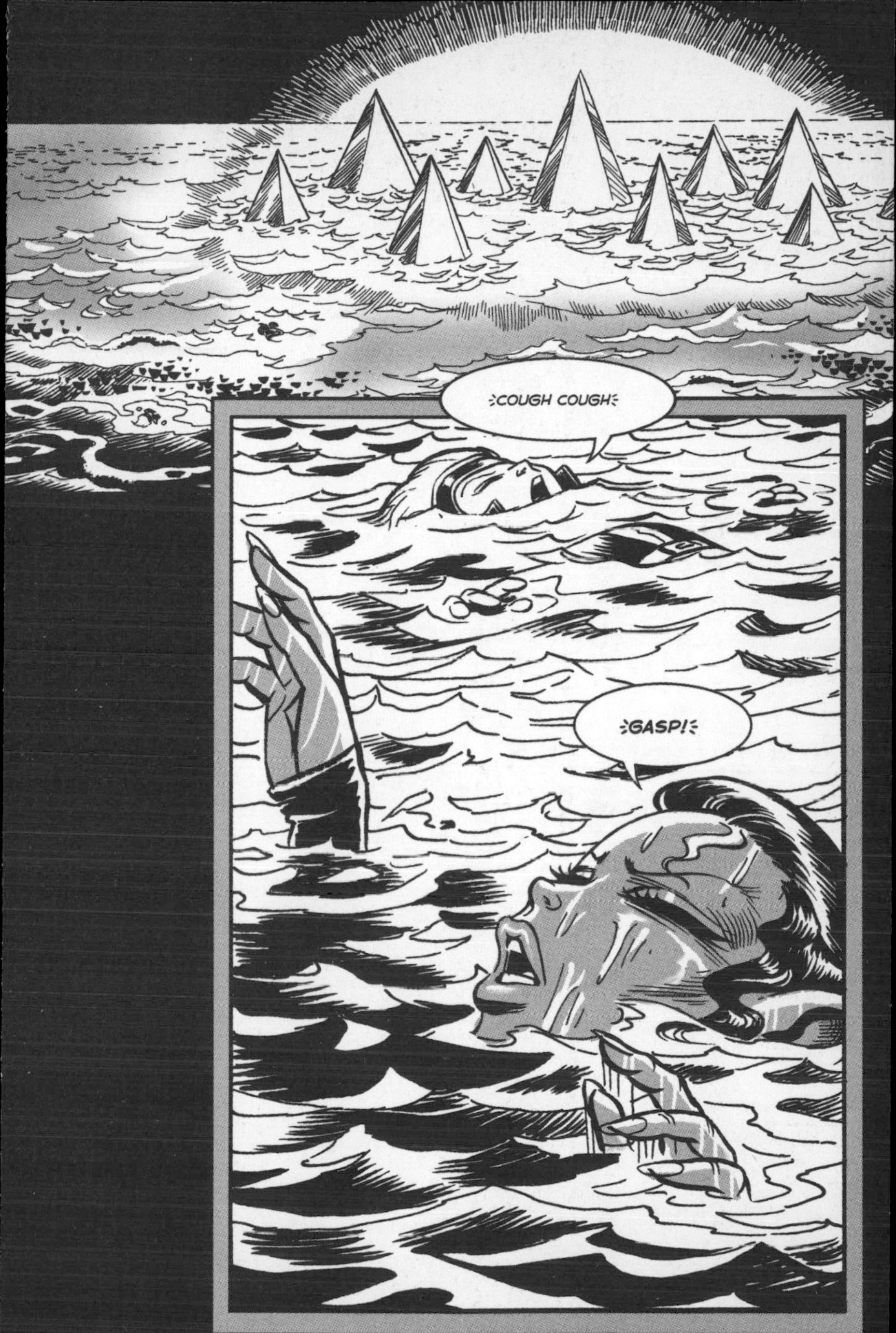
COUGH COUGH
GASP!

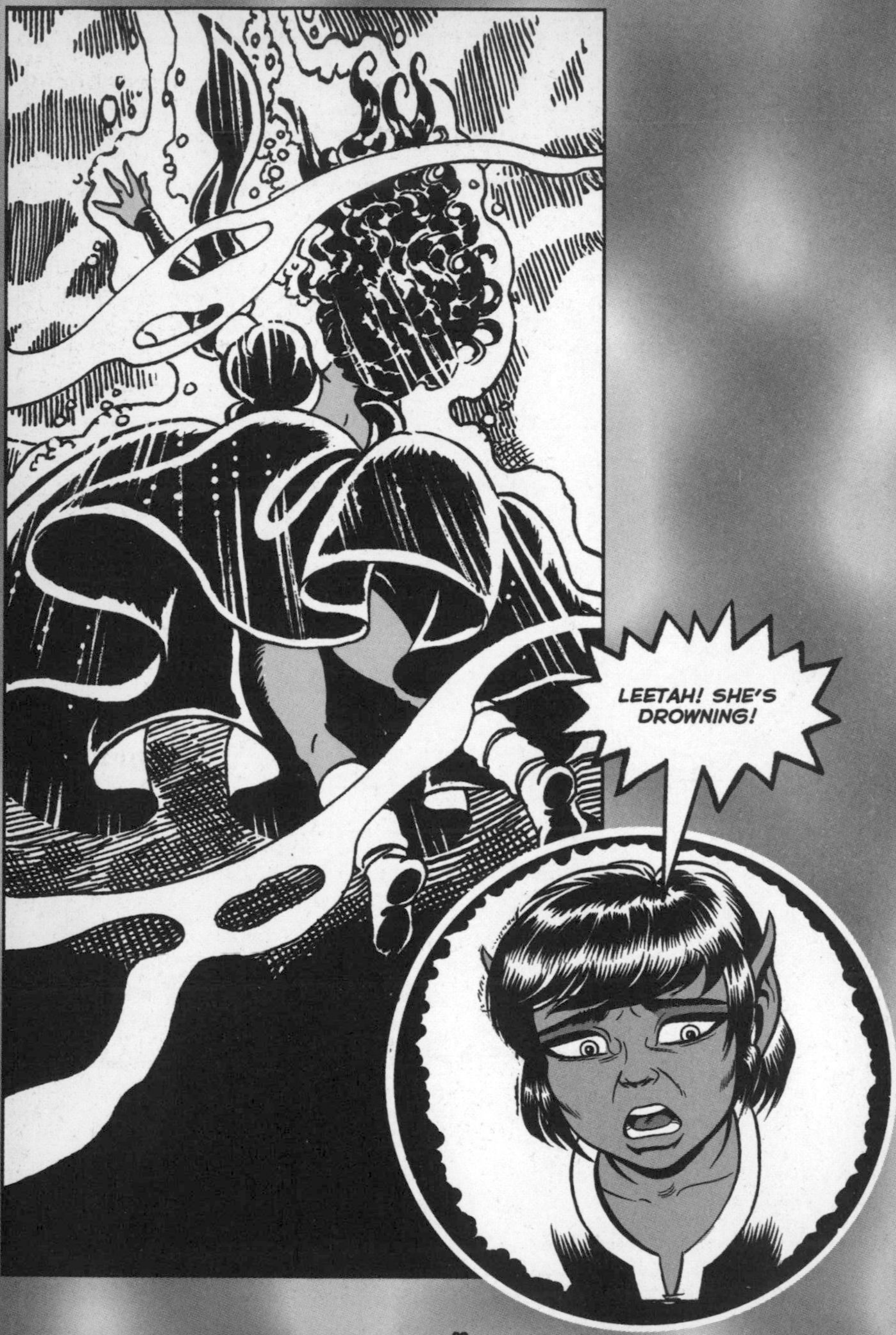
LEETAH! SHE'S DROWNING!

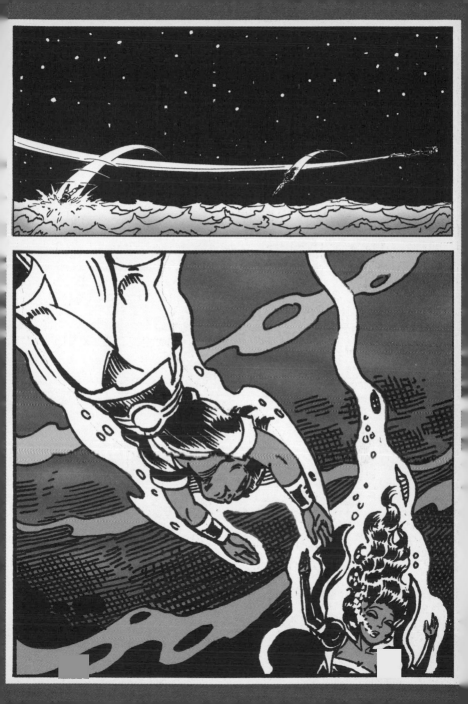

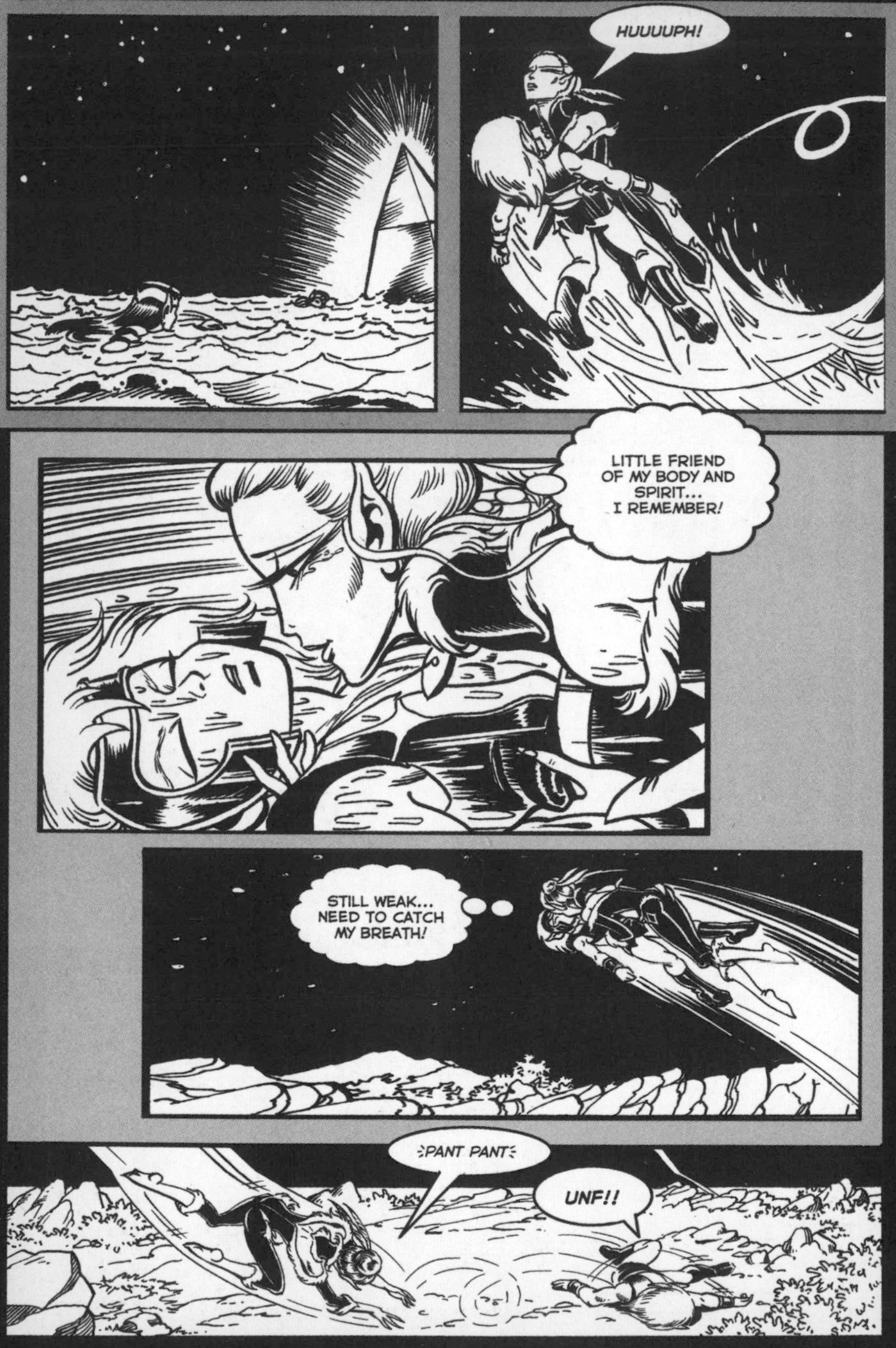
HUUUUPH!
LITTLE FRIEND OF MY BODY AND SPIRIT... I REMEMBER!
STILL WEAK... NEED TO CATCH MY BREATH!
PANT PANT
UNF!!

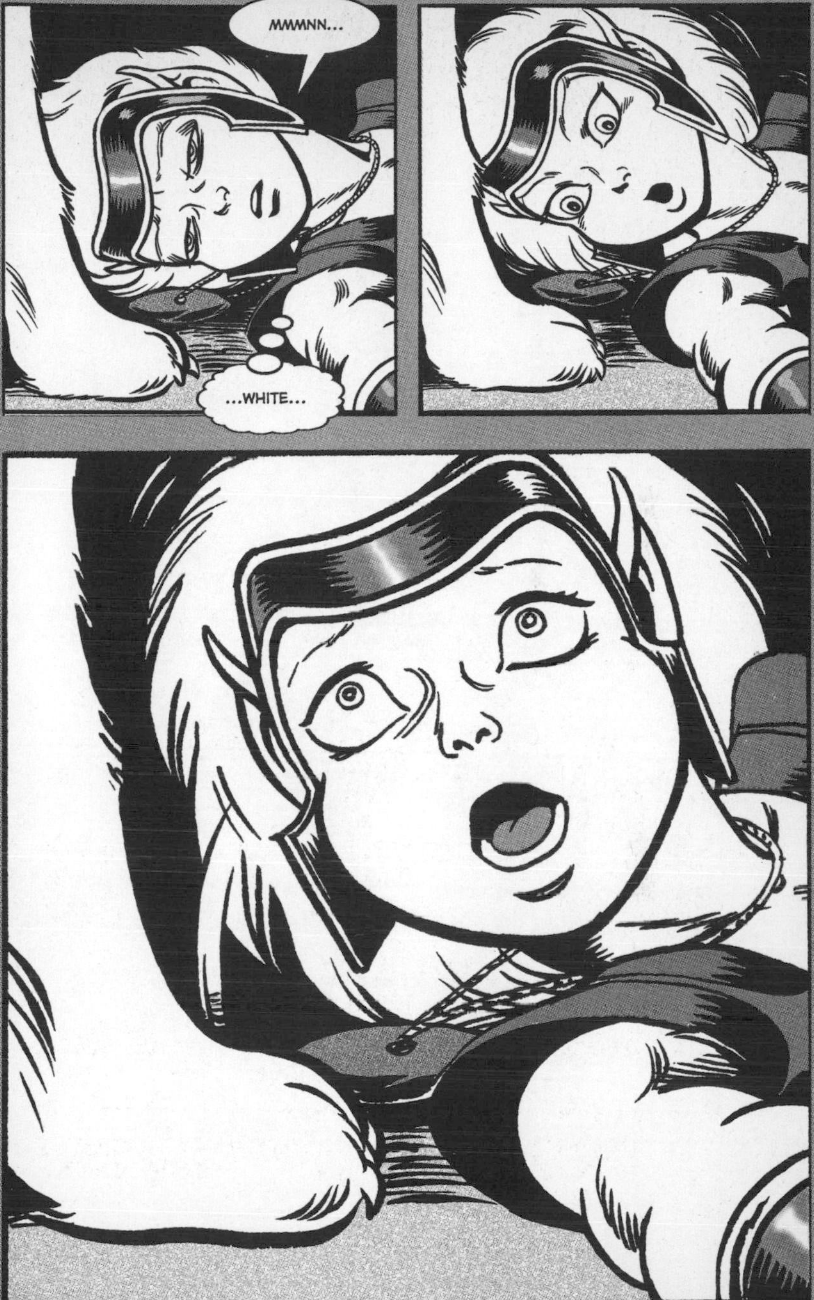
MMMNN...
...WHITE...

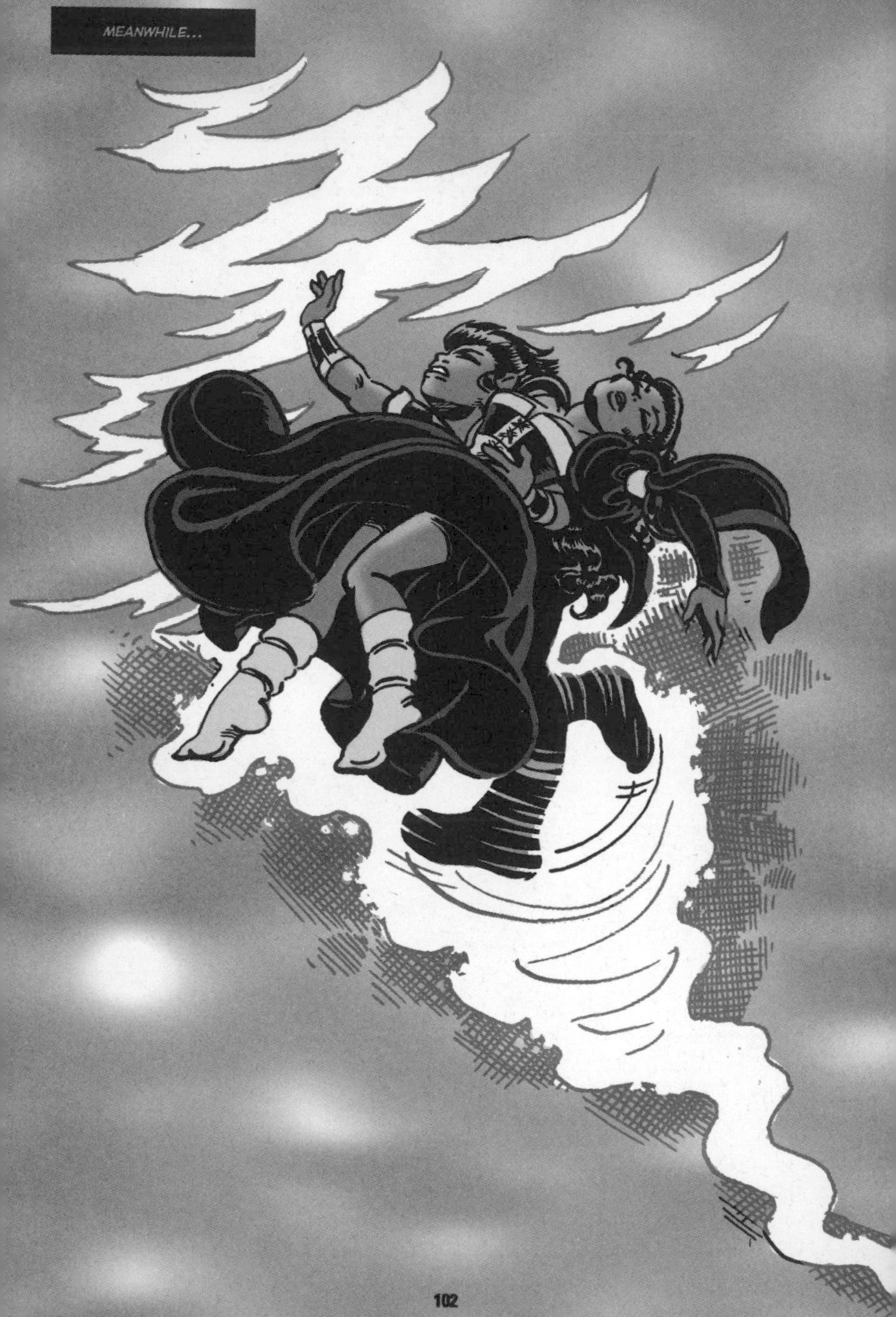
MEANWHILE...

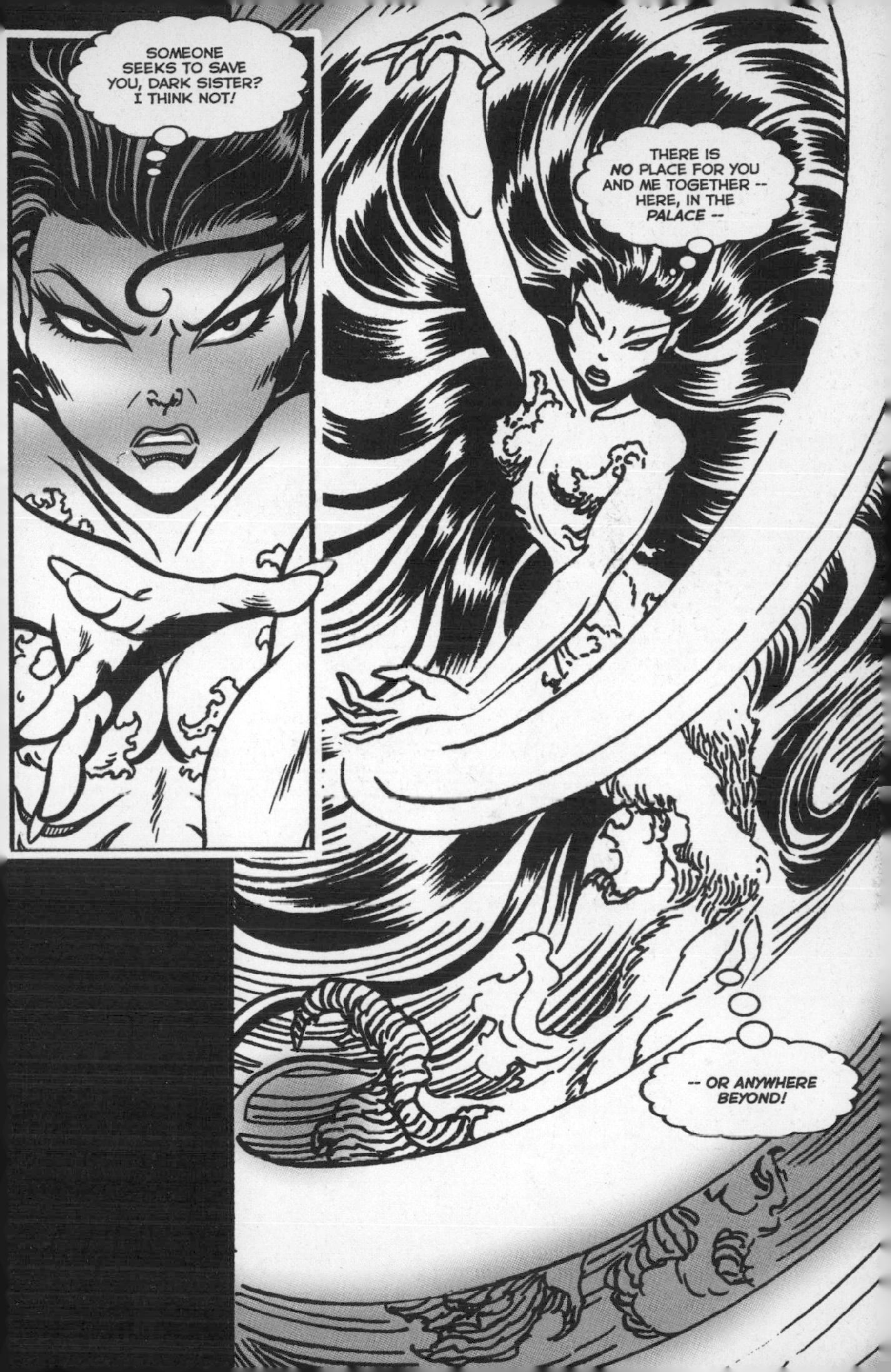
SOMEONE SEEKS TO SAVE YOU, DARK SISTER? I THINK NOT!
THERE IS NO PLACE FOR YOU AND ME TOGETHER -- HERE, IN THE PALACE --
-- OR ANYWHERE BEYOND!

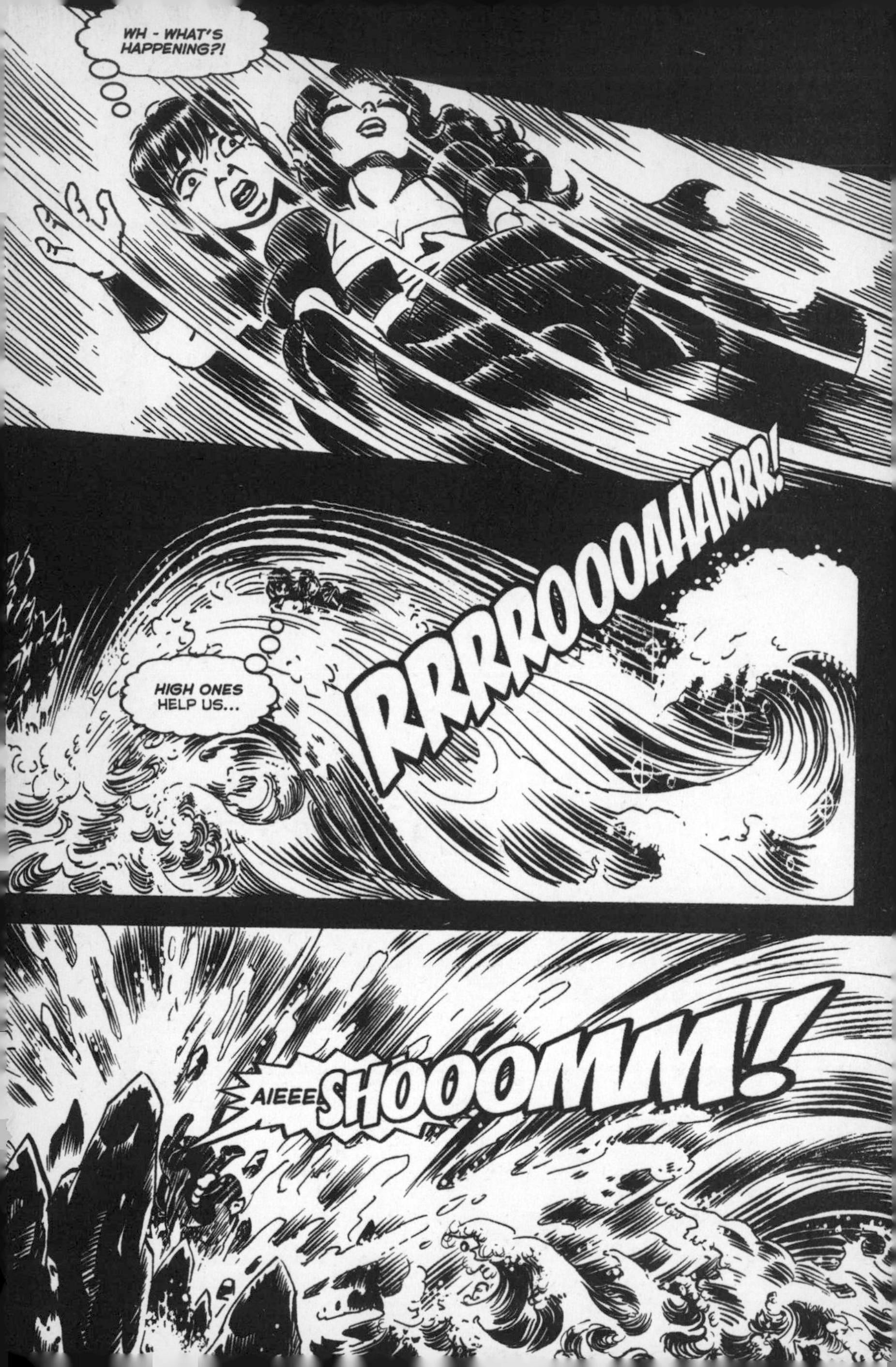
WH - WHAT'S HAPPENING?!
RRRROOOOAAARRR!
HIGH ONES HELP US...
AIEEE
SHOOOMMM!

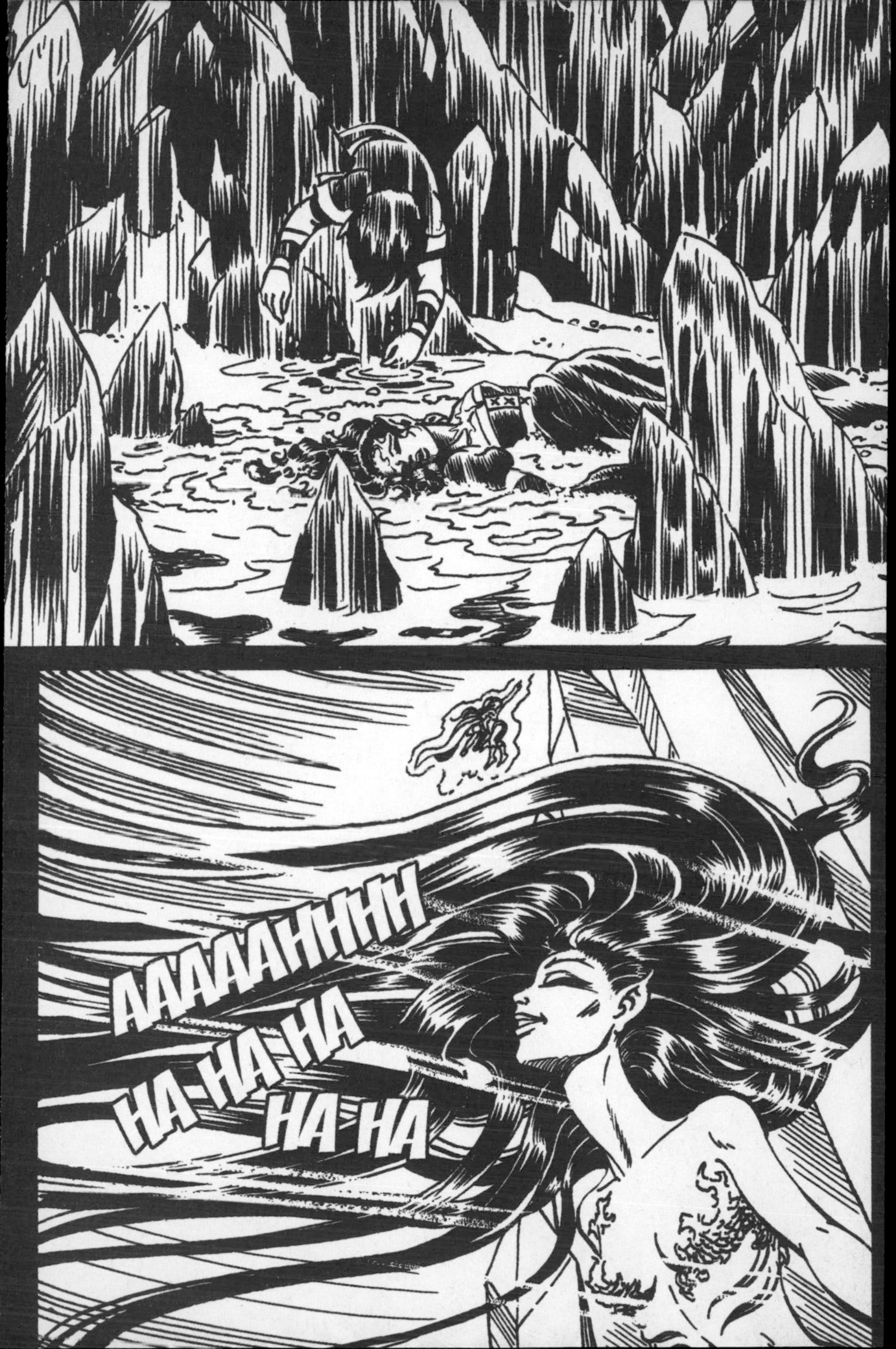
AAAAAHHHH
HA-HA-HA
HA HA

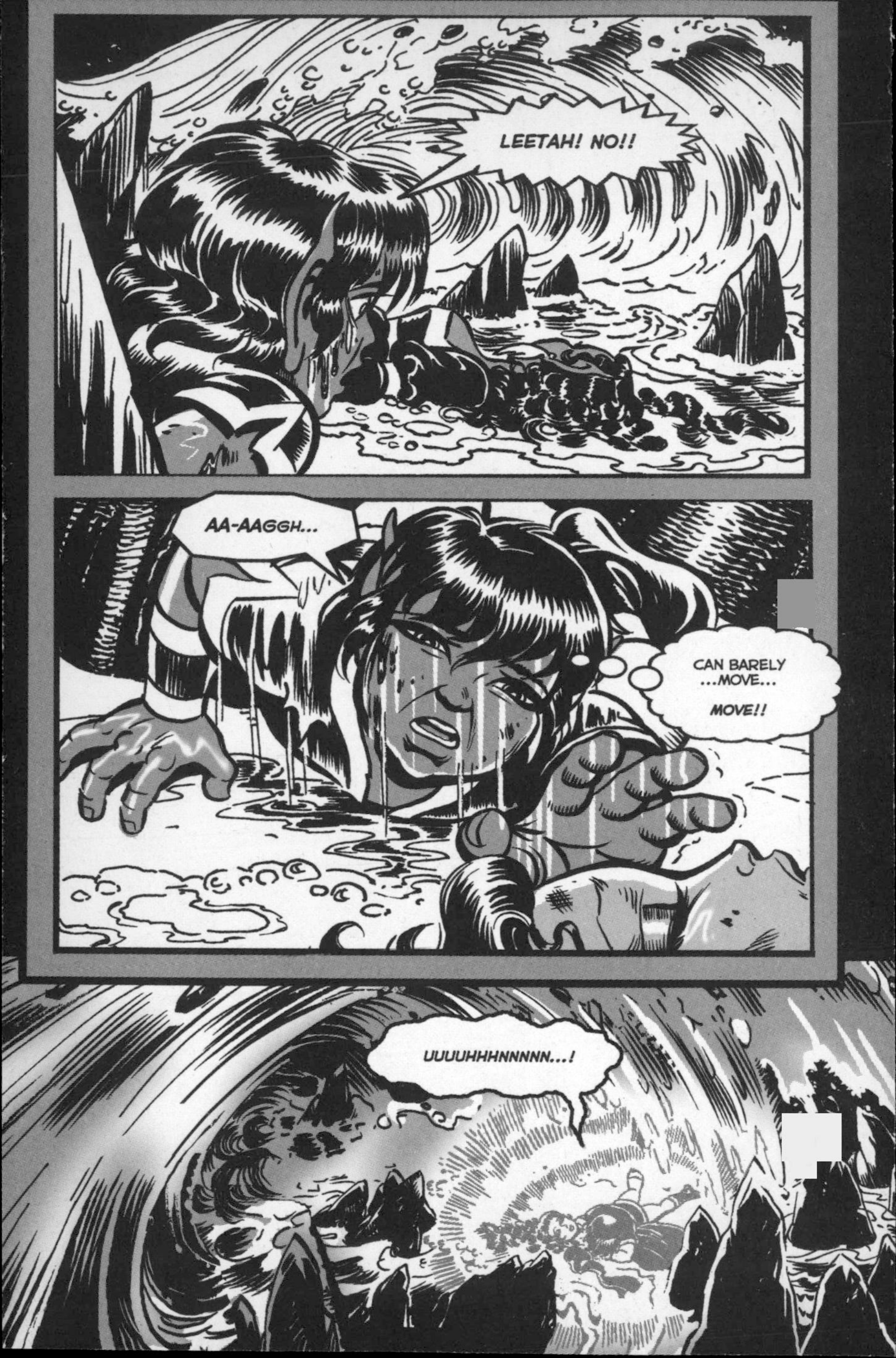
LEETAH! NO!!
AA-AAGGH...
CAN BARELY ...MOVE...
MOVE!!
UUUUHHHNNNNN...!

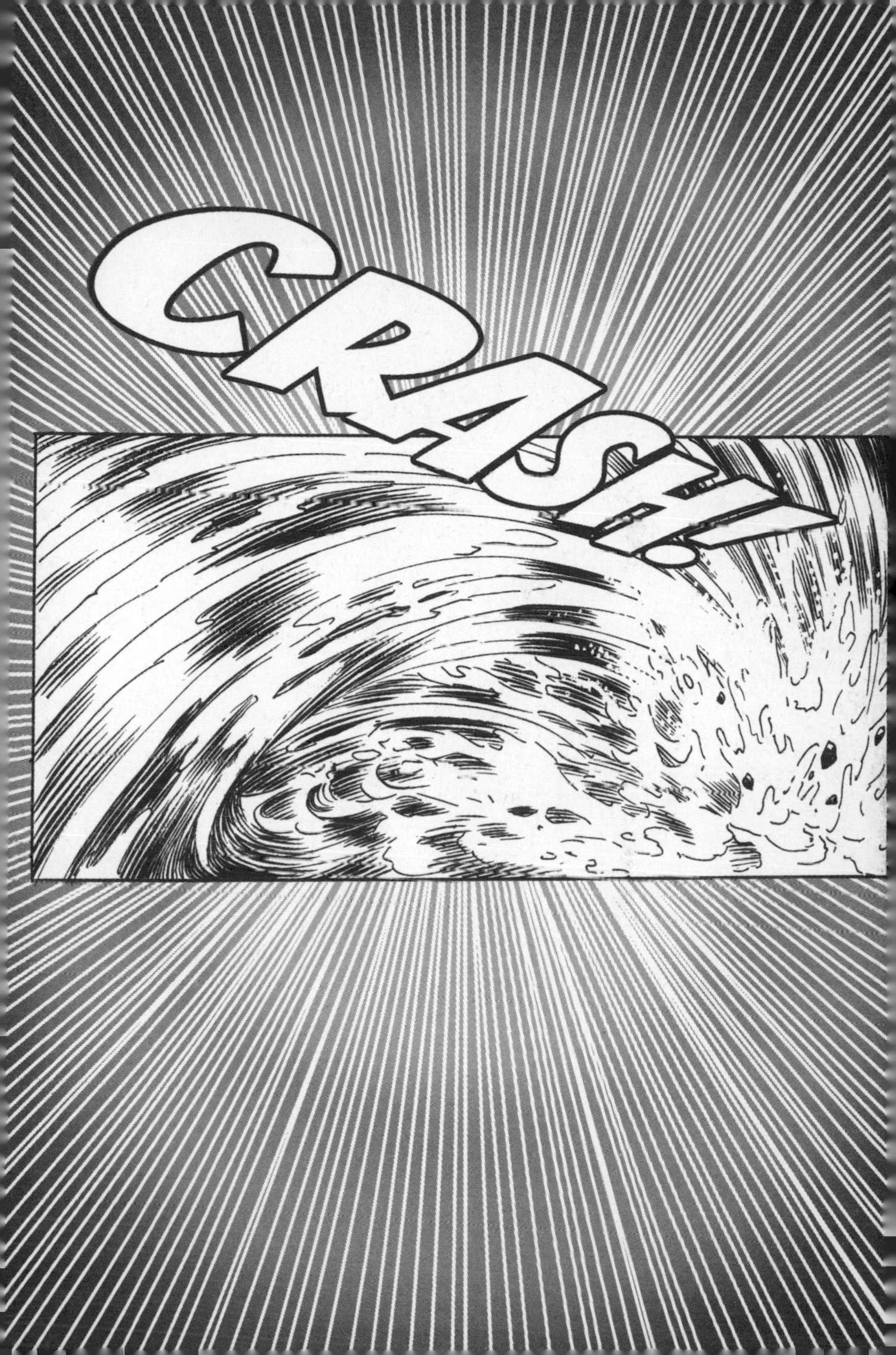
CRASH!

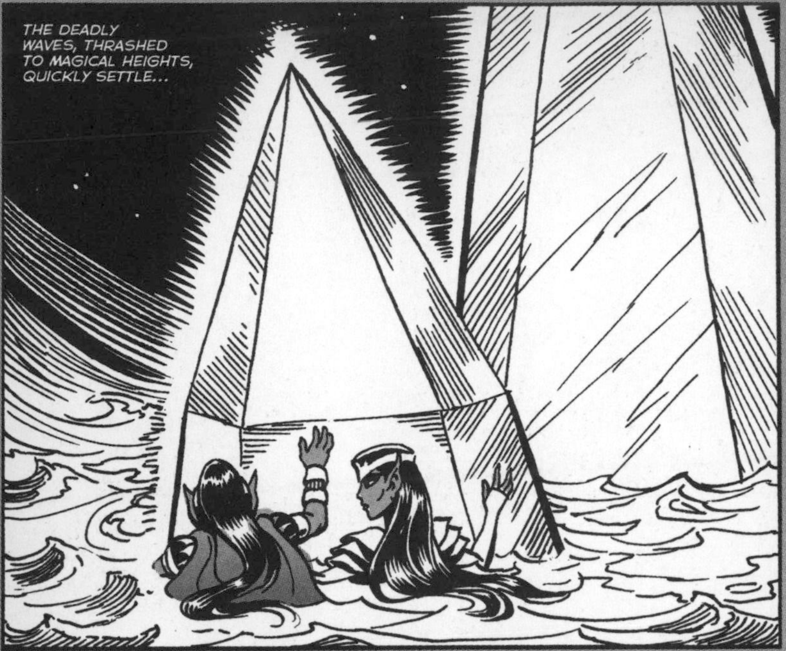
THE DEADLY WAVES, THRASHED TO MAGICAL HEIGHTS, QUICKLY SETTLE...

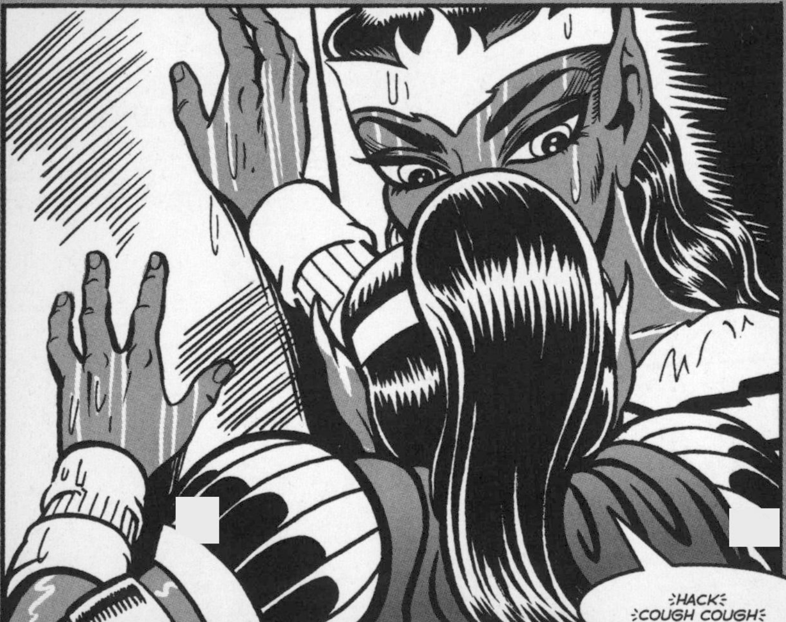
HACK
COUGH COUGH

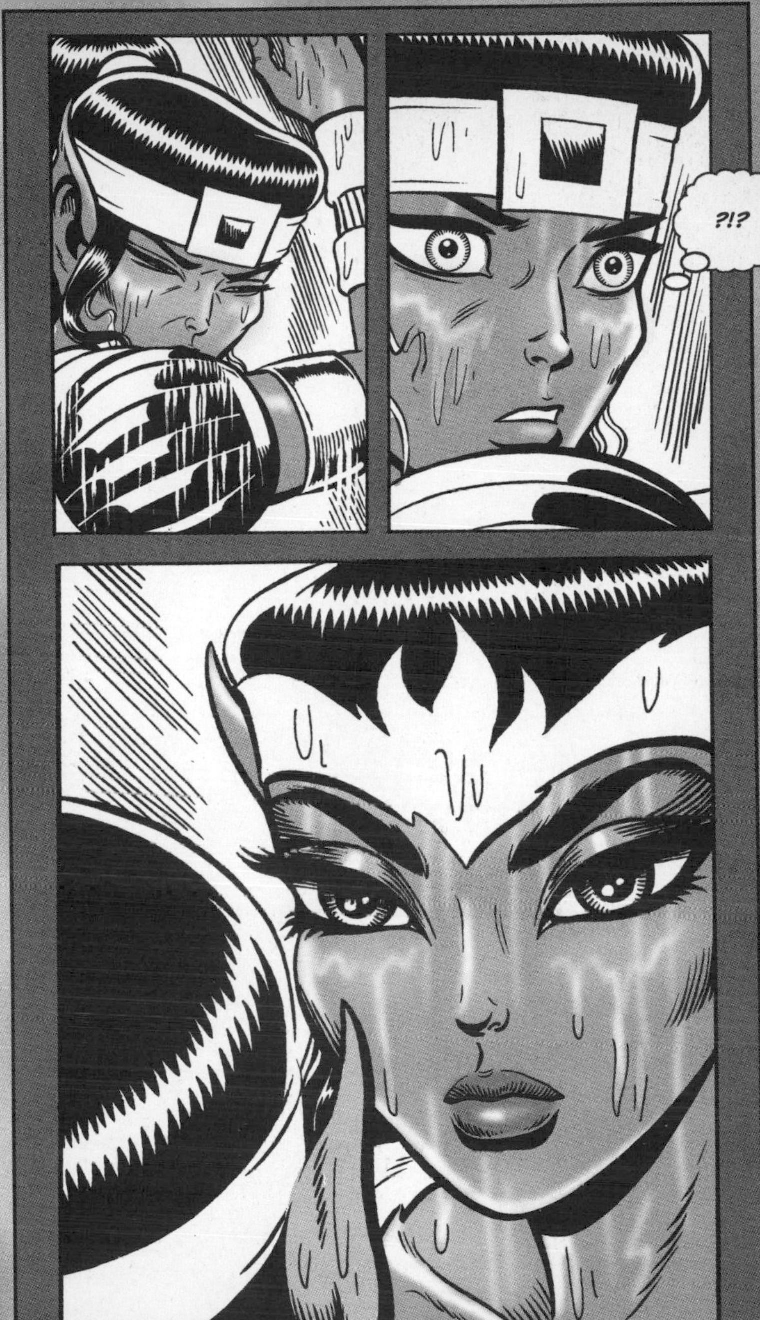
?!?

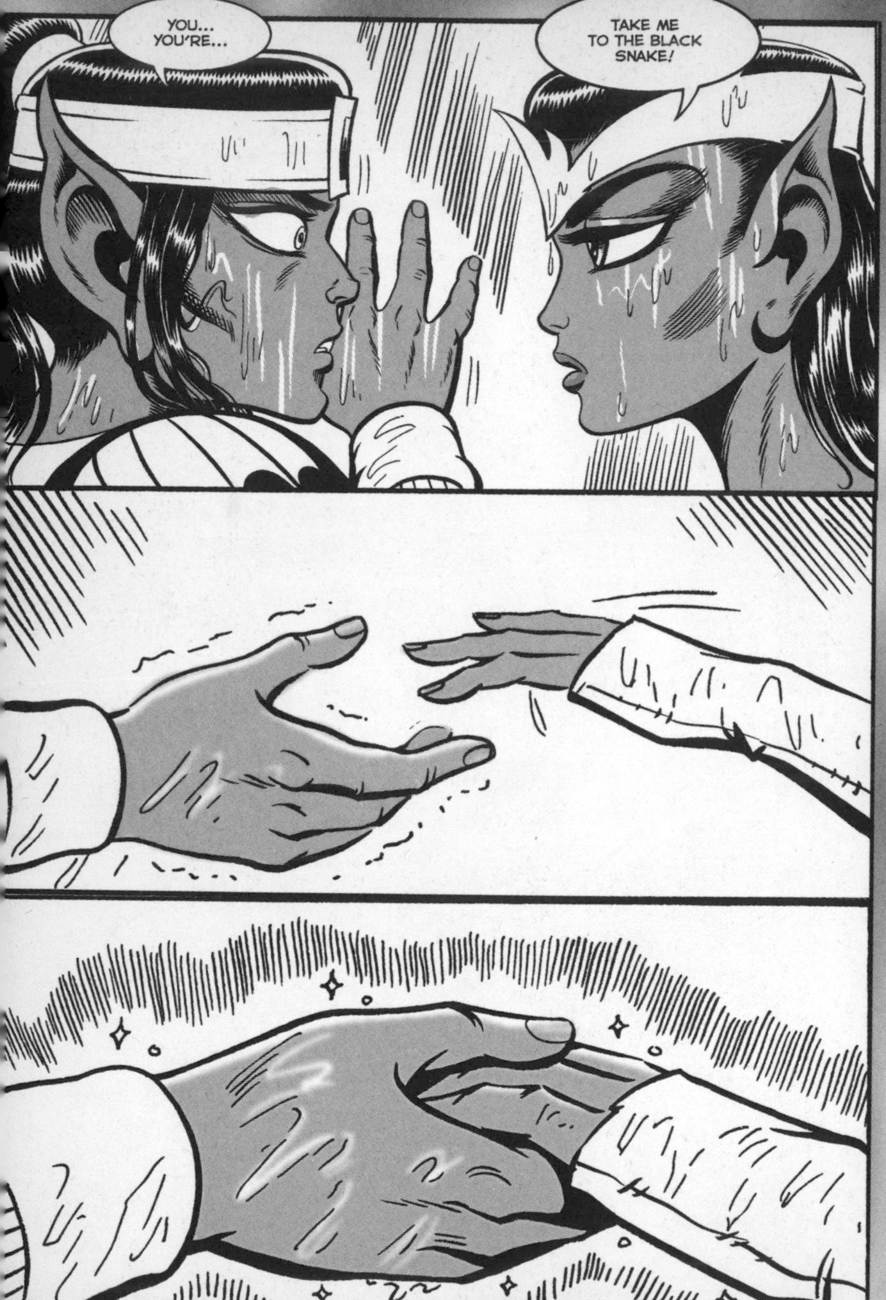
YOU... YOU'RE...
TAKE ME TO THE BLACK SNAKE!

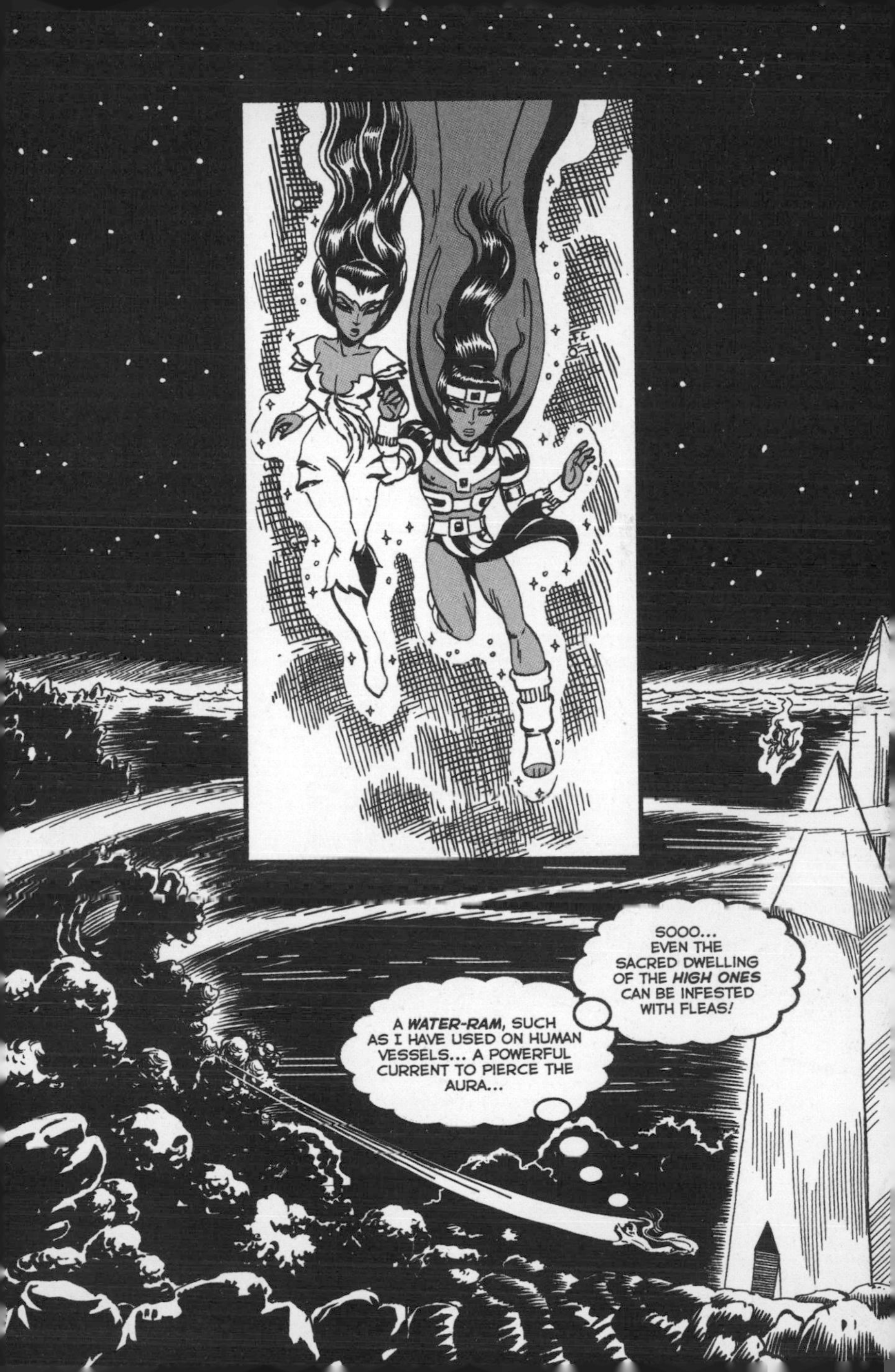
SOOO... EVEN THE SACRED DWELLING OF THE HIGH ONES CAN BE INFESTED WITH FLEAS!
A WATER-RAM, SUCH AS I HAVE USED ON HUMAN VESSELS... A POWERFUL CURRENT TO PIERCE THE AURA...

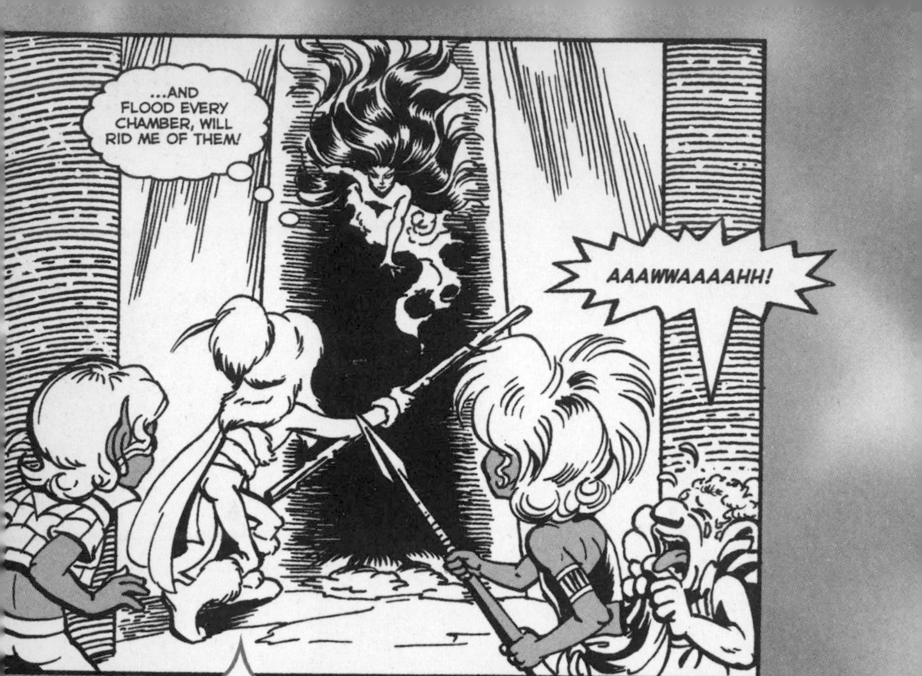
...AND FLOOD EVERY CHAMBER, WILL RID ME OF THEM!
AAAWWAAAAHH!

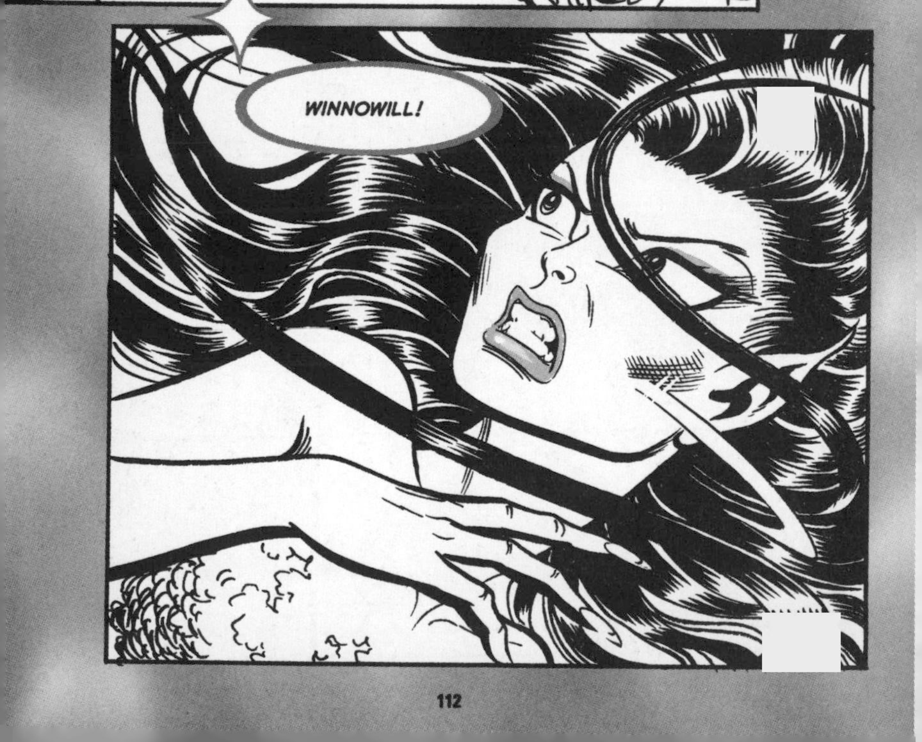
WINNOWILL!

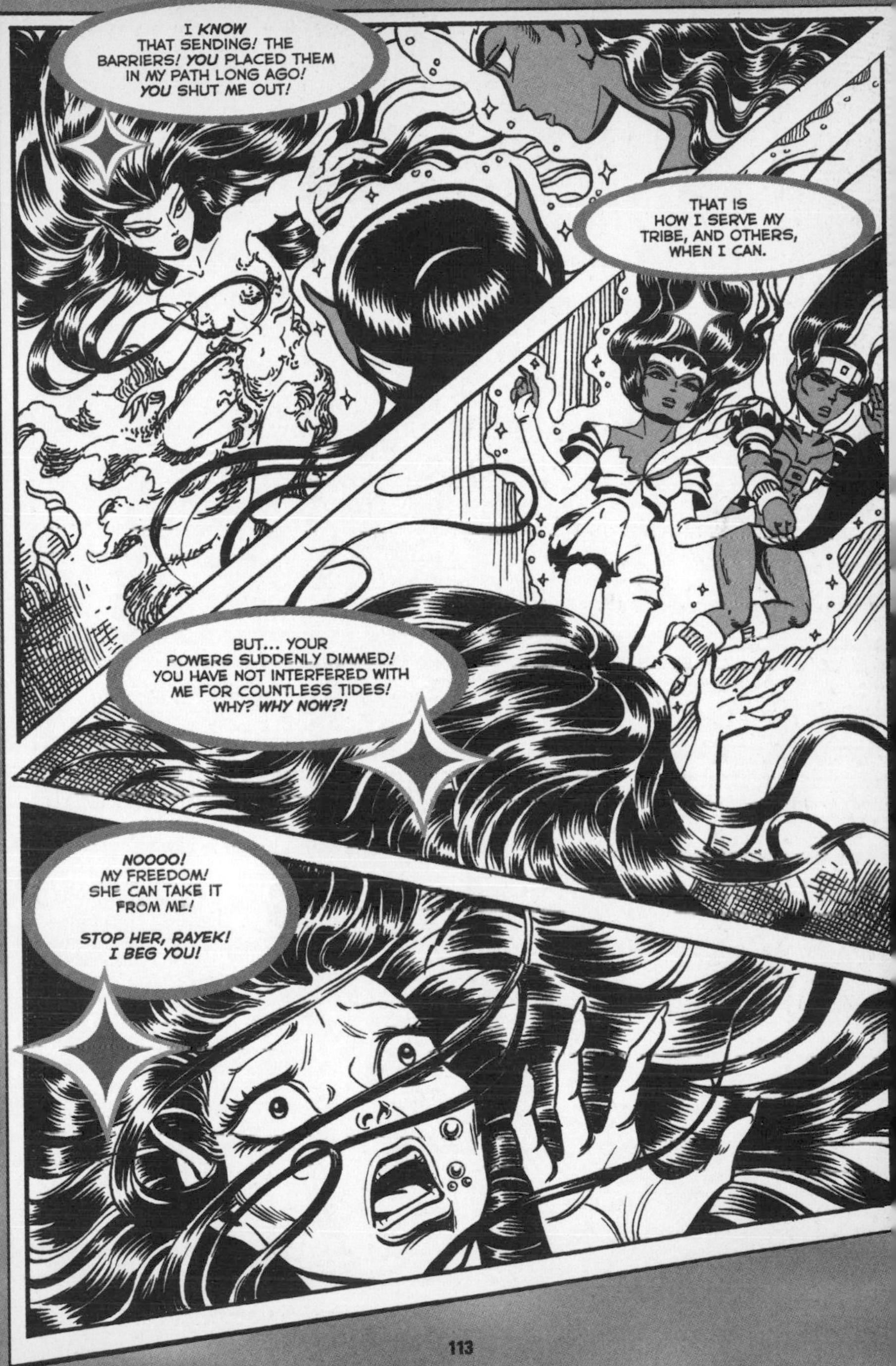
I KNOW THAT SENDING! THE BARRIERS! YOU PLACED THEM IN MY PATH LONG AGO! YOU SHUT ME OUT!
THAT IS HOW I SERVE MY TRIBE, AND OTHERS, WHEN I CAN.
BUT... YOUR POWERS SUDDENLY DIMMED! YOU HAVE NOT INTERFERED WITH ME FOR COUNTLESS TIDES! WHY? WHY NOW?!
NOOOO! MY FREEDOM! SHE CAN TAKE IT FROM ME!
STOP HER, RAYEK! I BEG YOU!

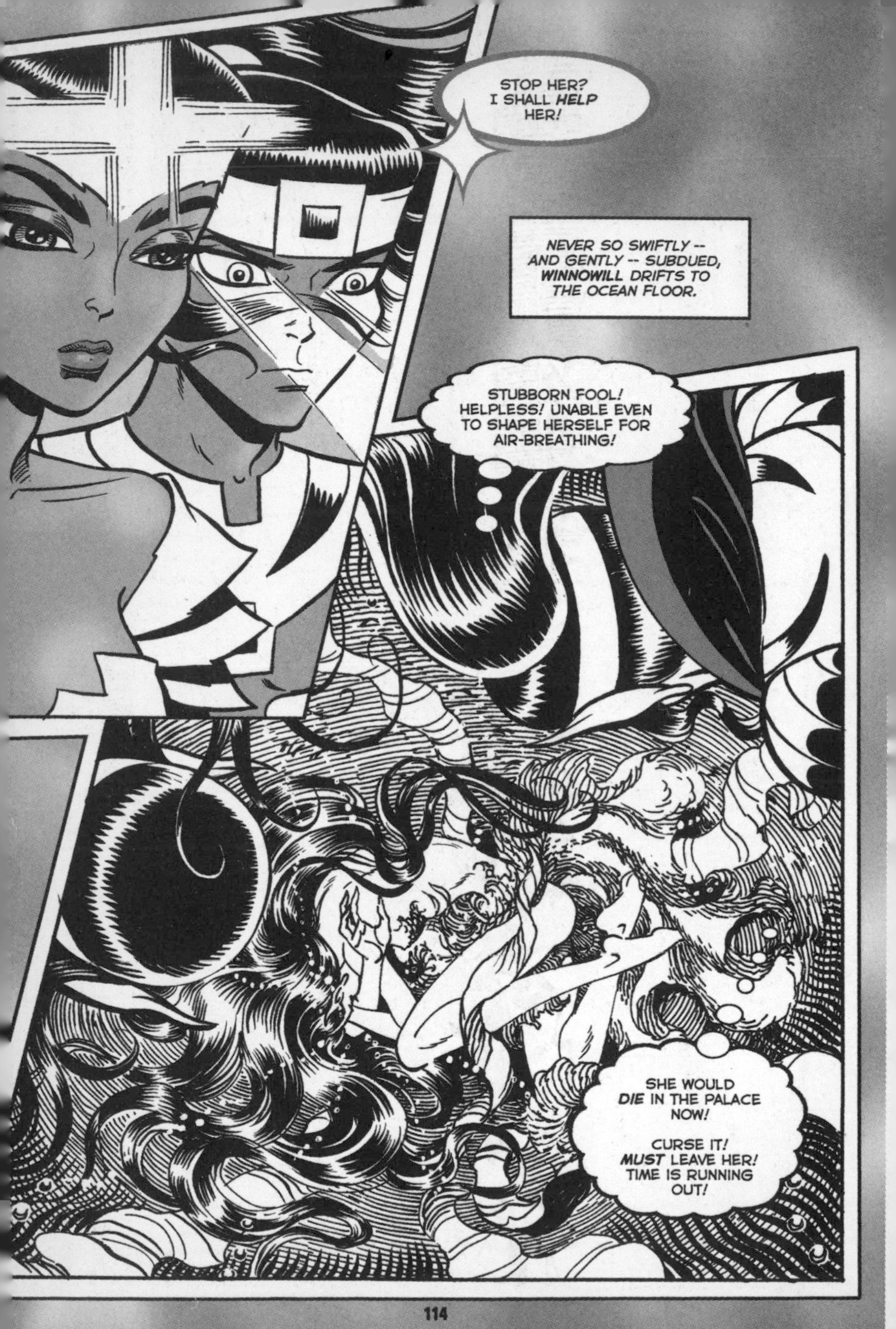
STOP HER? I SHALL ***HELP*** HER!
NEVER SO SWIFTLY -- AND GENTLY -- SUBDUED, WINNOWILL DRIFTS TO THE OCEAN FLOOR.
STUBBORN FOOL! HELPLESS! UNABLE EVEN TO SHAPE HERSELF FOR AIR-BREATHING!
SHE WOULD ***DIE*** IN THE PALACE NOW!
CURSE IT! ***MUST*** LEAVE HER! TIME IS RUNNING OUT!

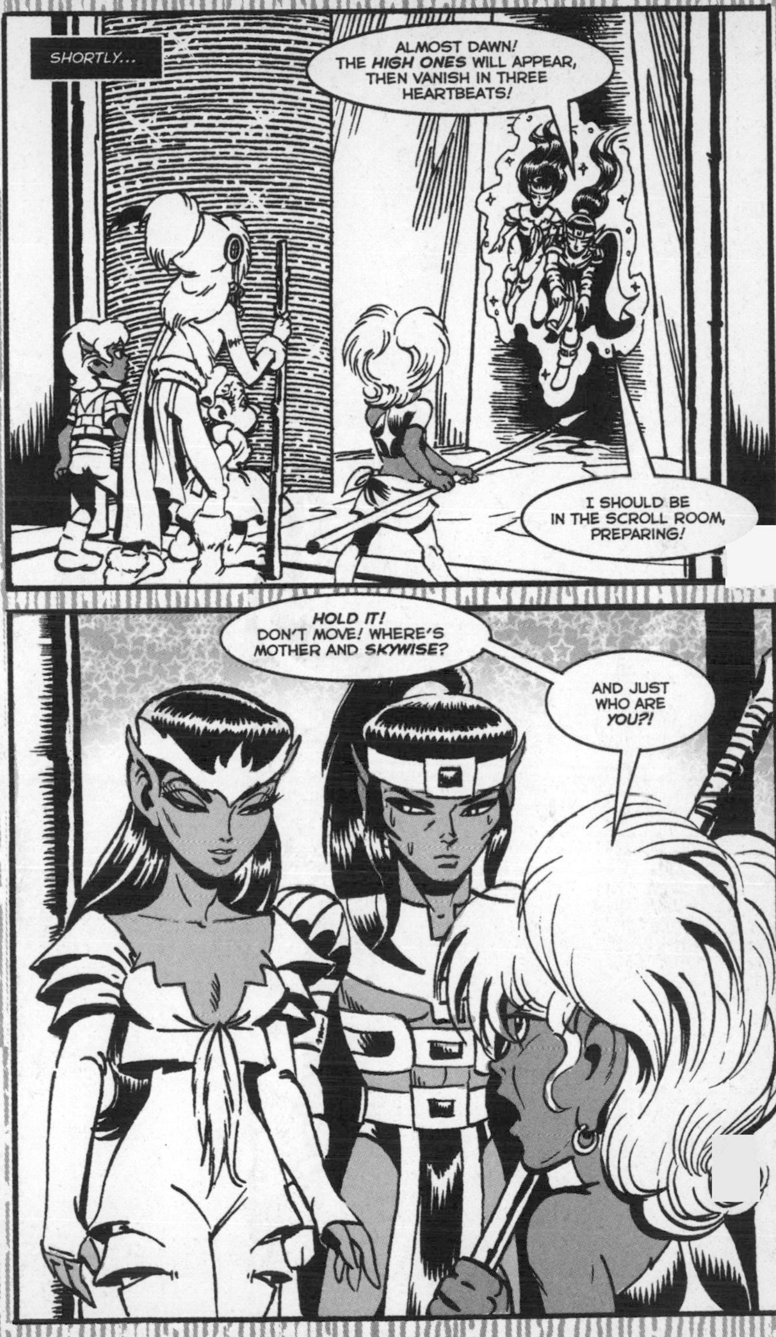
SHORTLY...
ALMOST DAWN! THE HIGH ONES WILL APPEAR, THEN VANISH IN THREE HEARTBEATS!
I SHOULD BE IN THE SCROLL ROOM, PREPARING!
HOLD IT! DON'T MOVE! WHERE'S MOTHER AND SKYWISE?
AND JUST WHO ARE YOU?!

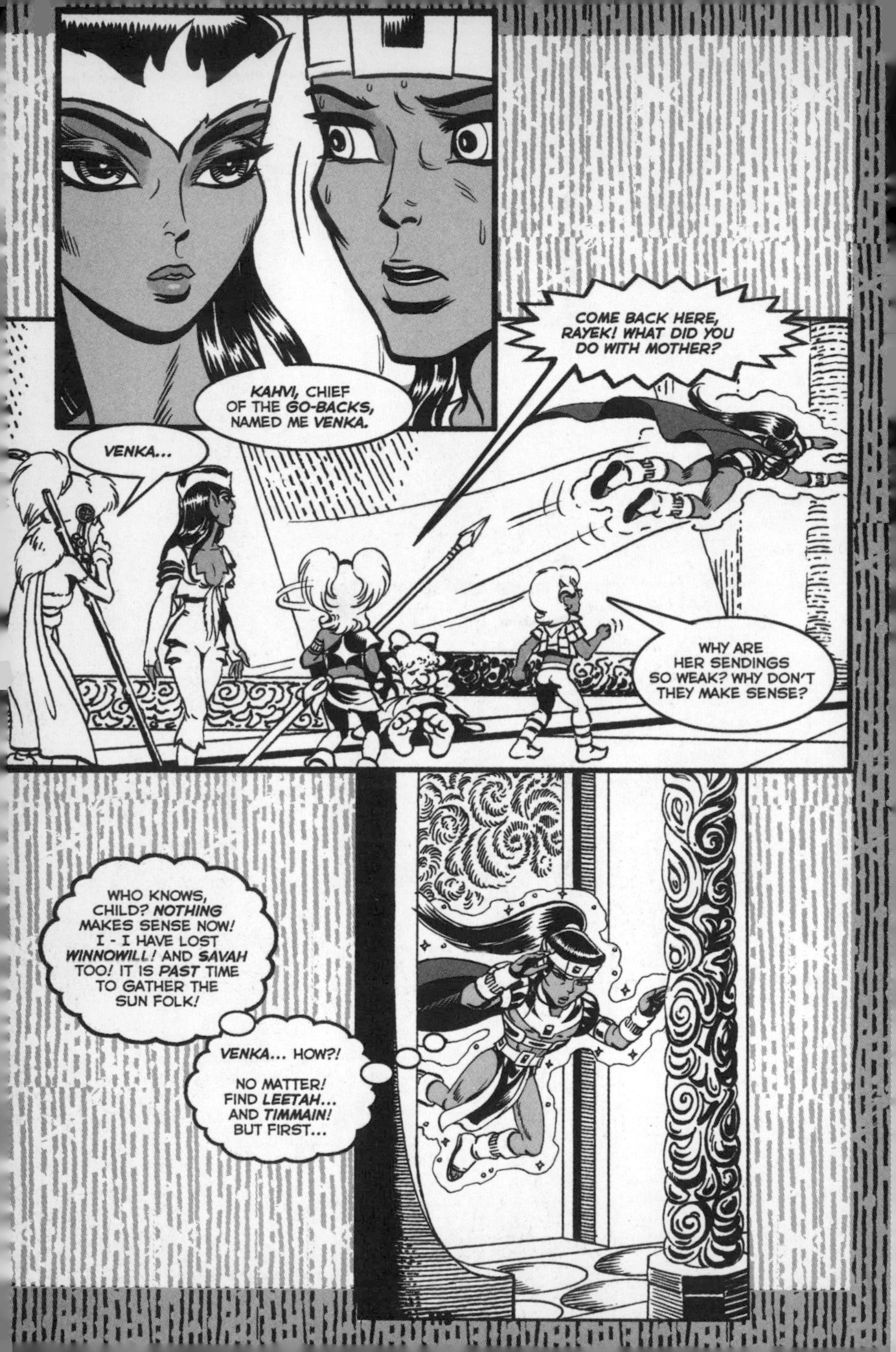
KAHVI, CHIEF OF THE GO-BACKS, NAMED ME VENKA.
VENKA...
COME BACK HERE, RAYEK! WHAT DID YOU DO WITH MOTHER?
WHY ARE HER SENDINGS SO WEAK? WHY DON'T THEY MAKE SENSE?
WHO KNOWS, CHILD? NOTHING MAKES SENSE NOW! I - I HAVE LOST WINNOWILL! AND SAVAH TOO! IT IS PAST TIME TO GATHER THE SUN FOLK!
VENKA... HOW?!
NO MATTER! FIND LEETAH... AND TIMMAIN! BUT FIRST...

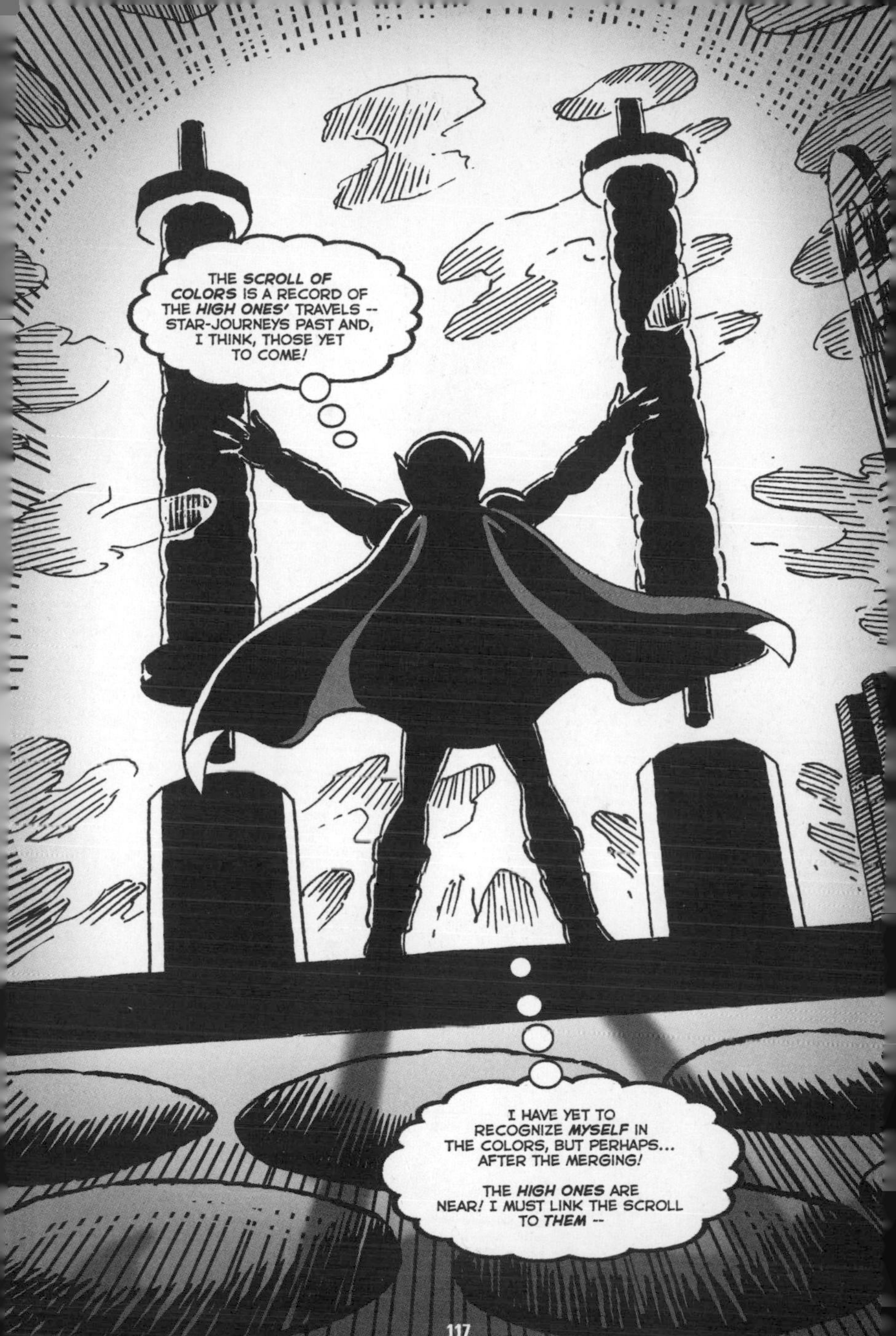
THE SCROLL OF COLORS IS A RECORD OF THE HIGH ONES' TRAVELS -- STAR-JOURNEYS PAST AND, I THINK, THOSE YET TO COME!
I HAVE YET TO RECOGNIZE MYSELF IN THE COLORS, BUT PERHAPS... AFTER THE MERGING!
THE HIGH ONES ARE NEAR! I MUST LINK THE SCROLL TO THEM --

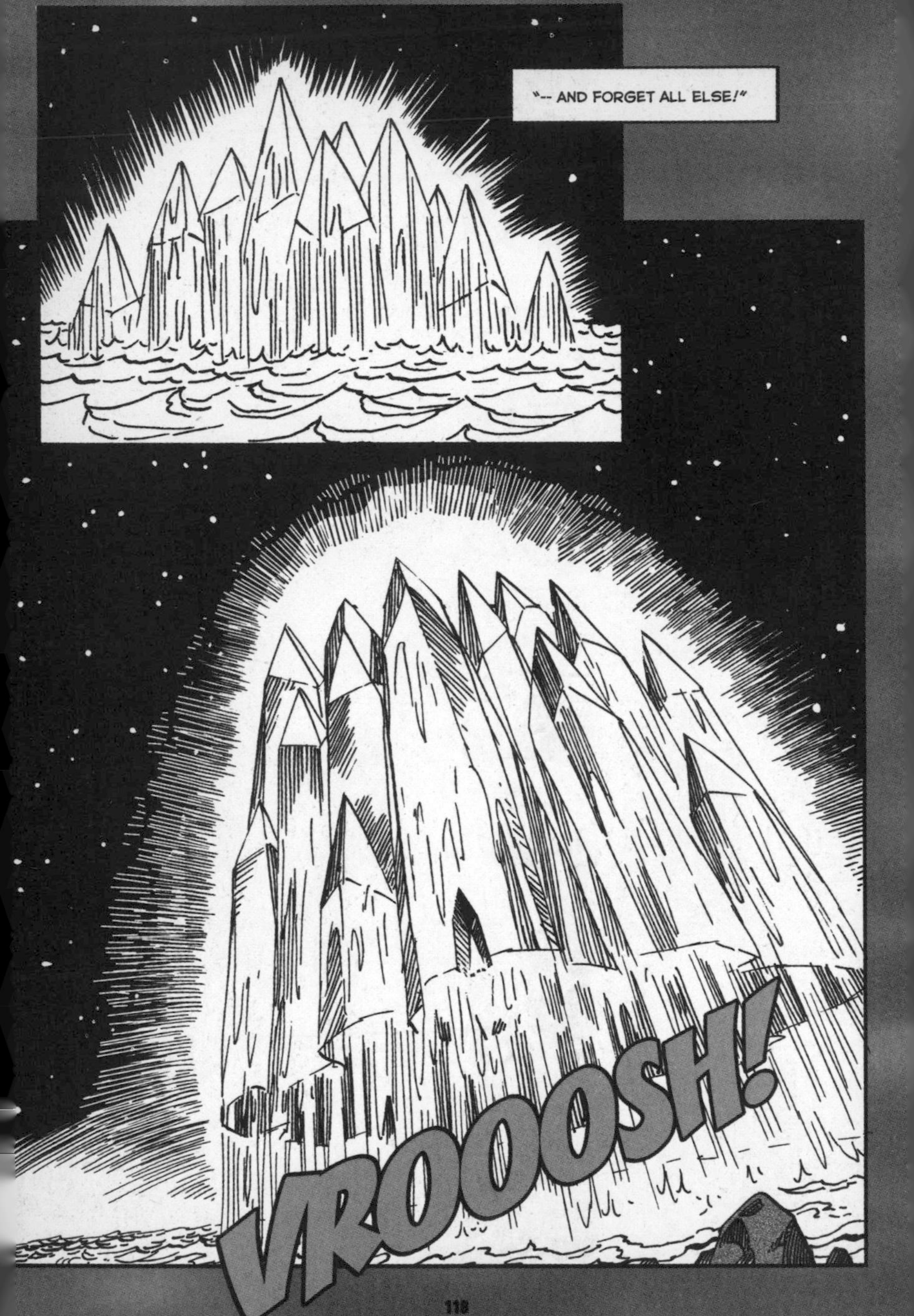
"-- AND FORGET ALL ELSE!"
VROOOSH!

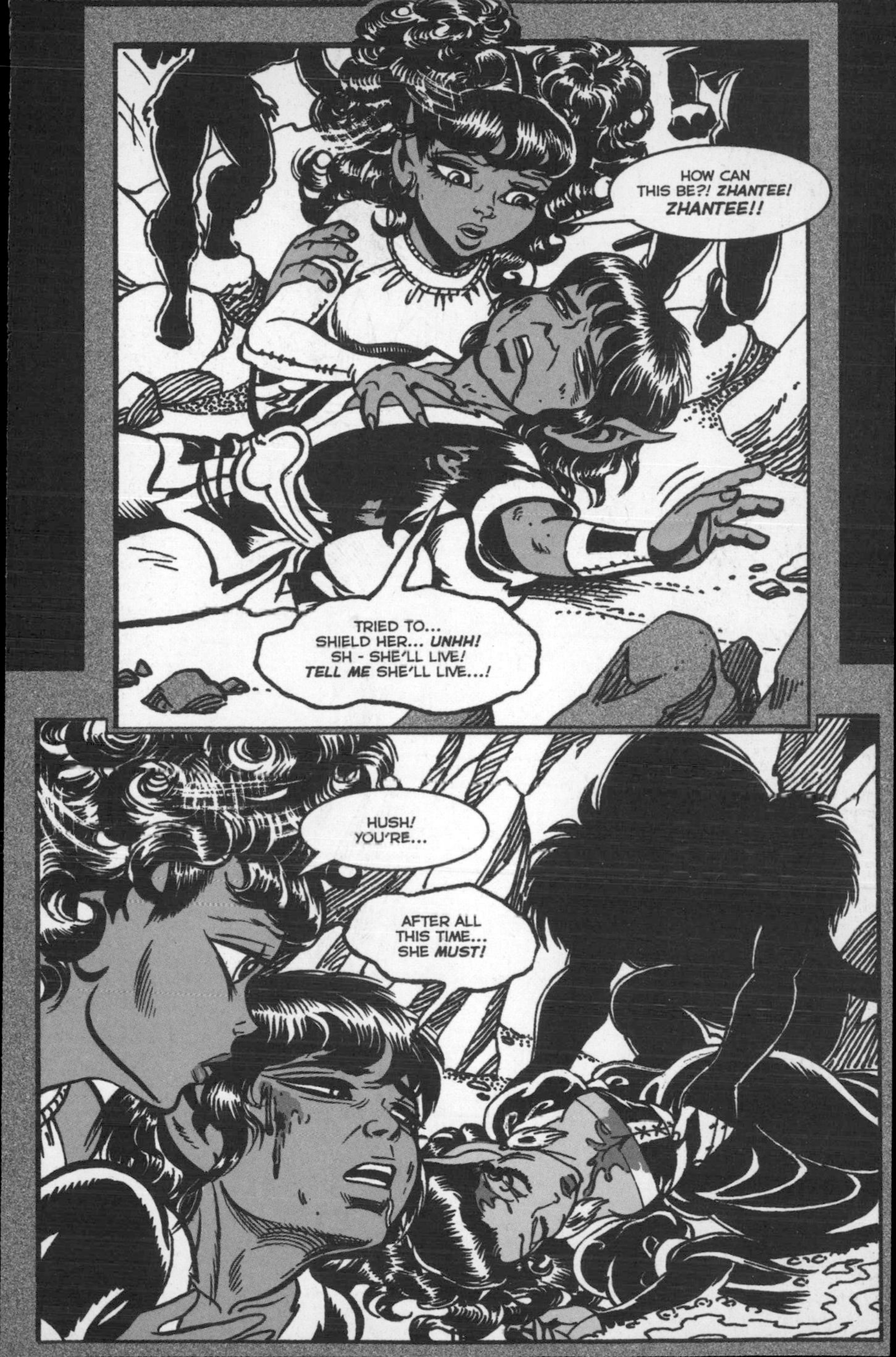
HOW CAN THIS BE?! ZHANTEE! ZHANTEE!!
TRIED TO... SHIELD HER... UNHH! SH - SHE'LL LIVE! TELL ME SHE'LL LIVE...!
HUSH! YOU'RE...
AFTER ALL THIS TIME... SHE MUST!

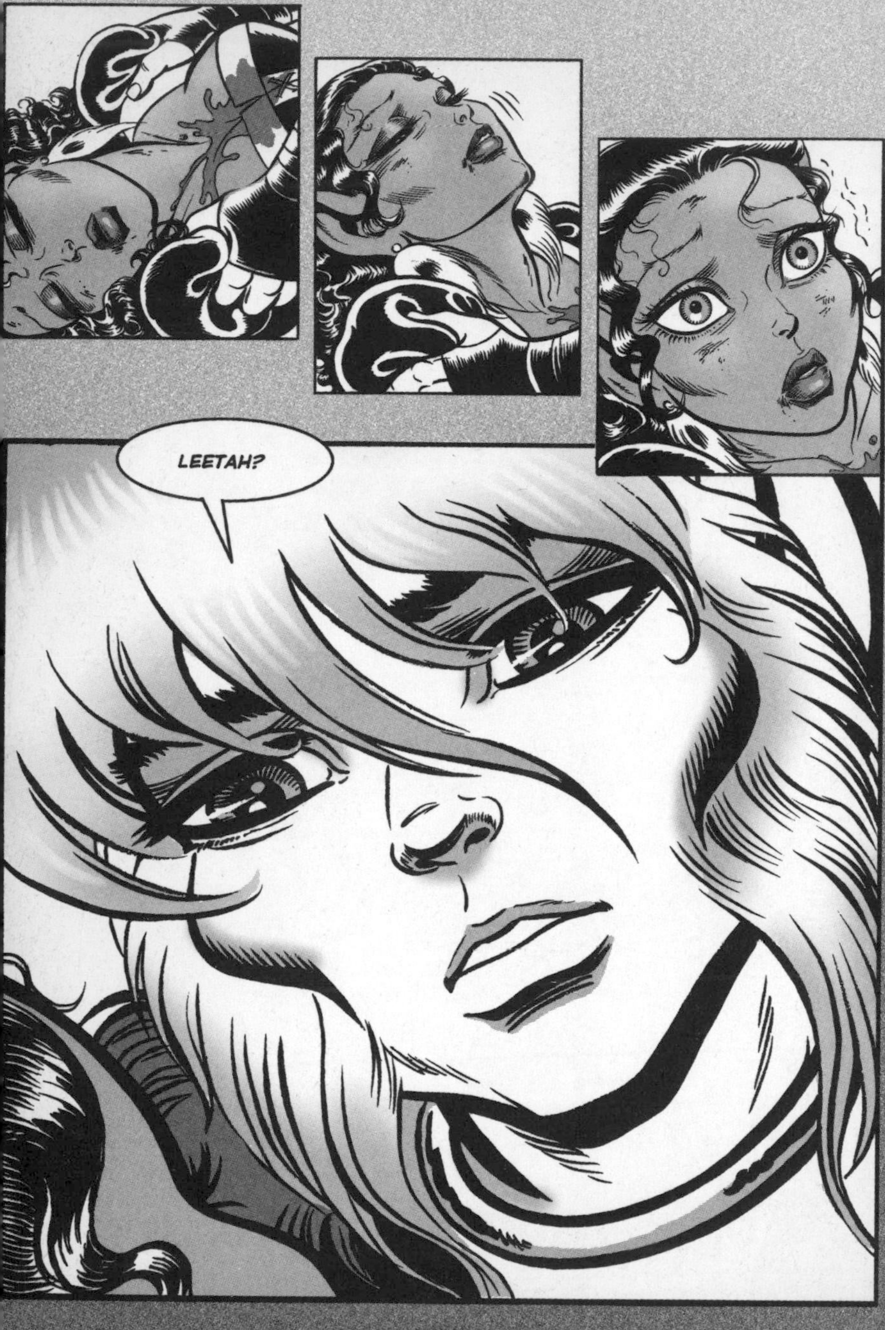
LEETAH?

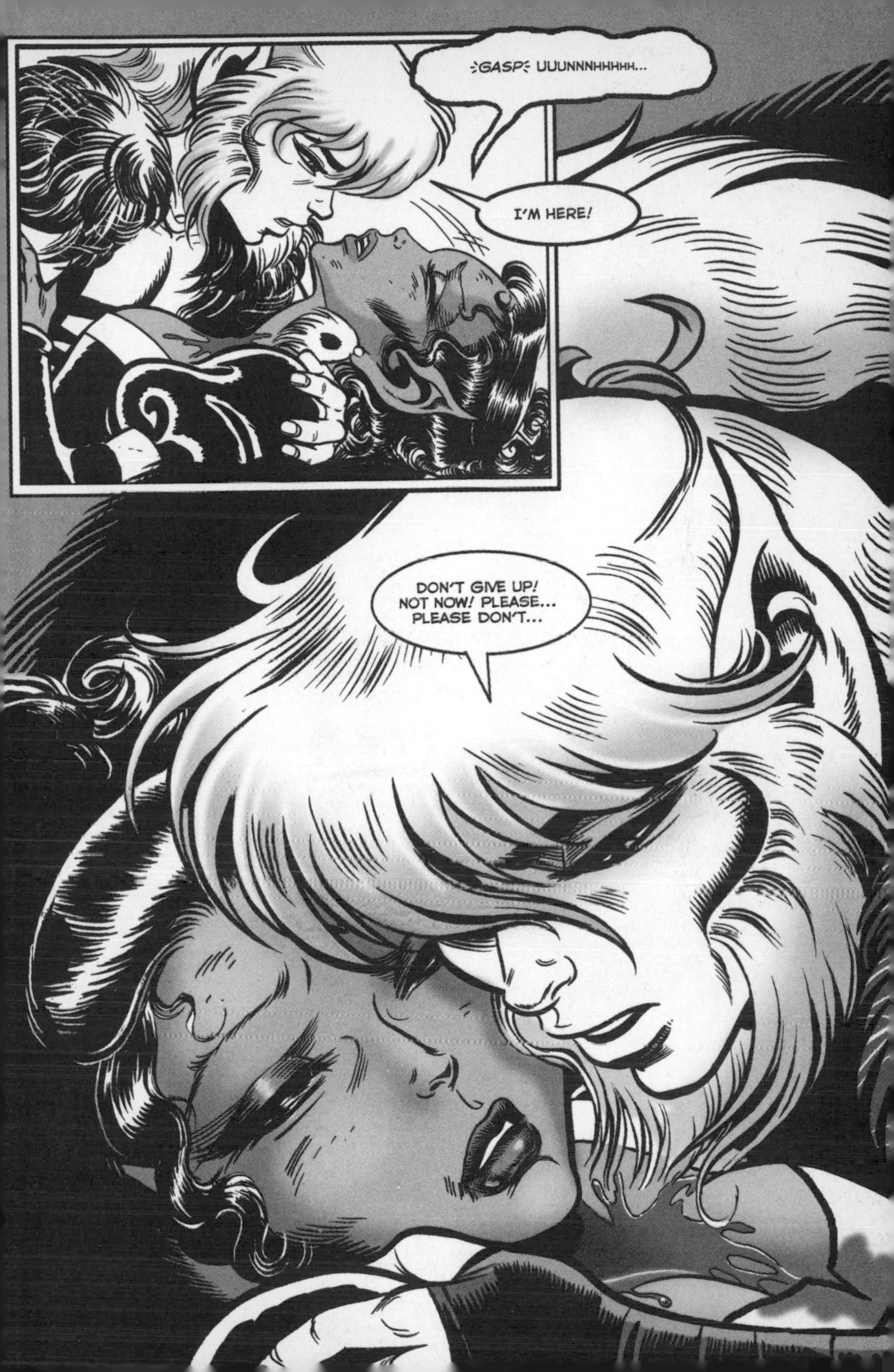

:GASP: UUUNNNHHHHH...
I'M HERE!
DON'T GIVE UP! NOT NOW! PLEASE... PLEASE DON'T...

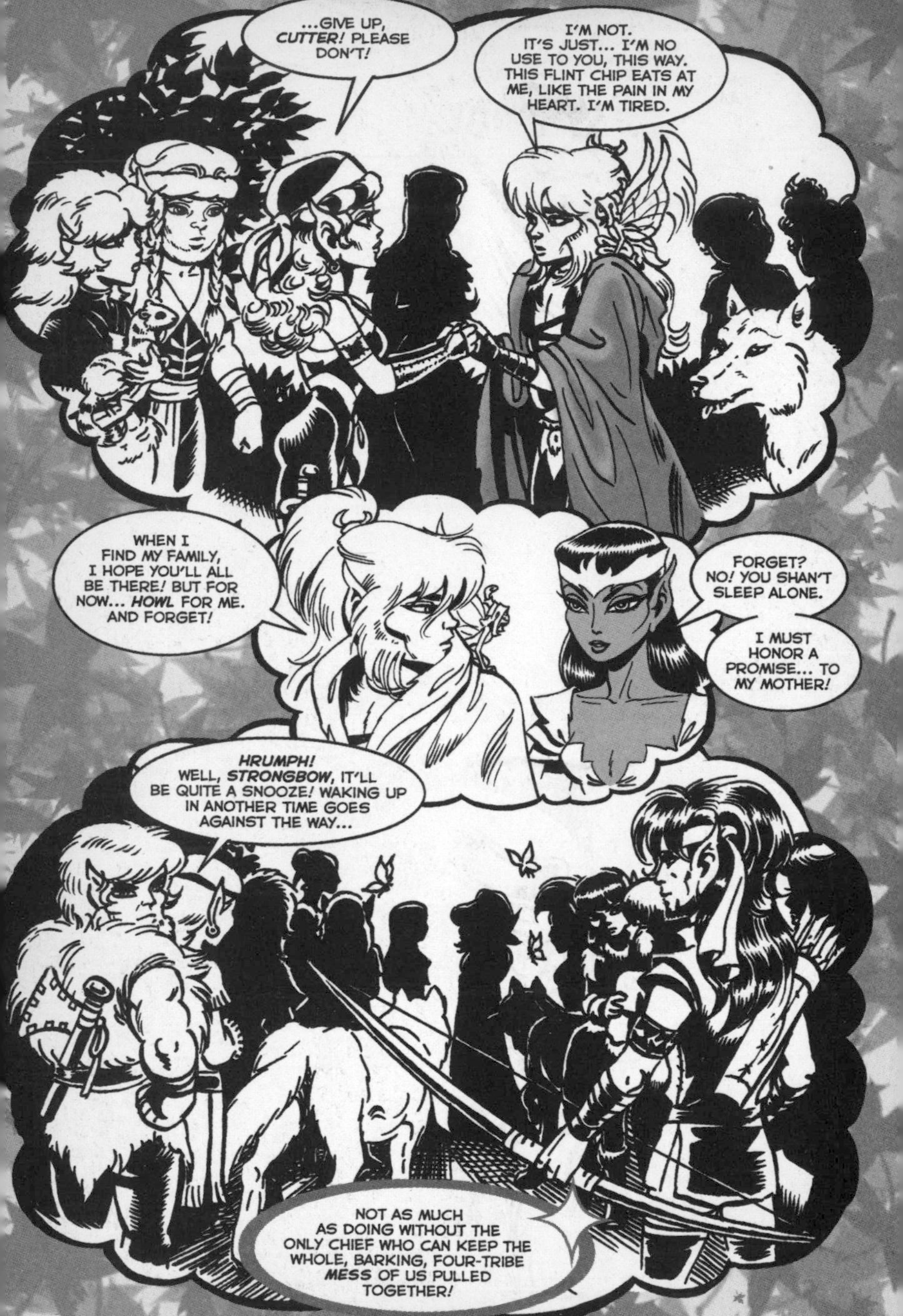
...GIVE UP, CUTTER! PLEASE DON'T!
I'M NOT. IT'S JUST... I'M NO USE TO YOU, THIS WAY. THIS FLINT CHIP EATS AT ME, LIKE THE PAIN IN MY HEART. I'M TIRED.
WHEN I FIND MY FAMILY, I HOPE YOU'LL ALL BE THERE! BUT FOR NOW... HOWL FOR ME. AND FORGET!
FORGET? NO! YOU SHAN'T SLEEP ALONE.
I MUST HONOR A PROMISE... TO MY MOTHER!
HRUMPH! WELL, STRONGBOW, IT'LL BE QUITE A SNOOZE! WAKING UP IN ANOTHER TIME GOES AGAINST THE WAY...
NOT AS MUCH AS DOING WITHOUT THE ONLY CHIEF WHO CAN KEEP THE WHOLE, BARKING, FOUR-TRIBE MESS OF US PULLED TOGETHER!

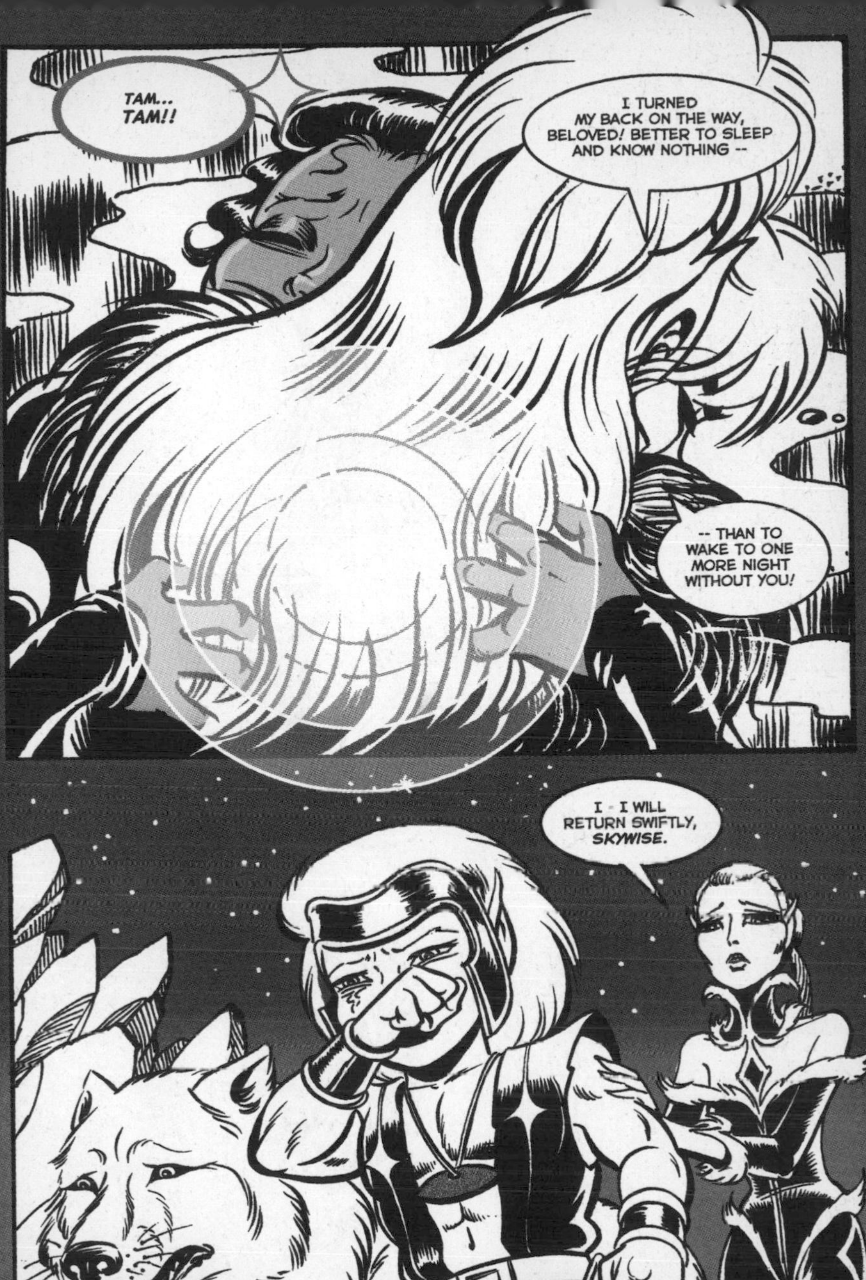
TAM... TAM!!
I TURNED MY BACK ON THE WAY, BELOVED! BETTER TO SLEEP AND KNOW NOTHING --
-- THAN TO WAKE TO ONE MORE NIGHT WITHOUT YOU!
I - I WILL RETURN SWIFTLY, SKYWISE.

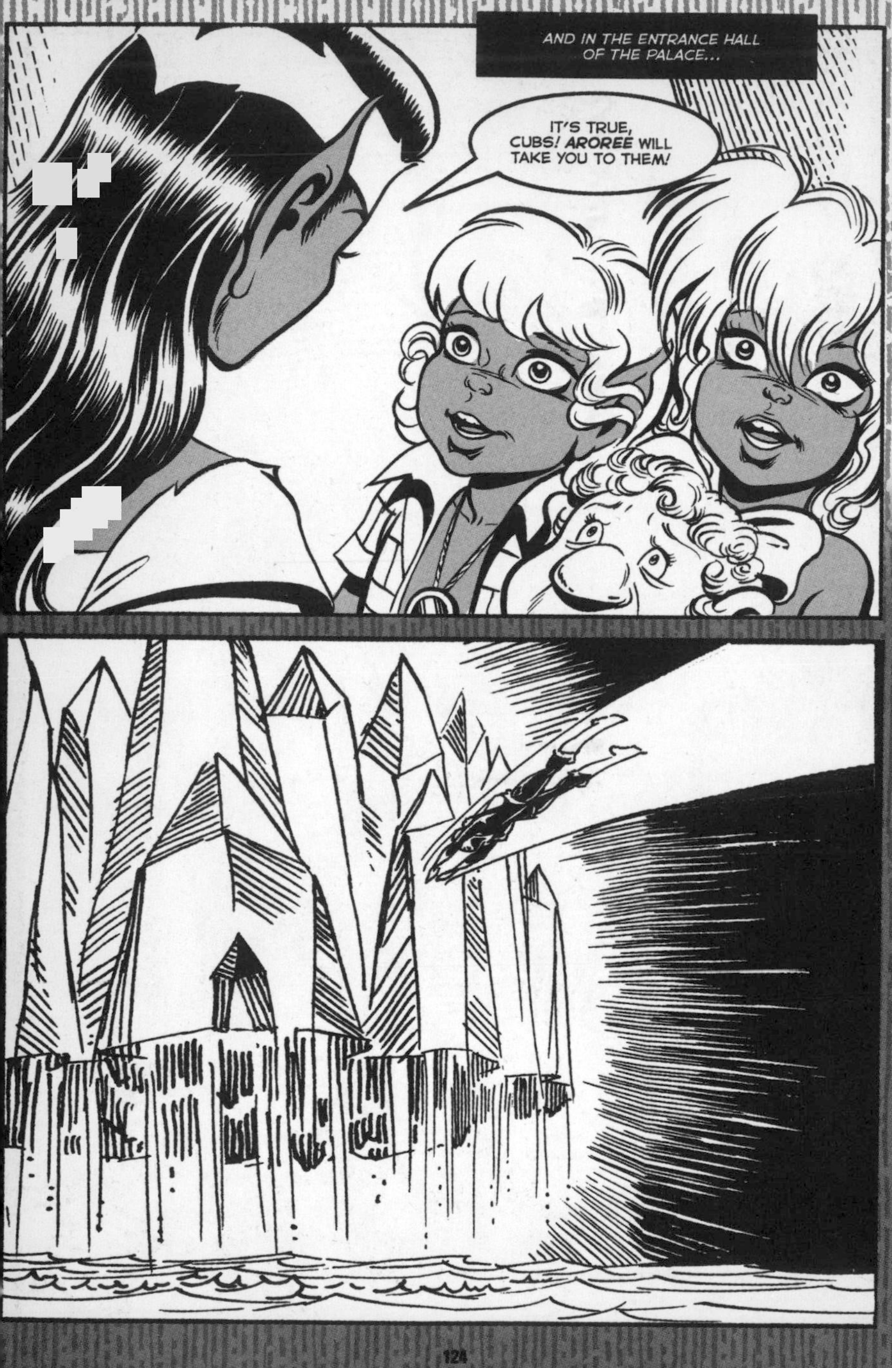
AND IN THE ENTRANCE HALL OF THE PALACE...
IT'S TRUE, CUBS! AROREE WILL TAKE YOU TO THEM!

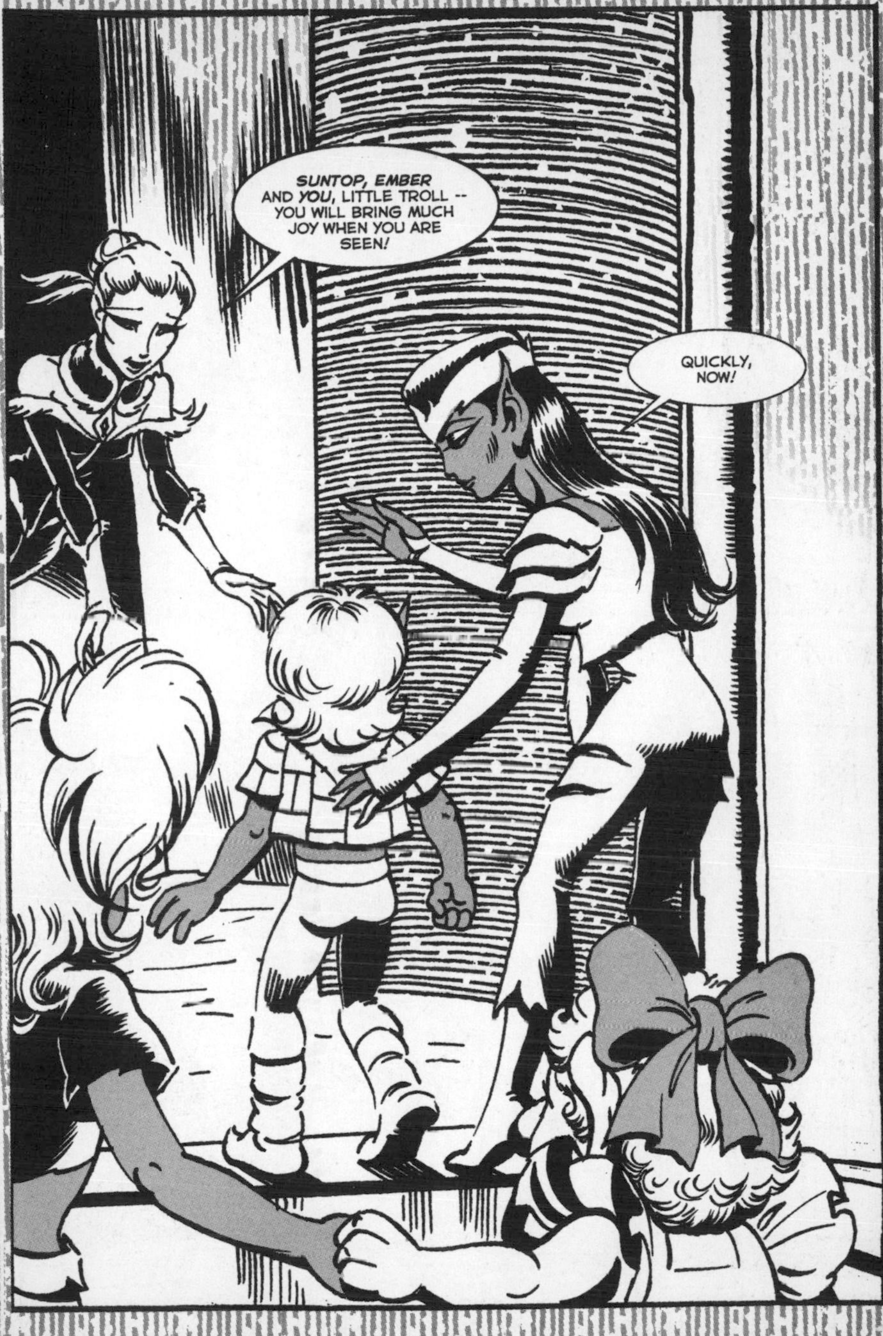
SUNTOP, EMBER AND YOU, LITTLE TROLL -- YOU WILL BRING MUCH JOY WHEN YOU ARE SEEN!
QUICKLY, NOW!

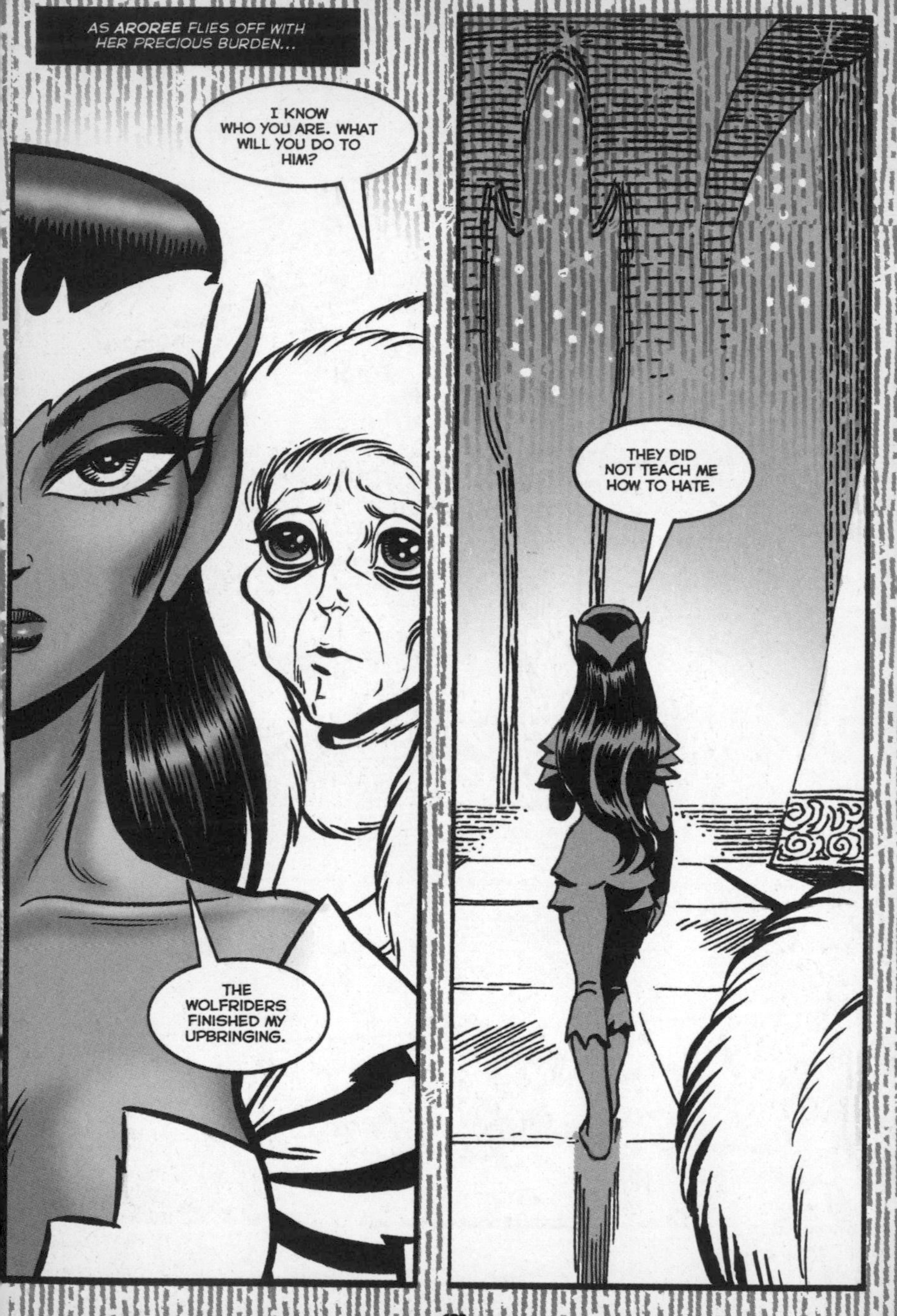
AS AROREE FLIES OFF WITH HER PRECIOUS BURDEN...
I KNOW WHO YOU ARE. WHAT WILL YOU DO TO HIM?
THE WOLFRIDERS FINISHED MY UPBRINGING.
THEY DID NOT TEACH ME HOW TO HATE.

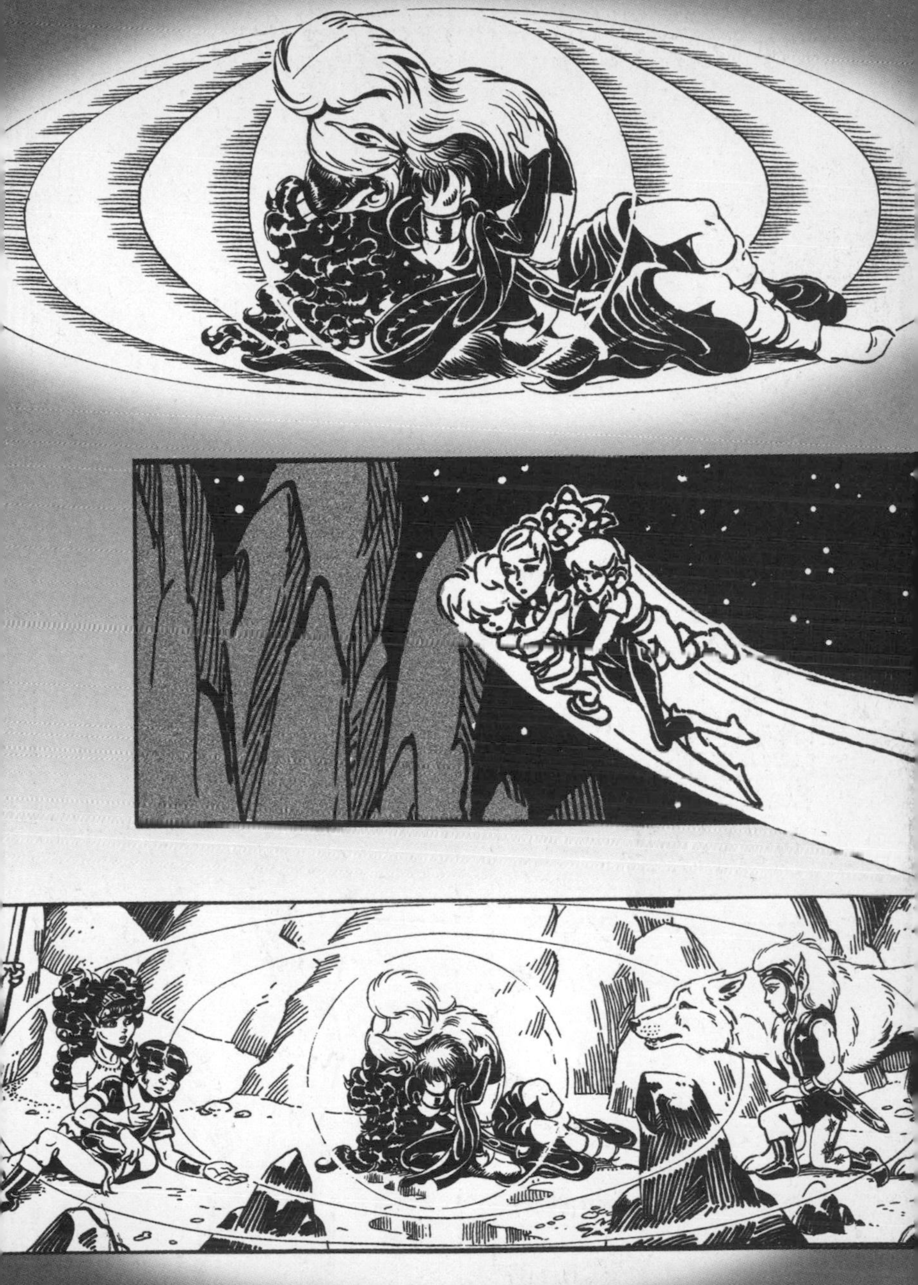

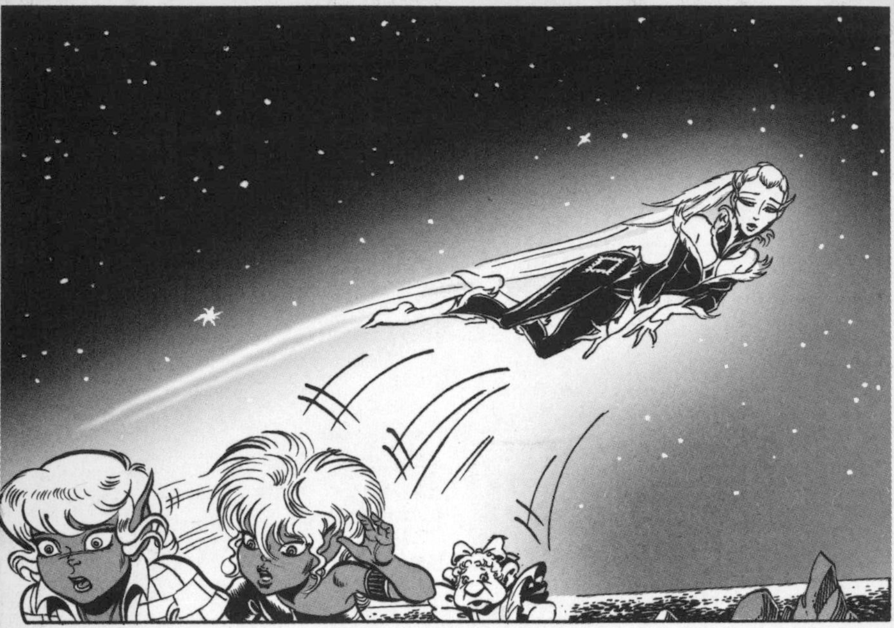

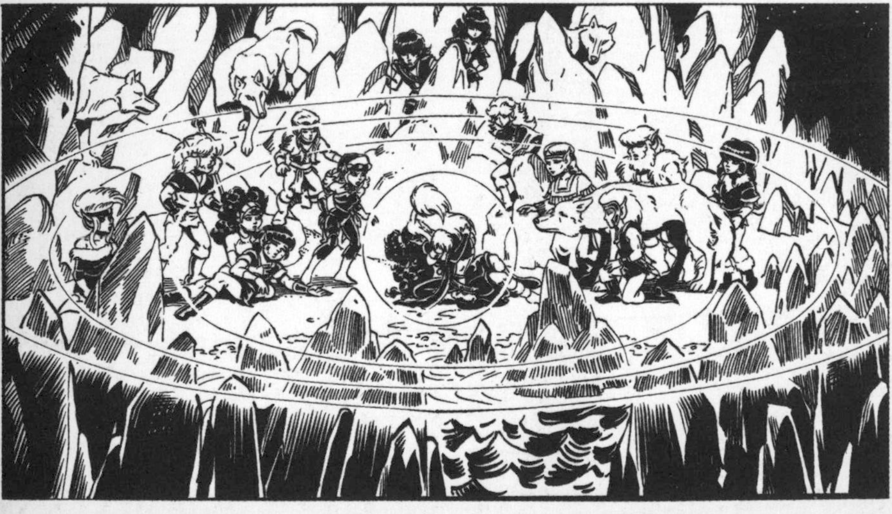

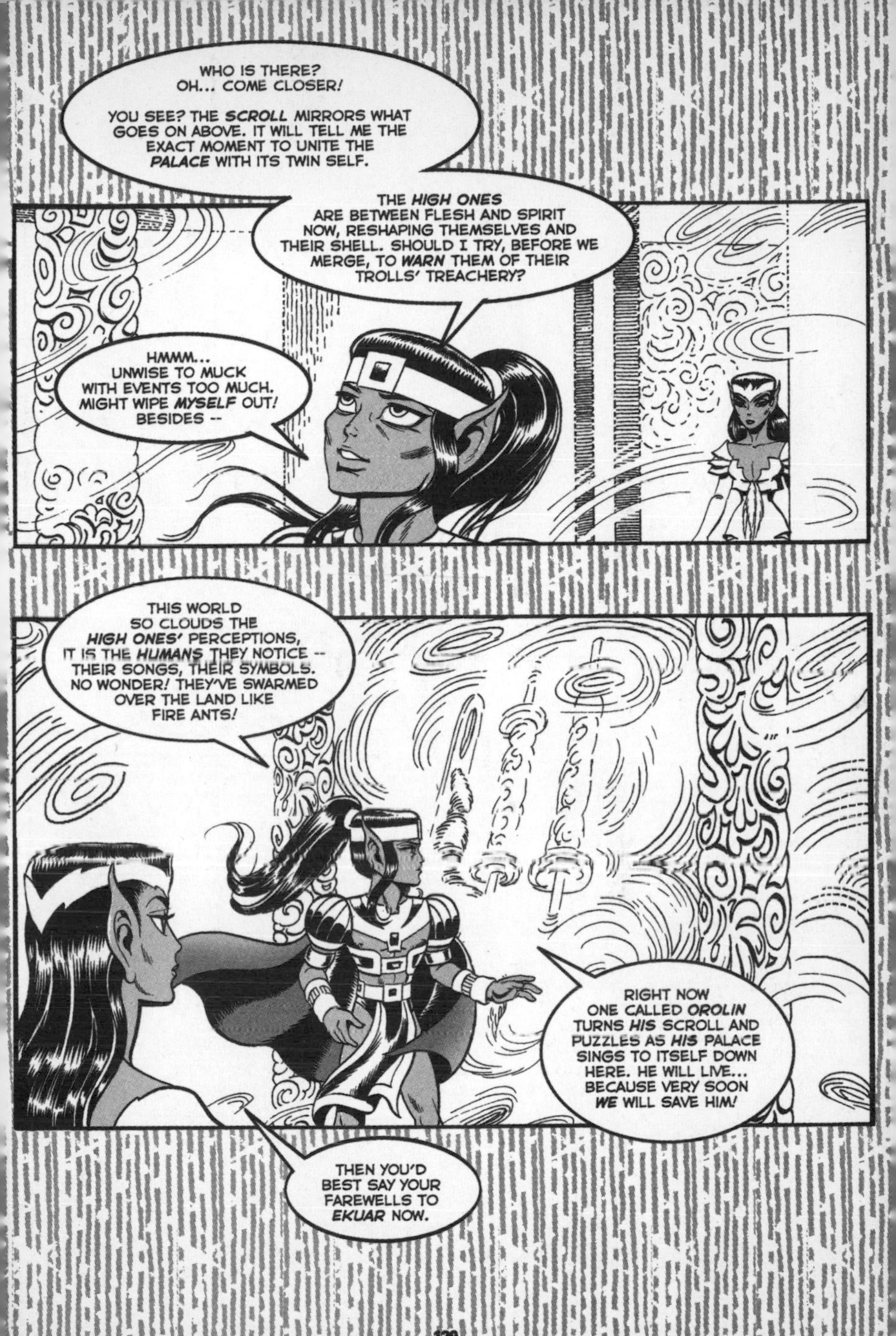
WHO IS THERE? OH... COME CLOSER! YOU SEE? THE SCROLL MIRRORS WHAT GOES ON ABOVE. IT WILL TELL ME THE EXACT MOMENT TO UNITE THE PALACE WITH ITS TWIN SELF.
THE HIGH ONES ARE BETWEEN FLESH AND SPIRIT NOW, RESHAPING THEMSELVES AND THEIR SHELL. SHOULD I TRY, BEFORE WE MERGE, TO WARN THEM OF THEIR TROLLS' TREACHERY?
HMMM... UNWISE TO MUCK WITH EVENTS TOO MUCH. MIGHT WIPE MYSELF OUT! BESIDES --
THIS WORLD SO CLOUDS THE HIGH ONES' PERCEPTIONS, IT IS THE HUMANS THEY NOTICE -- THEIR SONGS, THEIR SYMBOLS. NO WONDER! THEY'VE SWARMED OVER THE LAND LIKE FIRE ANTS!
RIGHT NOW ONE CALLED OROLIN TURNS HIS SCROLL AND PUZZLES AS HIS PALACE SINGS TO ITSELF DOWN HERE. HE WILL LIVE... BECAUSE VERY SOON WE WILL SAVE HIM!
THEN YOU'D BEST SAY YOUR FAREWELLS TO EKUAR NOW.

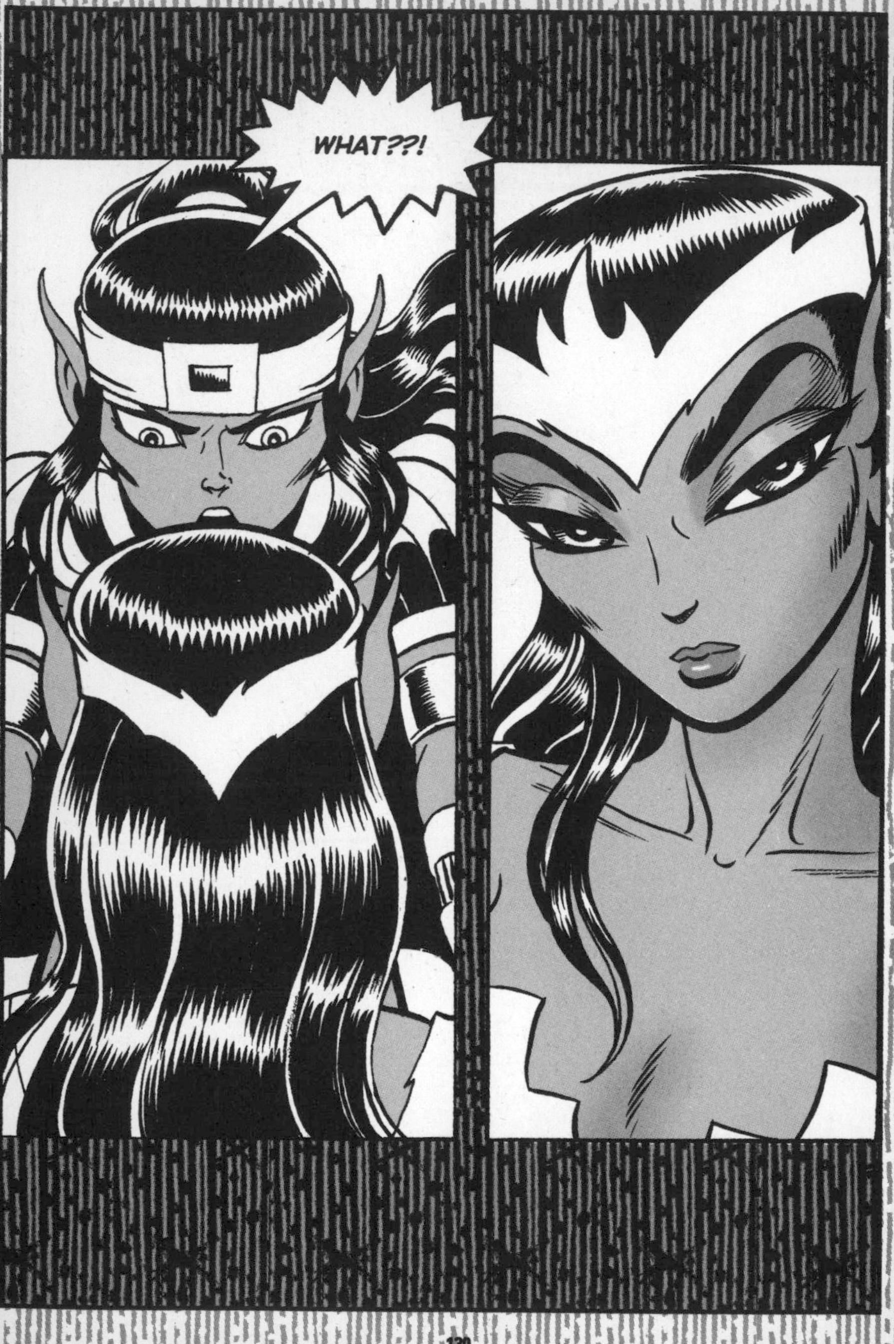
WHAT??!

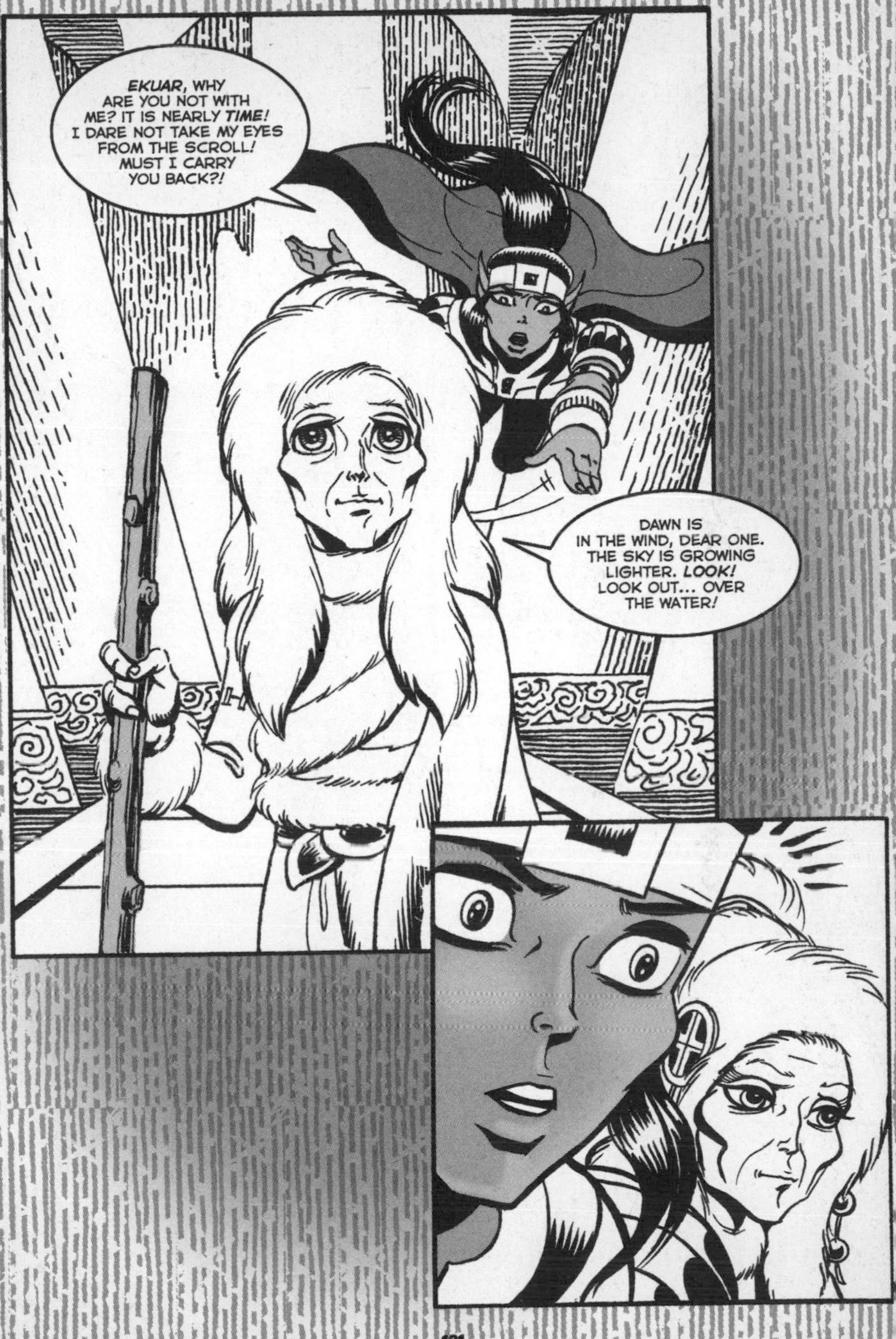
EKUAR, WHY ARE YOU NOT WITH ME? IT IS NEARLY *TIME!* I DARE NOT TAKE MY EYES FROM THE SCROLL! MUST I CARRY YOU BACK?!
DAWN IS IN THE WIND, DEAR ONE. THE SKY IS GROWING LIGHTER. *LOOK!* LOOK OUT... OVER THE WATER!

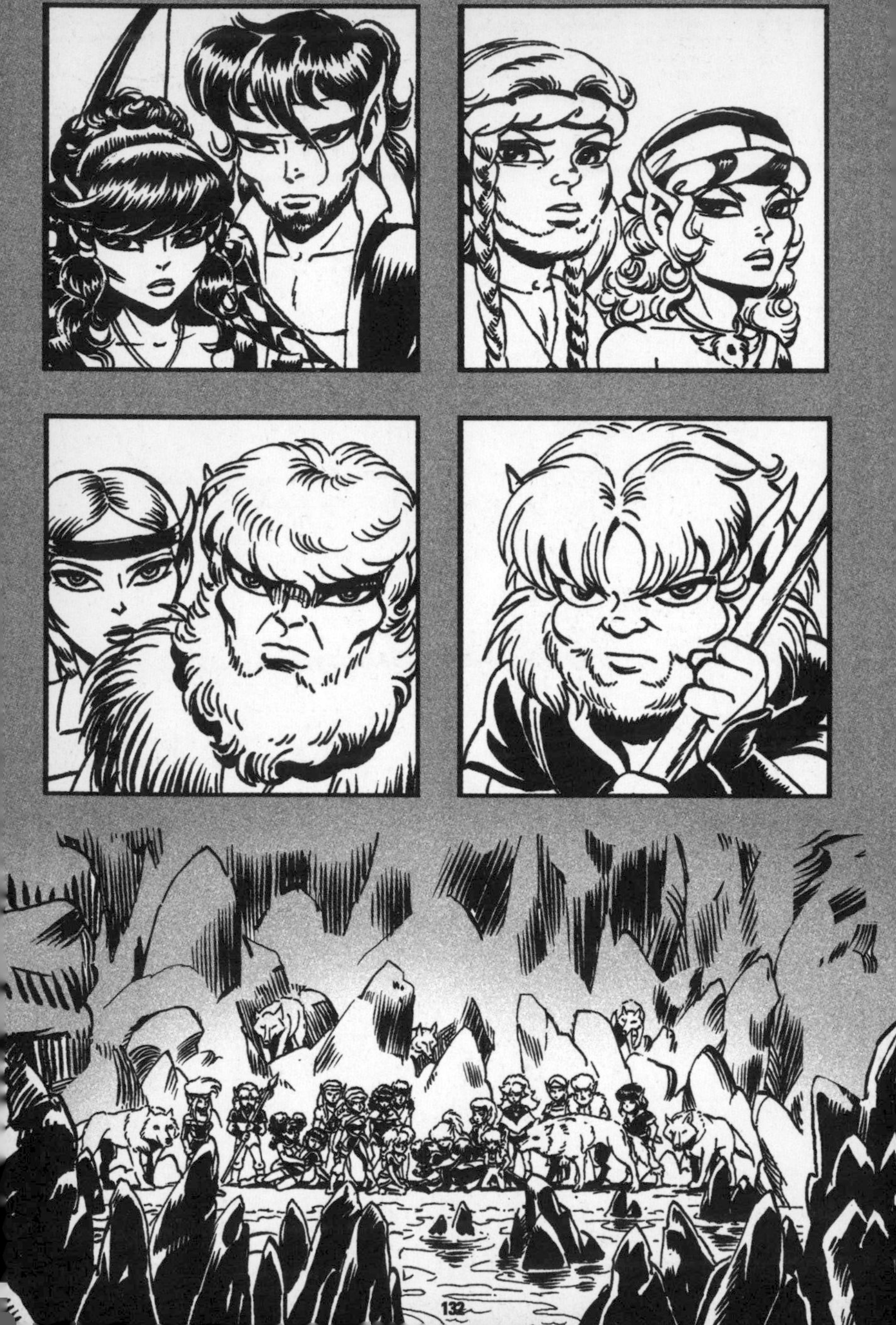

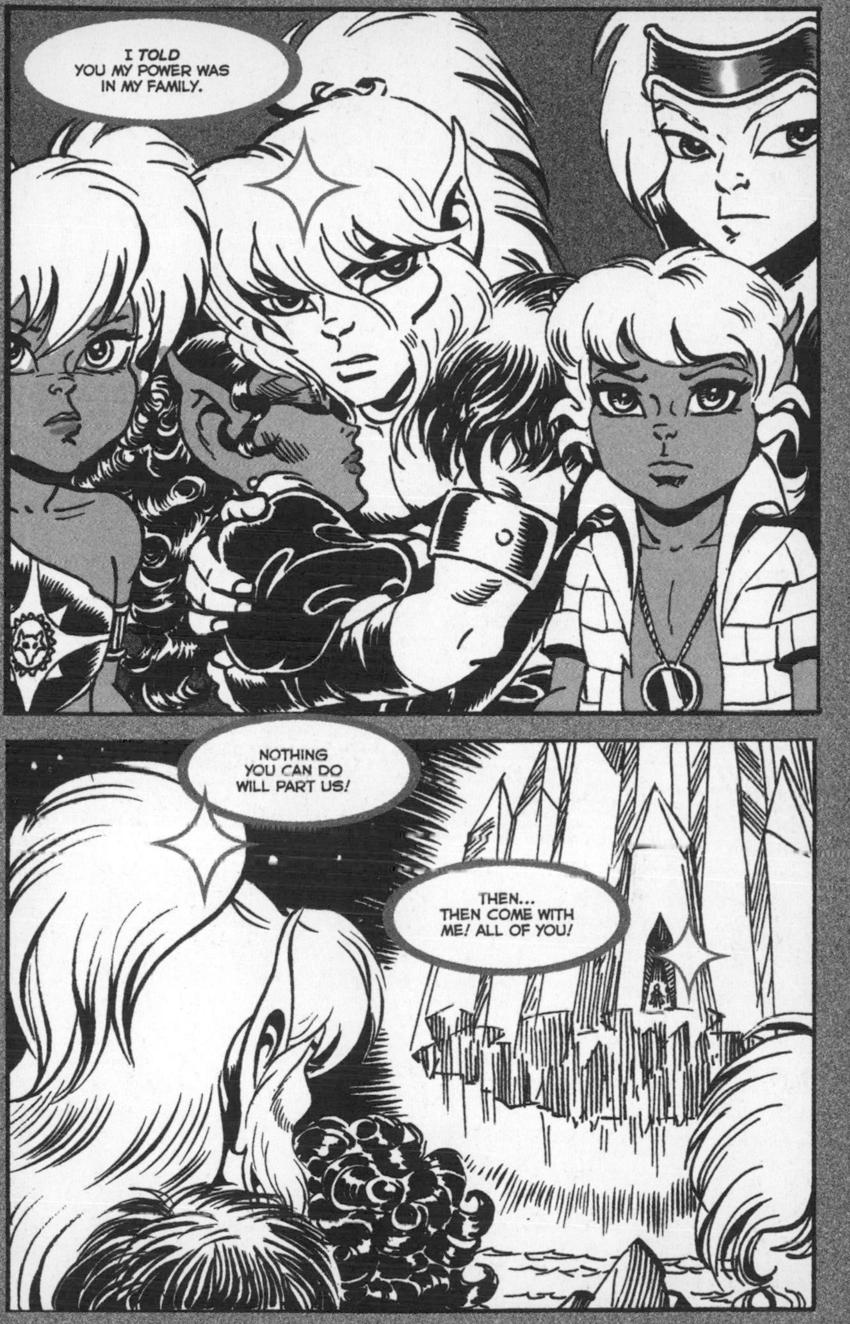
I *TOLD* YOU MY POWER WAS IN MY FAMILY.
NOTHING YOU CAN DO WILL PART US!
THEN... THEN COME WITH ME! ALL OF YOU!

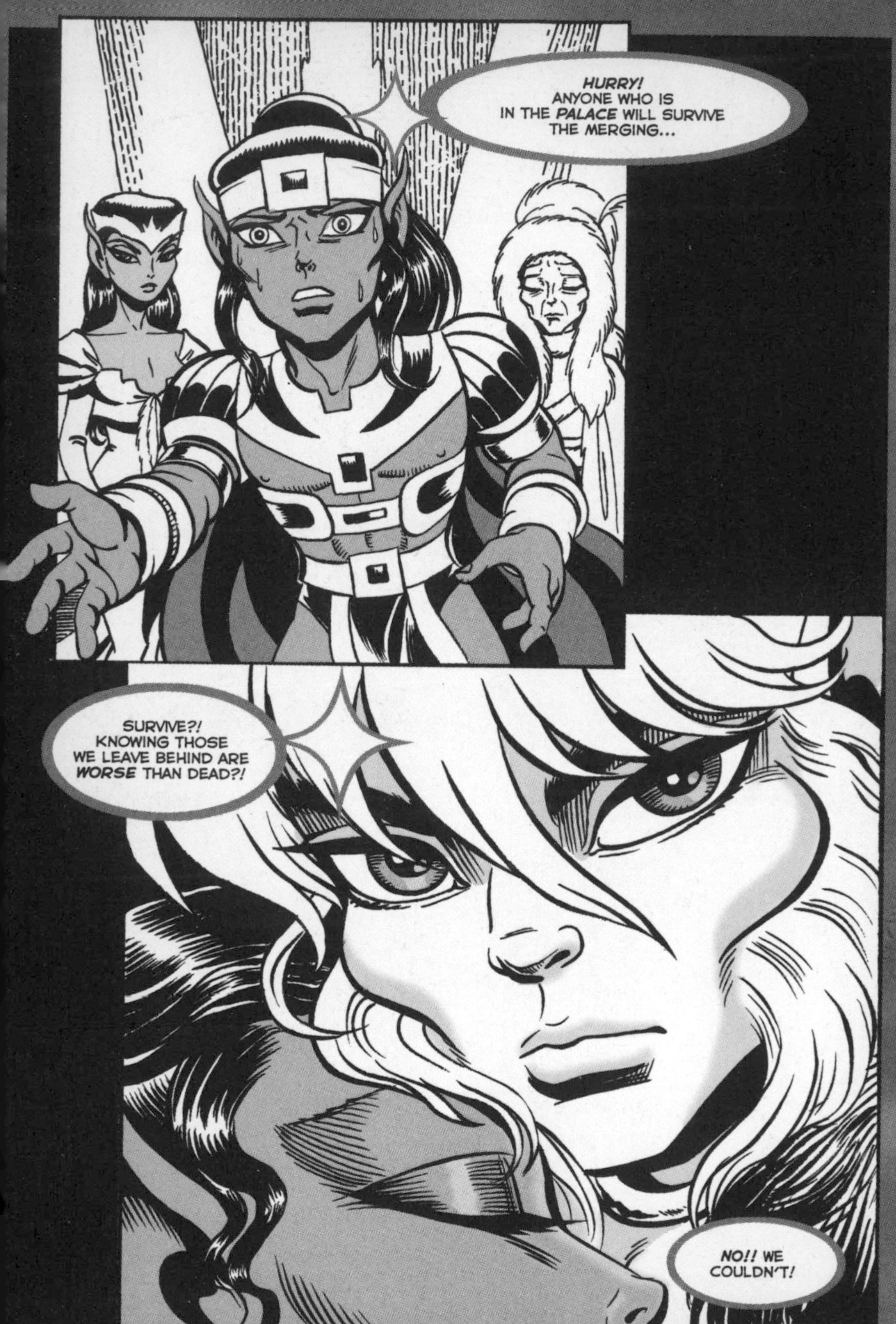
HURRY! ANYONE WHO IS IN THE PALACE WILL SURVIVE THE MERGING...
SURVIVE?! KNOWING THOSE WE LEAVE BEHIND ARE WORSE THAN DEAD?!
NO!! WE COULDN'T!

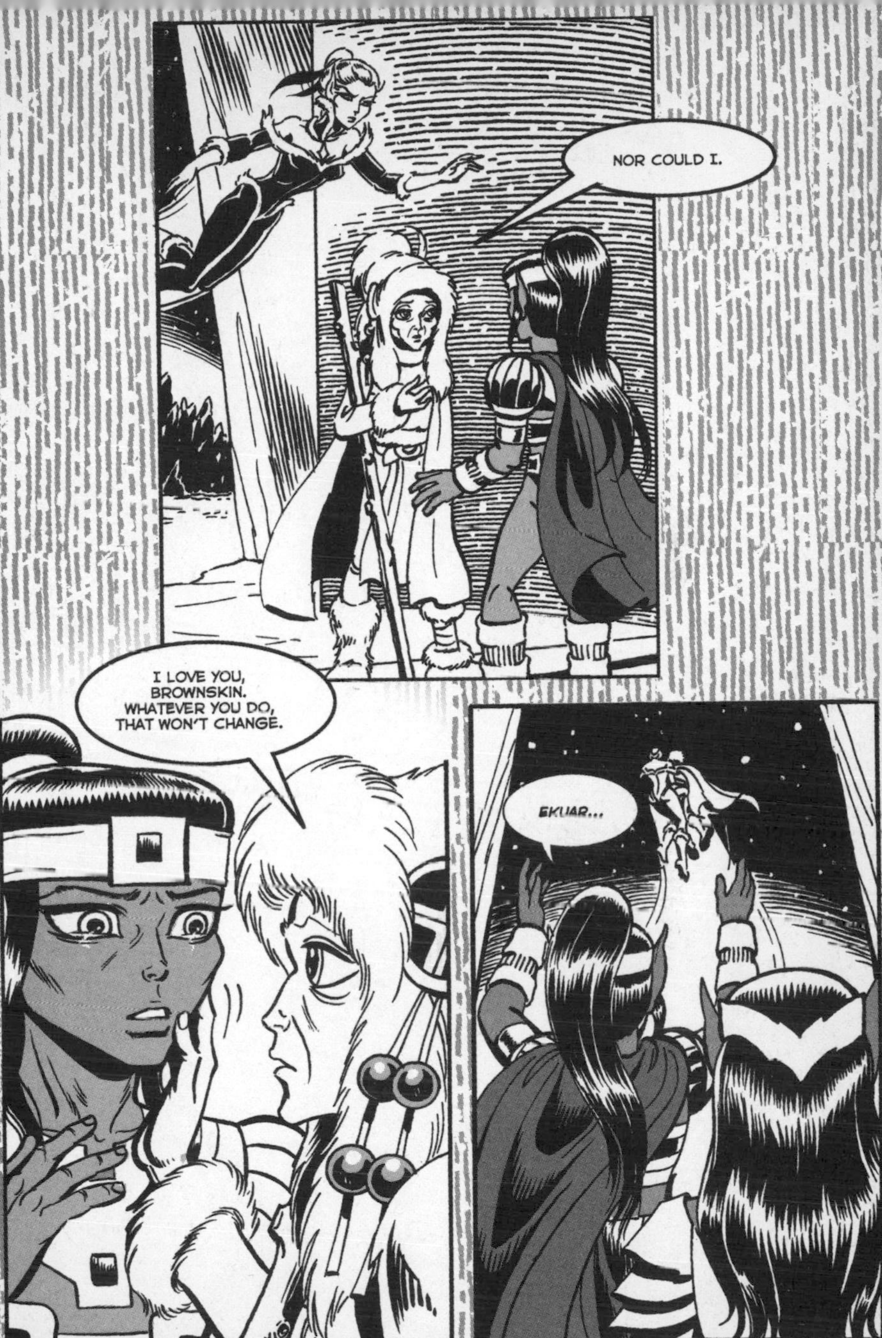
NOR COULD I.
I LOVE YOU, BROWNSKIN. WHATEVER YOU DO, THAT WON'T CHANGE.
EKUAR...

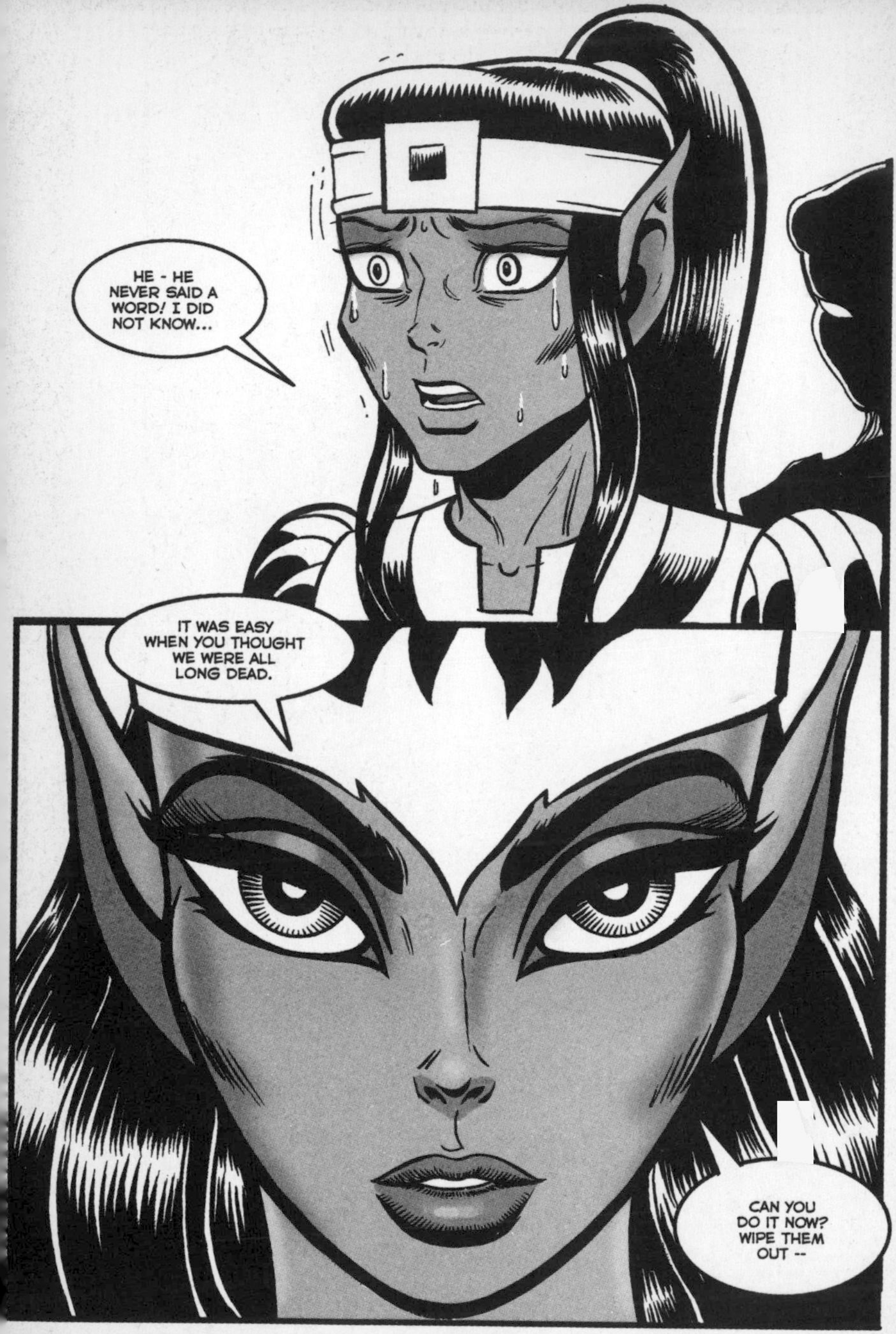
HE - HE NEVER SAID A WORD! I DID NOT KNOW...
IT WAS EASY WHEN YOU THOUGHT WE WERE ALL LONG DEAD.
CAN YOU DO IT NOW? WIPE THEM OUT --

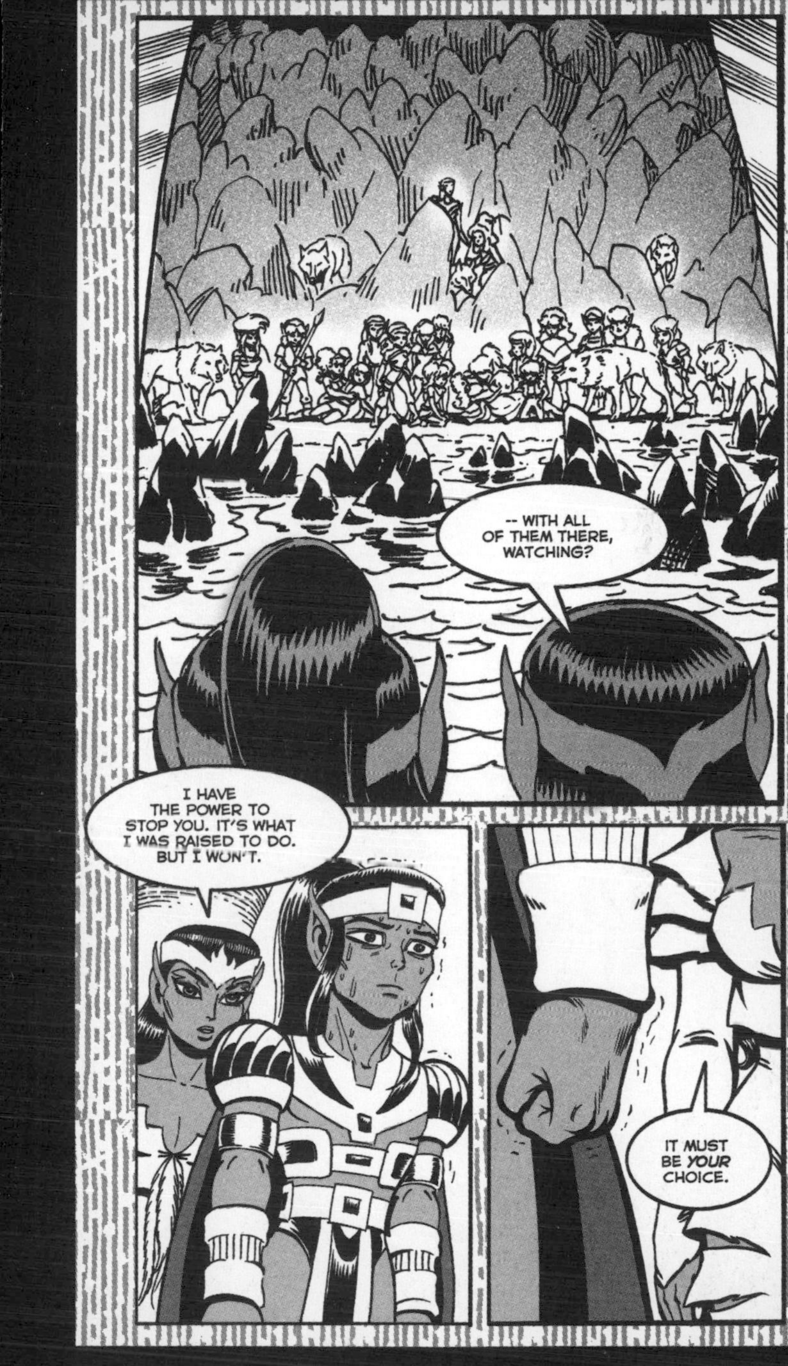
-- WITH ALL OF THEM THERE, WATCHING?
I HAVE THE POWER TO STOP YOU. IT'S WHAT I WAS RAISED TO DO. BUT I WON'T.
IT MUST BE *YOUR* CHOICE.

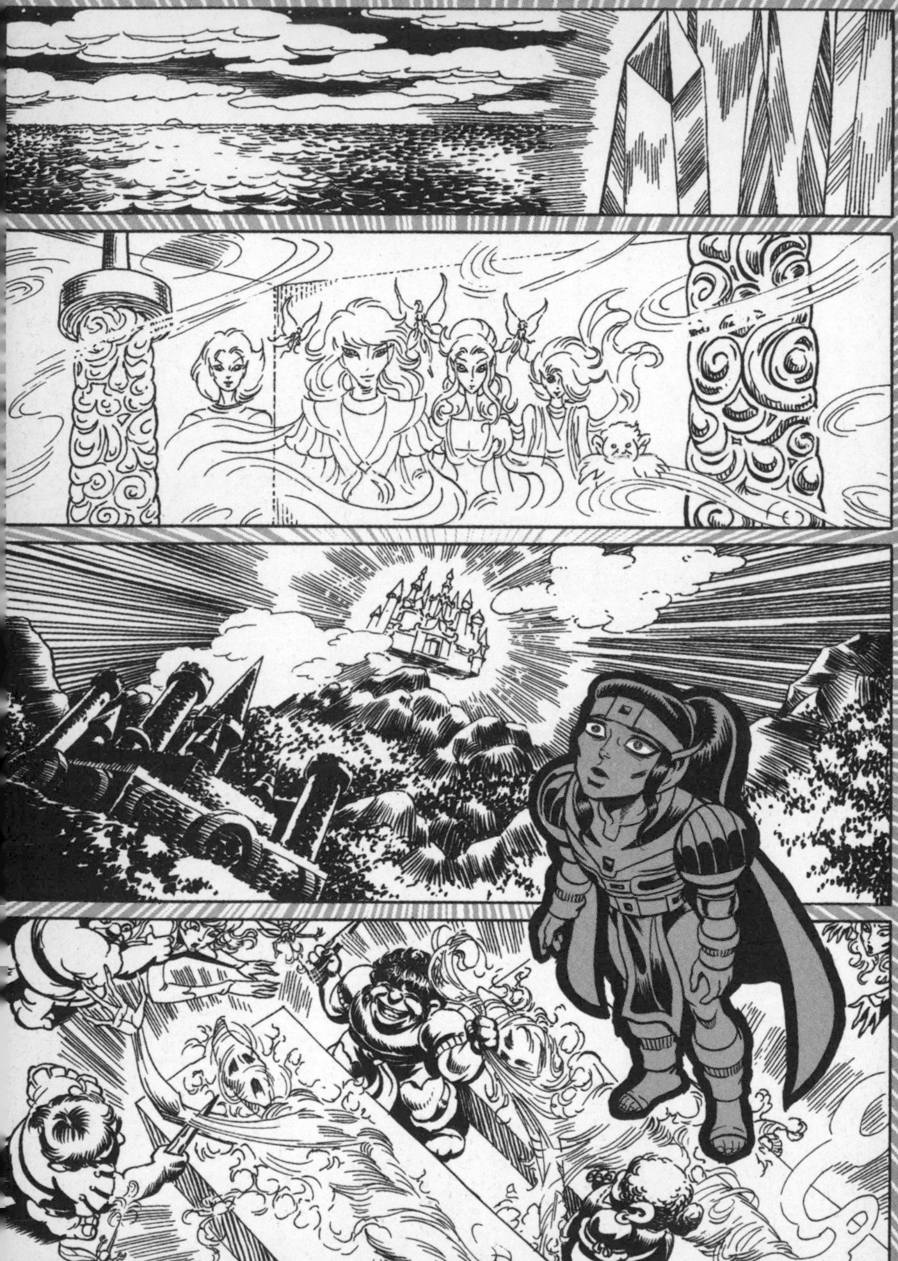

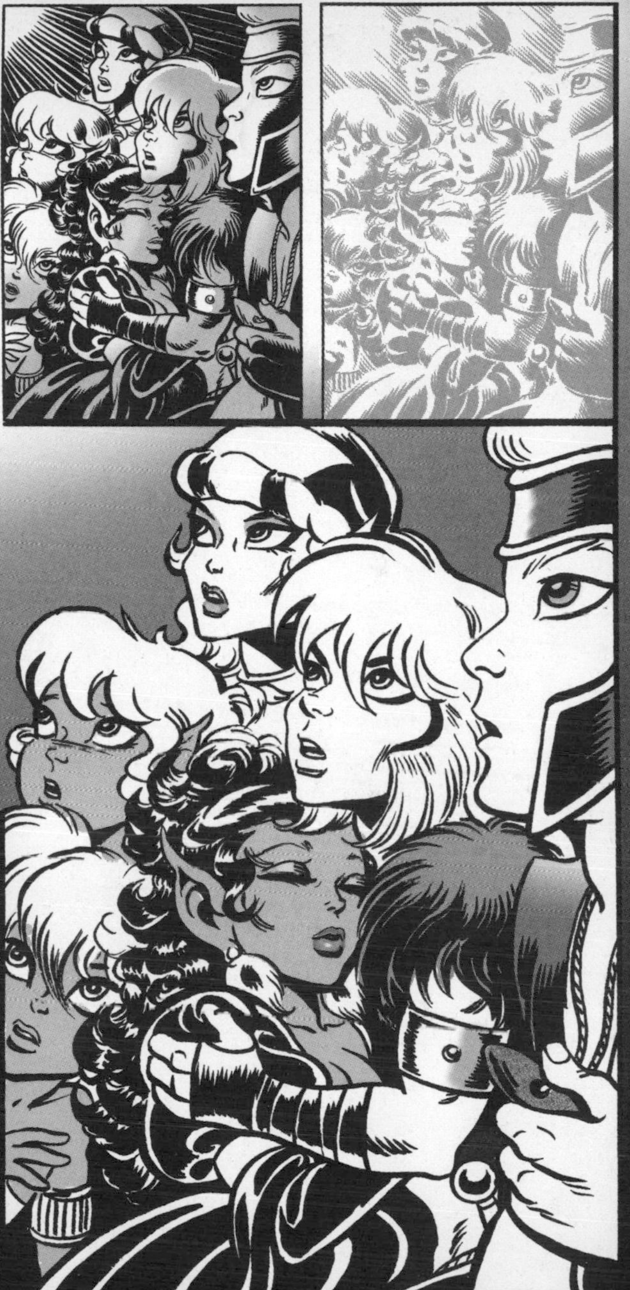

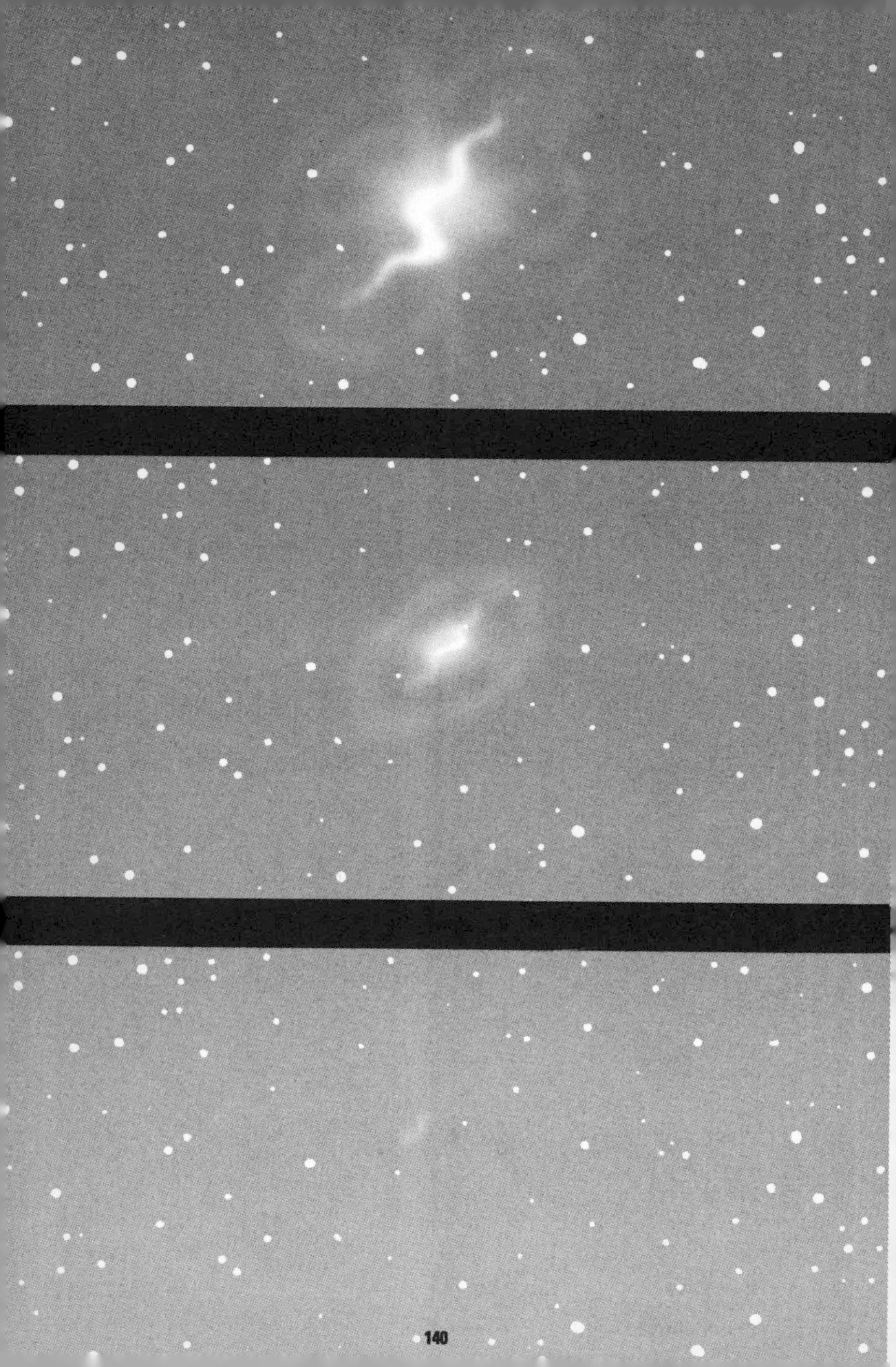

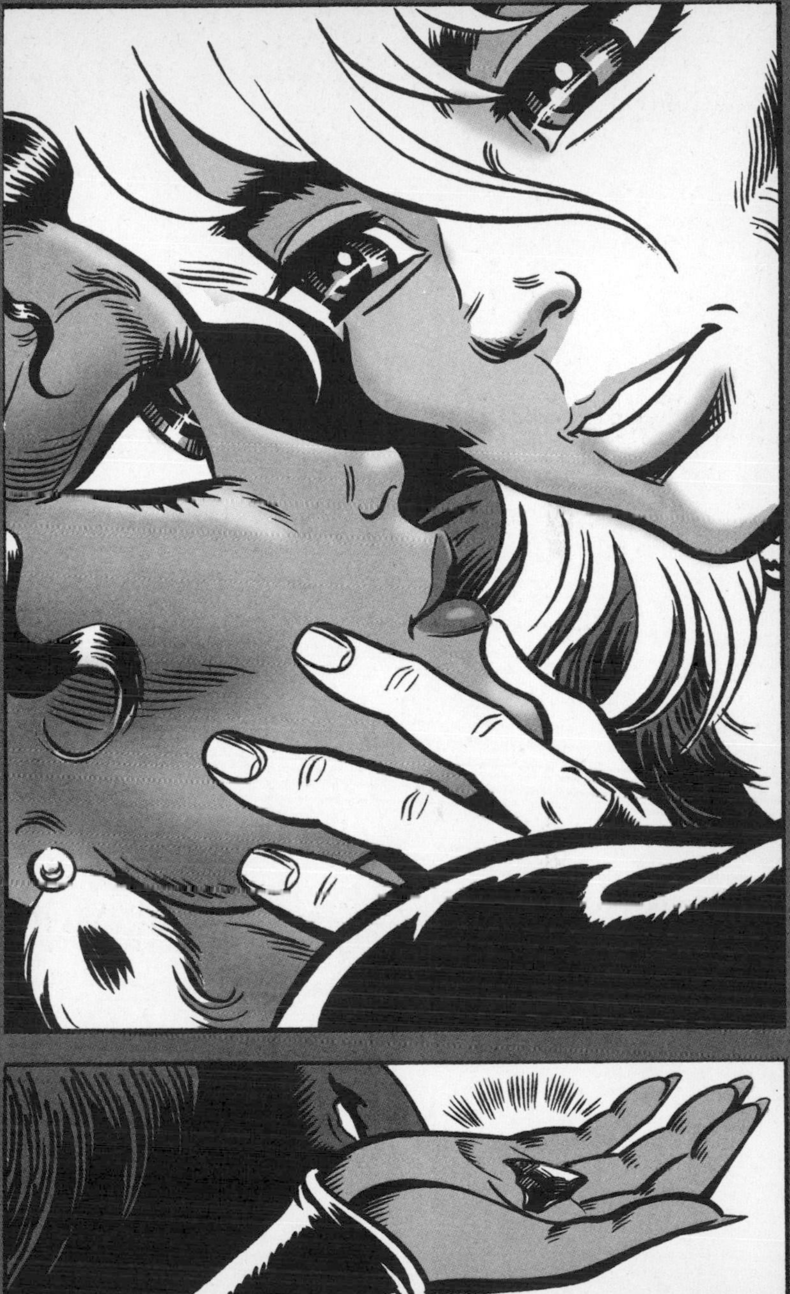

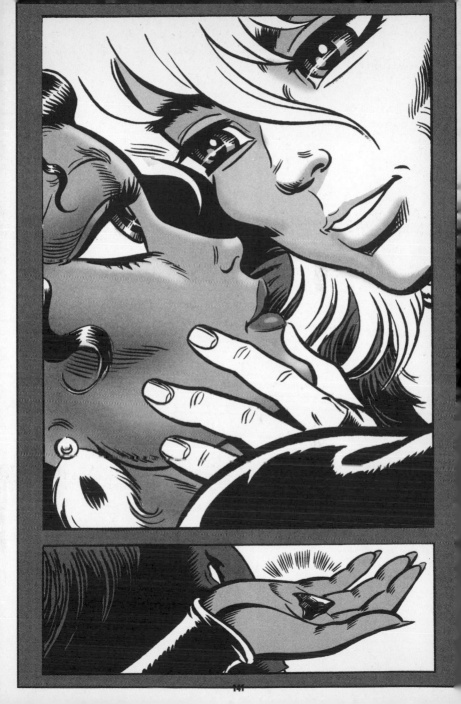

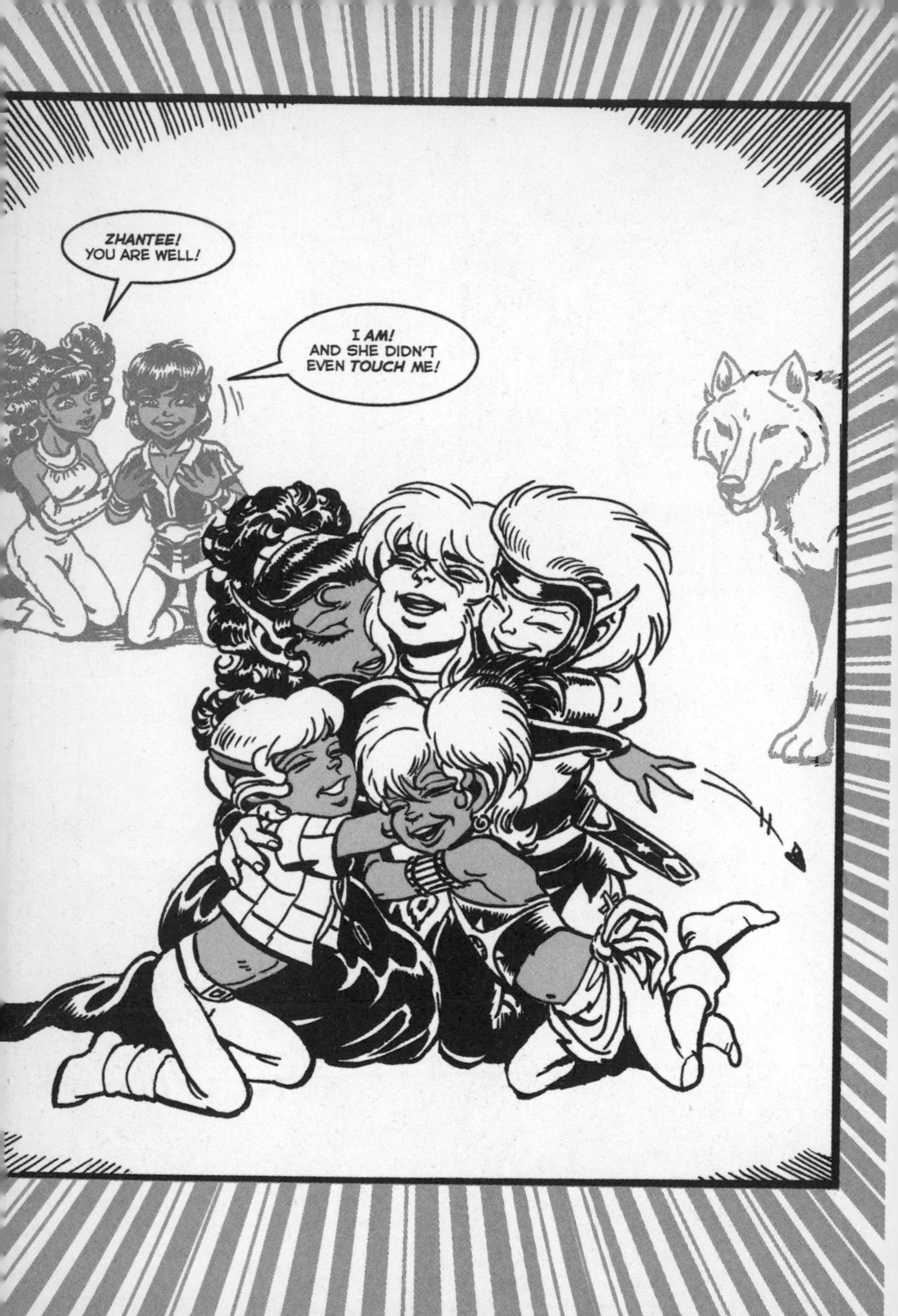
ZHANTEE! YOU ARE WELL!
I AM! AND SHE DIDN'T EVEN TOUCH ME!

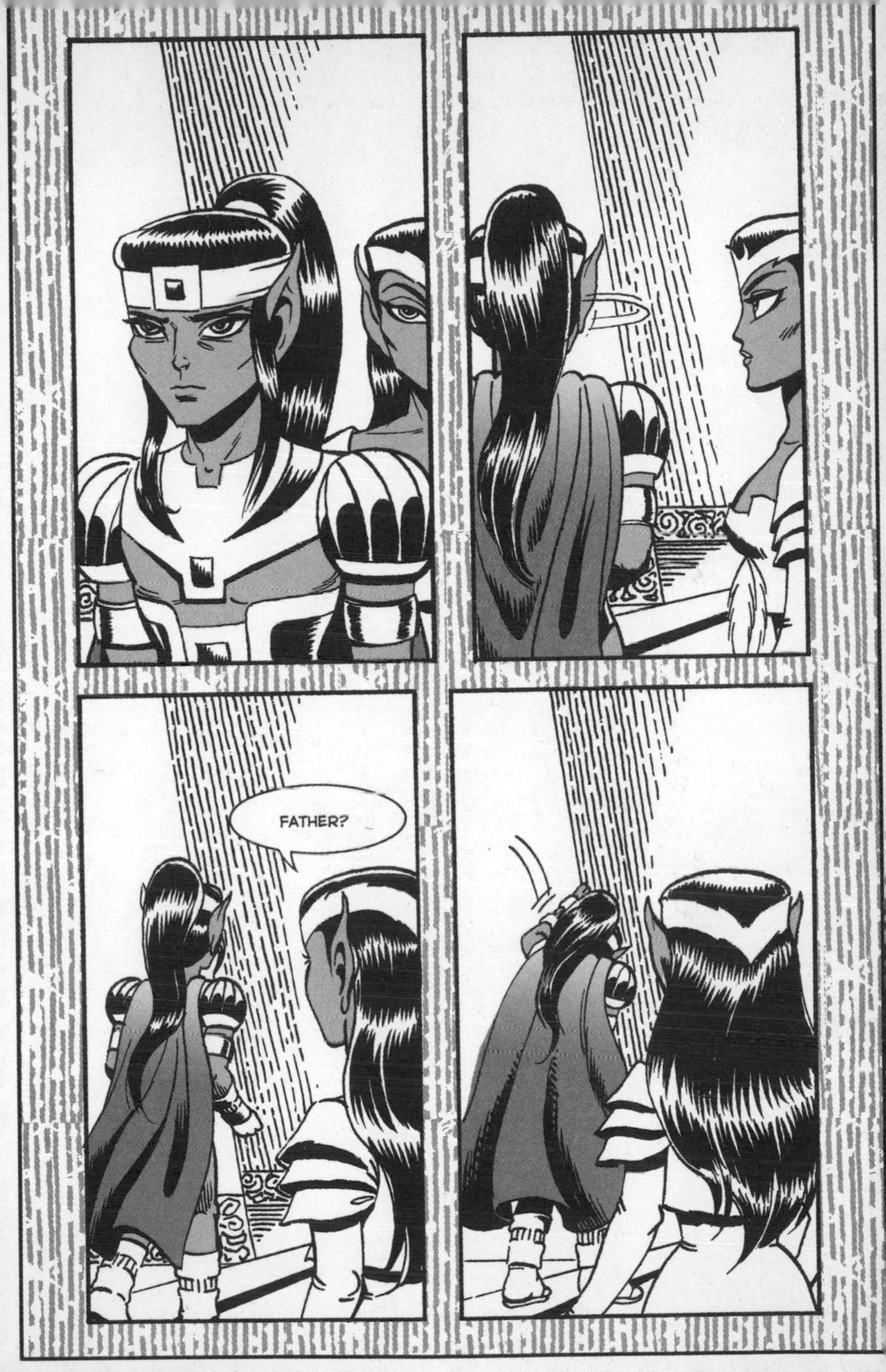
FATHER?

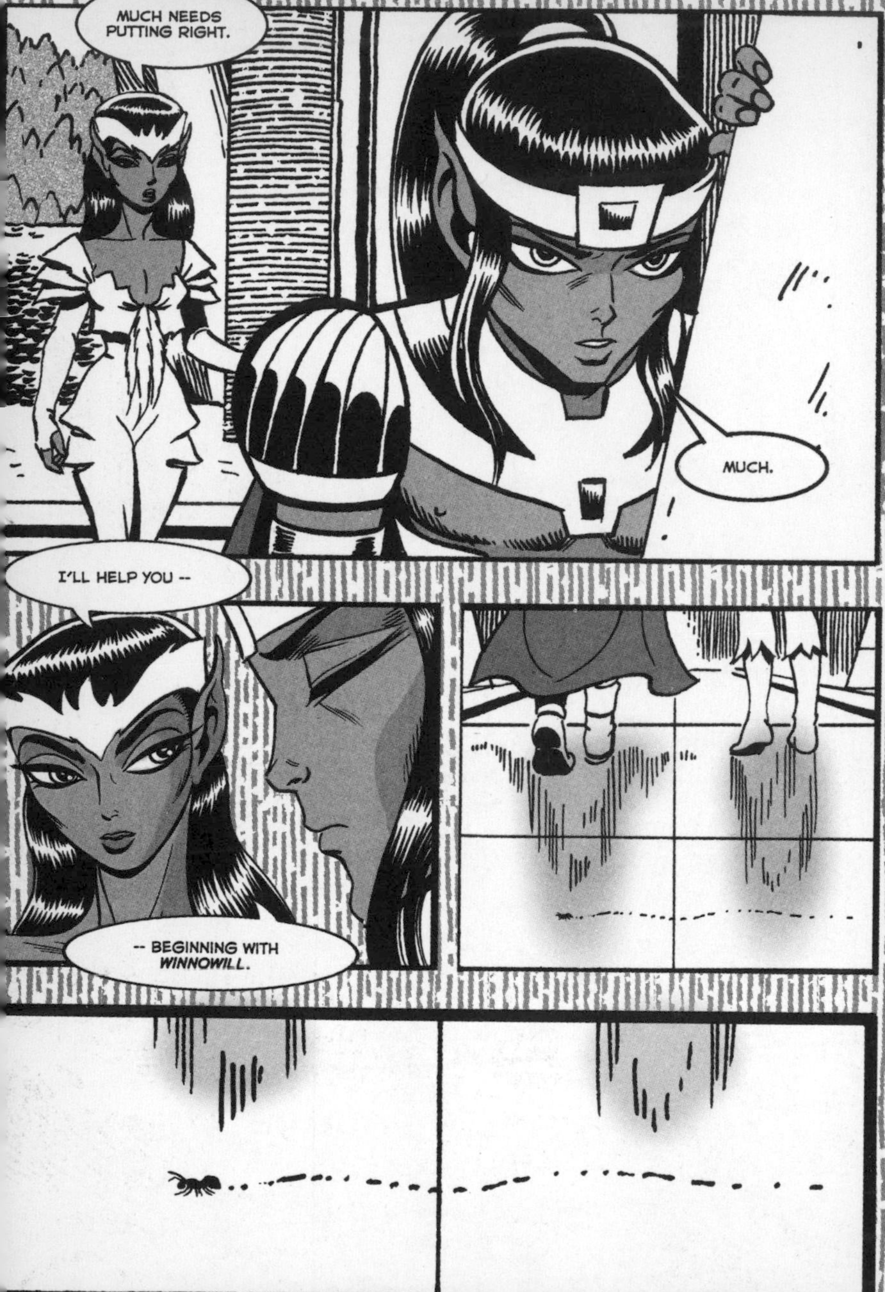
MUCH NEEDS PUTTING RIGHT.
MUCH.
I'LL HELP YOU --
-- BEGINNING WITH *WINNOWILL*.

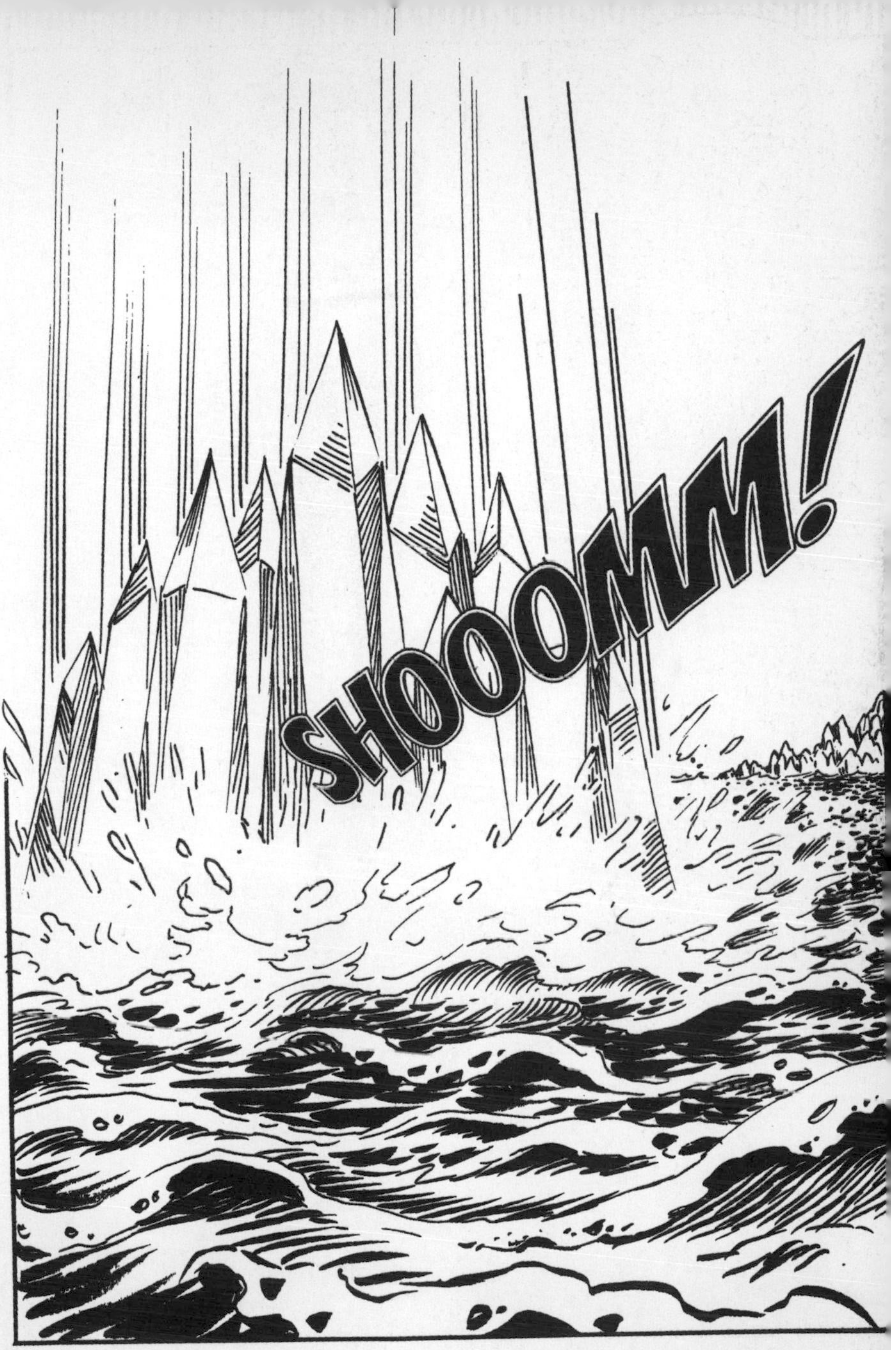
SHOOOOMM!

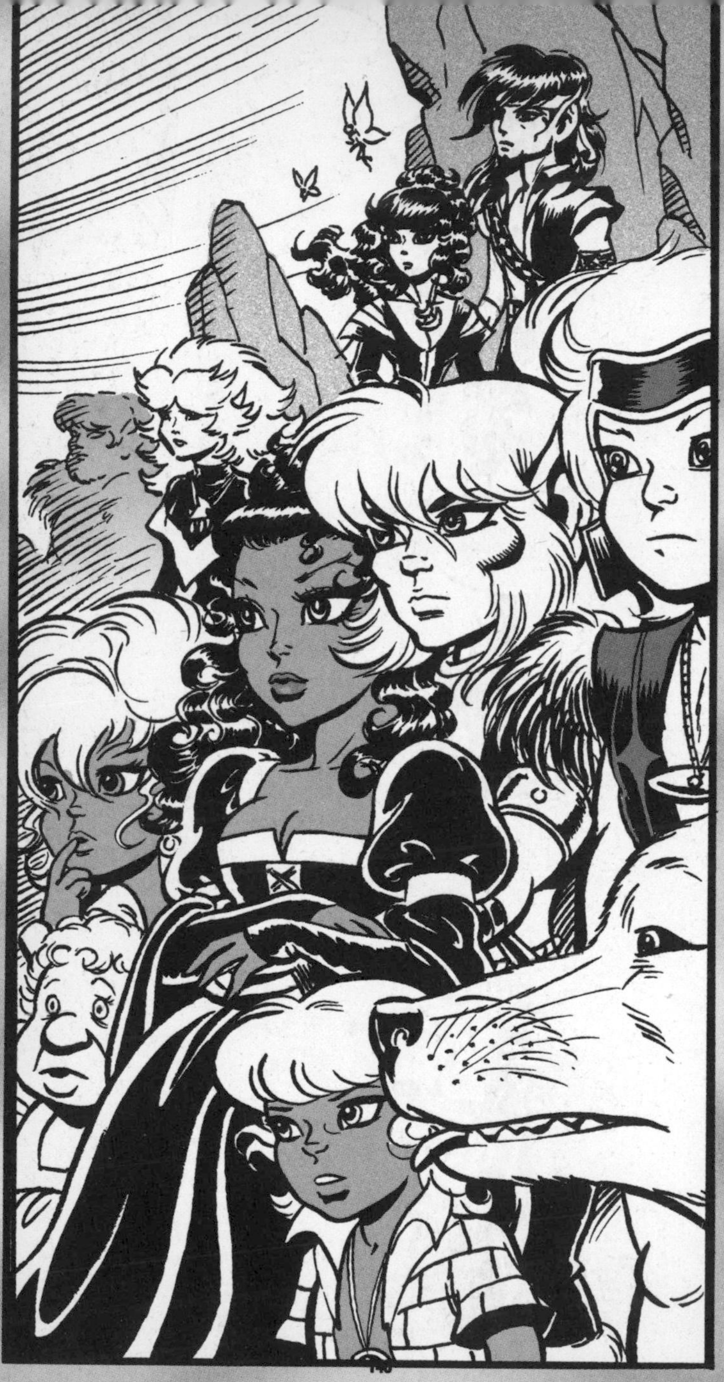

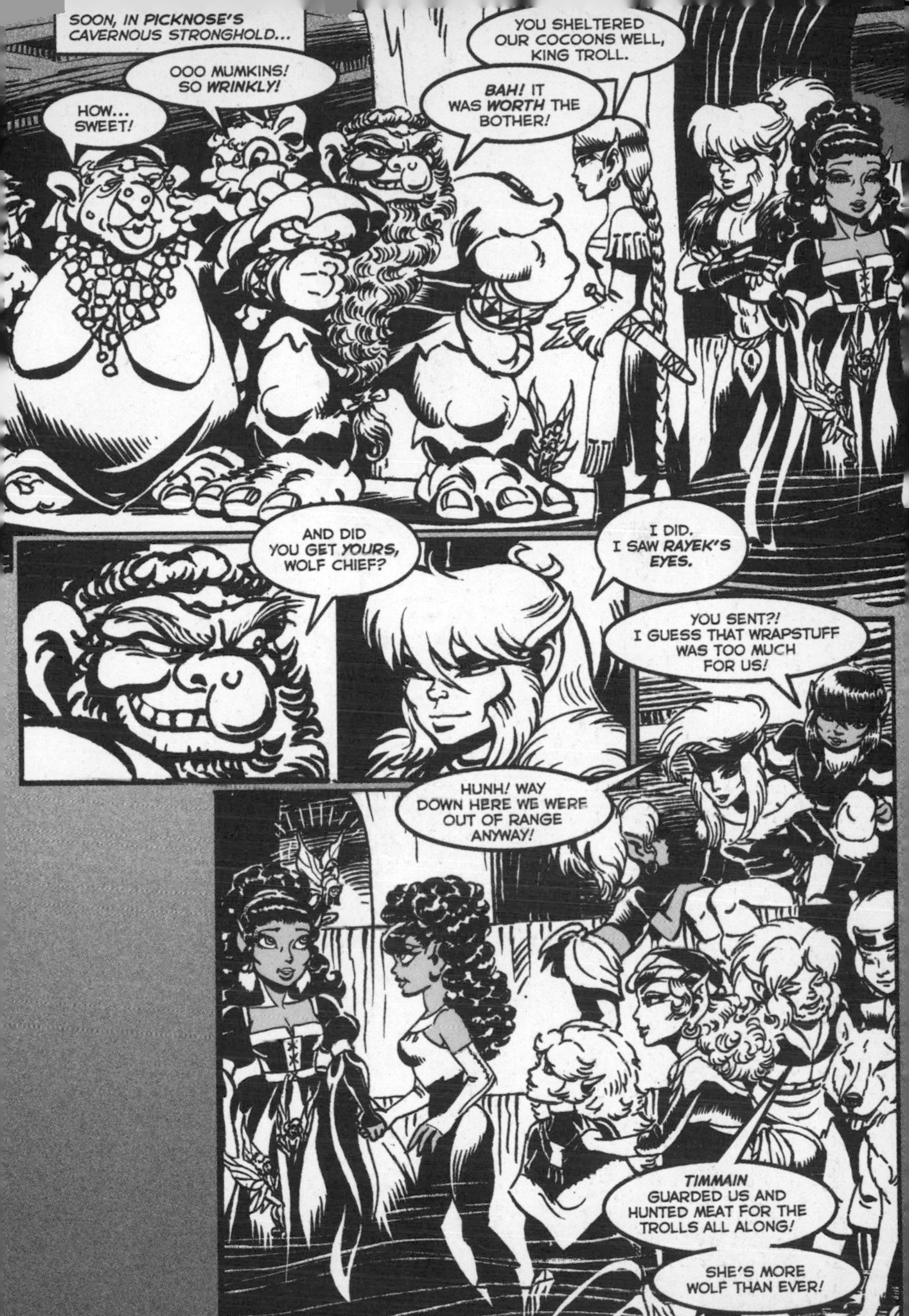
SOON, IN PICKNOSE'S CAVERNOUS STRONGHOLD...
YOU SHELTERED OUR COCOONS WELL, KING TROLL.
OOO MUMKINS! SO WRINKLY!
HOW... SWEET!
BAH! IT WAS WORTH THE BOTHER!
AND DID YOU GET YOURS, WOLF CHIEF?
I DID. I SAW RAYEK'S EYES.
YOU SENT?! I GUESS THAT WRAPSTUFF WAS TOO MUCH FOR US!
HUNH! WAY DOWN HERE WE WERE OUT OF RANGE ANYWAY!
TIMMAIN GUARDED US AND HUNTED MEAT FOR THE TROLLS ALL ALONG!
SHE'S MORE WOLF THAN EVER!

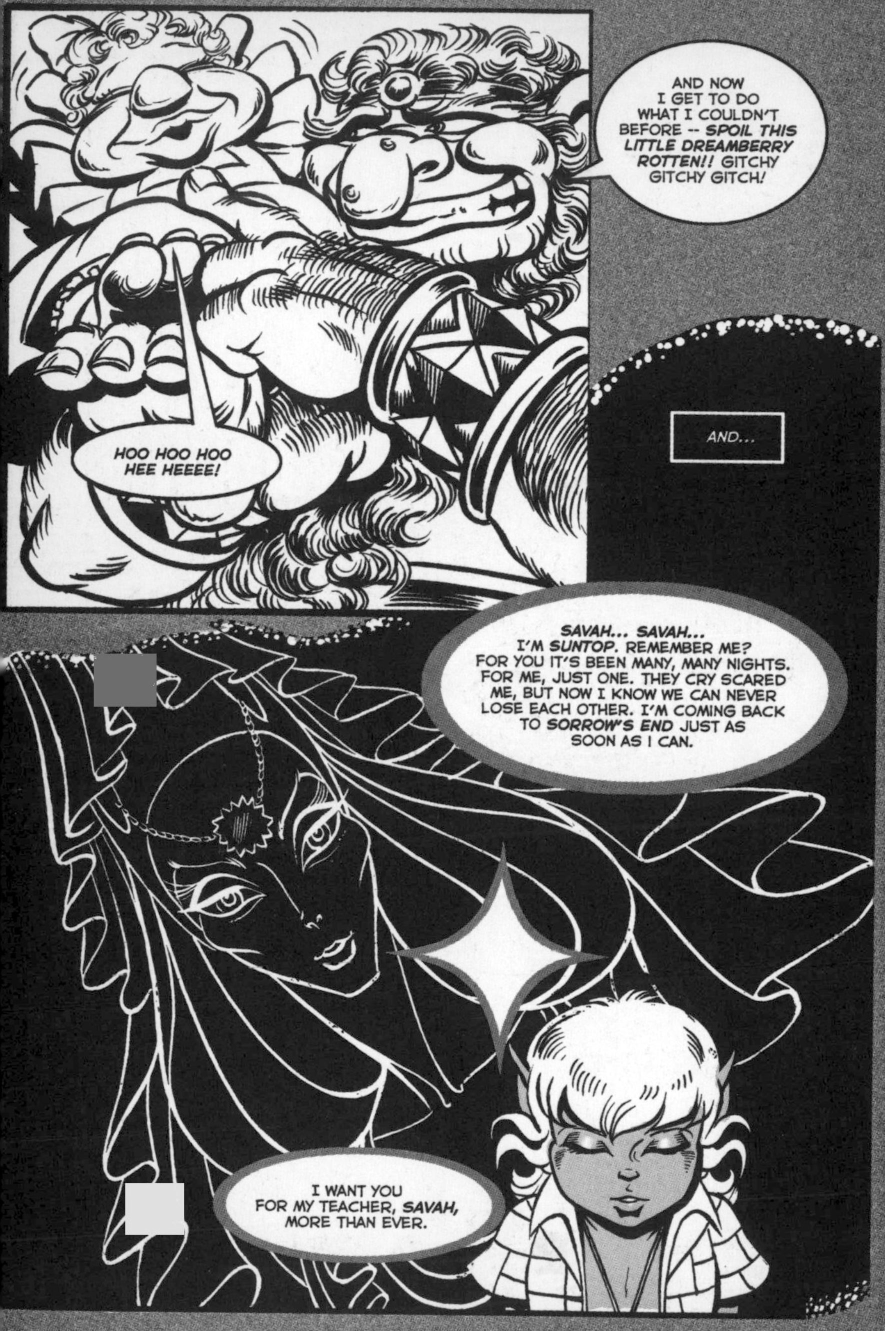
AND NOW I GET TO DO WHAT I COULDN'T BEFORE -- SPOIL THIS LITTLE DREAMBERRY ROTTEN!! GITCHY GITCHY GITCH!
HOO HOO HOO HEE HEEEE!
AND...
SAVAH... SAVAH... I'M SUNTOP. REMEMBER ME? FOR YOU IT'S BEEN MANY, MANY NIGHTS. FOR ME, JUST ONE. THEY CRY SCARED ME, BUT NOW I KNOW WE CAN NEVER LOSE EACH OTHER. I'M COMING BACK TO SORROW'S END JUST AS SOON AS I CAN.
I WANT YOU FOR MY TEACHER, SAVAH, MORE THAN EVER.

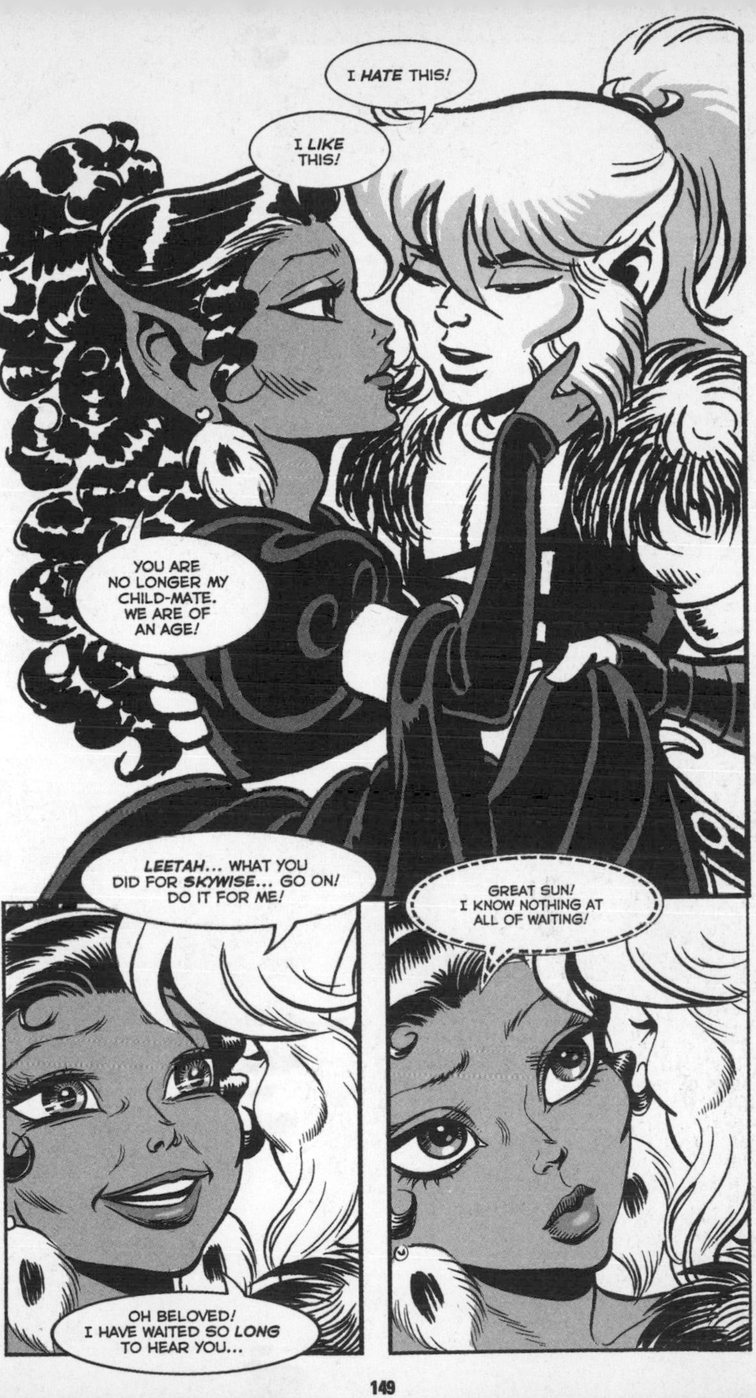
I HATE THIS!
I LIKE THIS!
YOU ARE NO LONGER MY CHILD-MATE. WE ARE OF AN AGE!
LEETAH... WHAT YOU DID FOR SKYWISE... GO ON! DO IT FOR ME!
GREAT SUN! I KNOW NOTHING AT ALL OF WAITING!
OH BELOVED! I HAVE WAITED SO LONG TO HEAR YOU...

"WHEN **SKYWISE** ASKED FOR TIME, IT WAS FROM HIS HEART. ONLY THE **TRIAL** YOU'VE ENDURED MAKES YOU SPEAK NOW. WHEN YOUR HEART IS CLEAR, ASK ME AGAIN."

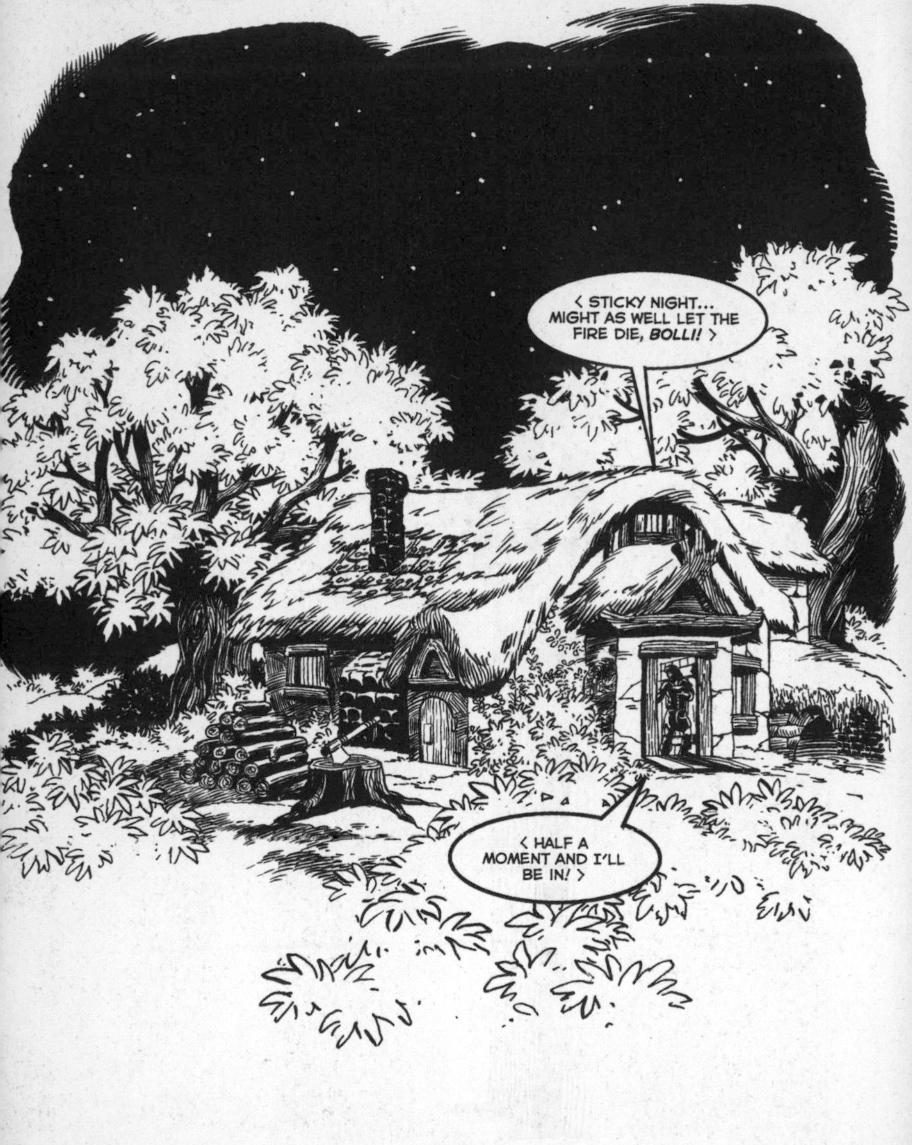

< STICKY NIGHT... MIGHT AS WELL LET THE FIRE DIE, BOLLI! >
< HALF A MOMENT AND I'LL BE IN! >

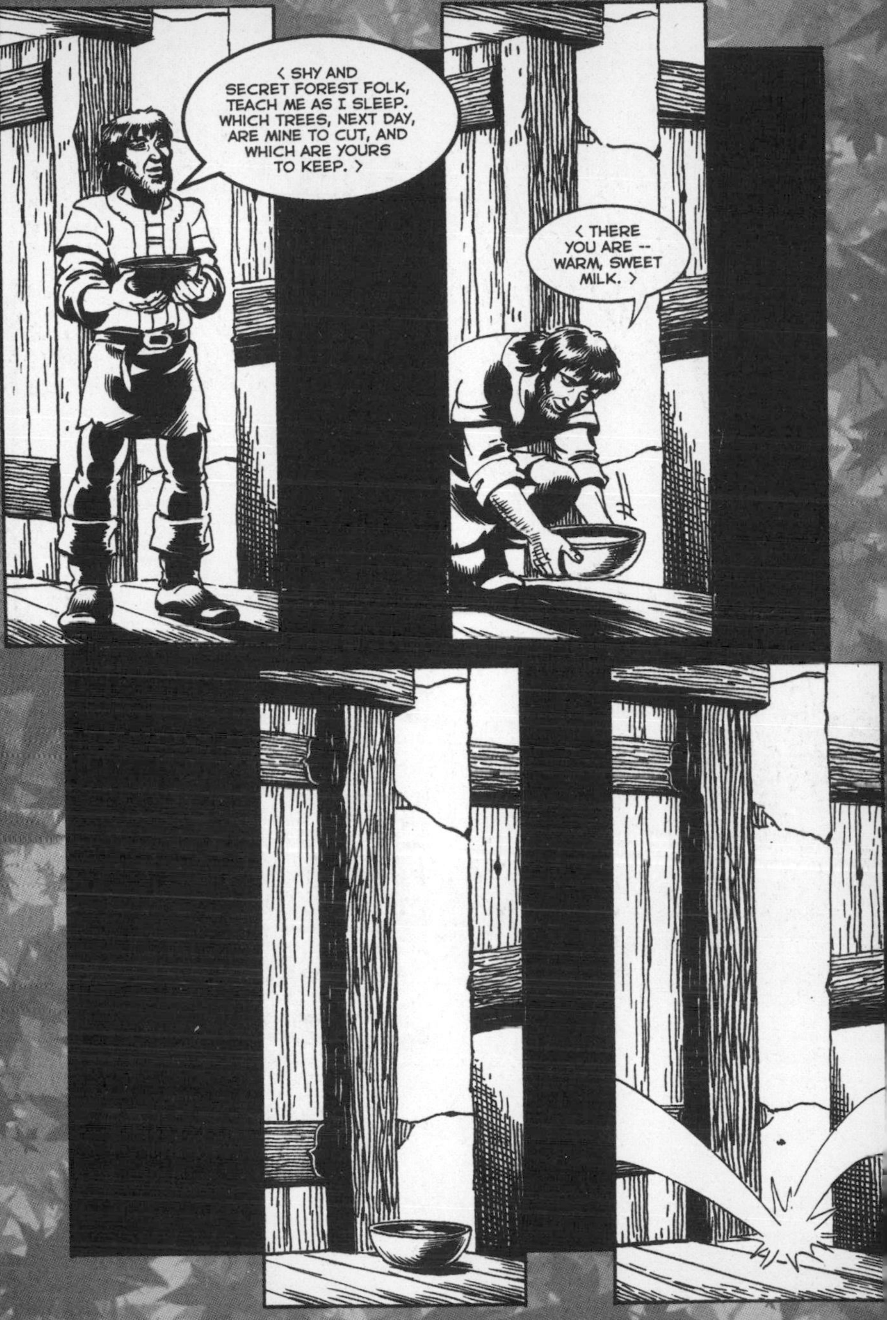
< SHY AND SECRET FOREST FOLK, TEACH ME AS I SLEEP. WHICH TREES, NEXT DAY, ARE MINE TO CUT, AND WHICH ARE YOURS TO KEEP. >
< THERE YOU ARE -- WARM, SWEET MILK. >

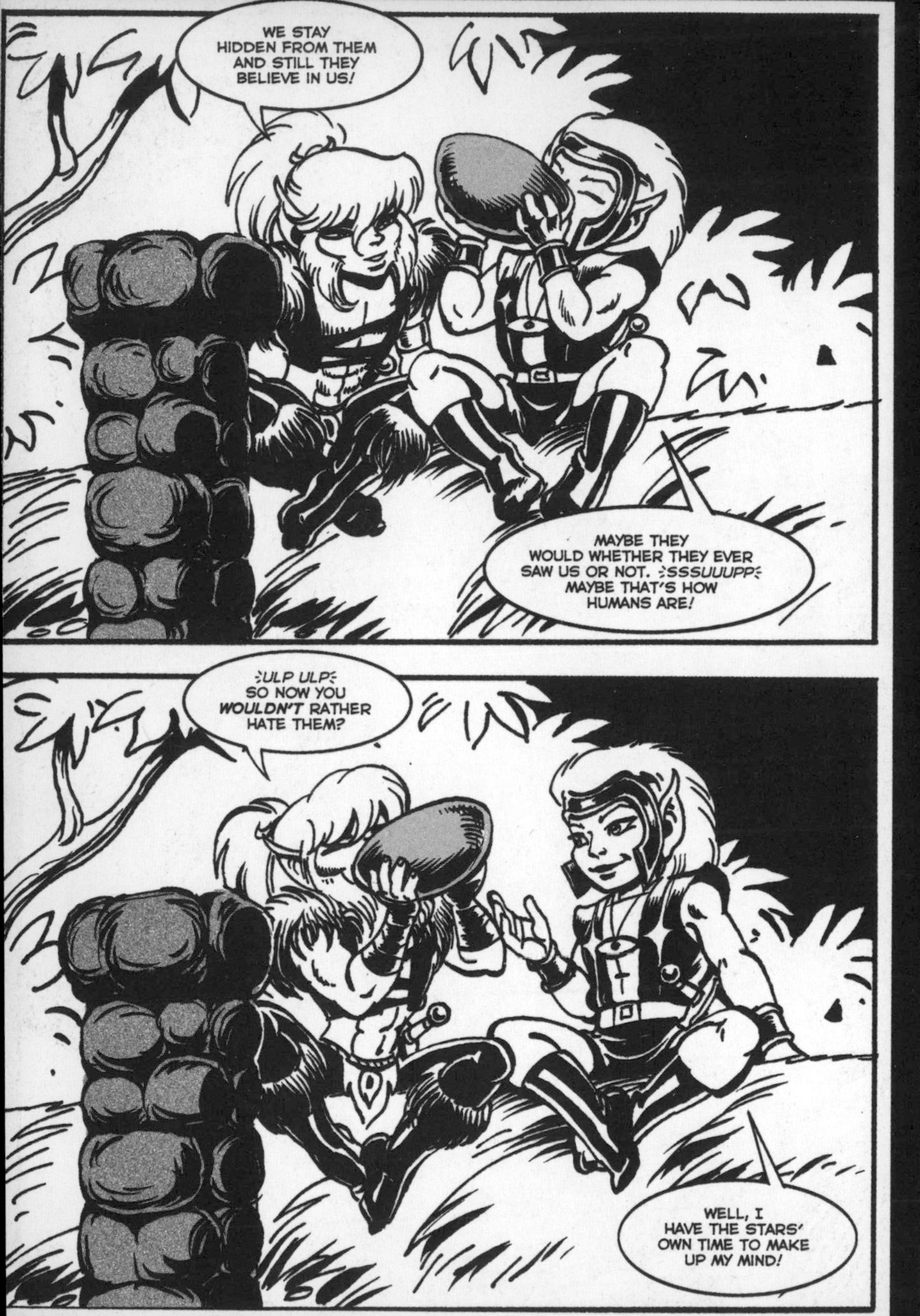
WE STAY HIDDEN FROM THEM AND STILL THEY BELIEVE IN US!
MAYBE THEY WOULD WHETHER THEY EVER SAW US OR NOT. *SSSUUUPP* MAYBE THAT'S HOW HUMANS ARE!
ULP ULP SO NOW YOU *WOULDN'T* RATHER HATE THEM?
WELL, I HAVE THE STARS' OWN TIME TO MAKE UP MY MIND!

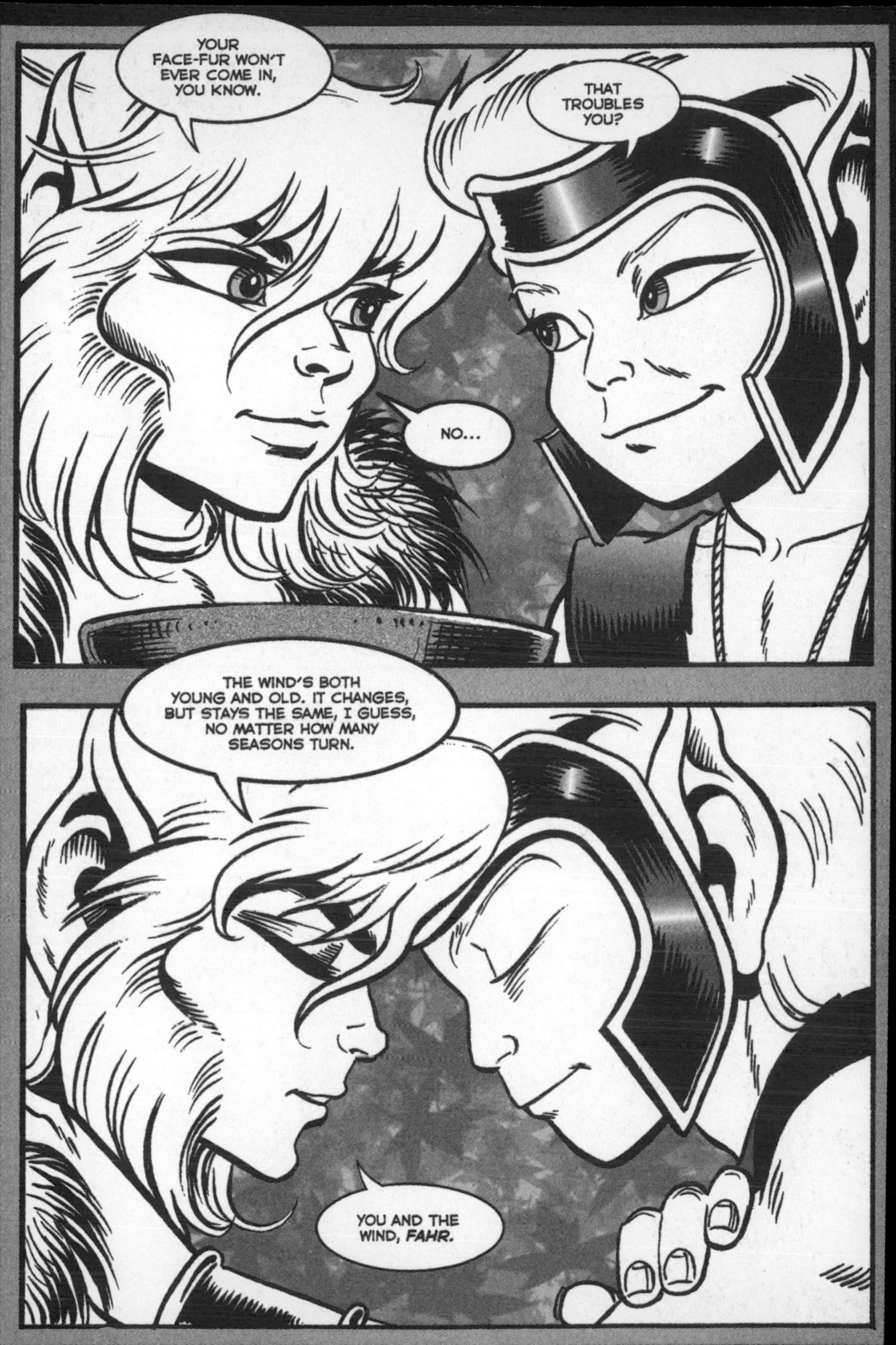
YOUR FACE-FUR WON'T EVER COME IN, YOU KNOW.
THAT TROUBLES YOU?
NO...
THE WIND'S BOTH YOUNG AND OLD. IT CHANGES, BUT STAYS THE SAME, I GUESS, NO MATTER HOW MANY SEASONS TURN.
YOU AND THE WIND, *FAHR.*

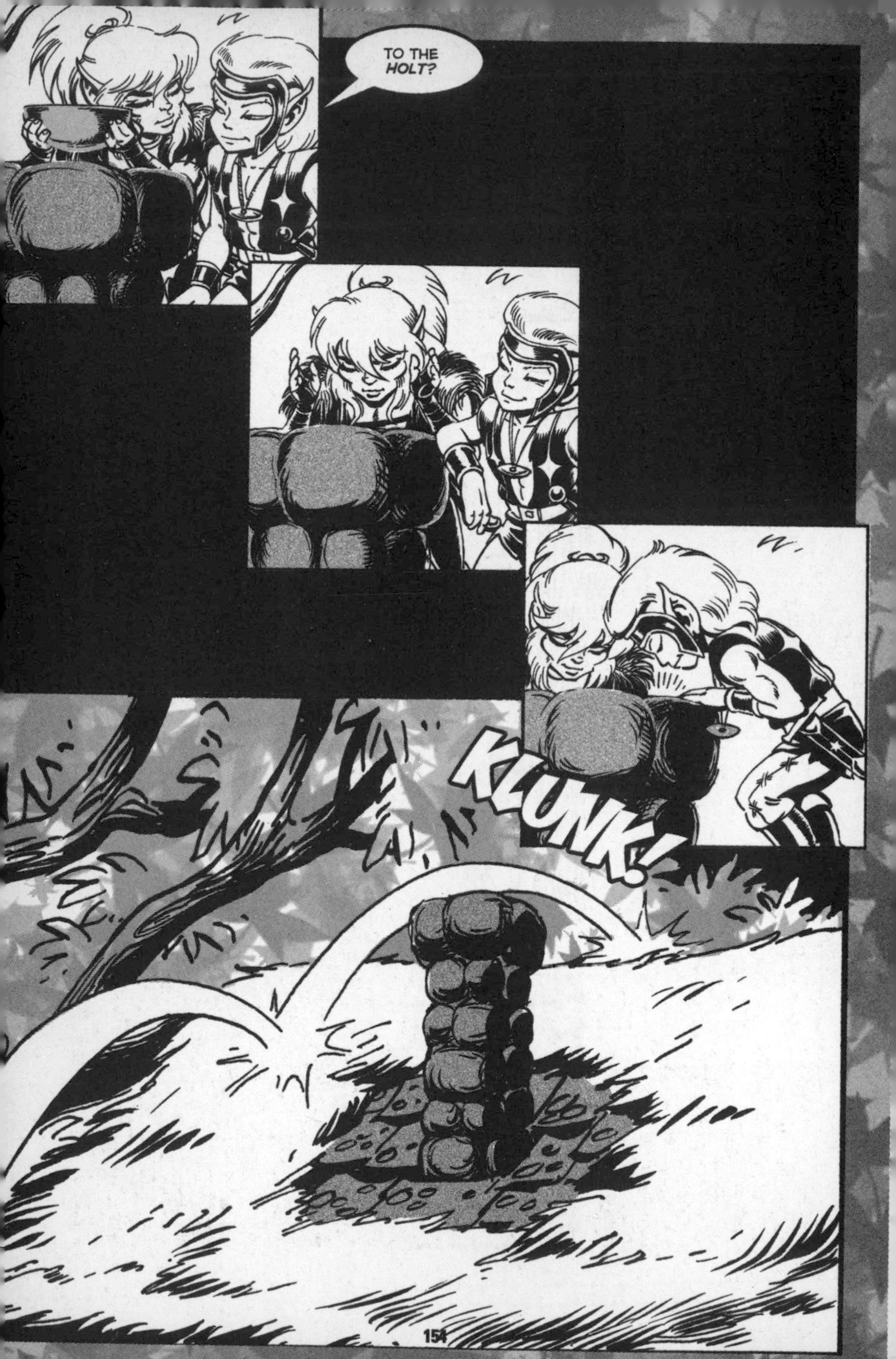
TO THE *HOLT?*
KLUNK!

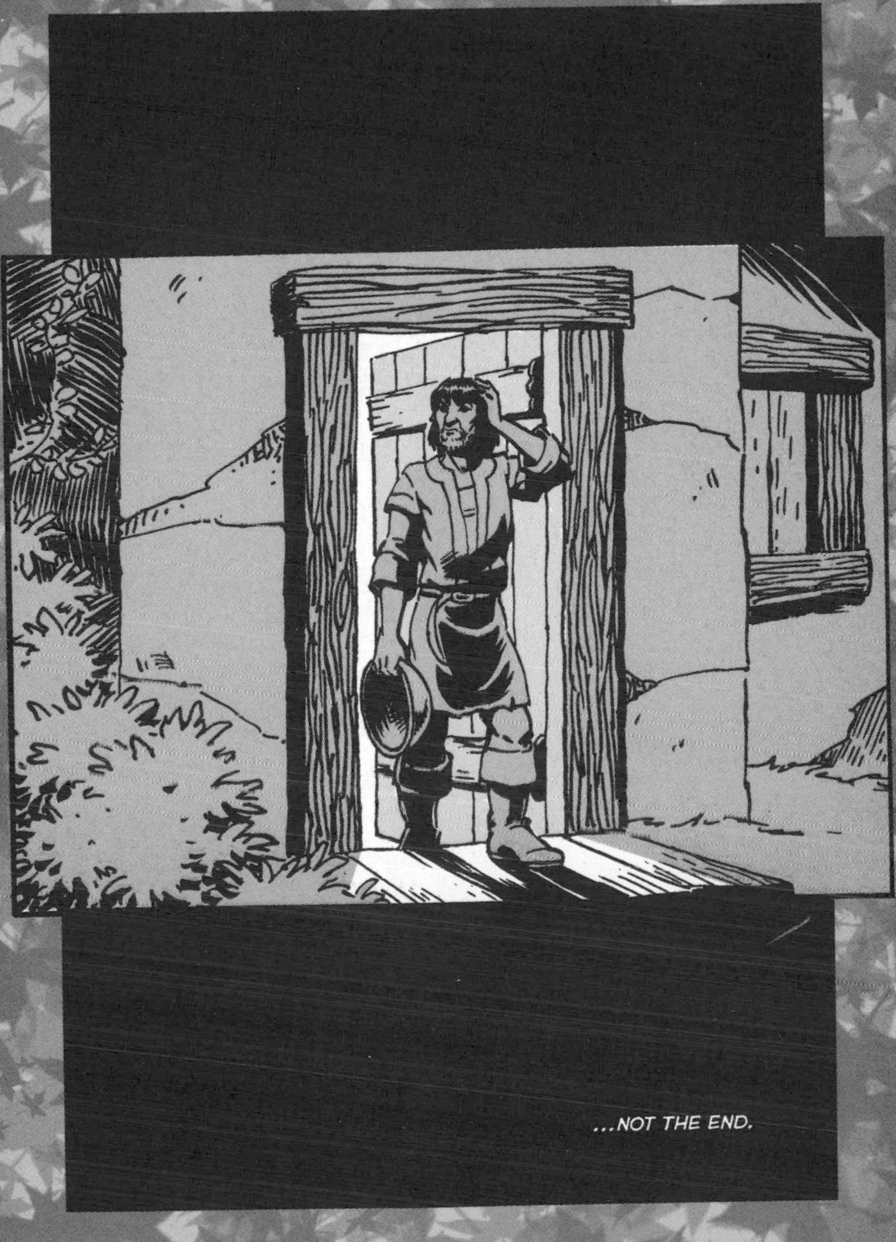
...NOT THE END.

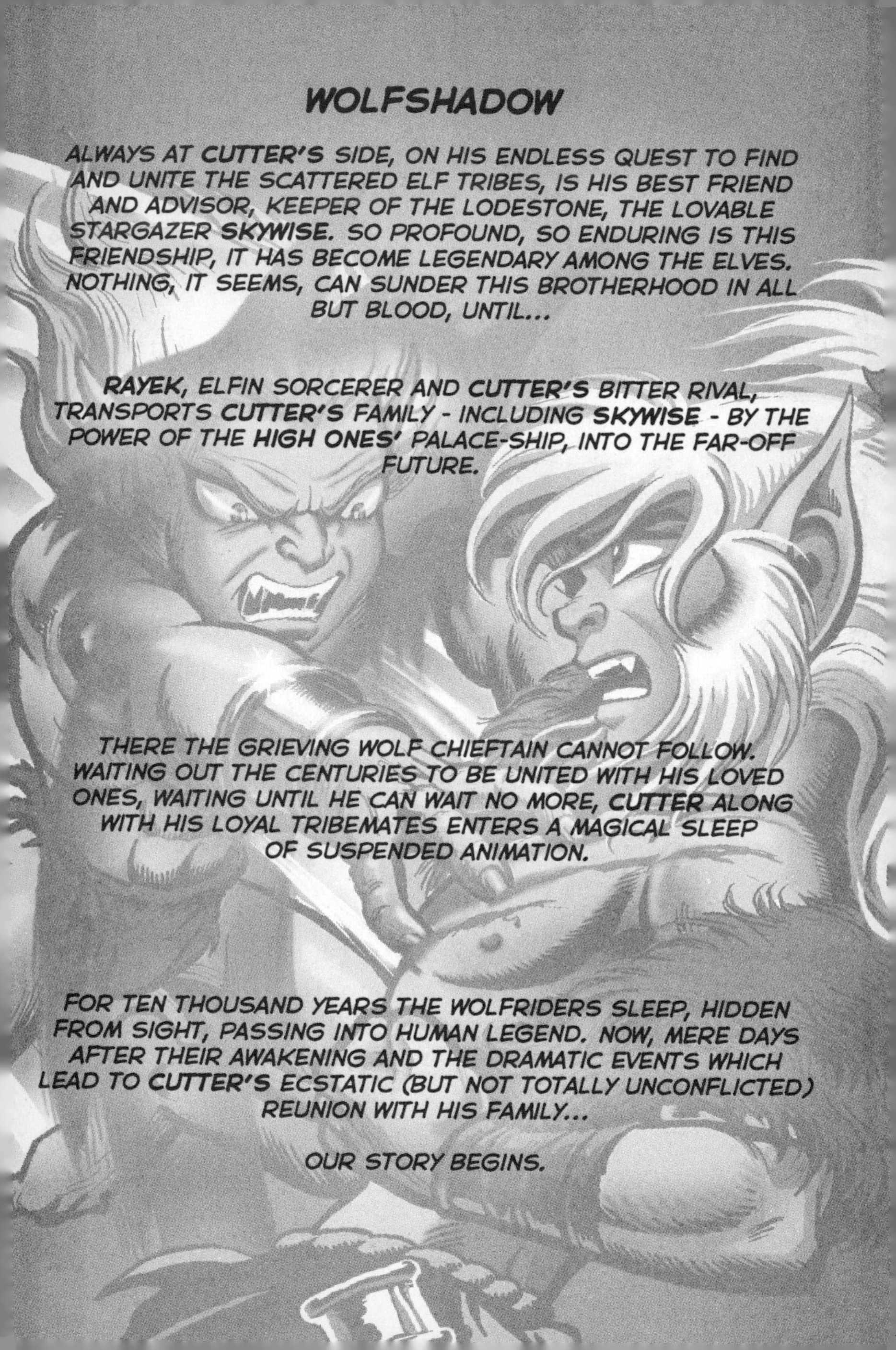

WOLFSHADOW

ALWAYS AT **CUTTER'S** SIDE, ON HIS ENDLESS QUEST TO FIND AND UNITE THE SCATTERED ELF TRIBES, IS HIS BEST FRIEND AND ADVISOR, KEEPER OF THE LODESTONE, THE LOVABLE STARGAZER **SKYWISE**. SO PROFOUND, SO ENDURING IS THIS FRIENDSHIP, IT HAS BECOME LEGENDARY AMONG THE ELVES. NOTHING, IT SEEMS, CAN SUNDER THIS BROTHERHOOD IN ALL BUT BLOOD, UNTIL...

RAYEK, ELFIN SORCERER AND **CUTTER'S** BITTER RIVAL, TRANSPORTS **CUTTER'S** FAMILY - INCLUDING **SKYWISE** - BY THE POWER OF THE **HIGH ONES'** PALACE-SHIP, INTO THE FAR-OFF FUTURE.

THERE THE GRIEVING WOLF CHIEFTAIN CANNOT FOLLOW. WAITING OUT THE CENTURIES TO BE UNITED WITH HIS LOVED ONES, WAITING UNTIL HE CAN WAIT NO MORE, **CUTTER** ALONG WITH HIS LOYAL TRIBEMATES ENTERS A MAGICAL SLEEP OF SUSPENDED ANIMATION.

FOR TEN THOUSAND YEARS THE WOLFRIDERS SLEEP, HIDDEN FROM SIGHT, PASSING INTO HUMAN LEGEND. NOW, MERE DAYS AFTER THEIR AWAKENING AND THE DRAMATIC EVENTS WHICH LEAD TO **CUTTER'S** ECSTATIC (BUT NOT TOTALLY UNCONFLICTED) REUNION WITH HIS FAMILY...

OUR STORY BEGINS.

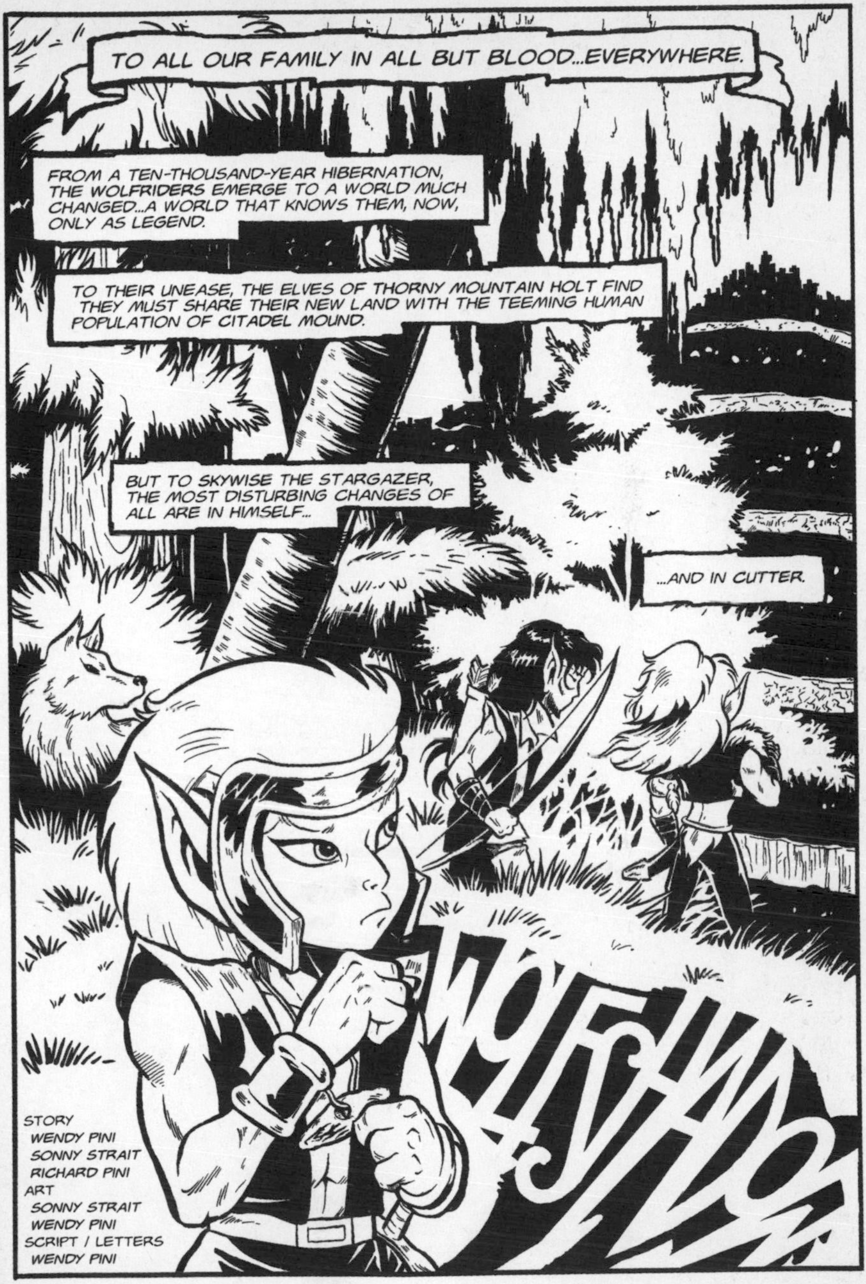
TO ALL OUR FAMILY IN ALL BUT BLOOD...EVERYWHERE.
FROM A TEN-THOUSAND-YEAR HIBERNATION, THE WOLFRIDERS EMERGE TO A WORLD MUCH CHANGED...A WORLD THAT KNOWS THEM, NOW, ONLY AS LEGEND.
TO THEIR UNEASE, THE ELVES OF THORNY MOUNTAIN HOLT FIND THEY MUST SHARE THEIR NEW LAND WITH THE TEEMING HUMAN POPULATION OF CITADEL MOUND.
BUT TO SKYWISE THE STARGAZER, THE MOST DISTURBING CHANGES OF ALL ARE IN HIMSELF...
...AND IN CUTTER.
STORY
WENDY PINI
SONNY STRAIT
RICHARD PINI
ART
SONNY STRAIT
WENDY PINI
SCRIPT / LETTERS
WENDY PINI

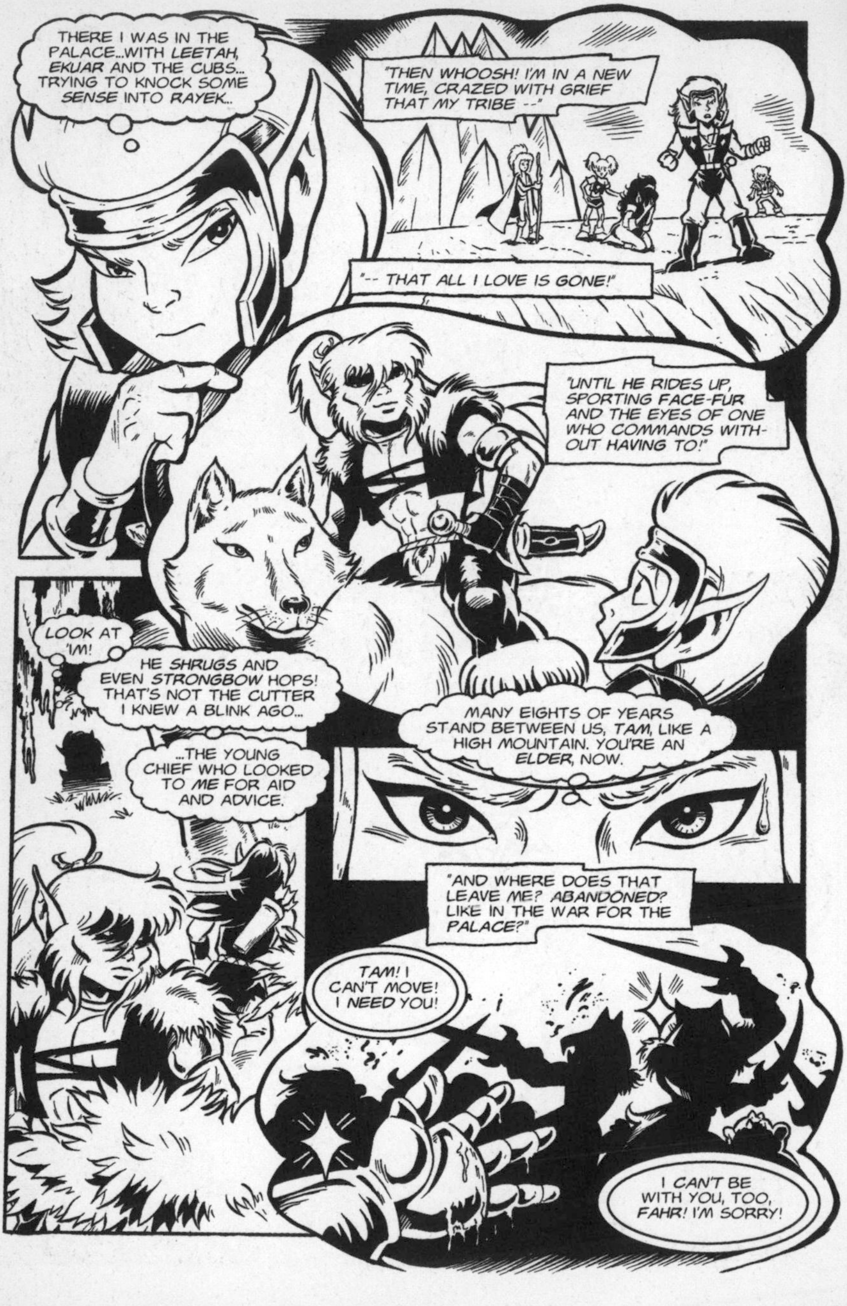

THERE I WAS IN THE PALACE...WITH LEETAH, EKUAR AND THE CUBS... TRYING TO KNOCK SOME SENSE INTO RAYEK...
"THEN WHOOSH! I'M IN A NEW TIME, CRAZED WITH GRIEF THAT MY TRIBE --"
"-- THAT ALL I LOVE IS GONE!"
"UNTIL HE RIDES UP, SPORTING FACE-FUR AND THE EYES OF ONE WHO COMMANDS WITH-OUT HAVING TO!"
LOOK AT 'IM!
HE SHRUGS AND EVEN STRONGBOW HOPS! THAT'S NOT THE CUTTER I KNEW A BLINK AGO...
...THE YOUNG CHIEF WHO LOOKED TO ME FOR AID AND ADVICE.
MANY EIGHTS OF YEARS STAND BETWEEN US, TAM, LIKE A HIGH MOUNTAIN. YOU'RE AN ELDER, NOW.
"AND WHERE DOES THAT LEAVE ME? ABANDONED? LIKE IN THE WAR FOR THE PALACE?"
TAM! I CAN'T MOVE! I NEED YOU!
I CAN'T BE WITH YOU, TOO, FAHR! I'M SORRY!

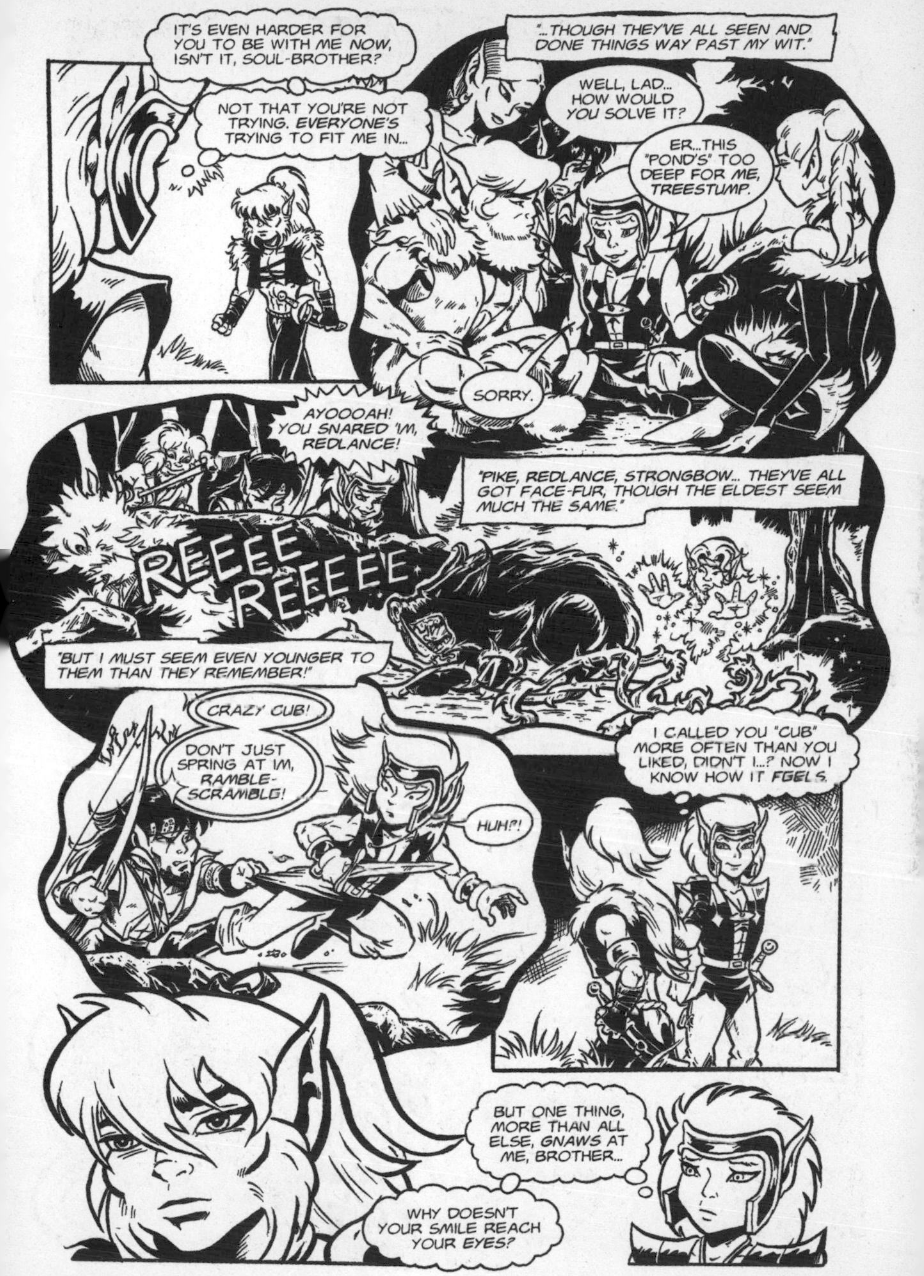
IT'S EVEN HARDER FOR YOU TO BE WITH ME NOW, ISN'T IT, SOUL-BROTHER?
NOT THAT YOU'RE NOT TRYING. EVERYONE'S TRYING TO FIT ME IN...
"...THOUGH THEY'VE ALL SEEN AND DONE THINGS WAY PAST MY WIT."
WELL, LAD... HOW WOULD YOU SOLVE IT?
ER...THIS "POND'S" TOO DEEP FOR ME, TREESTUMP.
SORRY.
AYOOOAH! YOU SNARED 'IM, REDLANCE!
"PIKE, REDLANCE, STRONGBOW... THEY'VE ALL GOT FACE-FUR, THOUGH THE ELDEST SEEM MUCH THE SAME."
REEEE REEEEEE
"BUT I MUST SEEM EVEN YOUNGER TO THEM THAN THEY REMEMBER!"
CRAZY CUB!
DON'T JUST SPRING AT 'IM, RAMBLE-SCRAMBLE!
HUH?!
I CALLED YOU "CUB" MORE OFTEN THAN YOU LIKED, DIDN'T I...? NOW I KNOW HOW IT FEELS.
BUT ONE THING, MORE THAN ALL ELSE, GNAWS AT ME, BROTHER...
WHY DOESN'T YOUR SMILE REACH YOUR EYES?

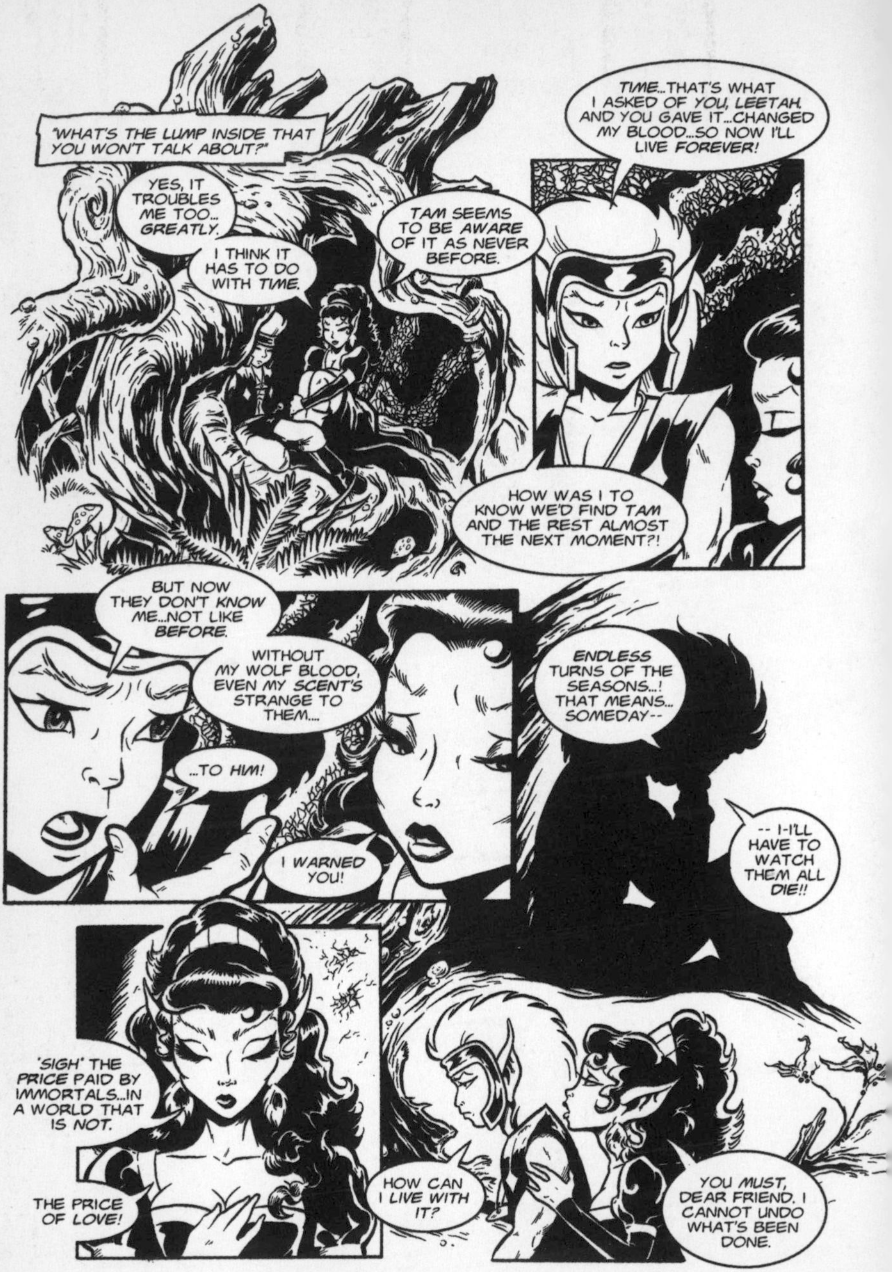
"WHAT'S THE LUMP INSIDE THAT YOU WON'T TALK ABOUT?"
YES, IT TROUBLES ME TOO... GREATLY.
I THINK IT HAS TO DO WITH TIME.
TAM SEEMS TO BE AWARE OF IT AS NEVER BEFORE.
TIME...THAT'S WHAT I ASKED OF YOU, LEETAH. AND YOU GAVE IT...CHANGED MY BLOOD...SO NOW I'LL LIVE FOREVER!
HOW WAS I TO KNOW WE'D FIND TAM AND THE REST ALMOST THE NEXT MOMENT?!
BUT NOW THEY DON'T KNOW ME...NOT LIKE BEFORE.
WITHOUT MY WOLF BLOOD, EVEN MY SCENT'S STRANGE TO THEM....
...TO HIM!
I WARNED YOU!
ENDLESS TURNS OF THE SEASONS...! THAT MEANS... SOMEDAY--
-- I-I'LL HAVE TO WATCH THEM ALL DIE!!
'SIGH' THE PRICE PAID BY IMMORTALS...IN A WORLD THAT IS NOT.
THE PRICE OF LOVE!
HOW CAN I LIVE WITH IT?
YOU MUST, DEAR FRIEND. I CANNOT UNDO WHAT'S BEEN DONE.

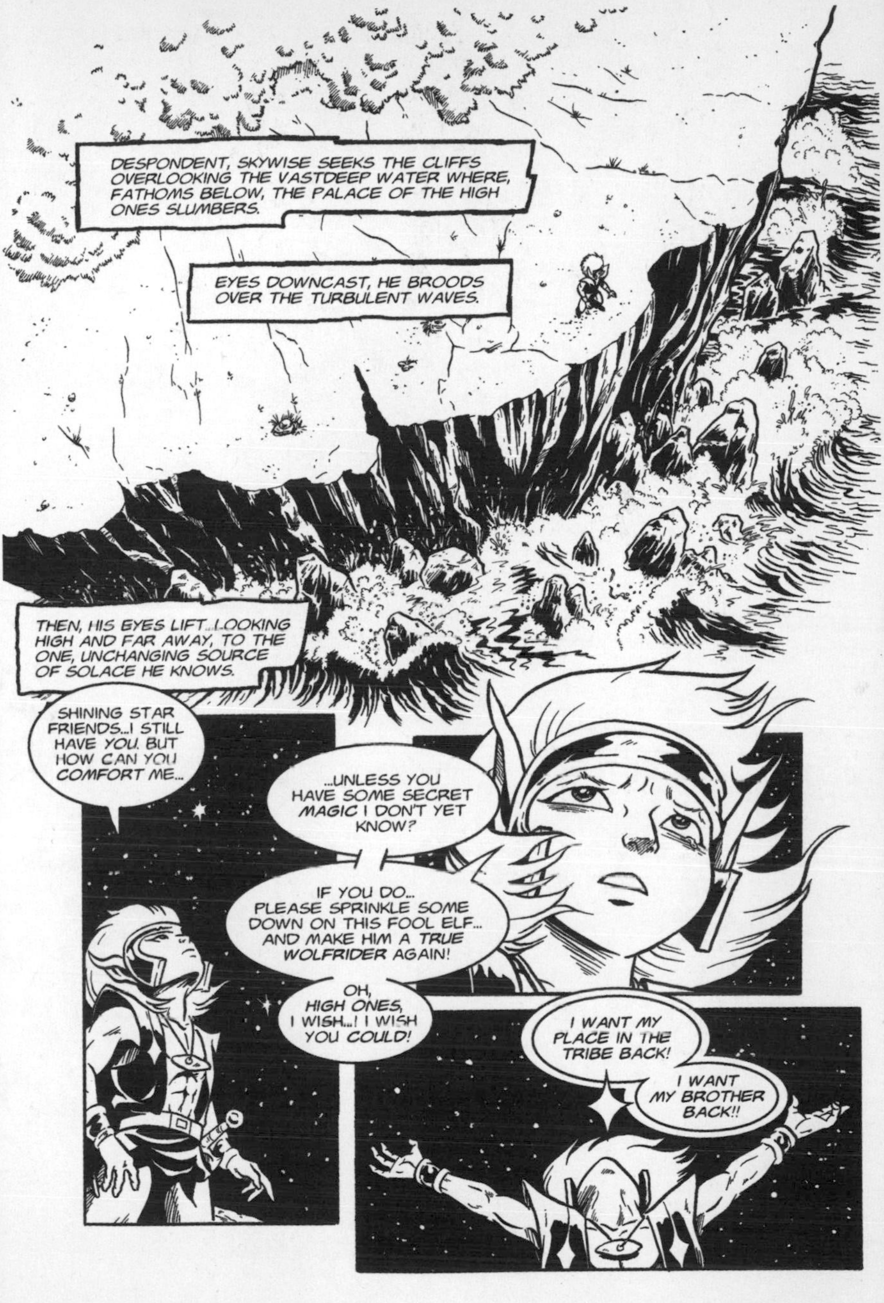

DESPONDENT, SKYWISE SEEKS THE CLIFFS OVERLOOKING THE VASTDEEP WATER WHERE, FATHOMS BELOW, THE PALACE OF THE HIGH ONES SLUMBERS.
EYES DOWNCAST, HE BROODS OVER THE TURBULENT WAVES.
THEN, HIS EYES LIFT...LOOKING HIGH AND FAR AWAY, TO THE ONE, UNCHANGING SOURCE OF SOLACE HE KNOWS.
SHINING STAR FRIENDS...I STILL HAVE YOU. BUT HOW CAN YOU COMFORT ME...
...UNLESS YOU HAVE SOME SECRET MAGIC I DON'T YET KNOW?
IF YOU DO... PLEASE SPRINKLE SOME DOWN ON THIS FOOL ELF... AND MAKE HIM A TRUE WOLFRIDER AGAIN!
OH, HIGH ONES, I WISH...! I WISH YOU COULD!
I WANT MY PLACE IN THE TRIBE BACK!
I WANT MY BROTHER BACK!!

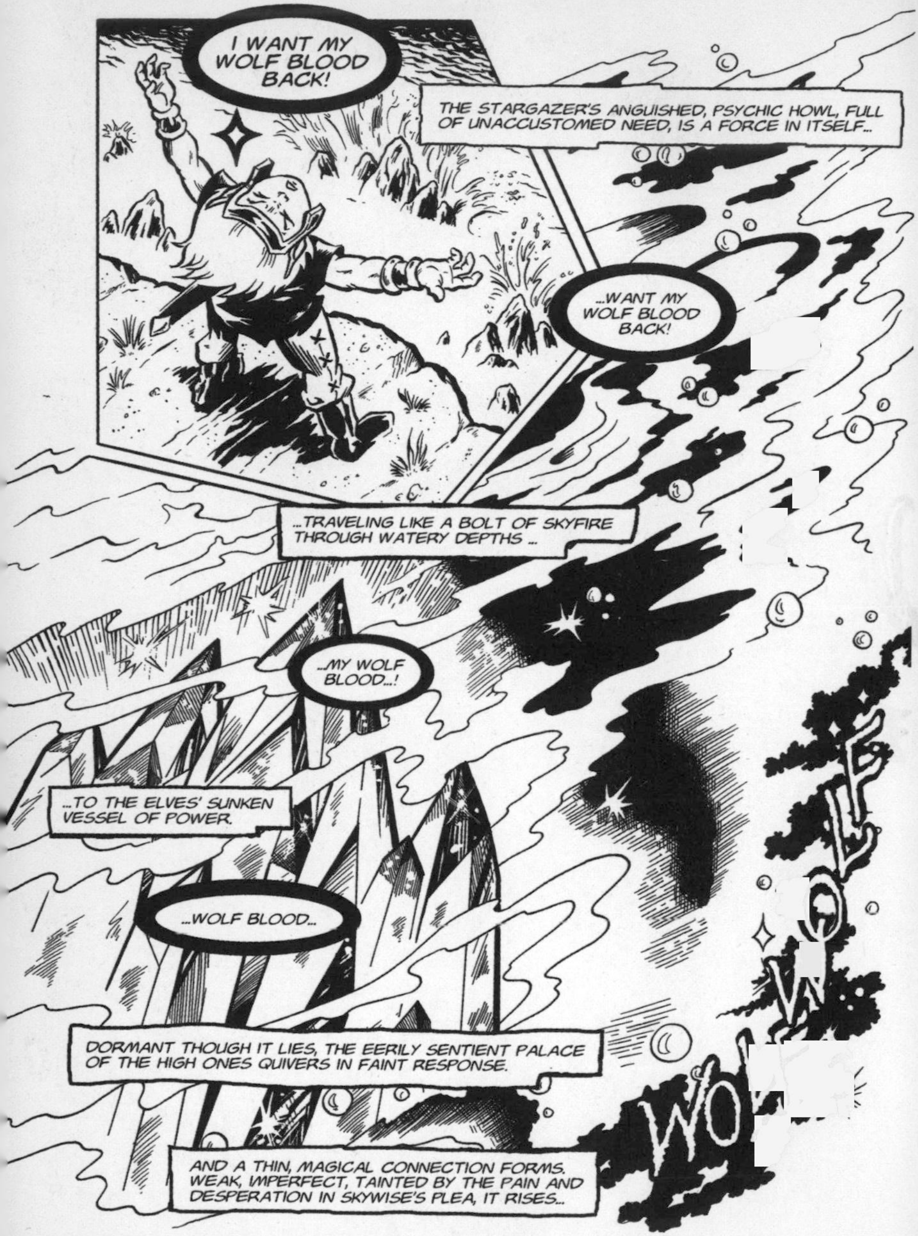
I WANT MY WOLF BLOOD BACK!
THE STARGAZER'S ANGUISHED, PSYCHIC HOWL, FULL OF UNACCUSTOMED NEED, IS A FORCE IN ITSELF...
...WANT MY WOLF BLOOD BACK!
...TRAVELING LIKE A BOLT OF SKYFIRE THROUGH WATERY DEPTHS ...
...MY WOLF BLOOD...!
...TO THE ELVES' SUNKEN VESSEL OF POWER.
...WOLF BLOOD...
DORMANT THOUGH IT LIES, THE EERILY SENTIENT PALACE OF THE HIGH ONES QUIVERS IN FAINT RESPONSE.
AND A THIN, MAGICAL CONNECTION FORMS. WEAK, IMPERFECT, TAINTED BY THE PAIN AND DESPERATION IN SKYWISE'S PLEA, IT RISES...

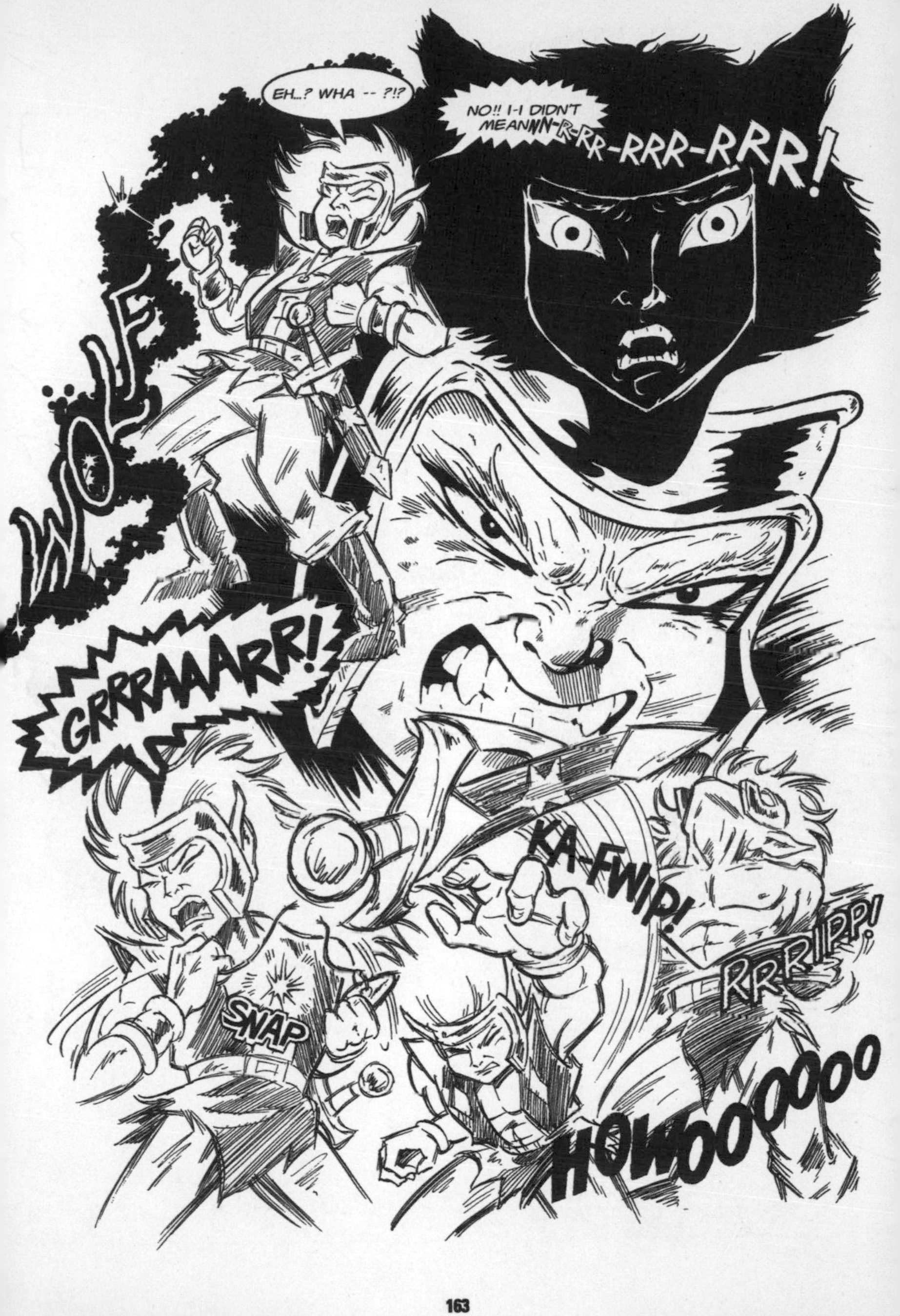
EH..? WHA -- ?!?
NO!! I-I DIDN'T MEANNN-R-RR-RRR-RRR!
WOLF
GRRRAAARR!
KA-FWIP!
RRRIPP!
SNAP
HOWOOOOOOO

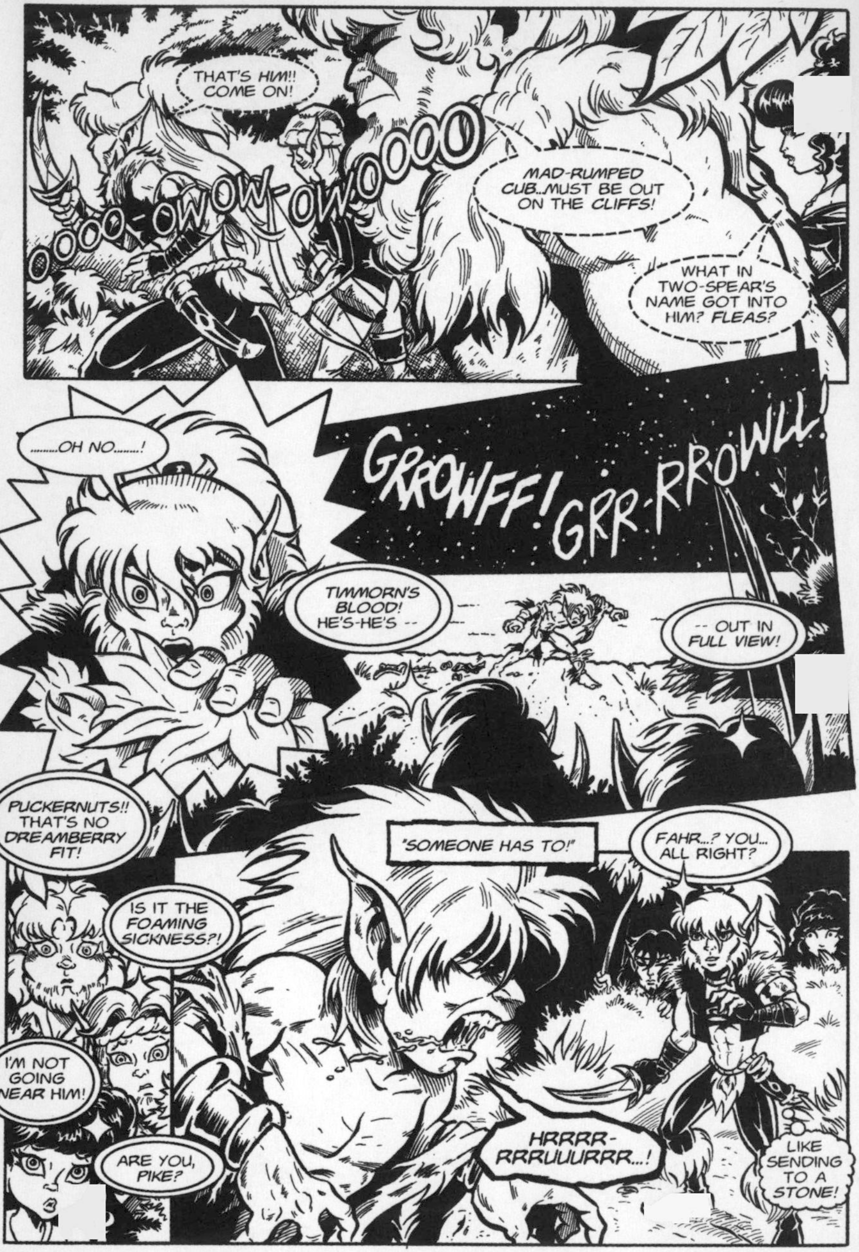
THAT'S HIM!! COME ON!
OOOO-OWOW-OW-OWOOOO
MAD-RUMPED CUB..MUST BE OUT ON THE CLIFFS!
WHAT IN TWO-SPEAR'S NAME GOT INTO HIM? FLEAS?
........OH NO........!
GRROWFF! GRR-RROWLL!
TIMMORN'S BLOOD! HE'S-HE'S --
-- OUT IN FULL VIEW!
PUCKERNUTS!! THAT'S NO DREAMBERRY FIT!
"SOMEONE HAS TO!"
FAHR...? YOU... ALL RIGHT?
IS IT THE FOAMING SICKNESS?!
I'M NOT GOING NEAR HIM!
ARE YOU, PIKE?
HRRRR-RRRUUURRR...!
LIKE SENDING TO A STONE!

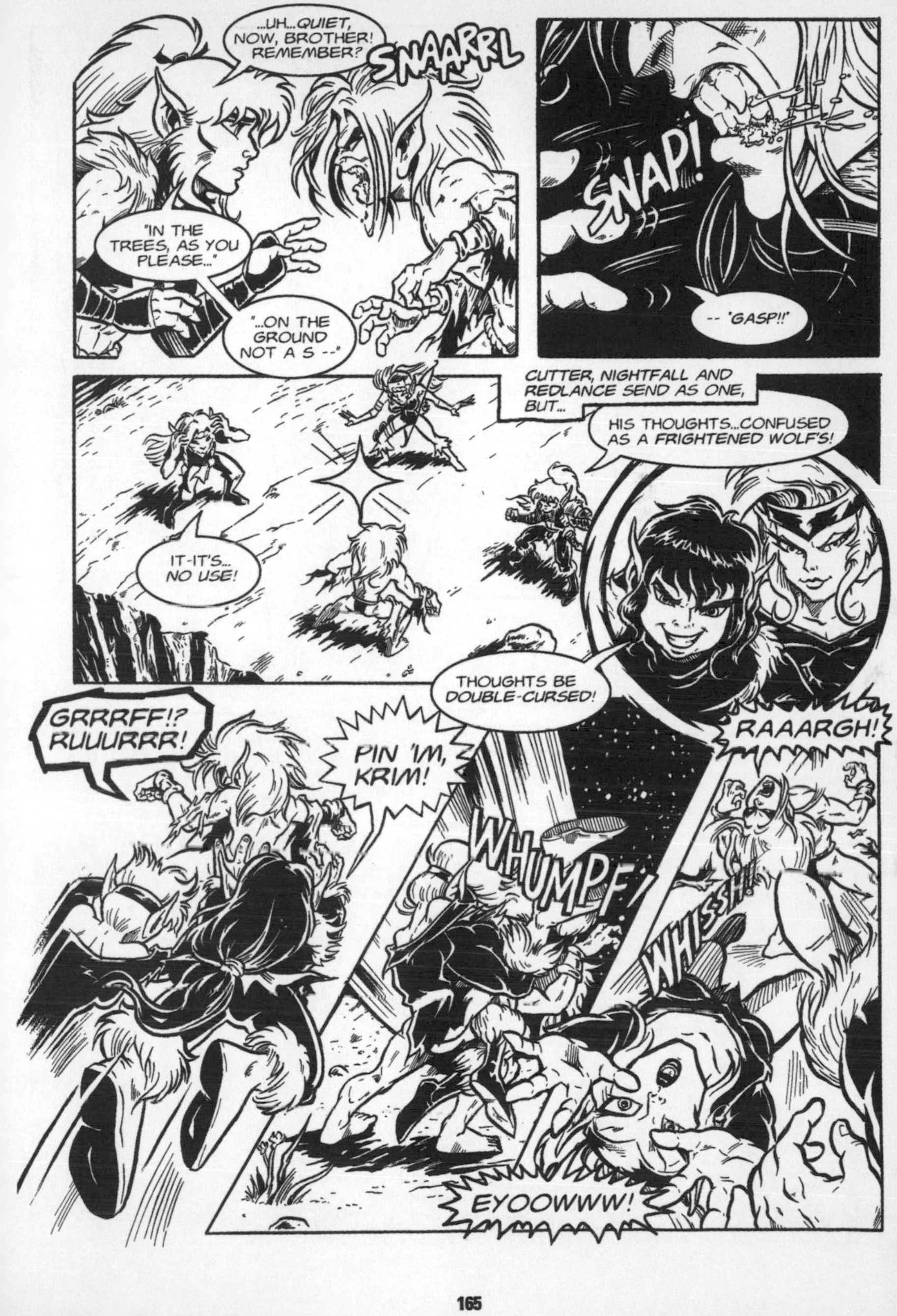
...UH...QUIET, NOW, BROTHER! REMEMBER?
SNAARRL
"IN THE TREES, AS YOU PLEASE..."
"...ON THE GROUND NOT A S --"
SNAP!
-- 'GASP!!'
CUTTER, NIGHTFALL AND REDLANCE SEND AS ONE, BUT...
HIS THOUGHTS...CONFUSED AS A FRIGHTENED WOLF'S!
IT-IT'S... NO USE!
THOUGHTS BE DOUBLE-CURSED!
GRRRFF!? RUUURRR!
PIN 'IM, KRIM!
RAAARGH!
WHUMPF!
WHISSH!
EYOOWWW!

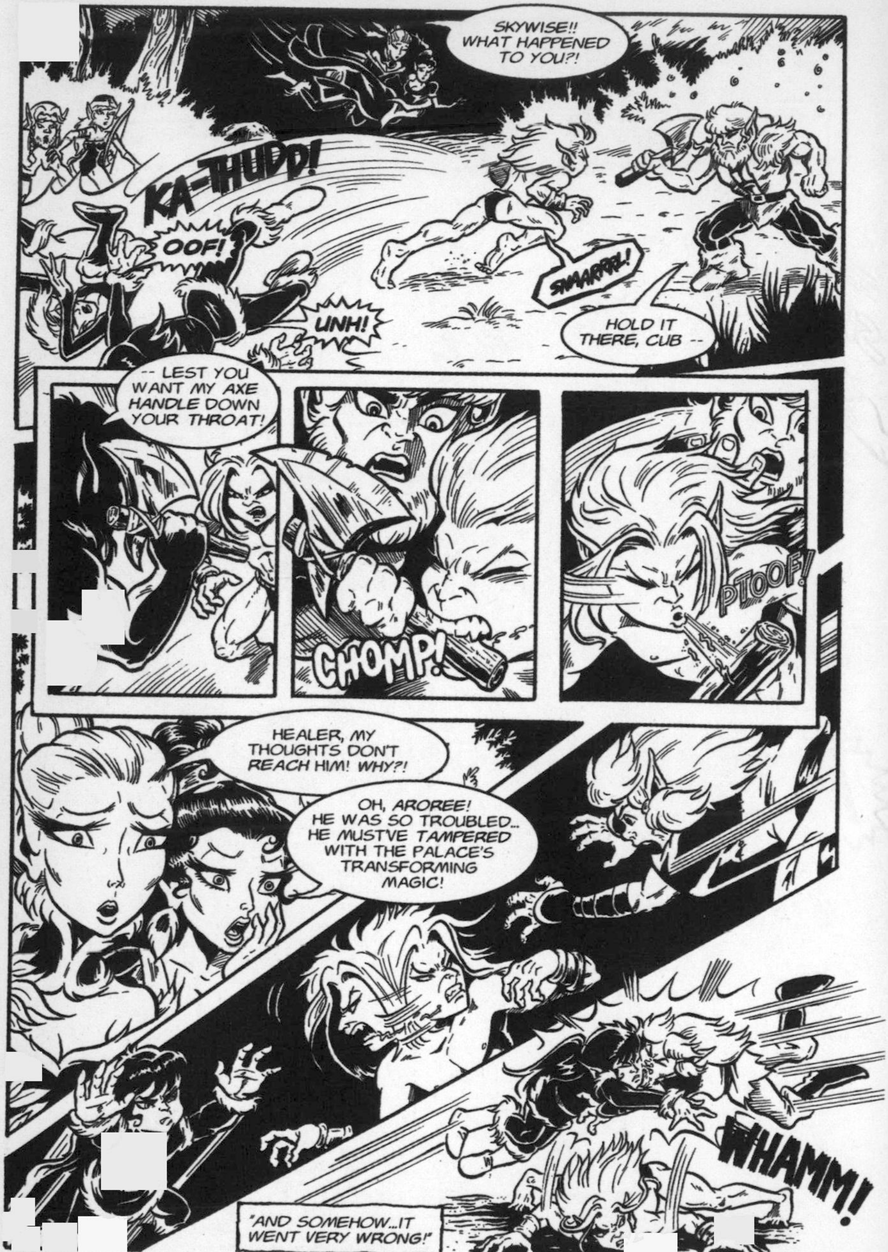
SKYWISE!! WHAT HAPPENED TO YOU?!
KA-THUDD!
OOF!
UNH!
SNARRRL!
HOLD IT THERE, CUB --
-- LEST YOU WANT MY AXE HANDLE DOWN YOUR THROAT!
CHOMP!
PTOOF!
HEALER, MY THOUGHTS DON'T REACH HIM! WHY?!
OH, AROREE! HE WAS SO TROUBLED... HE MUST'VE TAMPERED WITH THE PALACE'S TRANSFORMING MAGIC!
WHAMM!
"AND SOMEHOW...IT WENT VERY WRONG!"

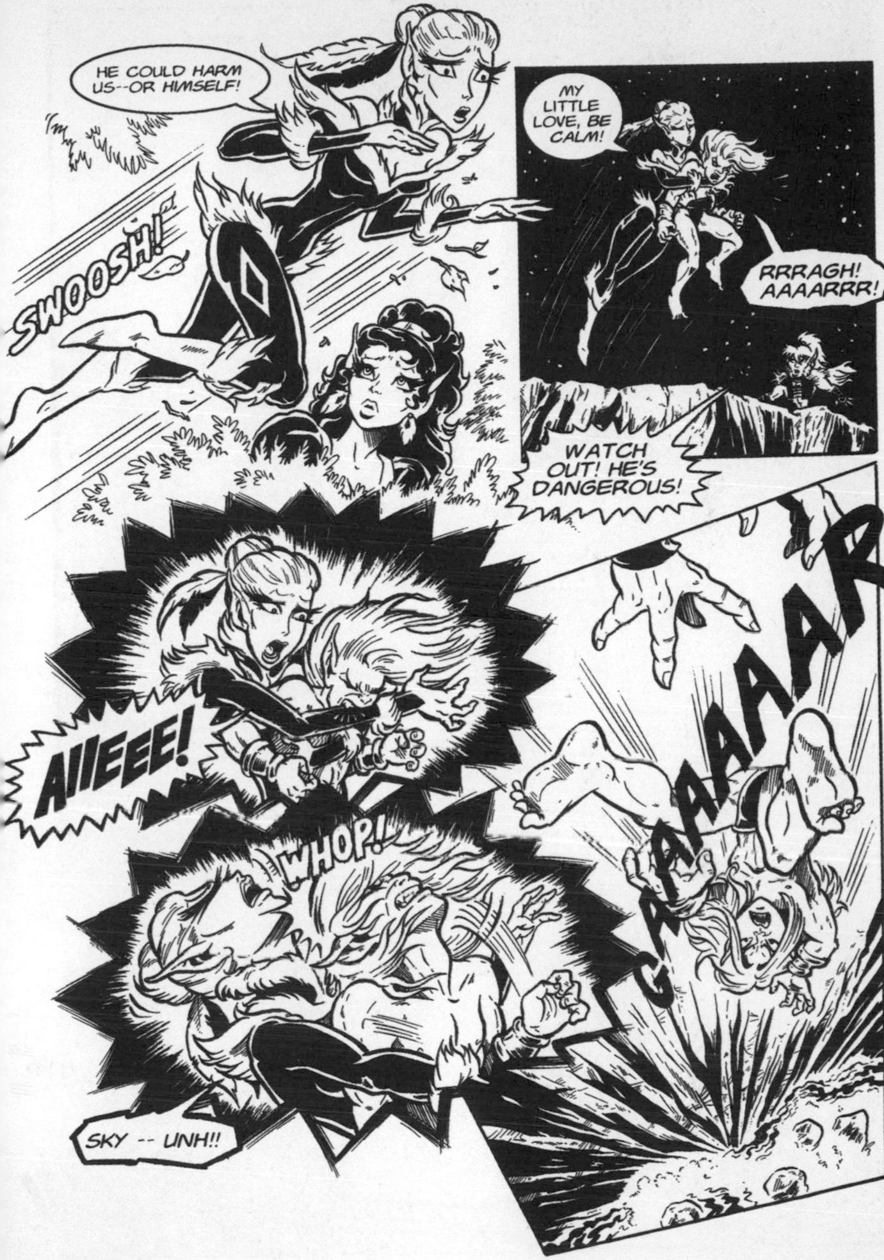
HE COULD HARM US--OR HIMSELF!
SWOOSH!
MY LITTLE LOVE, BE CALM!
RRRAGH! AAAARRR!
WATCH OUT! HE'S DANGEROUS!
AIIEEE!
GAAAAAR
WHOP!
SKY -- UNH!!

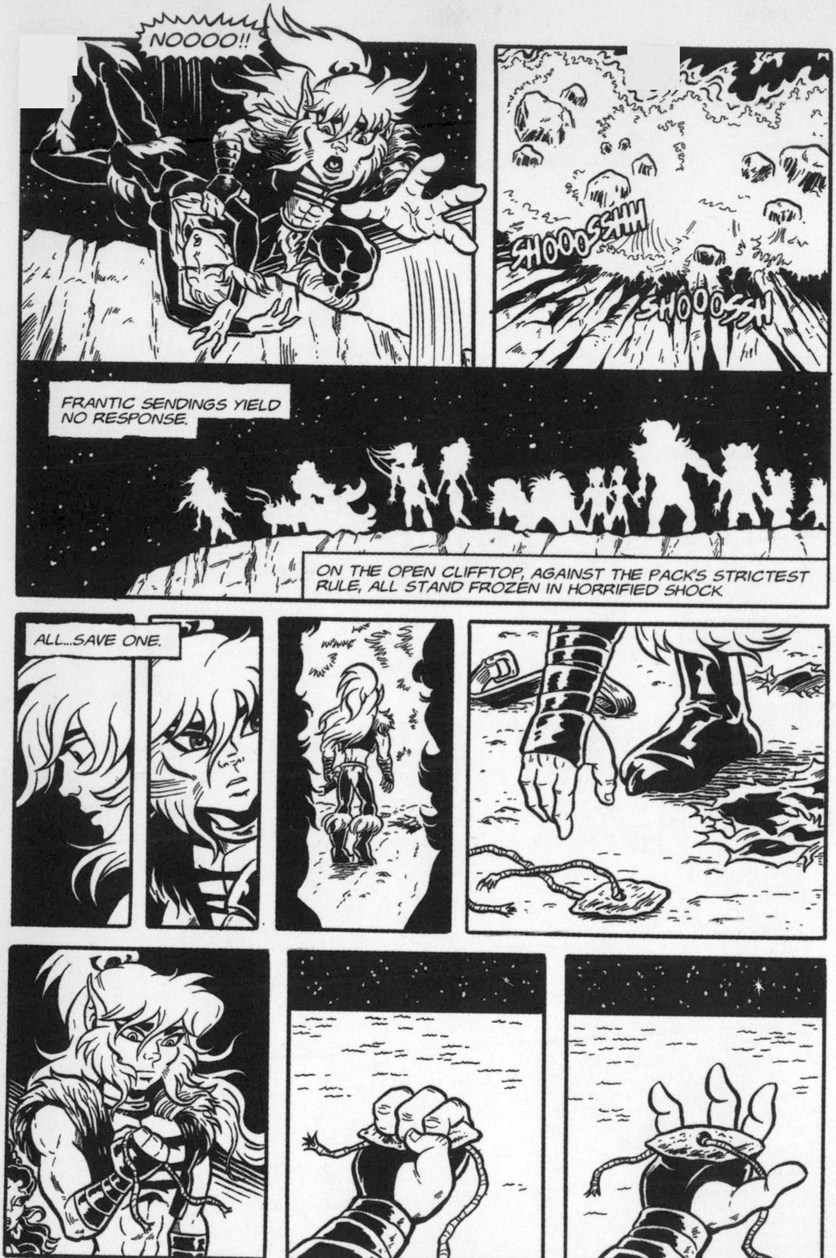
NOOOO!!
SHOOOSHHH
SHOOOSSH
FRANTIC SENDINGS YIELD NO RESPONSE.
ON THE OPEN CLIFFTOP, AGAINST THE PACK'S STRICTEST RULE, ALL STAND FROZEN IN HORRIFIED SHOCK.
ALL...SAVE ONE.

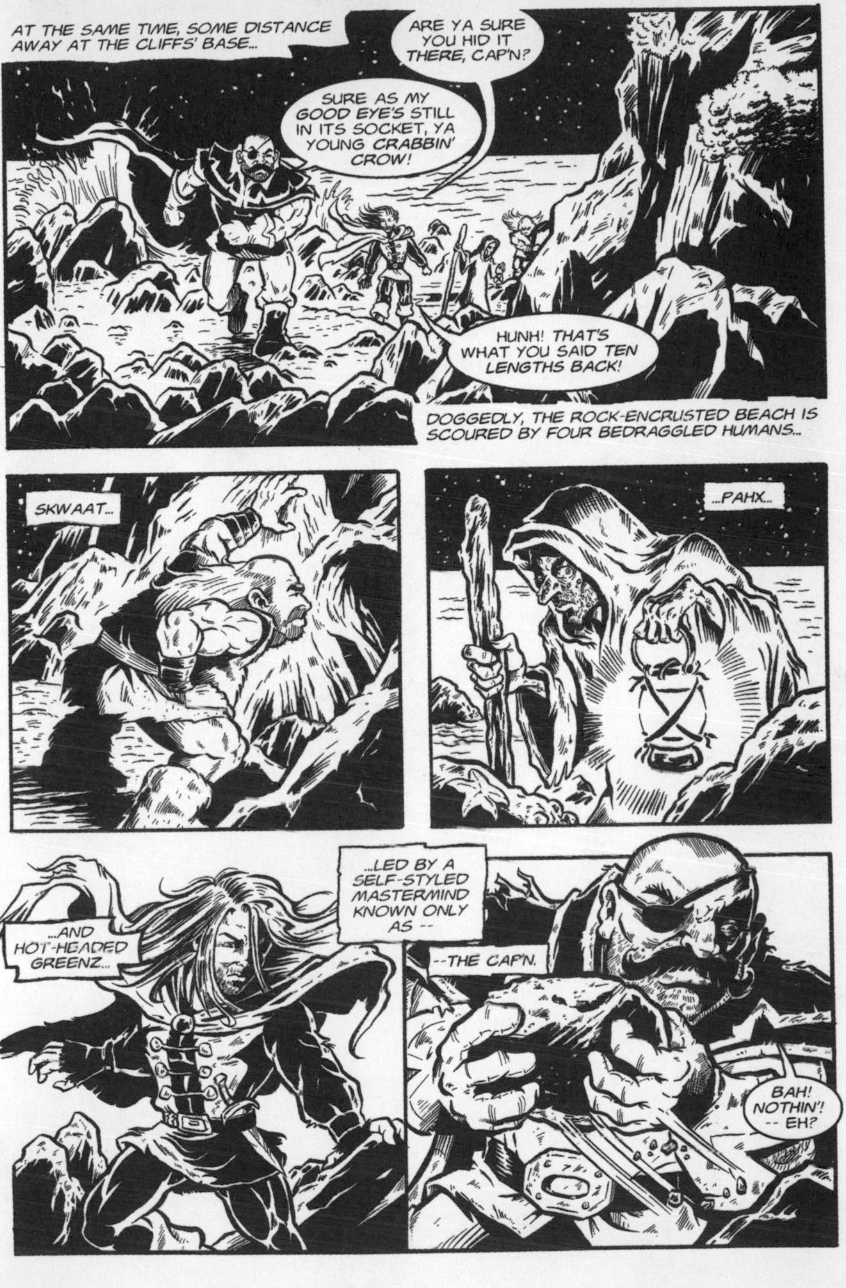
AT THE SAME TIME, SOME DISTANCE AWAY AT THE CLIFFS' BASE...
ARE YA SURE YOU HID IT THERE, CAP'N?
SURE AS MY GOOD EYE'S STILL IN ITS SOCKET, YA YOUNG CRABBIN' CROW!
HUNH! THAT'S WHAT YOU SAID TEN LENGTHS BACK!
DOGGEDLY, THE ROCK-ENCRUSTED BEACH IS SCOURED BY FOUR BEDRAGGLED HUMANS...
SKWAAT...
...PAHX...
...AND HOT-HEADED GREENZ...
...LED BY A SELF-STYLED MASTERMIND KNOWN ONLY AS --
--THE CAP'N.
BAH! NOTHIN'! -- EH?

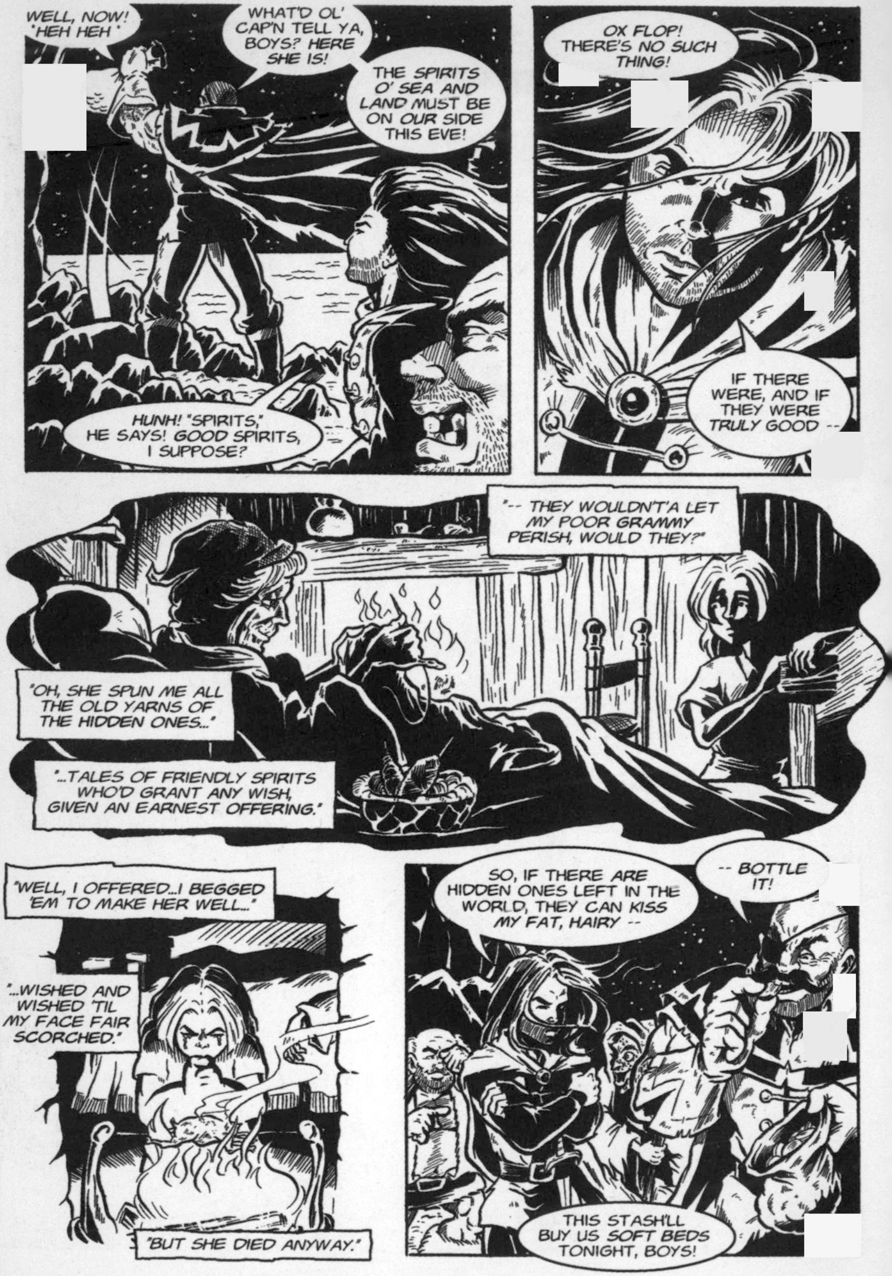
WELL, NOW! *HEH HEH*
WHAT'D OL' CAP'N TELL YA, BOYS? HERE SHE IS!
THE SPIRITS O' SEA AND LAND MUST BE ON OUR SIDE THIS EVE!
HUNH! "SPIRITS," HE SAYS! GOOD SPIRITS, I SUPPOSE?
OX FLOP! THERE'S NO SUCH THING!
IF THERE WERE, AND IF THEY WERE TRULY GOOD --
"-- THEY WOULDN'T'A LET MY POOR GRAMMY PERISH, WOULD THEY?"
"OH, SHE SPUN ME ALL THE OLD YARNS OF THE HIDDEN ONES..."
"...TALES OF FRIENDLY SPIRITS WHO'D GRANT ANY WISH, GIVEN AN EARNEST OFFERING."
"WELL, I OFFERED...I BEGGED 'EM TO MAKE HER WELL..."
"...WISHED AND WISHED 'TIL MY FACE FAIR SCORCHED."
"BUT SHE DIED ANYWAY."
SO, IF THERE ARE HIDDEN ONES LEFT IN THE WORLD, THEY CAN KISS MY FAT, HAIRY --
-- BOTTLE IT!
THIS STASH'LL BUY US SOFT BEDS TONIGHT, BOYS!

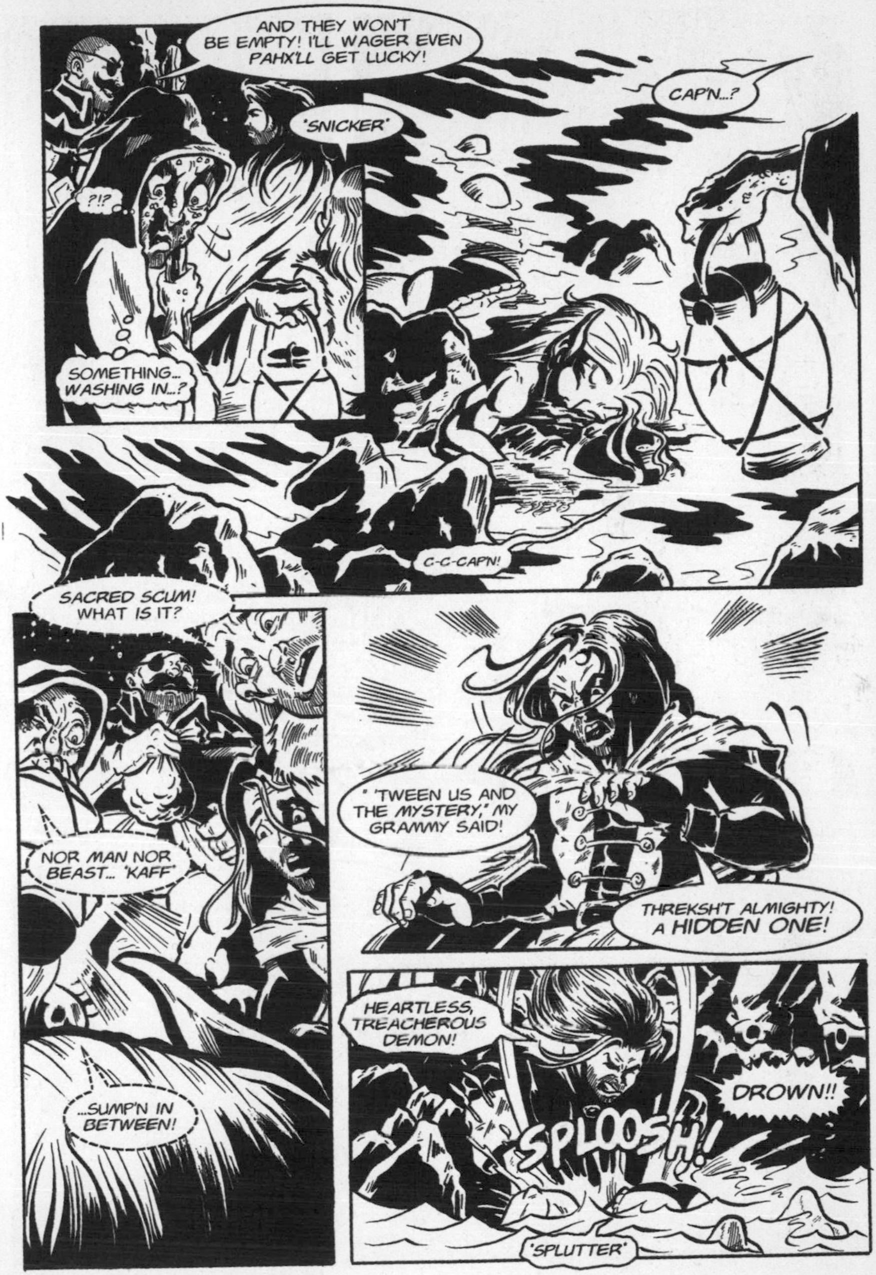
AND THEY WON'T BE EMPTY! I'LL WAGER EVEN PAHX'LL GET LUCKY!
'SNICKER'
?!?
SOMETHING... WASHING IN...?
CAP'N...?
C-C-CAP'N!
SACRED SCUM! WHAT IS IT?
NOR MAN NOR BEAST... 'KAFF'
...SUMP'N IN BETWEEN!
" 'TWEEN US AND THE MYSTERY," MY GRAMMY SAID!
THREKSH'T ALMIGHTY! A HIDDEN ONE!
HEARTLESS, TREACHEROUS DEMON!
DROWN!!
SPLOOSH!
'SPLUTTER'

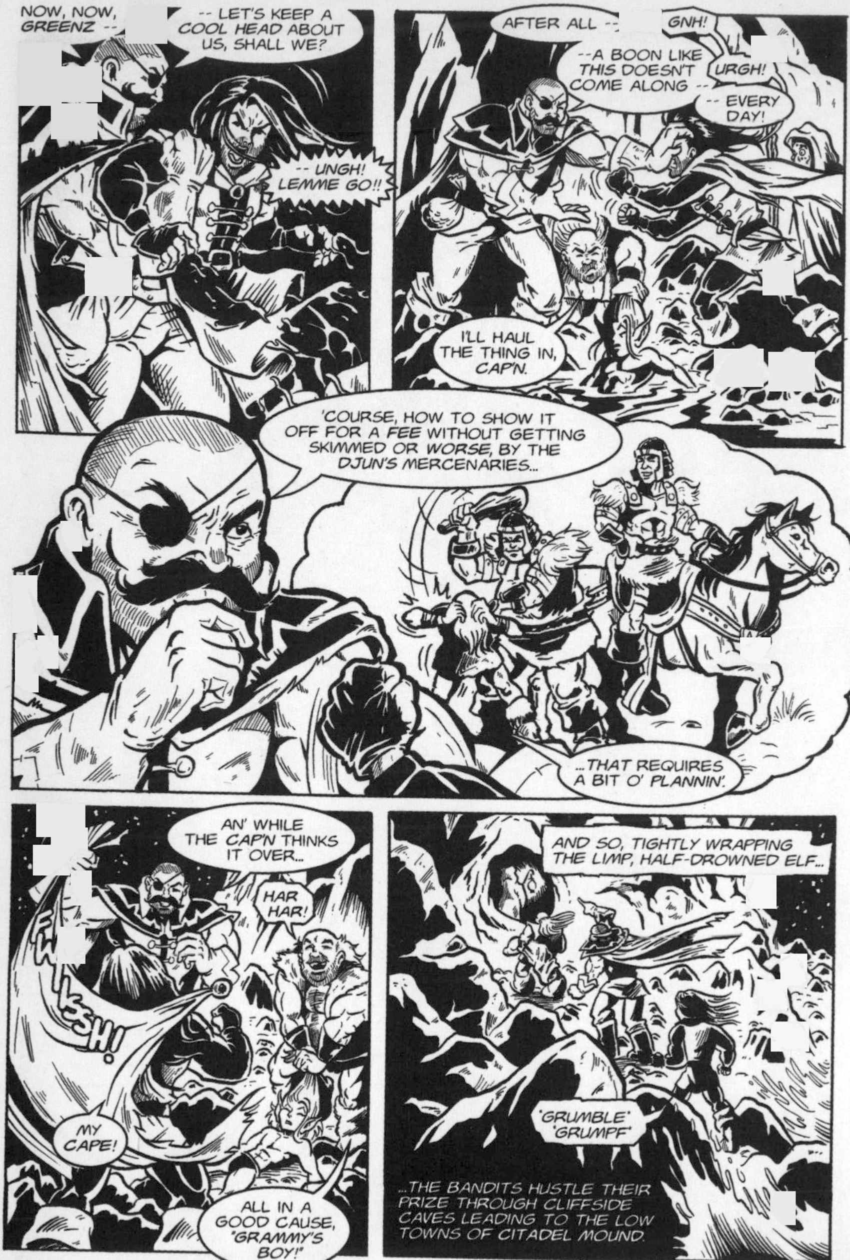
NOW, NOW, GREENZ --
-- LET'S KEEP A COOL HEAD ABOUT US, SHALL WE?
-- UNGH! LEMME GO!!
AFTER ALL --
GNH!
--A BOON LIKE THIS DOESN'T COME ALONG --
URGH!
-- EVERY DAY!
I'LL HAUL THE THING IN, CAP'N.
'COURSE, HOW TO SHOW IT OFF FOR A FEE WITHOUT GETTING SKIMMED OR WORSE, BY THE DJUN'S MERCENARIES...
...THAT REQUIRES A BIT O' PLANNIN'.
AN' WHILE THE CAP'N THINKS IT OVER...
HAR HAR!
FWHYSSH!
MY CAPE!
ALL IN A GOOD CAUSE, "GRAMMY'S BOY!"
AND SO, TIGHTLY WRAPPING THE LIMP, HALF-DROWNED ELF...
GRUMBLE
GRUMPF
...THE BANDITS HUSTLE THEIR PRIZE THROUGH CLIFFSIDE CAVES LEADING TO THE LOW TOWNS OF CITADEL MOUND.

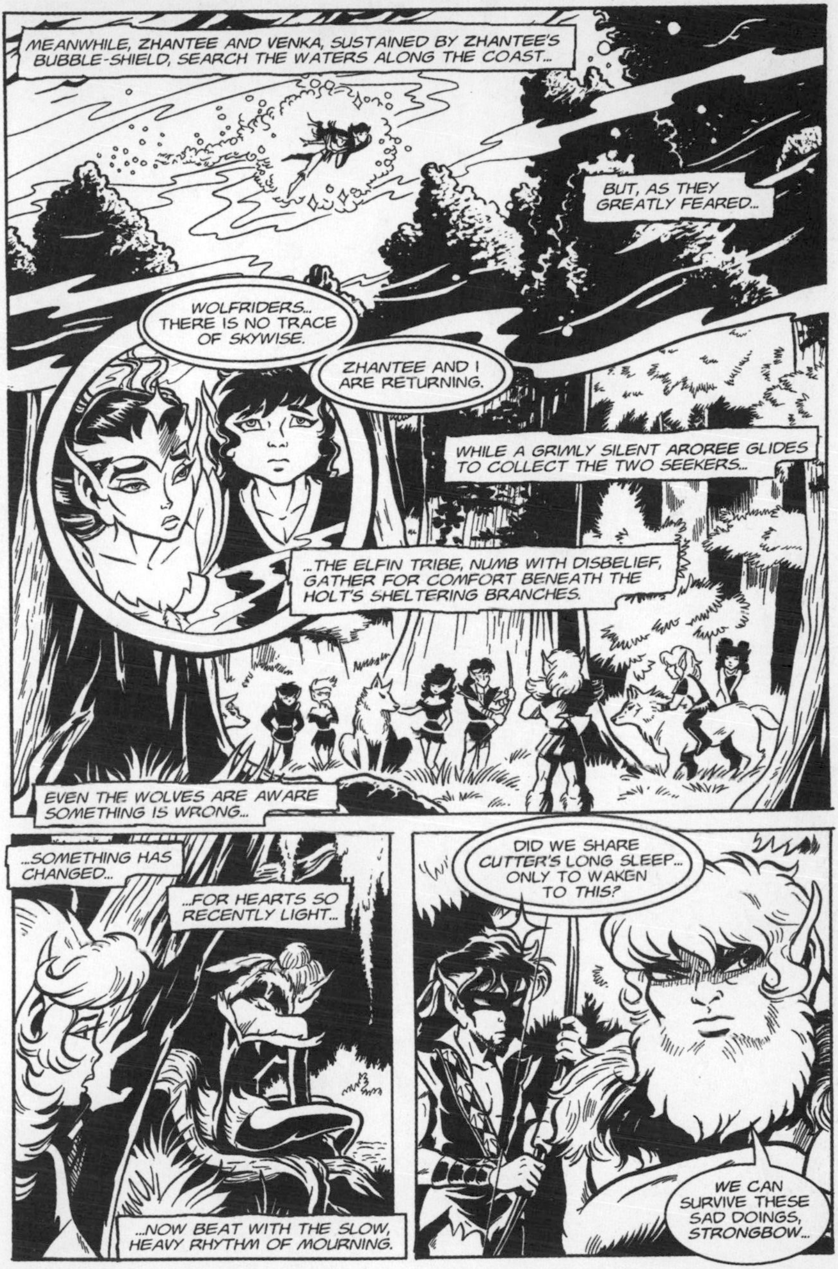
MEANWHILE, ZHANTEE AND VENKA, SUSTAINED BY ZHANTEE'S BUBBLE-SHIELD, SEARCH THE WATERS ALONG THE COAST...
BUT, AS THEY GREATLY FEARED...
WOLFRIDERS... THERE IS NO TRACE OF SKYWISE.
ZHANTEE AND I ARE RETURNING.
WHILE A GRIMLY SILENT AROREE GLIDES TO COLLECT THE TWO SEEKERS...
...THE ELFIN TRIBE, NUMB WITH DISBELIEF, GATHER FOR COMFORT BENEATH THE HOLT'S SHELTERING BRANCHES.
EVEN THE WOLVES ARE AWARE SOMETHING IS WRONG...
...SOMETHING HAS CHANGED...
...FOR HEARTS SO RECENTLY LIGHT...
...NOW BEAT WITH THE SLOW, HEAVY RHYTHM OF MOURNING.
DID WE SHARE CUTTER'S LONG SLEEP... ONLY TO WAKEN TO THIS?
WE CAN SURVIVE THESE SAD DOINGS, STRONGBOW...

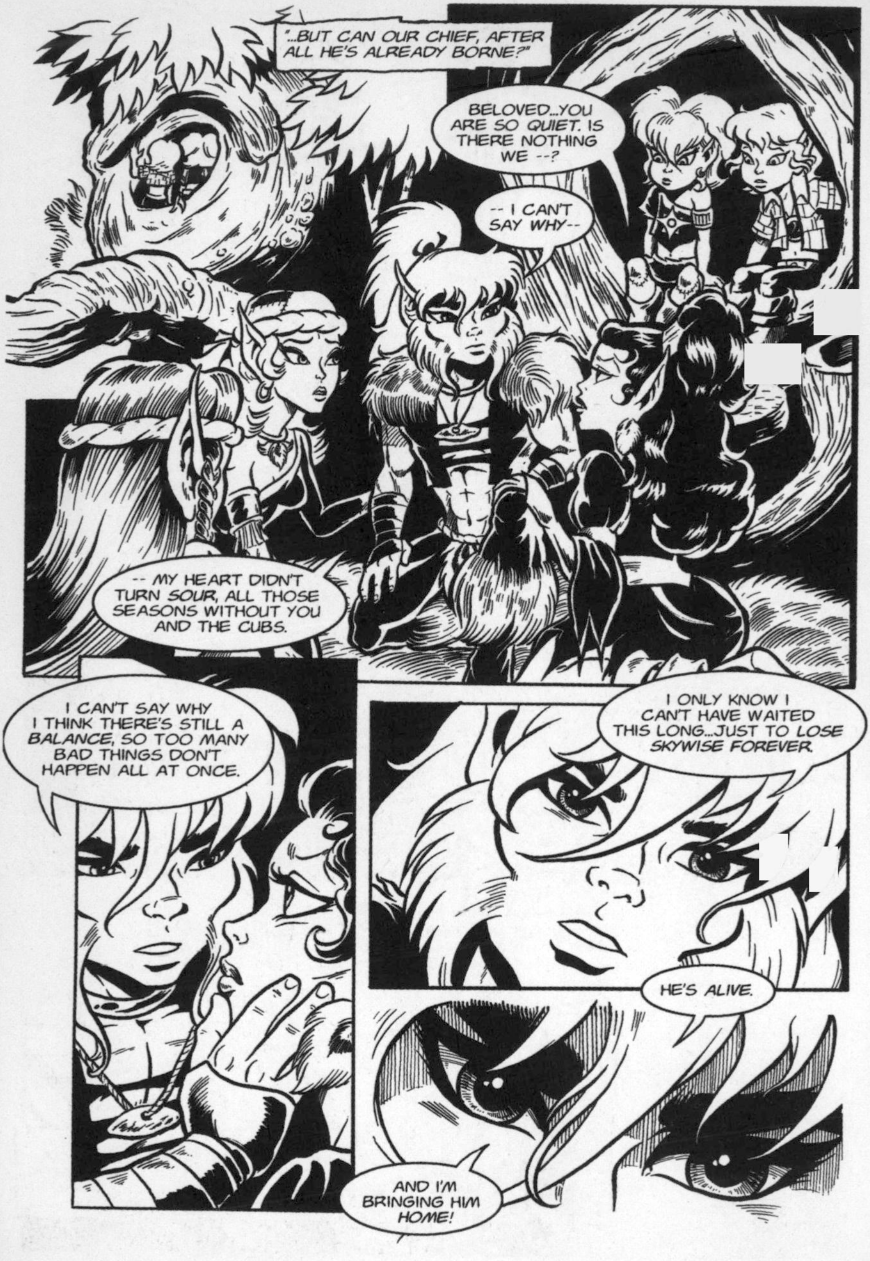
"...BUT CAN OUR CHIEF, AFTER ALL HE'S ALREADY BORNE?"
BELOVED...YOU ARE SO QUIET. IS THERE NOTHING WE --?
-- I CAN'T SAY WHY--
-- MY HEART DIDN'T TURN SOUR, ALL THOSE SEASONS WITHOUT YOU AND THE CUBS.
I CAN'T SAY WHY I THINK THERE'S STILL A BALANCE, SO TOO MANY BAD THINGS DON'T HAPPEN ALL AT ONCE.
I ONLY KNOW I CAN'T HAVE WAITED THIS LONG...JUST TO LOSE SKYWISE FOREVER.
HE'S ALIVE.
AND I'M BRINGING HIM HOME!

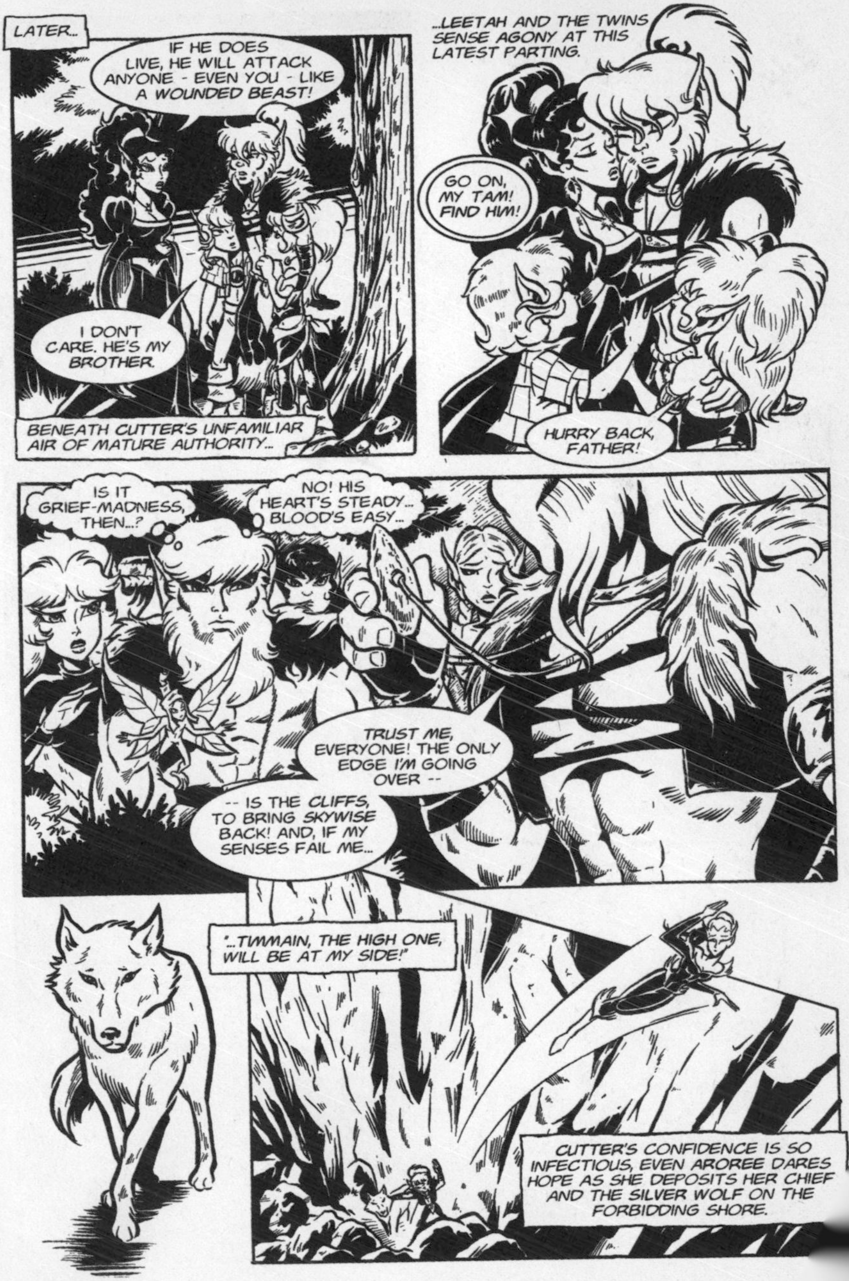
LATER...
IF HE DOES LIVE, HE WILL ATTACK ANYONE - EVEN YOU - LIKE A WOUNDED BEAST!
I DON'T CARE. HE'S MY BROTHER.
BENEATH CUTTER'S UNFAMILIAR AIR OF MATURE AUTHORITY...
...LEETAH AND THE TWINS SENSE AGONY AT THIS LATEST PARTING.
GO ON, MY TAM! FIND HIM!
HURRY BACK, FATHER!
IS IT GRIEF-MADNESS, THEN...?
NO! HIS HEART'S STEADY... BLOOD'S EASY...
TRUST ME, EVERYONE! THE ONLY EDGE I'M GOING OVER --
-- IS THE CLIFFS, TO BRING SKYWISE BACK! AND, IF MY SENSES FAIL ME...
"...TIMMAIN, THE HIGH ONE, WILL BE AT MY SIDE!"
CUTTER'S CONFIDENCE IS SO INFECTIOUS, EVEN AROREE DARES HOPE AS SHE DEPOSITS HER CHIEF AND THE SILVER WOLF ON THE FORBIDDING SHORE.

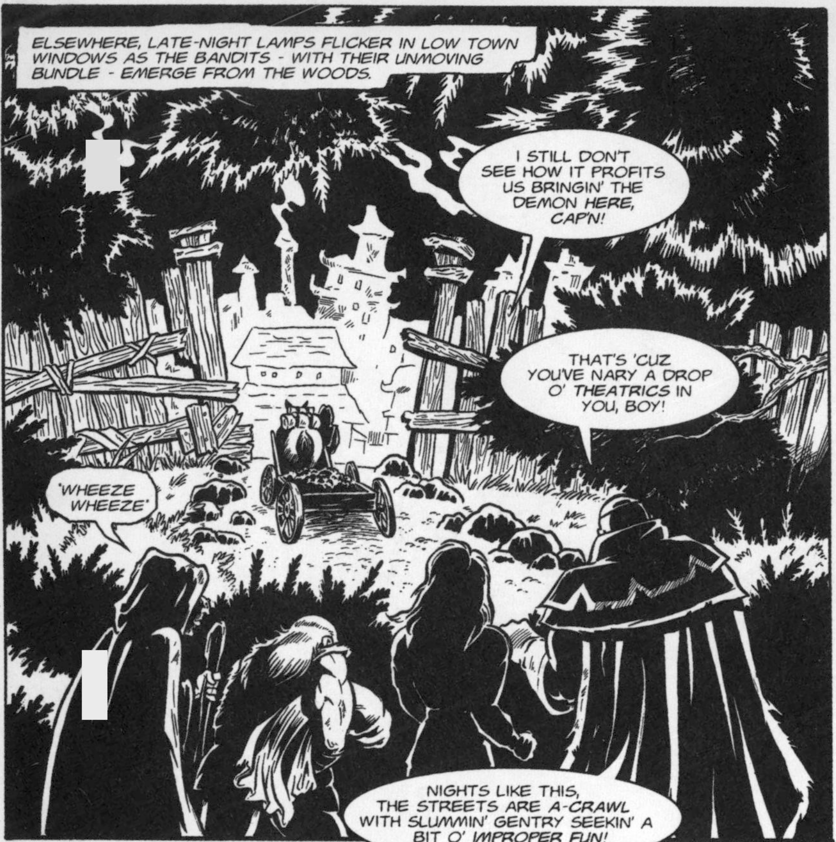
ELSEWHERE, LATE-NIGHT LAMPS FLICKER IN LOW TOWN WINDOWS AS THE BANDITS - WITH THEIR UNMOVING BUNDLE - EMERGE FROM THE WOODS.
I STILL DON'T SEE HOW IT PROFITS US BRINGIN' THE DEMON HERE, CAP'N!
THAT'S 'CUZ YOU'VE NARY A DROP O' THEATRICS IN YOU, BOY!
WHEEZE WHEEZE
NIGHTS LIKE THIS, THE STREETS ARE A-CRAWL WITH SLUMMIN' GENTRY SEEKIN' A BIT O' IMPROPER FUN!

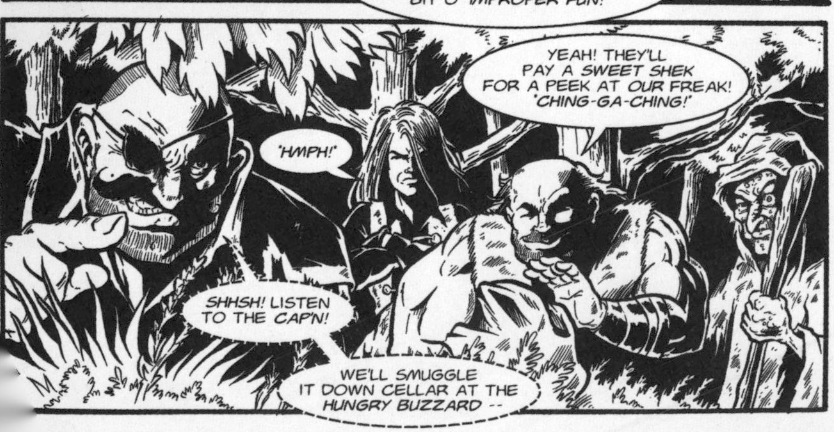
YEAH! THEY'LL PAY A SWEET SHEK FOR A PEEK AT OUR FREAK! *CHING-GA-CHING!*
HMPH!
SHHSH! LISTEN TO THE CAP'N!
WE'LL SMUGGLE IT DOWN CELLAR AT THE HUNGRY BUZZARD --

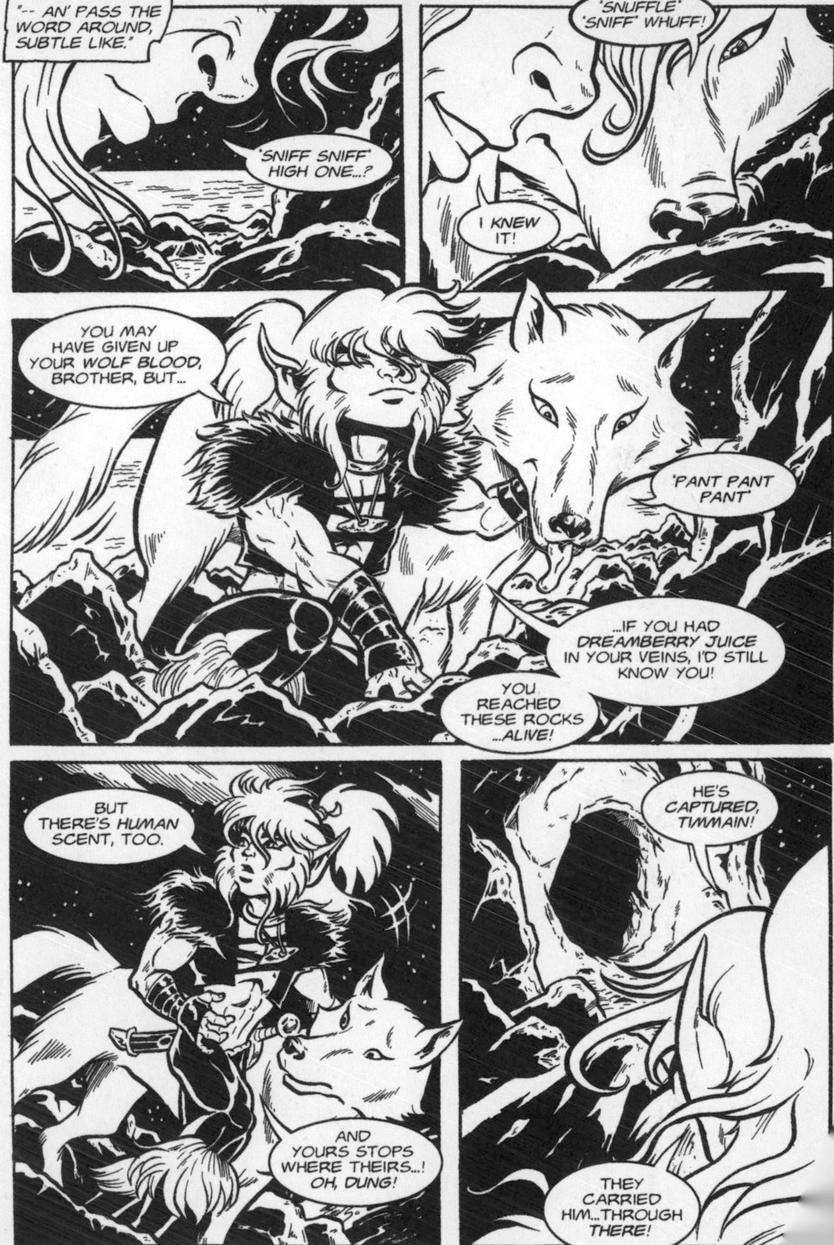
"-- AN' PASS THE WORD AROUND, SUBTLE LIKE."
'SNIFF SNIFF' HIGH ONE...?
'SNUFFLE' 'SNIFF' WHUFF!
I KNEW IT!
YOU MAY HAVE GIVEN UP YOUR WOLF BLOOD, BROTHER, BUT...
'PANT PANT PANT'
...IF YOU HAD DREAMBERRY JUICE IN YOUR VEINS, I'D STILL KNOW YOU!
YOU REACHED THESE ROCKS ...ALIVE!
BUT THERE'S HUMAN SCENT, TOO.
AND YOURS STOPS WHERE THEIRS...! OH, DUNG!
HE'S CAPTURED, TIMMAIN!
THEY CARRIED HIM...THROUGH THERE!

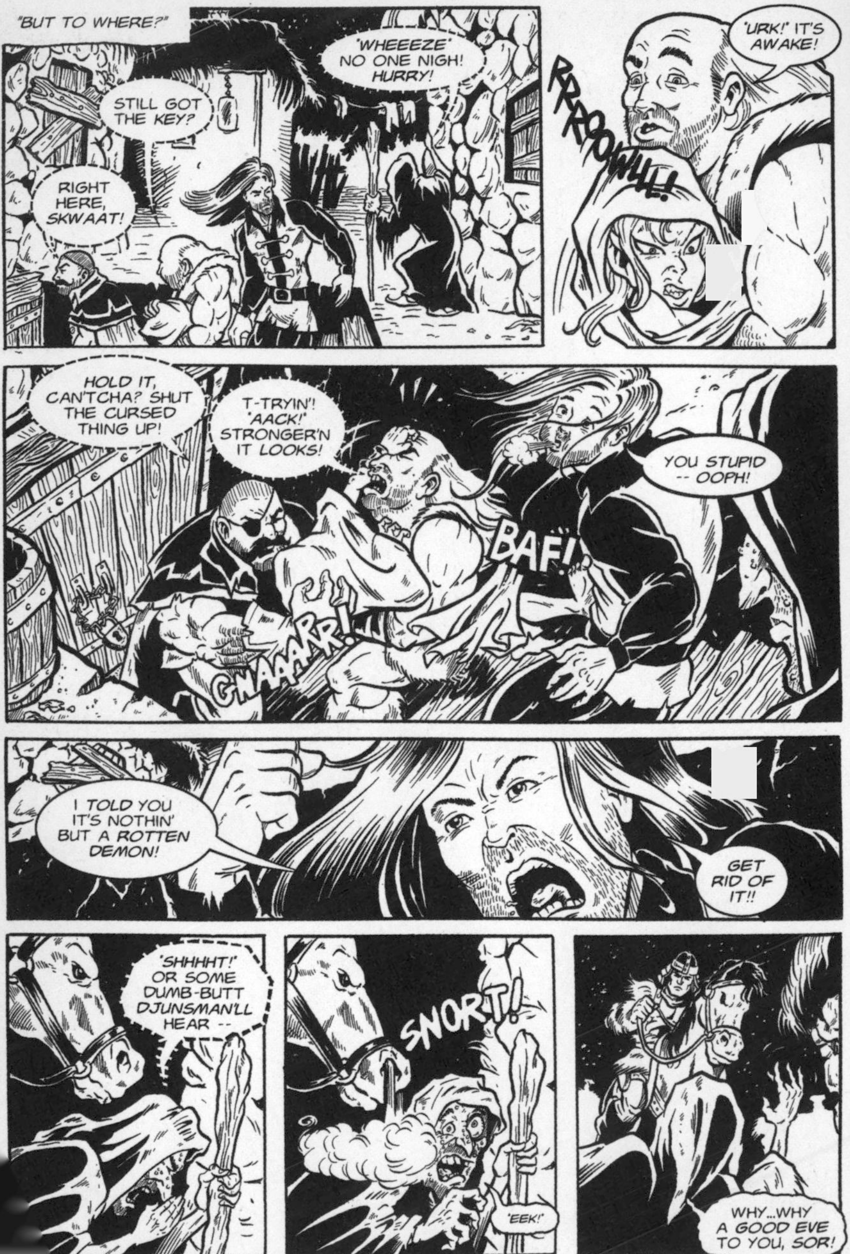
"BUT TO WHERE?"
'WHEEEZE' NO ONE NIGH! HURRY!
STILL GOT THE KEY?
RIGHT HERE, SKWAAT!
RRRROOWLLL!
'URK!' IT'S AWAKE!
HOLD IT, CAN'TCHA? SHUT THE CURSED THING UP!
T-TRYIN'! 'AACK!' STRONGER'N IT LOOKS!
YOU STUPID -- OOPH!
BAF!
GNAAARRR!
I TOLD YOU IT'S NOTHIN' BUT A ROTTEN DEMON!
GET RID OF IT!!
'SHHHHT!' OR SOME DUMB-BUTT DJUNSMAN'LL HEAR --
SNORT!
'EEK!'
WHY...WHY A GOOD EVE TO YOU, SOR!

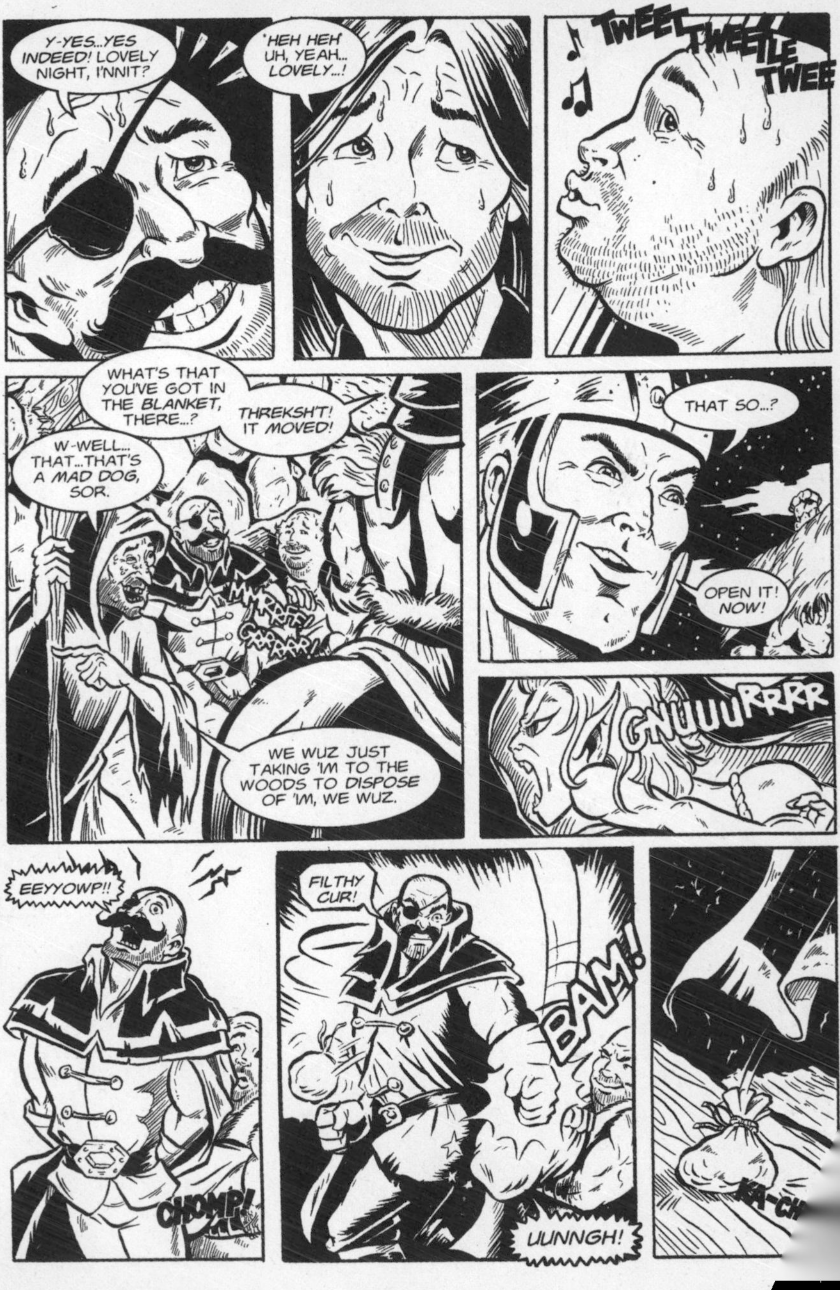

Y-YES...YES INDEED! LOVELY NIGHT, I'NNIT?
'HEH HEH' UH, YEAH... LOVELY...!
TWEET TWEETLE TWEE
WHAT'S THAT YOU'VE GOT IN THE BLANKET, THERE...?
THREKSH'T! IT MOVED!
W-WELL... THAT...THAT'S A MAD DOG, SOR.
WE WUZ JUST TAKING 'IM TO THE WOODS TO DISPOSE OF 'IM, WE WUZ.
THAT SO...?
OPEN IT! NOW!
GNUUURRRR
EEYYOWP!!
CHOMP!
FILTHY CUR!
BAM!
UUNNGH!
KA-CH

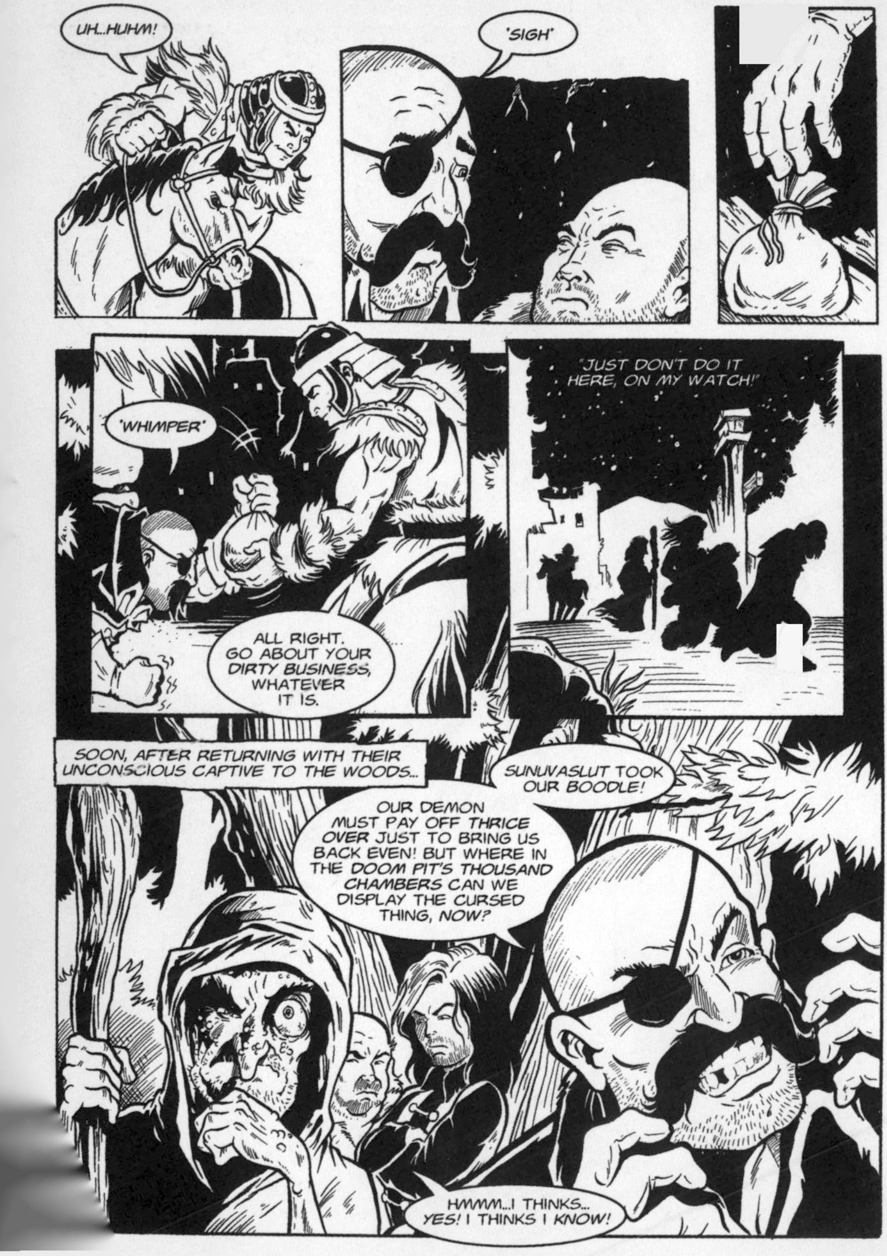
UH..HUHM!
'SIGH'
'WHIMPER'
ALL RIGHT. GO ABOUT YOUR DIRTY BUSINESS, WHATEVER IT IS.
"JUST DON'T DO IT HERE, ON MY WATCH!"
SOON, AFTER RETURNING WITH THEIR UNCONSCIOUS CAPTIVE TO THE WOODS...
SUNUVASLUT TOOK OUR BOODLE!
OUR DEMON MUST PAY OFF THRICE OVER JUST TO BRING US BACK EVEN! BUT WHERE IN THE DOOM PIT'S THOUSAND CHAMBERS CAN WE DISPLAY THE CURSED THING, NOW?
HMMM...I THINKS... YES! I THINKS I KNOW!

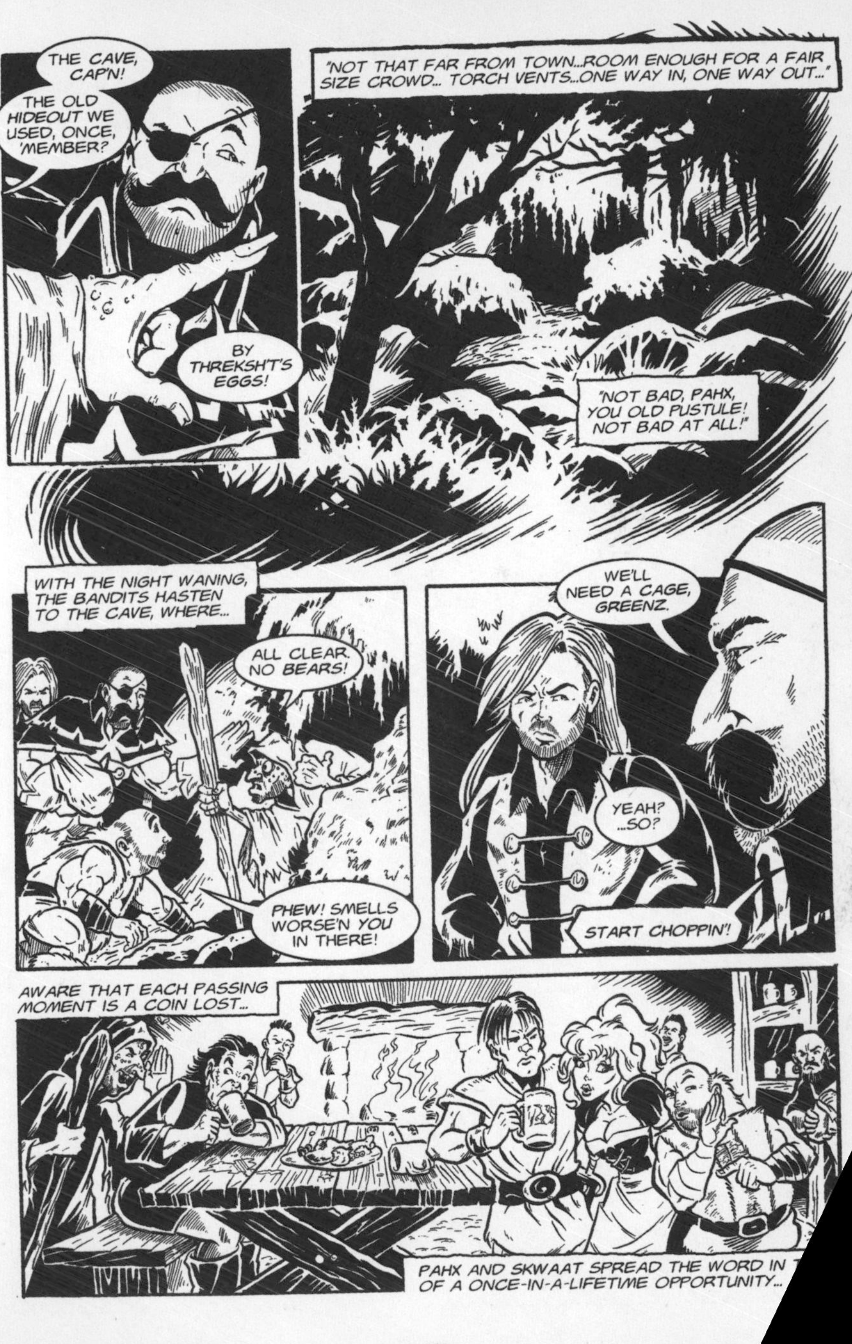
THE CAVE, CAP'N!
THE OLD HIDEOUT WE USED, ONCE, 'MEMBER?
BY THREKSHT'S EGGS!
"NOT THAT FAR FROM TOWN...ROOM ENOUGH FOR A FAIR SIZE CROWD... TORCH VENTS...ONE WAY IN, ONE WAY OUT..."
"NOT BAD, PAHX, YOU OLD PUSTULE! NOT BAD AT ALL!"
WITH THE NIGHT WANING, THE BANDITS HASTEN TO THE CAVE, WHERE...
ALL CLEAR. NO BEARS!
PHEW! SMELLS WORSE'N YOU IN THERE!
WE'LL NEED A CAGE, GREENZ.
YEAH? ...SO?
START CHOPPIN'!
AWARE THAT EACH PASSING MOMENT IS A COIN LOST...
PAHX AND SKWAAT SPREAD THE WORD IN T
OF A ONCE-IN-A-LIFETIME OPPORTUNITY...

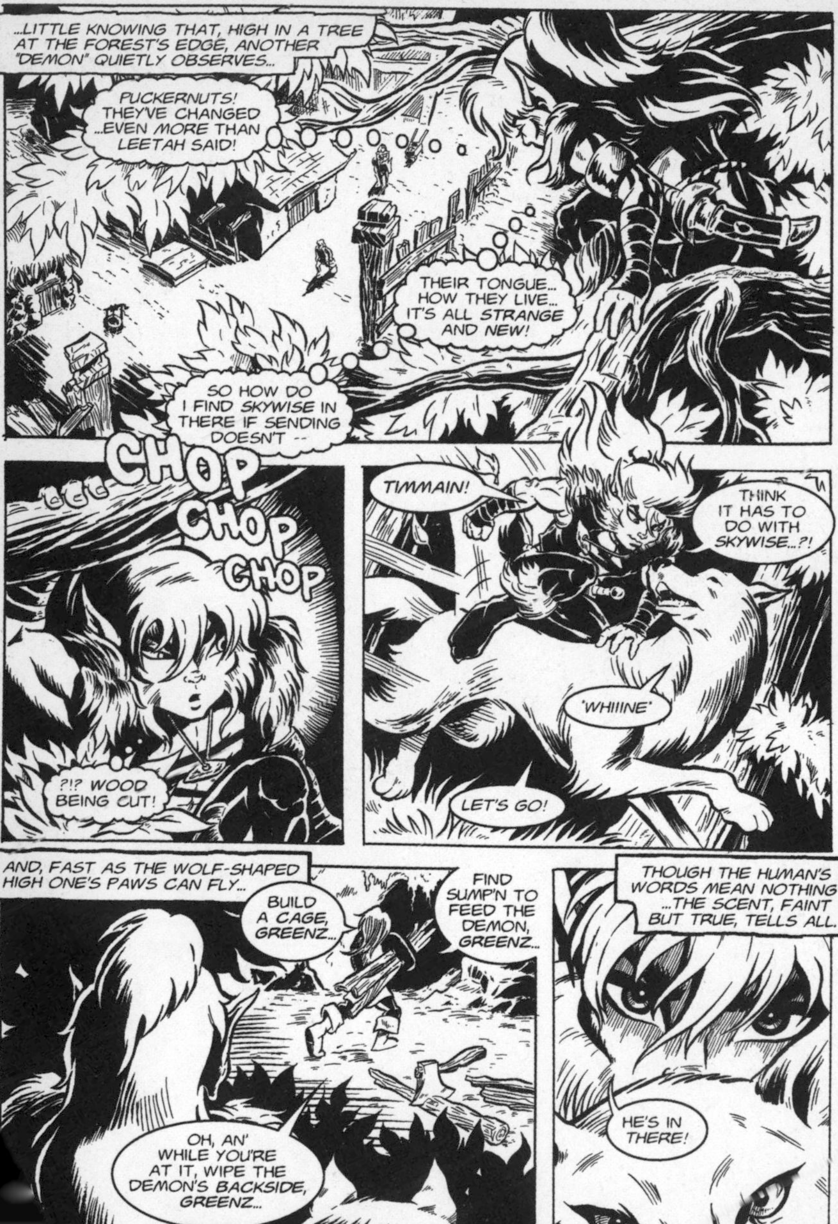
...LITTLE KNOWING THAT, HIGH IN A TREE AT THE FOREST'S EDGE, ANOTHER "DEMON" QUIETLY OBSERVES...
PUCKERNUTS! THEY'VE CHANGED ...EVEN MORE THAN LEETAH SAID!
THEIR TONGUE... HOW THEY LIVE... IT'S ALL STRANGE AND NEW!
SO HOW DO I FIND SKYWISE IN THERE IF SENDING DOESN'T --
CHOP
CHOP
CHOP
?!? WOOD BEING CUT!
TIMMAIN!
THINK IT HAS TO DO WITH SKYWISE...?!
WHIIINE
LET'S GO!
AND, FAST AS THE WOLF-SHAPED HIGH ONE'S PAWS CAN FLY...
BUILD A CAGE, GREENZ...
FIND SUMP'N TO FEED THE DEMON, GREENZ...
OH, AN' WHILE YOU'RE AT IT, WIPE THE DEMON'S BACKSIDE, GREENZ...
THOUGH THE HUMAN'S WORDS MEAN NOTHING ...THE SCENT, FAINT BUT TRUE, TELLS ALL.
HE'S IN THERE!

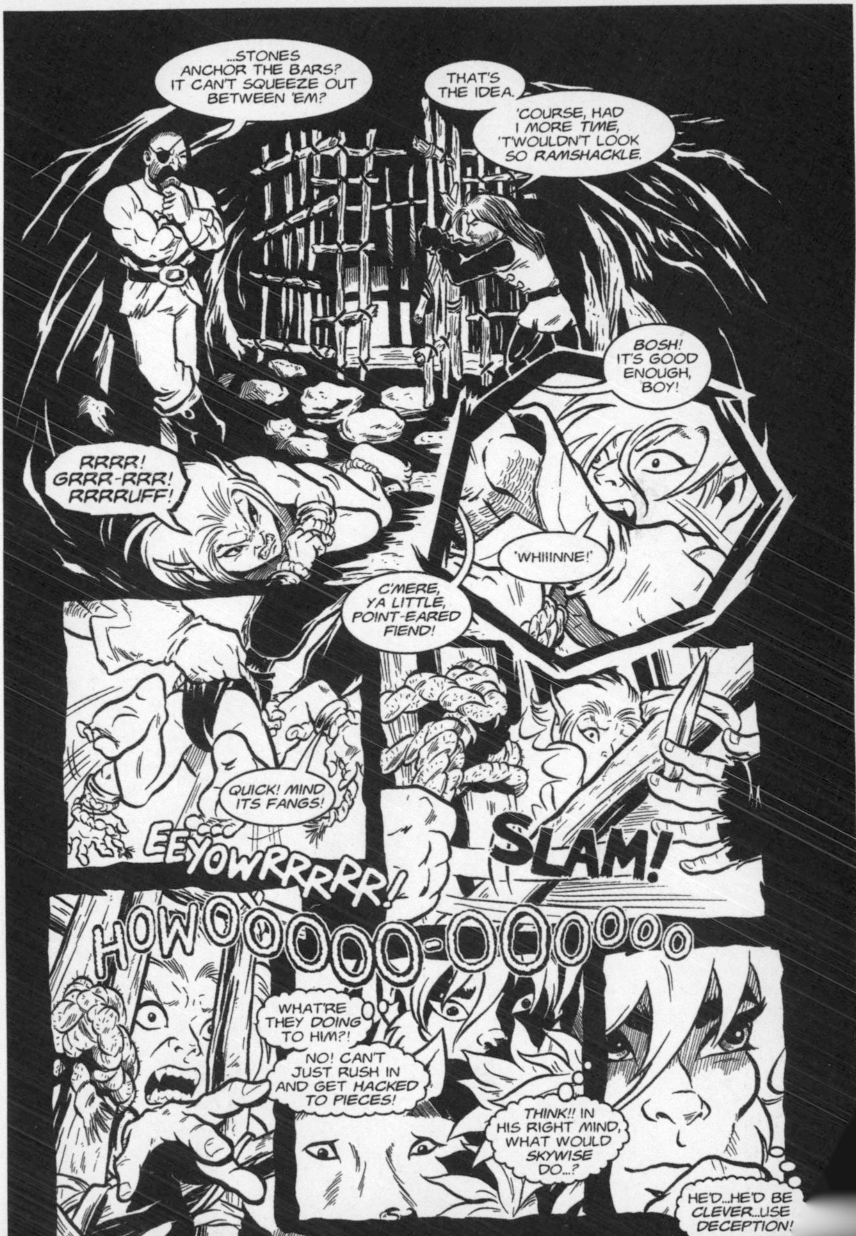
...STONES ANCHOR THE BARS? IT CAN'T SQUEEZE OUT BETWEEN 'EM?
THAT'S THE IDEA.
'COURSE, HAD I MORE TIME, 'TWOULDN'T LOOK SO RAMSHACKLE.
BOSH! IT'S GOOD ENOUGH, BOY!
RRRR! GRRR-RRR! RRRRUFF!
'WHIIINNE!'
C'MERE, YA LITTLE, POINT-EARED FIEND!
QUICK! MIND ITS FANGS!
EEYOWRRRRRR!
SLAM!
HOWOOOOOO-OOOOooo
WHAT'RE THEY DOING TO HIM?!
NO! CAN'T JUST RUSH IN AND GET HACKED TO PIECES!
THINK!! IN HIS RIGHT MIND, WHAT WOULD SKYWISE DO...?
HE'D...HE'D BE CLEVER...USE DECEPTION!

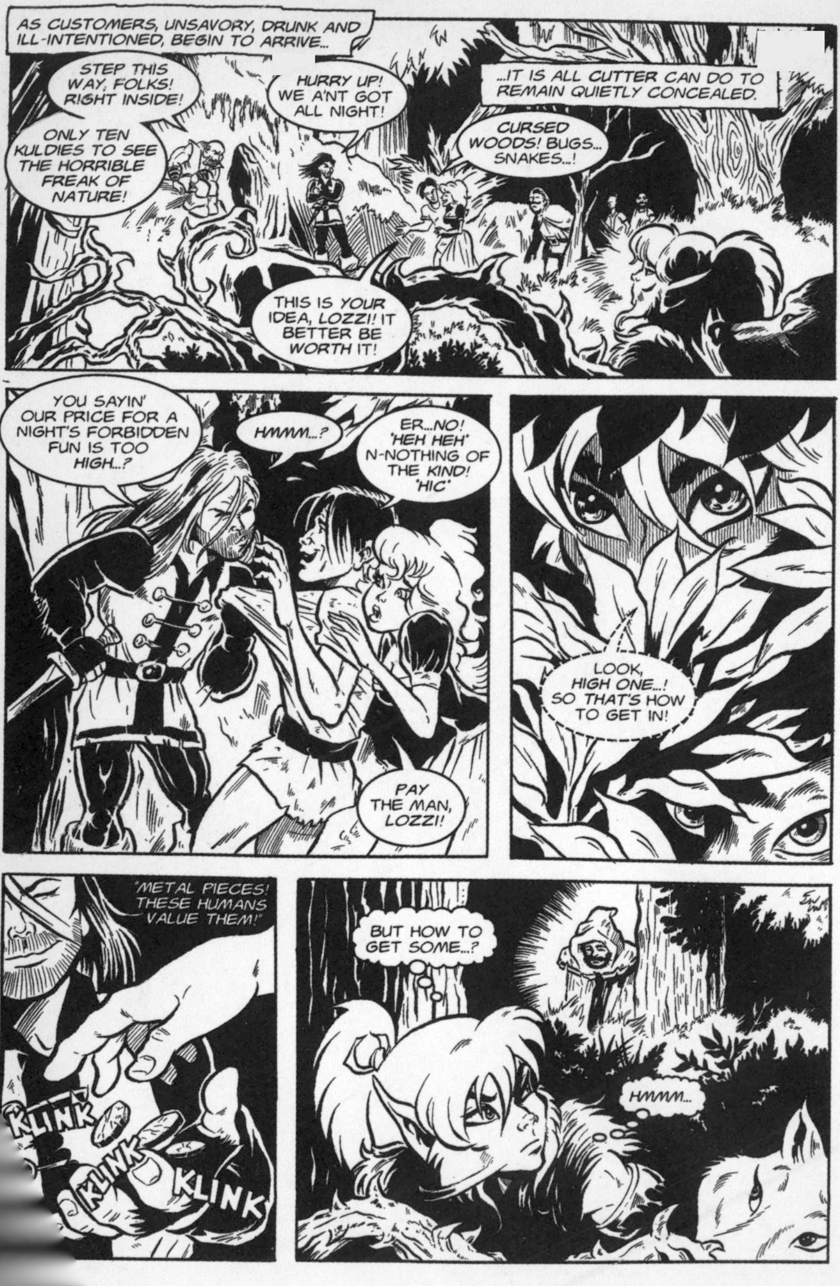
AS CUSTOMERS, UNSAVORY, DRUNK AND ILL-INTENTIONED, BEGIN TO ARRIVE...
STEP THIS WAY, FOLKS! RIGHT INSIDE!
ONLY TEN KULDIES TO SEE THE HORRIBLE FREAK OF NATURE!
HURRY UP! WE A'NT GOT ALL NIGHT!
...IT IS ALL CUTTER CAN DO TO REMAIN QUIETLY CONCEALED.
CURSED WOODS! BUGS... SNAKES...!
THIS IS YOUR IDEA, LOZZI! IT BETTER BE WORTH IT!
YOU SAYIN' OUR PRICE FOR A NIGHT'S FORBIDDEN FUN IS TOO HIGH...?
HMMM...?
ER...NO! 'HEH HEH' N-NOTHING OF THE KIND! 'HIC'
PAY THE MAN, LOZZI!
LOOK, HIGH ONE...! SO THAT'S HOW TO GET IN!
"METAL PIECES! THESE HUMANS VALUE THEM!"
KLINK
KLINK
KLINK
BUT HOW TO GET SOME...?
HMMM...

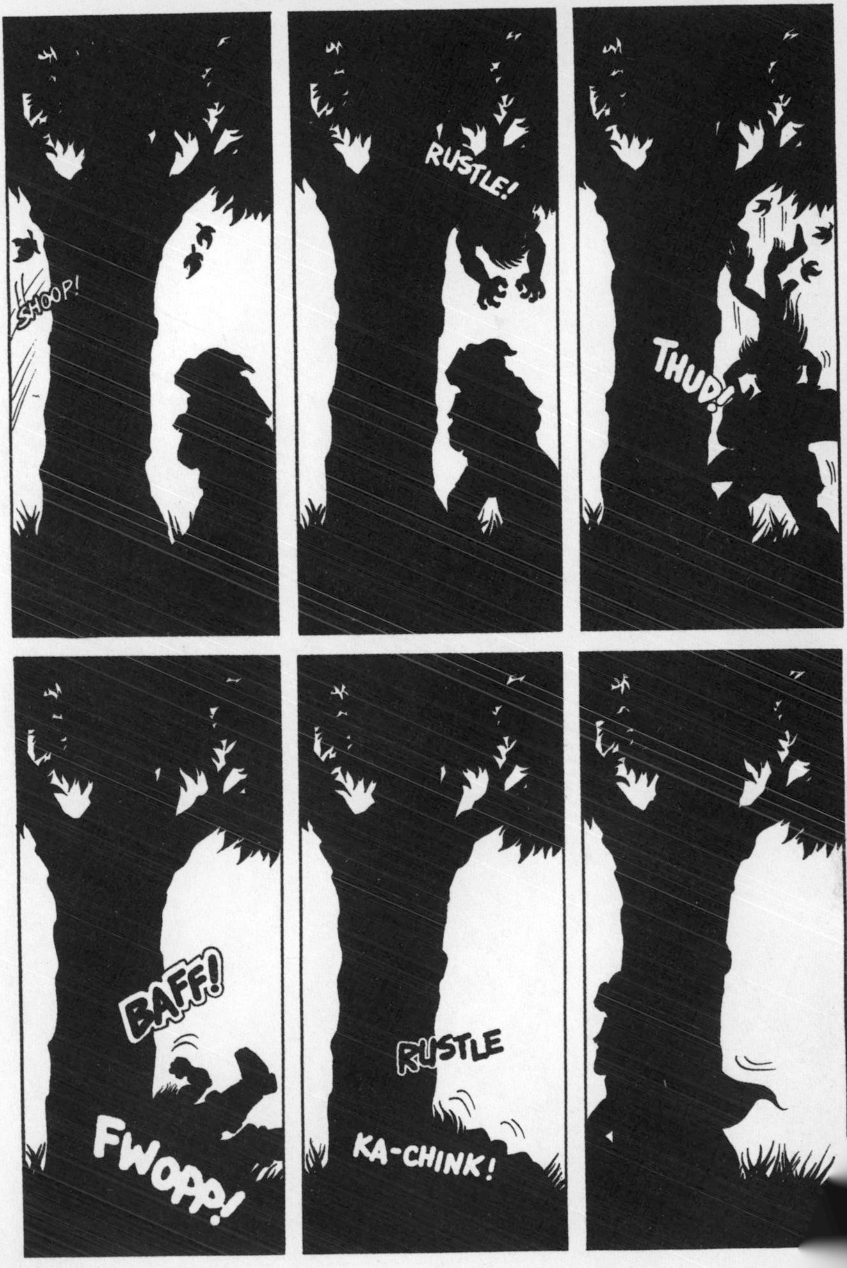
SHOOP!
RUSTLE!
THUD!
BAFF!
FWOPP!
RUSTLE
KA-CHINK!

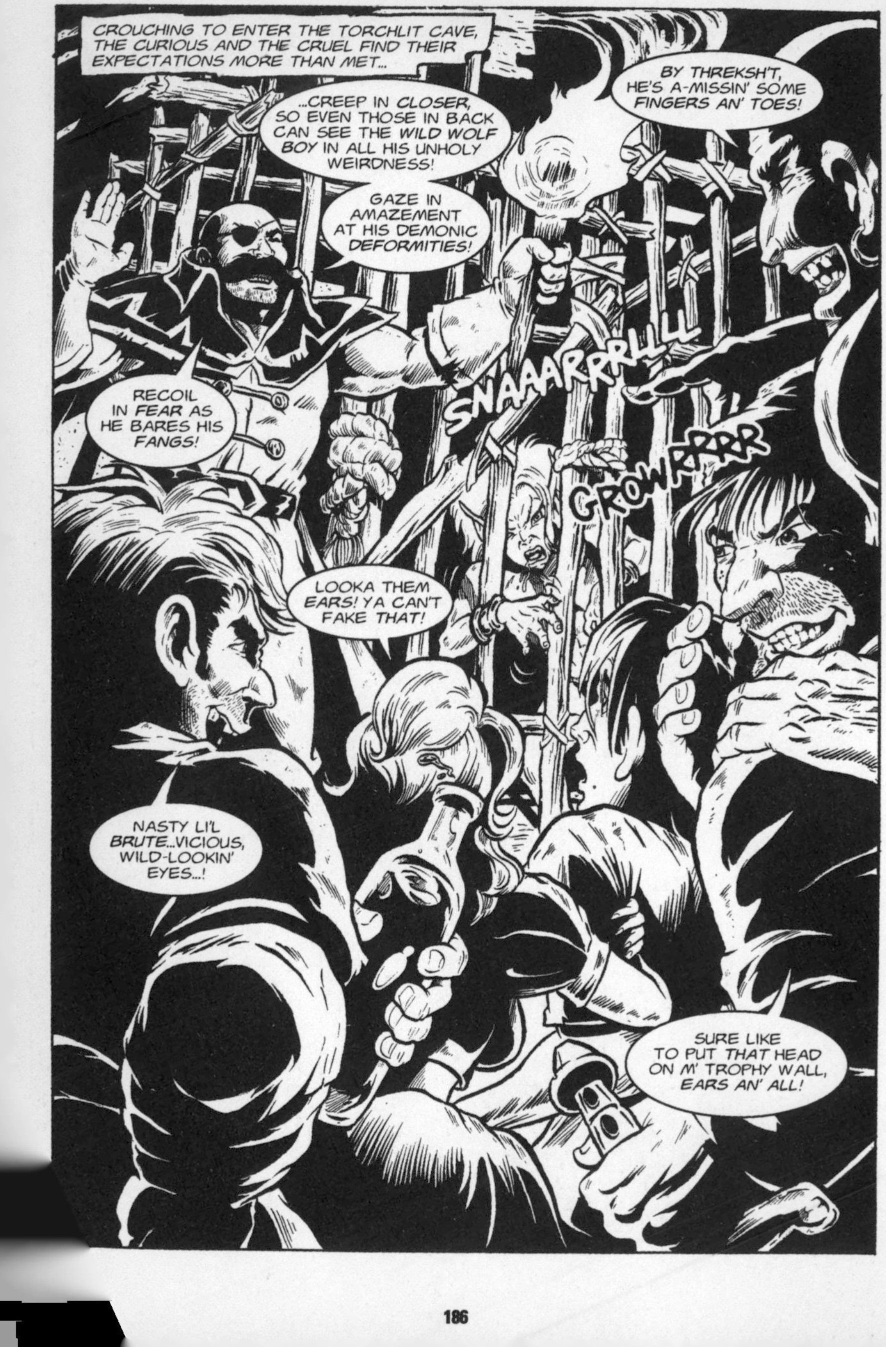
CROUCHING TO ENTER THE TORCHLIT CAVE, THE CURIOUS AND THE CRUEL FIND THEIR EXPECTATIONS MORE THAN MET...
...CREEP IN CLOSER, SO EVEN THOSE IN BACK CAN SEE THE WILD WOLF BOY IN ALL HIS UNHOLY WEIRDNESS!
GAZE IN AMAZEMENT AT HIS DEMONIC DEFORMITIES!
BY THREKSH'T, HE'S A-MISSIN' SOME FINGERS AN' TOES!
RECOIL IN FEAR AS HE BARES HIS FANGS!
SNAAARRRLLL
GROWRRRR
LOOKA THEM EARS! YA CAN'T FAKE THAT!
NASTY LI'L BRUTE...VICIOUS, WILD-LOOKIN' EYES...!
SURE LIKE TO PUT THAT HEAD ON M' TROPHY WALL, EARS AN' ALL!

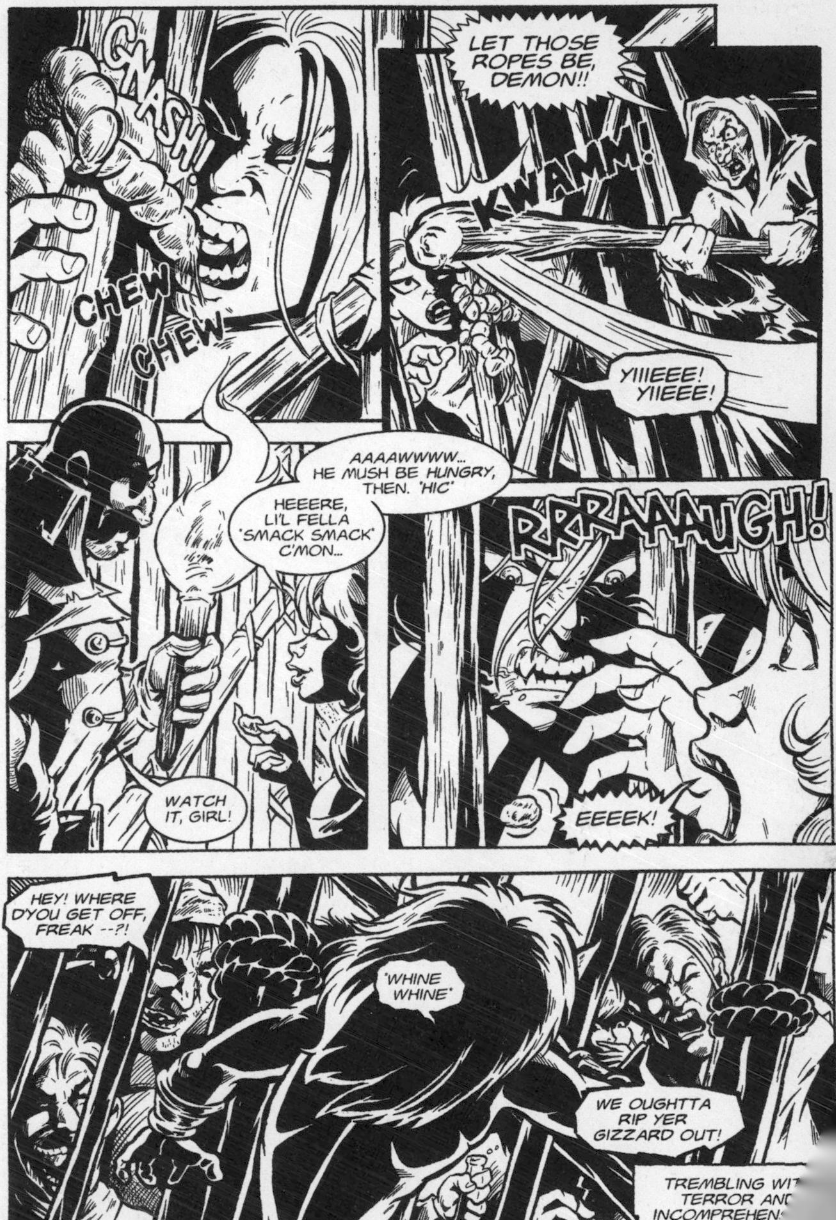
GNASH!
CHEW
CHEW
LET THOSE ROPES BE, DEMON!!
KWAMM!
YIIIEEE! YIIEEE!
AAAAWWWW... HE MUSH BE HUNGRY, THEN. *HIC*
HEEERE, LI'L FELLA *SMACK SMACK* C'MON...
WATCH IT, GIRL!
RRRAAAAUGH!
EEEEK!
HEY! WHERE D'YOU GET OFF, FREAK --?!
WHINE WHINE
WE OUGHTTA RIP YER GIZZARD OUT!
TREMBLING WIT TERROR AND INCOMPREHENS THE MAGIC-AD ELF PACES W

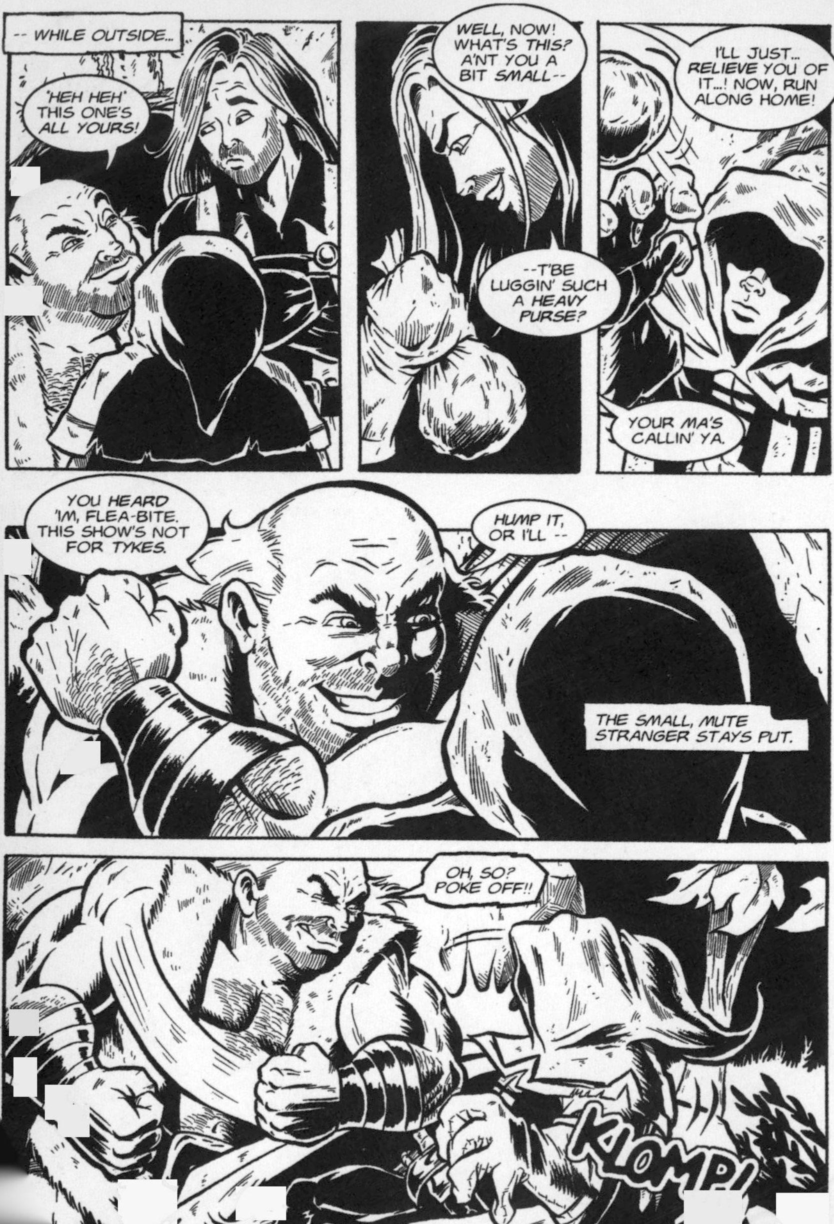
-- WHILE OUTSIDE...
'HEH HEH' THIS ONE'S ALL YOURS!
WELL, NOW! WHAT'S THIS? A'NT YOU A BIT SMALL--
--T'BE LUGGIN' SUCH A HEAVY PURSE?
I'LL JUST... RELIEVE YOU OF IT...! NOW, RUN ALONG HOME!
YOUR MA'S CALLIN' YA.
YOU HEARD 'IM, FLEA-BITE. THIS SHOW'S NOT FOR TYKES.
HUMP IT, OR I'LL --
THE SMALL, MUTE STRANGER STAYS PUT.
OH, SO? POKE OFF!!
KLOMP!

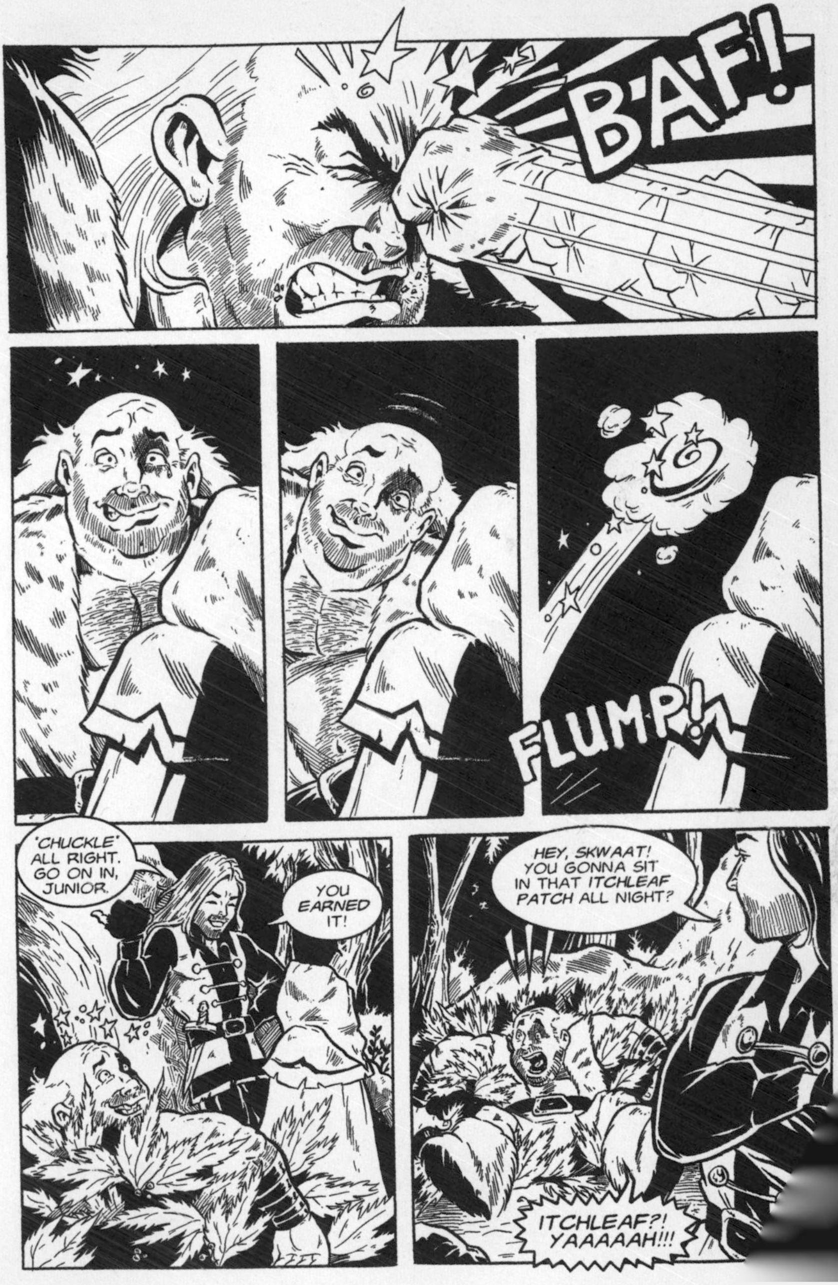
BAF!
FLUMP!
"CHUCKLE" ALL RIGHT. GO ON IN, JUNIOR.
YOU EARNED IT!
HEY, SKWAAT! YOU GONNA SIT IN THAT ITCHLEAF PATCH ALL NIGHT?
ITCHLEAF?! YAAAAAH!!!

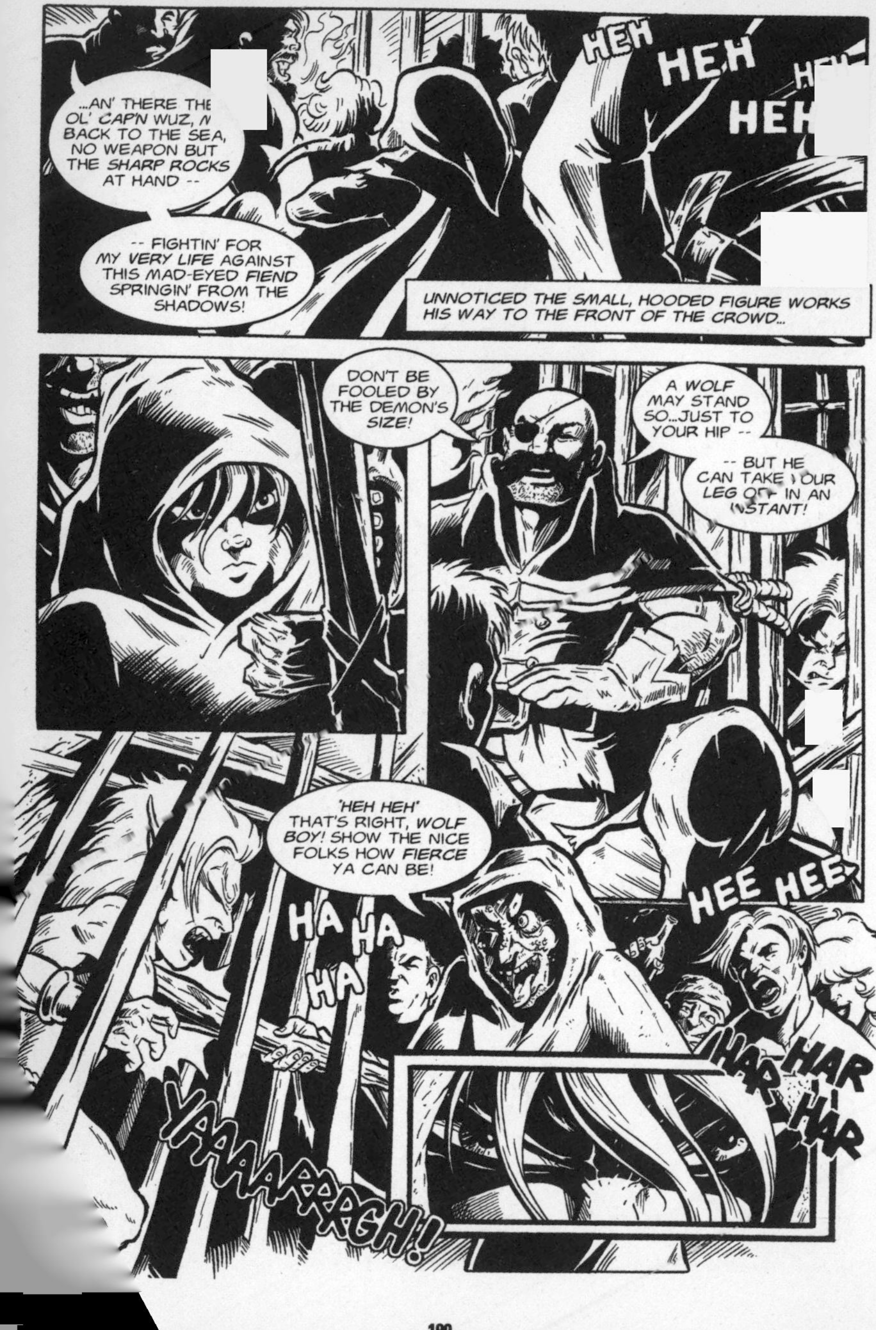
...AN' THERE THE OL' CAP'N WUZ, M BACK TO THE SEA, NO WEAPON BUT THE SHARP ROCKS AT HAND --
-- FIGHTIN' FOR MY VERY LIFE AGAINST THIS MAD-EYED FIEND SPRINGIN' FROM THE SHADOWS!
HEH HEH HEH
UNNOTICED THE SMALL, HOODED FIGURE WORKS HIS WAY TO THE FRONT OF THE CROWD...
DON'T BE FOOLED BY THE DEMON'S SIZE!
A WOLF MAY STAND SO...JUST TO YOUR HIP --
-- BUT HE CAN TAKE YOUR LEG OFF IN AN INSTANT!
'HEH HEH' THAT'S RIGHT, WOLF BOY! SHOW THE NICE FOLKS HOW FIERCE YA CAN BE!
HEE HEE
HA HA HA
HAR HAR HAR HAR
YAAAARRRGH!

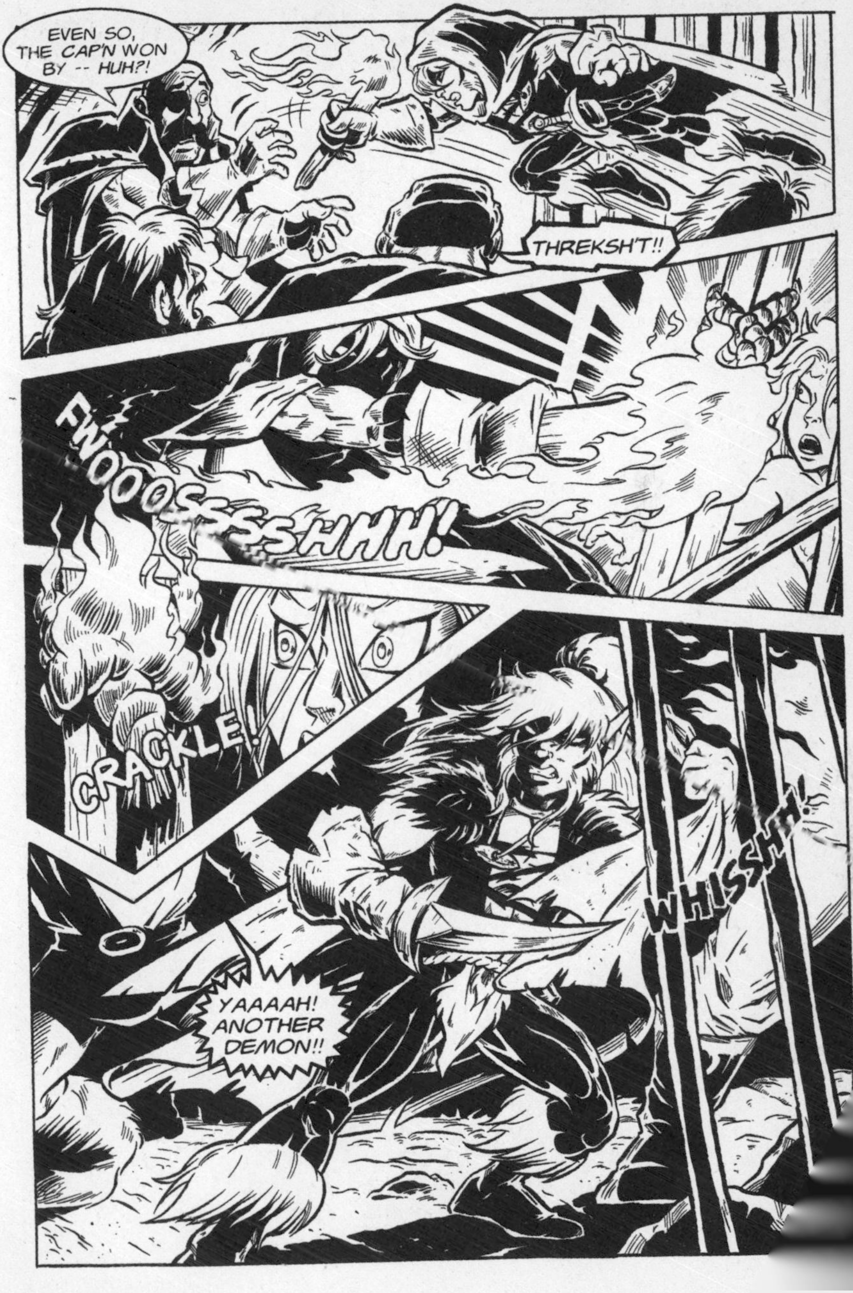
EVEN SO, THE CAP'N WON BY -- HUH?!
THREKSH'T!!
FWOOOSSSSHHHH!
CRACKLE!
WHISSHH!
YAAAAH! ANOTHER DEMON!!

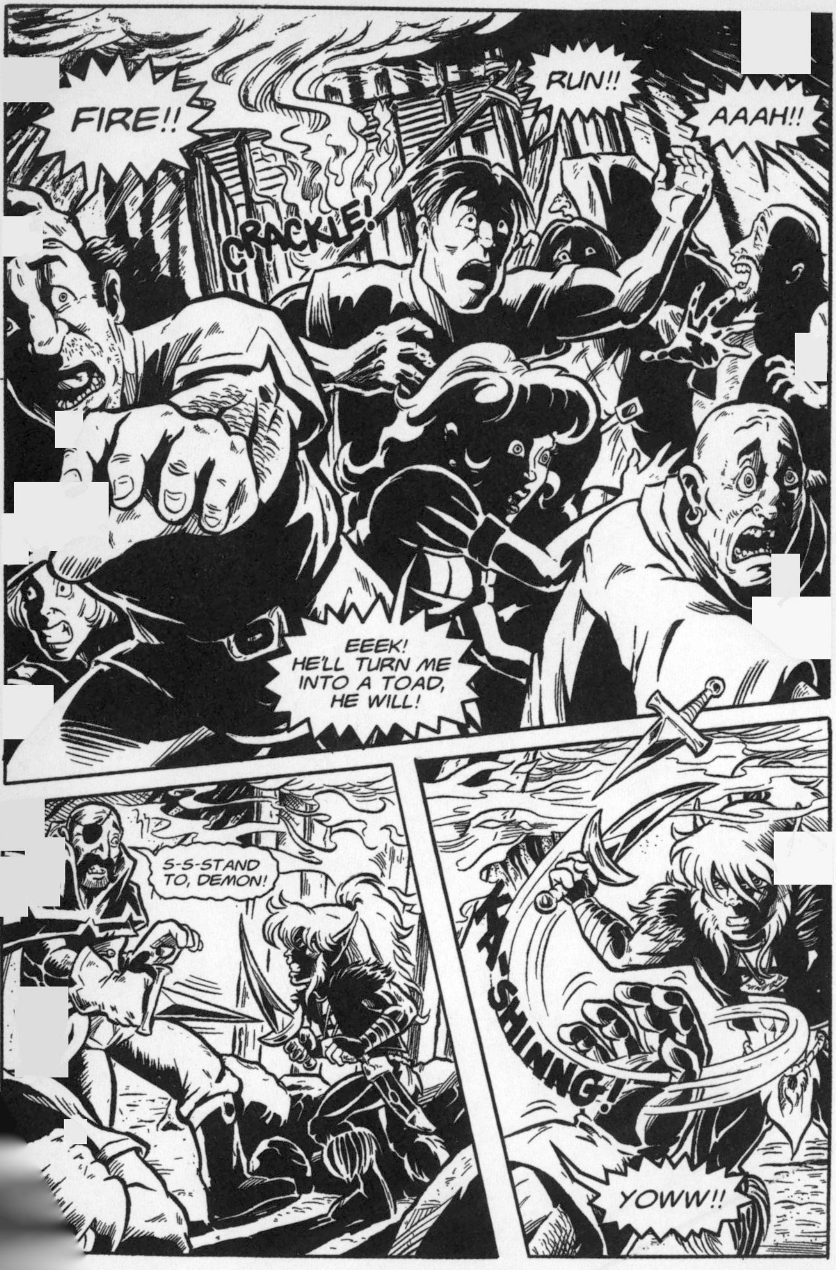
FIRE!!
CRACKLE!
RUN!!
AAAH!!
EEEK! HE'LL TURN ME INTO A TOAD, HE WILL!
S-S-STAND TO, DEMON!
KA-SHINNG!
YOWW!!

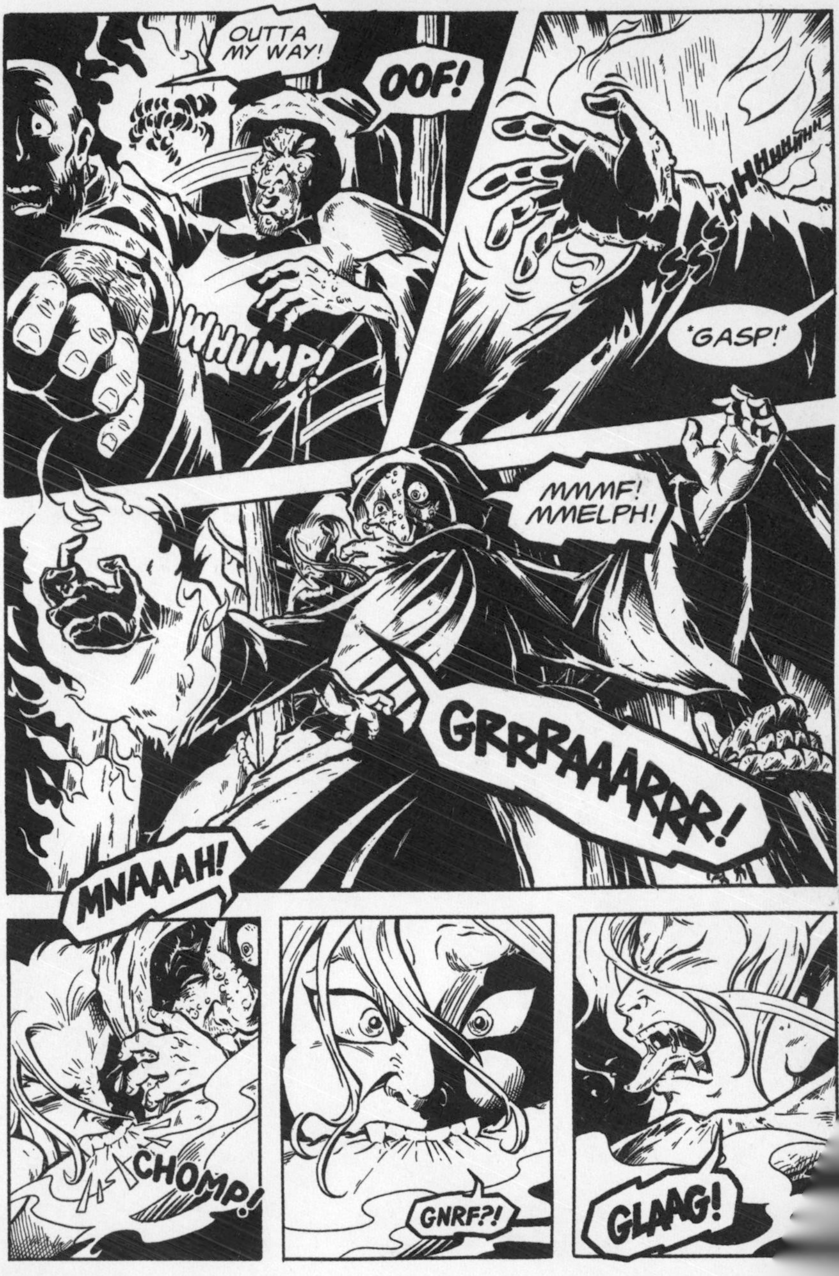
OUTTA MY WAY!
OOF!
WHUMP!
SSSHHHhhhhhhh
GASP!
MMMF! MMELPH!
GRRRAAAARRRR!
MNAAAH!
CHOMP!
GNRF?!
GLAAG!

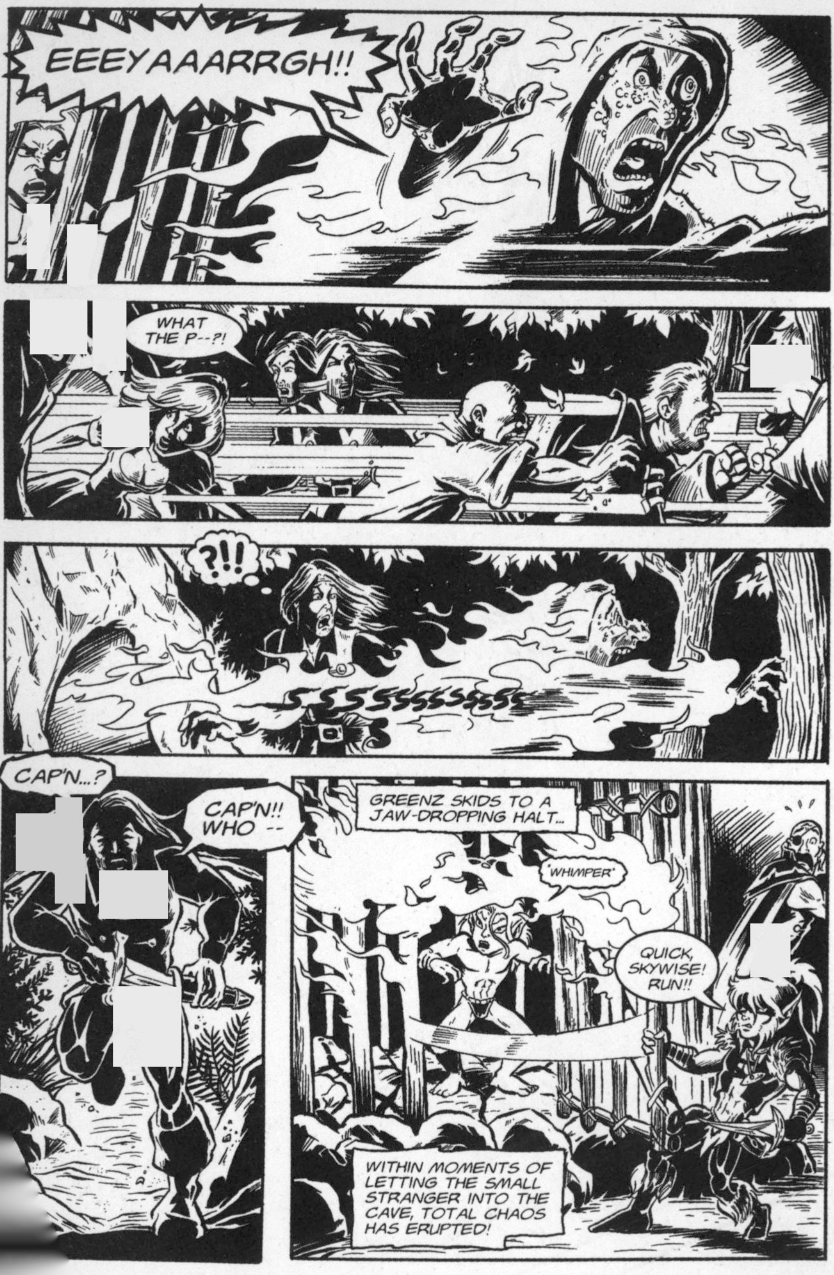
EEEYAAARRGH!!
WHAT THE P--?!
?!!
CAP'N...?
CAP'N!! WHO --
GREENZ SKIDS TO A JAW-DROPPING HALT...
WHIMPER
QUICK, SKYWISE! RUN!!
WITHIN MOMENTS OF LETTING THE SMALL STRANGER INTO THE CAVE, TOTAL CHAOS HAS ERUPTED!

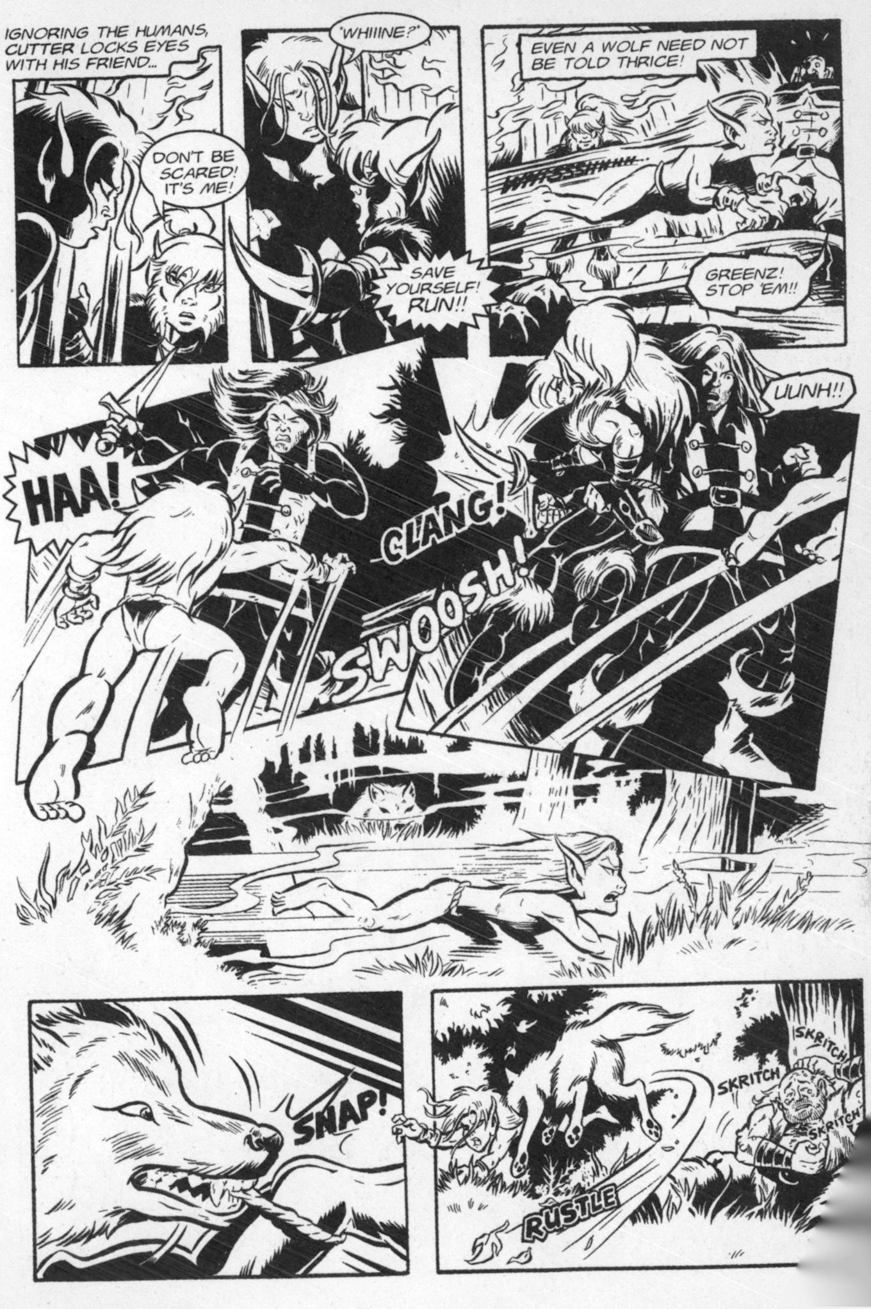
IGNORING THE HUMANS, CUTTER LOCKS EYES WITH HIS FRIEND...
DON'T BE SCARED! IT'S ME!
'WHIIINE?'
SAVE YOURSELF! RUN!!
EVEN A WOLF NEED NOT BE TOLD THRICE!
WHISSSHHHH...
GREENZ! STOP 'EM!!
HAA!
CLANG!
SWOOSH!
UUNH!!
SNAP!
RUSTLE
SKRITCH
SKRITCH
SKRITCH

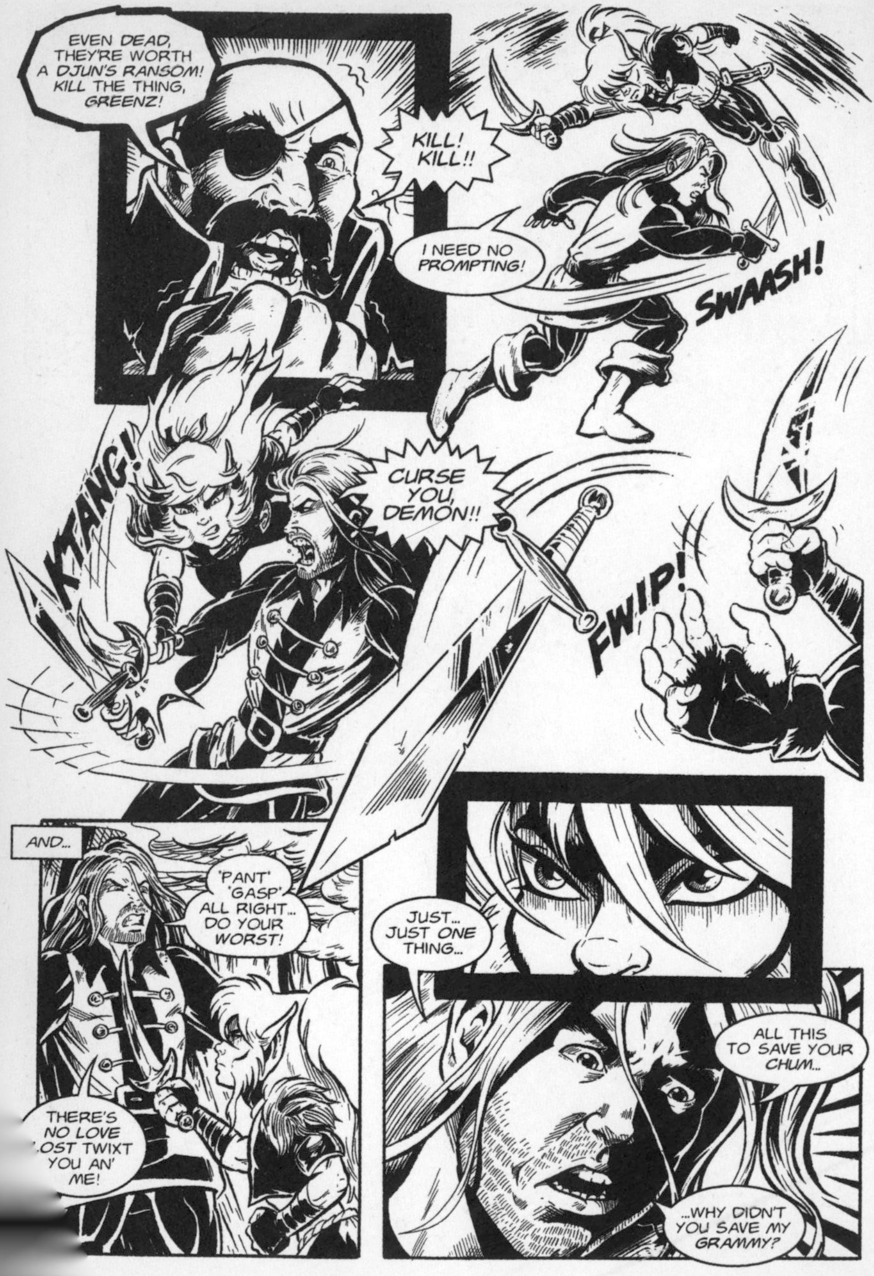
EVEN DEAD, THEY'RE WORTH A DJUN'S RANSOM! KILL THE THING, GREENZ!
KILL! KILL!!
I NEED NO PROMPTING!
SWAASH!
KTANG!
CURSE YOU, DEMON!!
FWIP!
AND...
'PANT' 'GASP' ALL RIGHT... DO YOUR WORST!
THERE'S NO LOVE LOST TWIXT YOU AN' ME!
JUST... JUST ONE THING...
ALL THIS TO SAVE YOUR CHUM...
...WHY DIDN'T YOU SAVE MY GRAMMY?

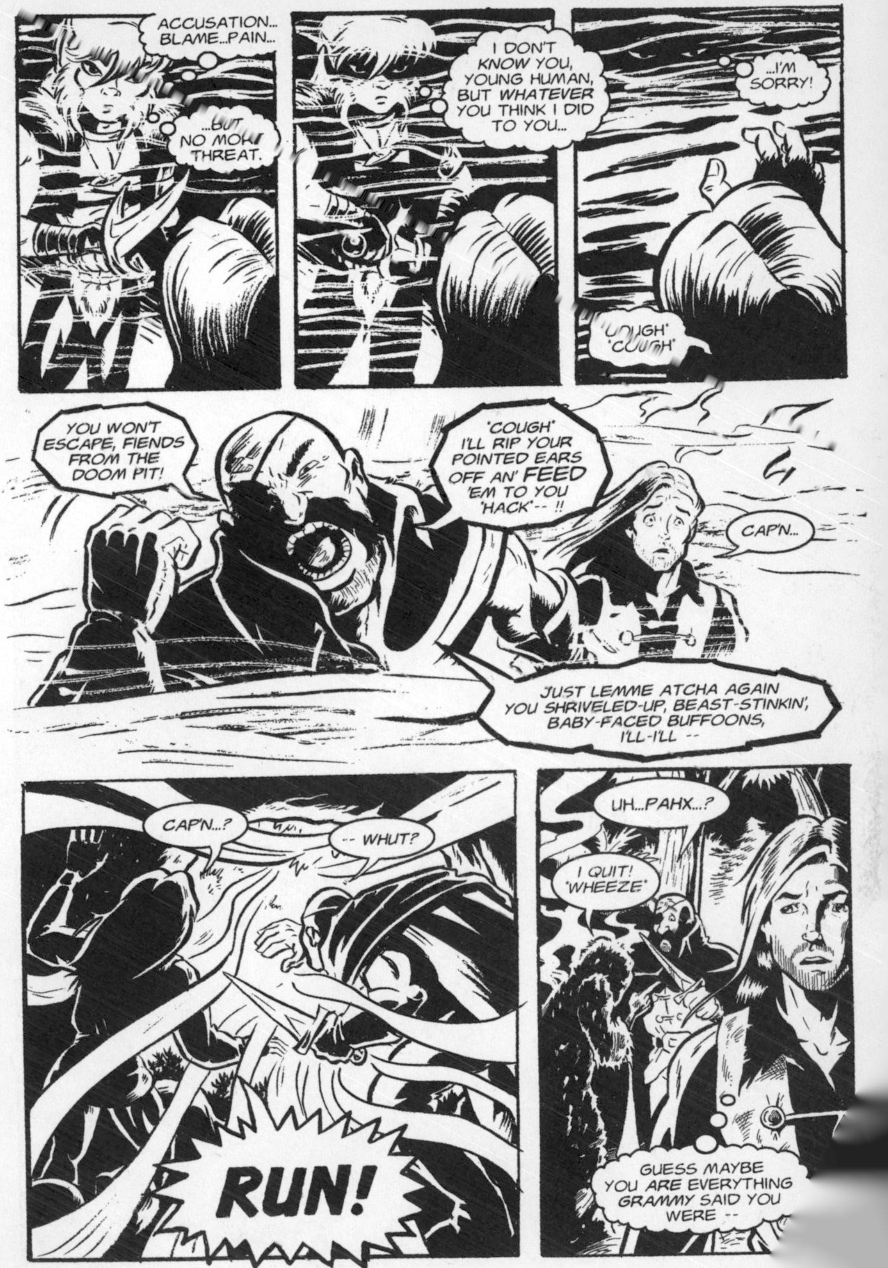
ACCUSATION... BLAME...PAIN...
...BUT NO MOR THREAT.
I DON'T KNOW YOU, YOUNG HUMAN, BUT WHATEVER YOU THINK I DID TO YOU...
...I'M SORRY!
'COUGH' 'COUGH'
YOU WON'T ESCAPE, FIENDS FROM THE DOOM PIT!
'COUGH' I'LL RIP YOUR POINTED EARS OFF AN' FEED 'EM TO YOU 'HACK'-- !!
CAP'N...
JUST LEMME ATCHA AGAIN YOU SHRIVELED-UP, BEAST-STINKIN', BABY-FACED BUFFOONS, I'LL-I'LL --
CAP'N...?
-- WHUT?
RUN!
UH...PAHX...?
I QUIT! 'WHEEZE'
GUESS MAYBE YOU ARE EVERYTHING GRAMMY SAID YOU WERE --

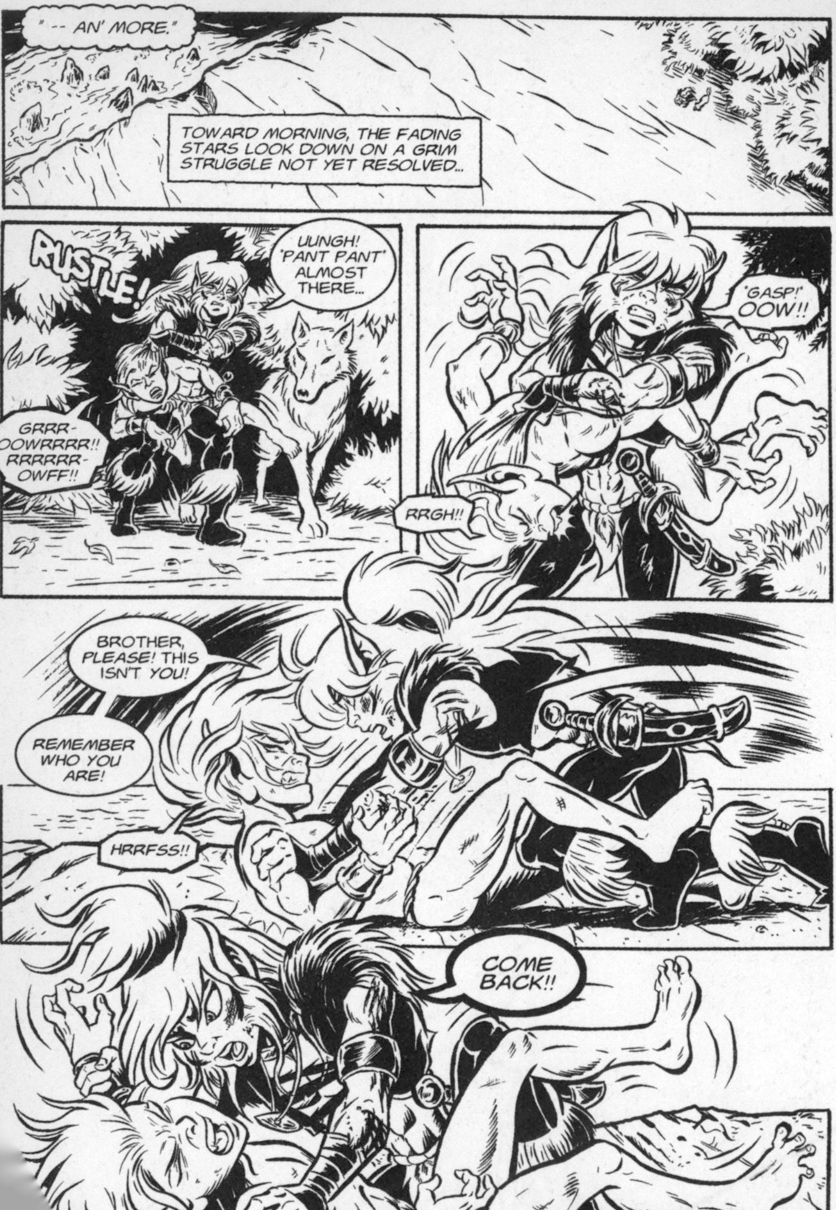
" -- AN' MORE."
TOWARD MORNING, THE FADING STARS LOOK DOWN ON A GRIM STRUGGLE NOT YET RESOLVED...
RUSTLE!
UUNGH! 'PANT PANT' ALMOST THERE...
GRRR-OOWRRRR!! RRRRRR-OWFF!!
'GASP!' OOW!!
RRGH!!
BROTHER, PLEASE! THIS ISN'T YOU!
REMEMBER WHO YOU ARE!
HRRFSS!!
COME BACK!!

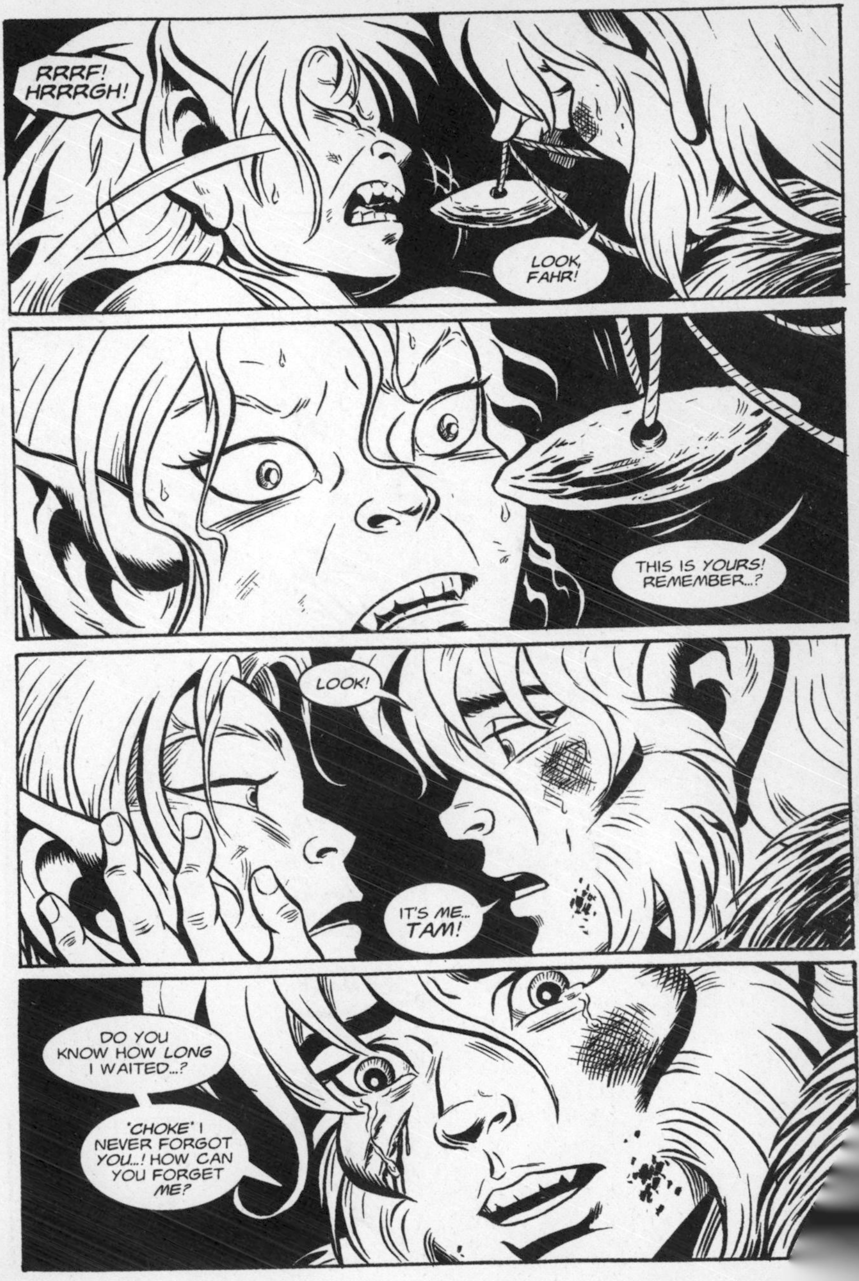
RRRF! HRRRGH!
LOOK, FAHR!
THIS IS YOURS! REMEMBER...?
LOOK!
IT'S ME... TAM!
DO YOU KNOW HOW LONG I WAITED...?
CHOKE I NEVER FORGOT YOU...! HOW CAN YOU FORGET ME?

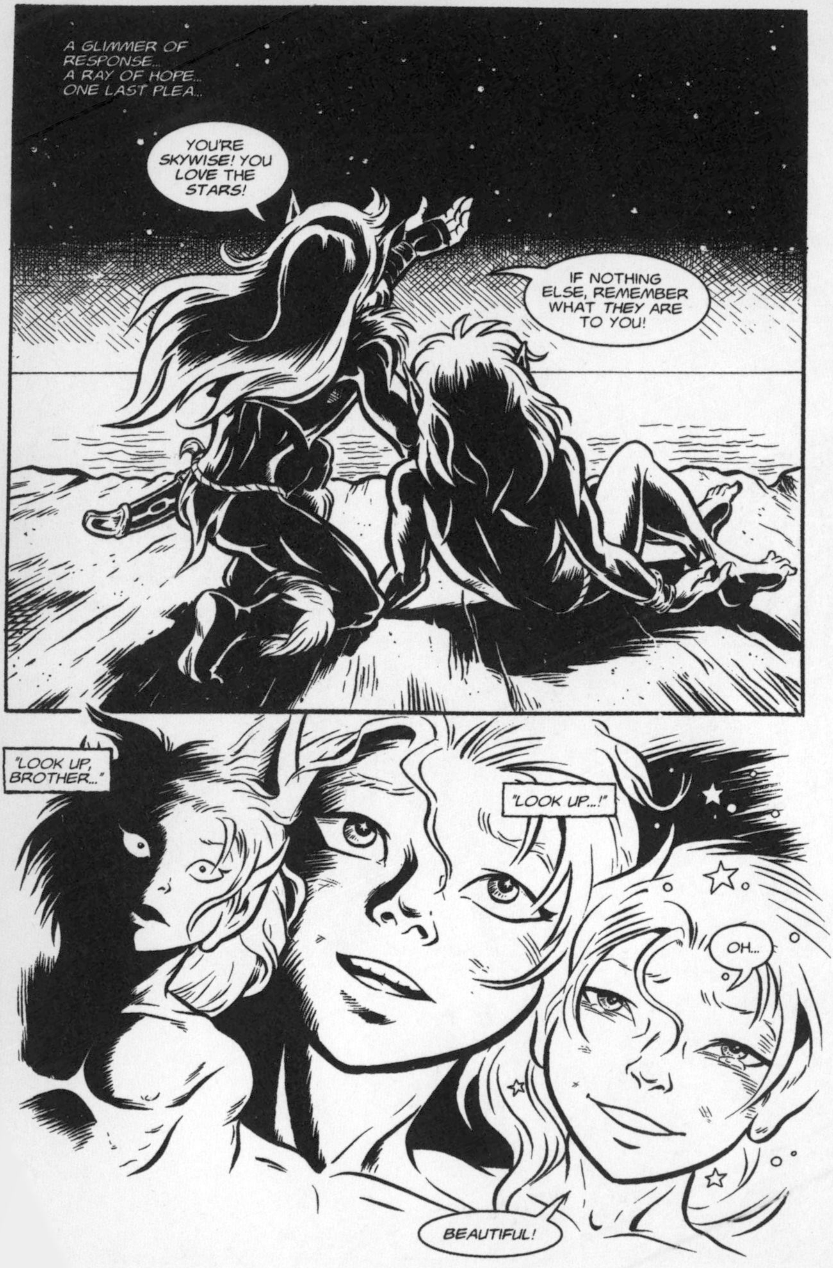
A GLIMMER OF RESPONSE... A RAY OF HOPE... ONE LAST PLEA...
YOU'RE SKYWISE! YOU LOVE THE STARS!
IF NOTHING ELSE, REMEMBER WHAT THEY ARE TO YOU!
"LOOK UP, BROTHER..."
"LOOK UP...!"
OH...
BEAUTIFUL!

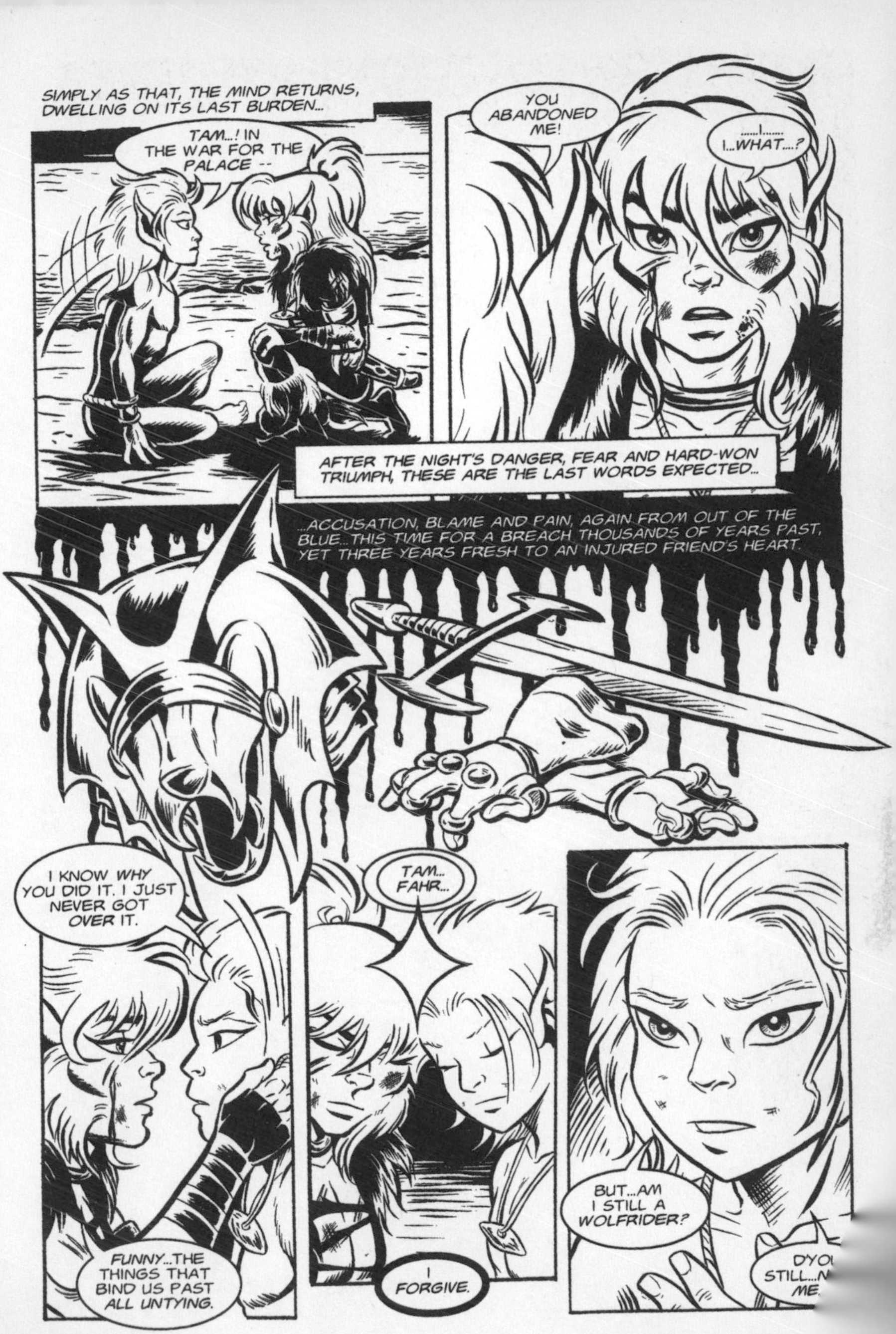
SIMPLY AS THAT, THE MIND RETURNS, DWELLING ON ITS LAST BURDEN...
TAM...! IN THE WAR FOR THE PALACE --
YOU ABANDONED ME!
......I...... I...WHAT....?
AFTER THE NIGHT'S DANGER, FEAR AND HARD-WON TRIUMPH, THESE ARE THE LAST WORDS EXPECTED...
...ACCUSATION, BLAME AND PAIN, AGAIN FROM OUT OF THE BLUE...THIS TIME FOR A BREACH THOUSANDS OF YEARS PAST, YET THREE YEARS FRESH TO AN INJURED FRIEND'S HEART.
I KNOW WHY YOU DID IT. I JUST NEVER GOT OVER IT.
FUNNY...THE THINGS THAT BIND US PAST ALL UNTYING.
TAM... FAHR...
I FORGIVE.
BUT...AM I STILL A WOLFRIDER?
D'YOU STILL...N ME

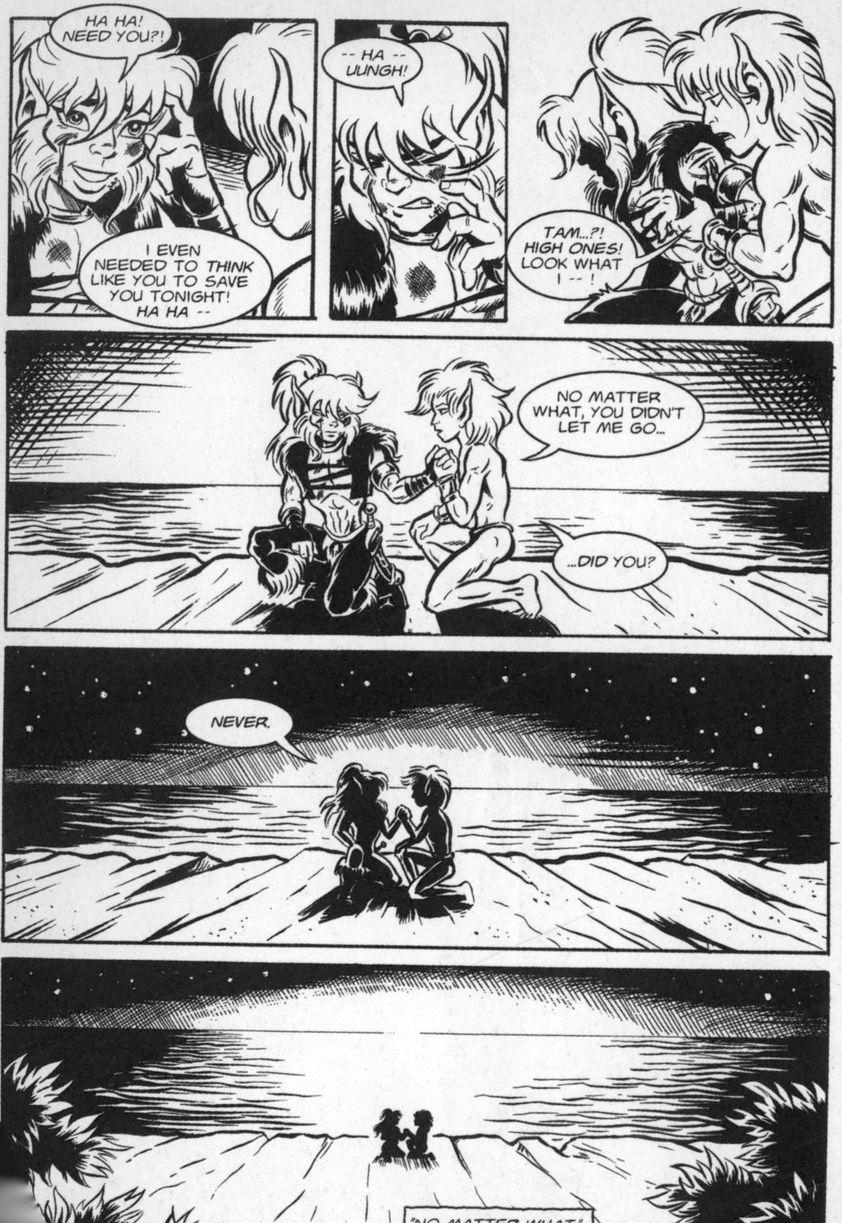
HA HA! NEED YOU?!
I EVEN NEEDED TO THINK LIKE YOU TO SAVE YOU TONIGHT! HA HA --
-- HA -- UUNGH!
TAM...?! HIGH ONES! LOOK WHAT I -- !
NO MATTER WHAT, YOU DIDN'T LET ME GO...
...DID YOU?
NEVER.
"NO MATTER WHAT."

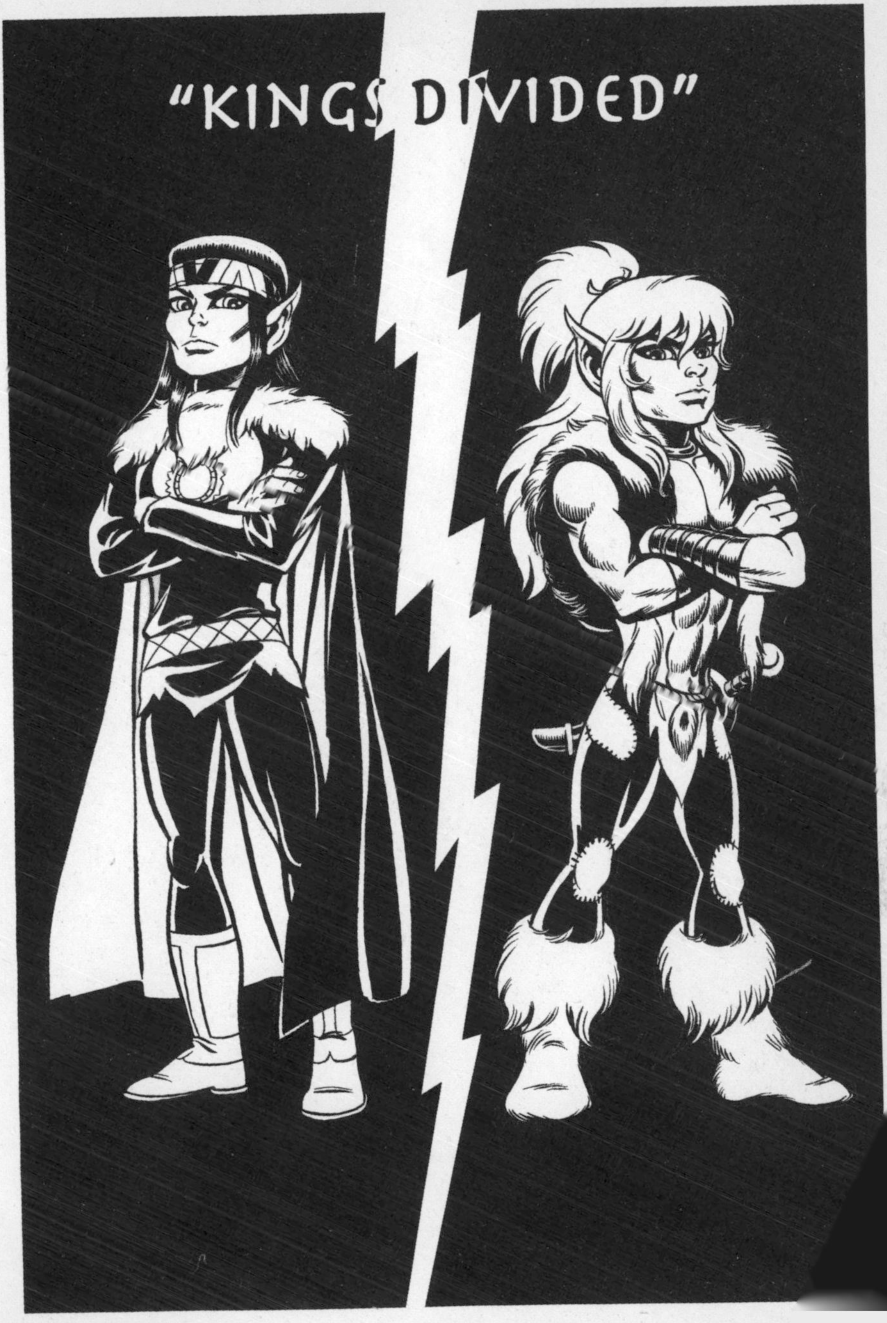
"KINGS DIVIDED"

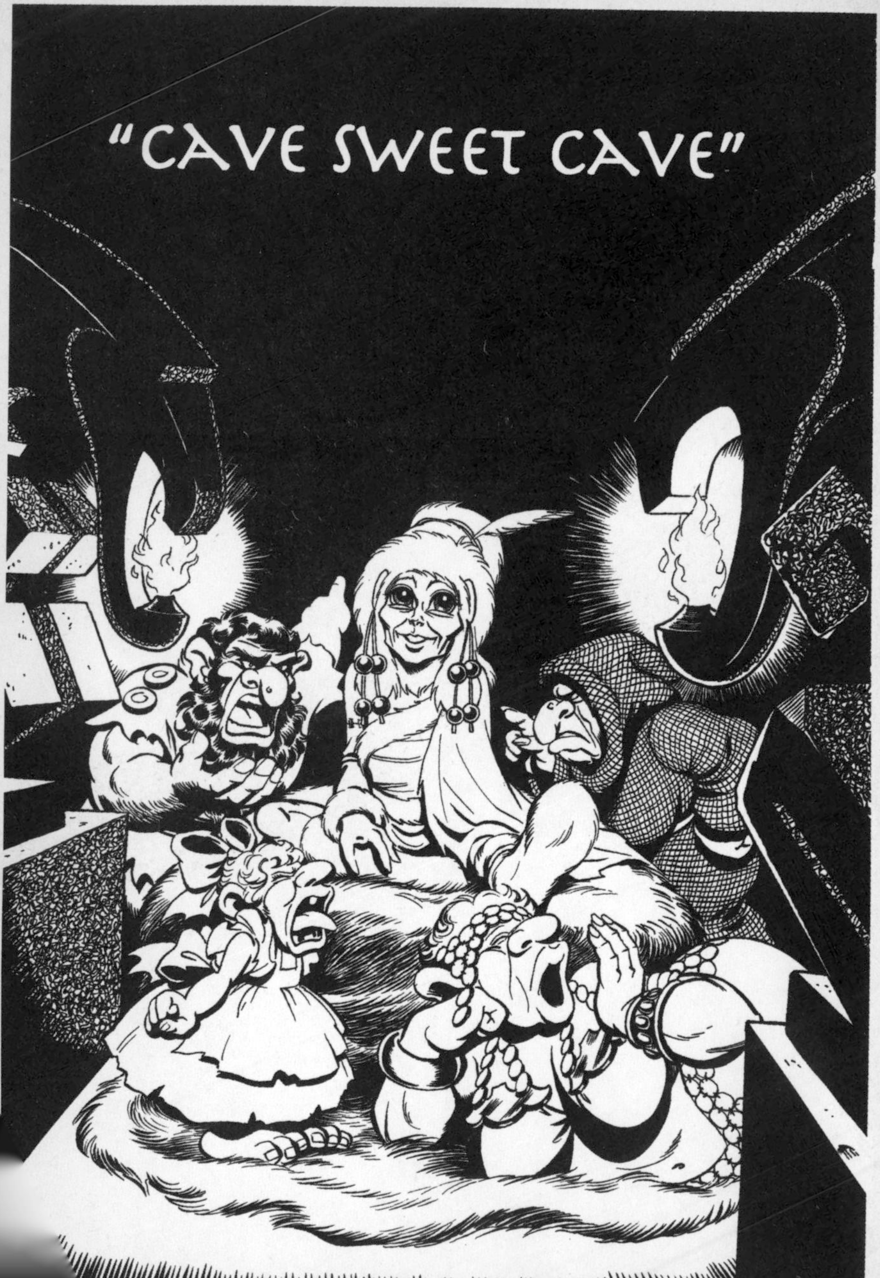
"CAVE SWEET CAVE"

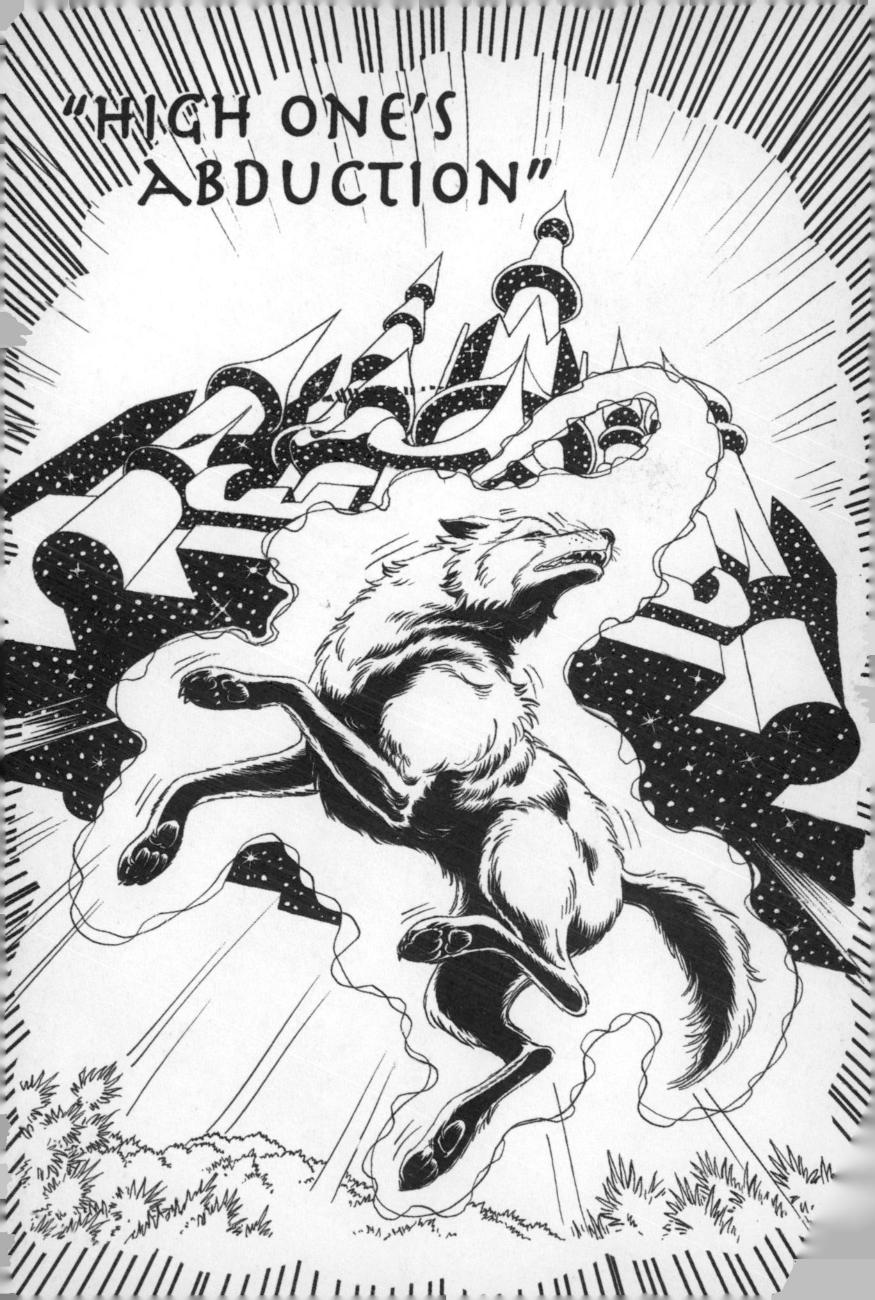
"HIGH ONE'S ABDUCTION"

IN THE
NEXT VOLUME

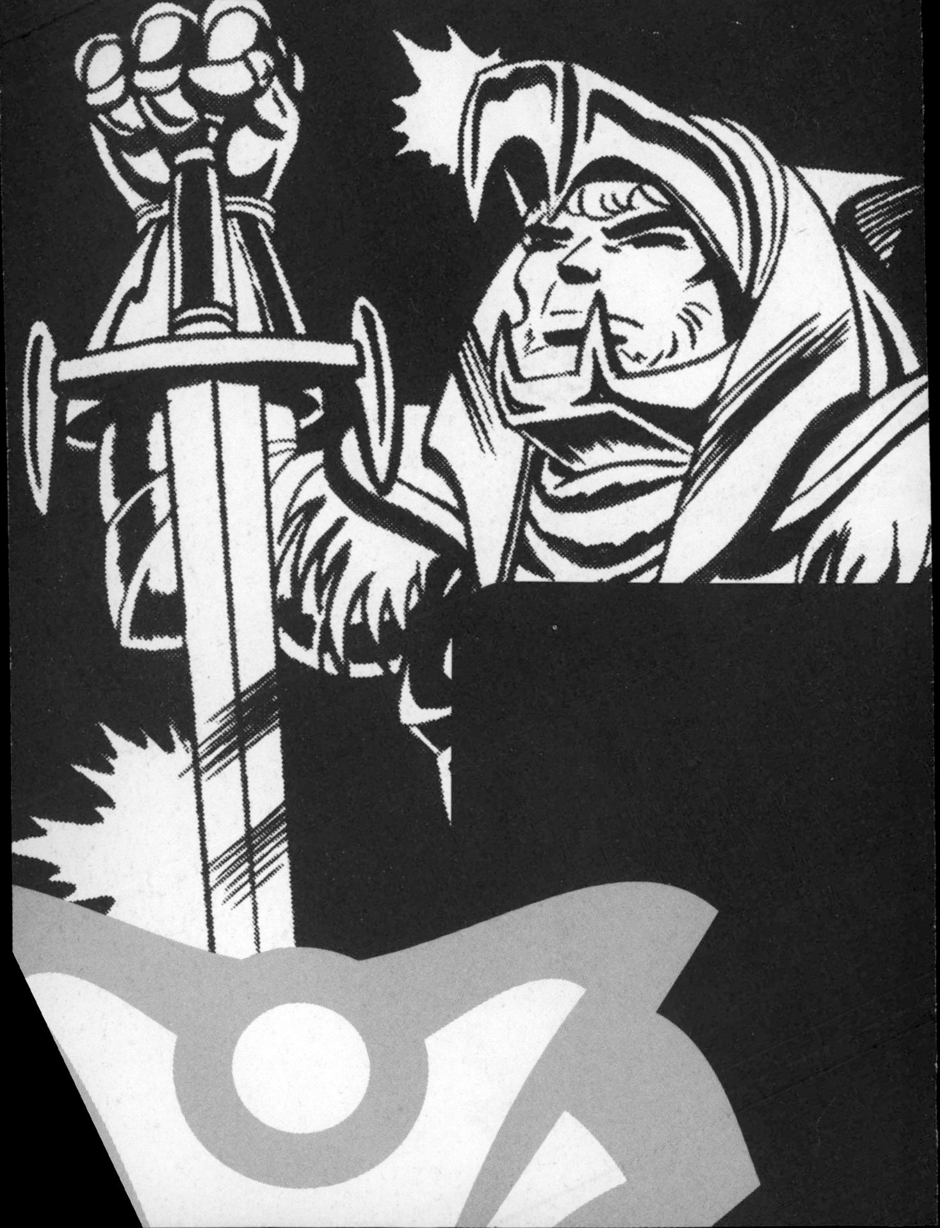

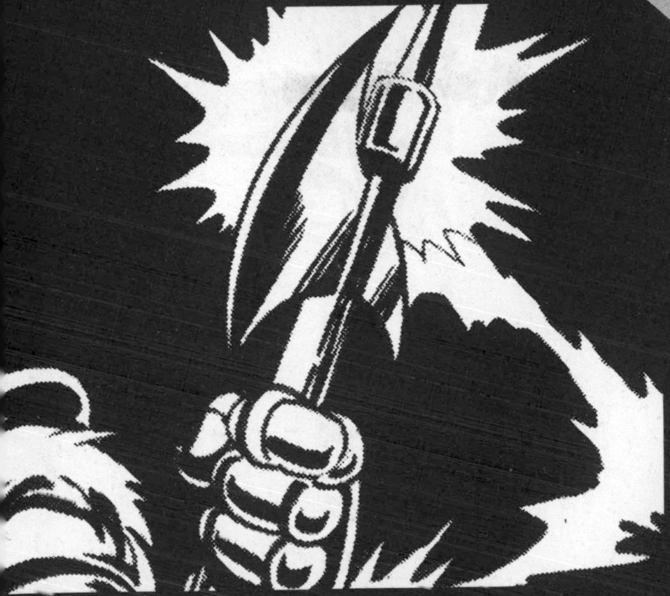

When Cutter's family and friends are stolen into the far future by jealous Rayek, the mortal Wolfrider chief and his warriors must make a fateful decision.

A single desperate hope lies within the folds of wrapstuff, magical Preserver webbing that allows the elves to slumber for centuries without harm. But the Wolfriders are tied to the future, and in strange dreams do they foresee their own doom?

Look for this latest addition in DC Comics' new library of ElfQuest stories in

FEBRUARY 2006